BIG HAIR AND PLASTIC GRASS

ALSO BY DAN EPSTEIN

Twentieth-Century Pop Culture

BIG HAIR AND PLASTIC GRASS

A Funky Ride Through Baseball
and America in the Swinging '70s

DAN EPSTEIN

Thomas Dunne Books
St. Martin's Press
New York

THOMAS DUNNE BOOKS.
An imprint of St. Martin's Press.

BIG HAIR AND PLASTIC GRASS. Copyright © 2010 by Dan Epstein.
All rights reserved. Printed in the United States of America. For information,
address St. Martin's Press, 175 Fifth Avenue, New York, N.Y. 10010.

www.thomasdunnebooks.com
www.stmartins.com

Library of Congress Cataloging-in-Publication Data

Epstein, Dan.
    Big hair and plastic grass : a funky ride through baseball and America in the
swinging '70s / Dan Epstein. — 1st ed.
        p. cm.
    ISBN 978-0-312-60754-8
    1. Baseball—United States—History—20th century.   2. Baseball—Social
aspects—United States—History—20th century.   3. Baseball players—United
States—History—20th century.   4. United States—History—1969–
5. Nineteen seventies.   I. Title.
    GV863.A1E67 2010
    796.3570973'09047—dc22

                                                                        2009045702

First Edition: June 2010

10 9 8 7 6 5 4 3 2 1

For my dad, Irwin,
who took me to my first American League game.

For my mother, Lyn,
who took me to my first National League game.

And for my grandpa Fred,
who gave me my first copy of the *Sporting News*.

CONTENTS

BIG HAIR AND PLASTIC GRASS

INTRODUCTION

It's been said that the "golden age of baseball" is an impossible thing to truly pinpoint or define, since it almost always refers to the era during which *you* first fell in love with the game. For my father, who grew up in the shadow of Ebbets Field and still considers Vin Scully "the new guy" on the Dodgers broadcasting team, the period from 1947 to 1955 was the golden age: Not only did it produce some of the greatest Brooklyn Dodger, New York Giant, and New York Yankee squads of all time, but it was also marked by the heroic (if long overdue) integration of the game, which helped pave the way for the increasing (and also long overdue) integration of American society.

For me, however, it all comes back to the 1970s. That's the decade when I attended my first major league game (a May 1976 contest between the Yankees and Tigers at Detroit's wonderfully creaky Tiger Stadium), collected my first baseball cards, and learned how to read a box score. To a kid whose first baseball movie was *The Bad News Bears*, legendary players like Ty Cobb, Babe Ruth, Hank Greenberg, and even Jackie Robinson seemed like old gods who'd roamed the earth in sepia tones, while Joe DiMaggio was the guy who did the TV commercials for Mr. Coffee. Hank Aaron and Reggie Jackson, on the other hand, were *real*; I know because I watched them break Babe Ruth's career and World Series home run records, respectively, on TV—*color* TV, no less.

Back then, I thought the Oakland A's green-and-gold uniforms were groovy, not garish; ditto for the Houston Astros' "tequila sunrise" jerseys. I still prefer the sleek, form-fitting look of '70s double knits to the softball tops and pajama bottoms so prevalent in the early twenty-first century, and I still think players who wear long hair, villainous mustaches, bushy sideburns, and voluminous Afros look way cooler than those who don't. I can't help it; I'm a child of the '70s.

These sorts of aesthetic preferences—and my deep, abiding love for the players, uniforms, and lore of the era—are admittedly subjective. What isn't subjective is the fact that the '70s were profoundly *different* from any baseball decade that preceded or followed. In his book *Talkin' Baseball: An Oral History of Baseball in the 1970s*, Phil Pepe writes that the 120 months that followed the New York Mets' surprising 1969 championship run "would bring more changes than the game had known in the first seven decades of the twentieth century," changes like the designated hitter, the free agent, and the World Series night game, all of which continue to affect baseball to this day. It was the decade when baseball— realizing that it could no longer afford to coast on its reputation as "the national pastime"—began learning how to market itself, however clumsily; as widely reviled as Charlie O. Finley and Bill Veeck were at the time, their carny-style promotions paved the way for the theme nights and bobble-head giveaways that all teams now regularly rely upon to put thousands of extra butts in the seats. It was also the decade when the players finally stood up to the owners and demanded greater control over their own destinies (and a larger slice of the financial pie); the 1972 players' strike was the first organized walkout in major league history, one that set the stage for the season-truncating labor actions of 1981 and 1994.

If the integration of baseball in the 1940s and '50s sparked changes in American culture, then the '70s was the decade where the changes in American culture turned back around and impacted baseball. Even during the turbulent 1960s, baseball players looked, spoke, and played as conservatively as their counterparts in decades past; the closest the game came to rubbing shoulders with contemporary popular culture was when the Beatles performed at Shea Stadium and Candlestick Park. In his book *The Tigers of '68*, George Cantor acknowledges this complete disconnect, citing as an example the July 23, 1967, doubleheader between the Yankees and Tigers at Tiger Stadium, which the teams played to completion while the deadliest, most destructive riot of the 1960s raged in the surrounding streets. "It was as if the stadium was wrapped in a cocoon," Cantor writes, "untouched by the catastrophe that was engulfing the city." He goes on to note that the era's "Vietnam protests and rallies, love-ins and acid trips were part of a parallel reality, one that did not intrude on baseball's space." In the 1970s, that cocoon would pop, and those two parallel realities would collide head-on, resulting in the most colorful era in baseball history.

Drugs, fashion, pop music, political upheaval, Black Power, the sexual revolution, gay liberation—all of these things left their mark upon '70s baseball in ways that would have been unthinkable just a few years earlier, and might be just as unthinkable now. For the first time in history, major league ballplayers felt comfortable letting their "freak flags" fly, sprouting bold Afros and wild facial hair, and expressing their opinions about everything from drugs and sex to Richard Nixon and the war in Vietnam. Instead of clean-cut heroes, there were flawed but talented players like Dick Allen and Reggie Jackson, and maverick owners like Veeck, Finley, and Ted Turner, all of whom seemed as cool and/or crazy as the antiheroes then populating the nation's movie screens. The increasing influence of black culture in American popular film and music paralleled the increased presence and influence of African-American players in and upon the sport, even down to what they wore on the field; after decades of drab, baggy wool uniforms, the '70s saw teams adopting double-knit polyester outfits whose gaudy color schemes and form-fitting tailoring reflected the flashy urban fashions of the day.

From 1970, when Dock Ellis pitched what was probably baseball's first and only LSD-assisted no-hitter, through 1979, when the infamous White Sox "Disco Demolition" promotion resulted in one of the worst on-field riots in baseball history, the sport exuded an edgy (and palpably exciting) anything-goes vibe, one that has long vanished from the game as we know it. In recent years, for example, the Atlanta Braves have held a "Faith Day" promotion, featuring performances by Christian rock bands and testimonials from Braves players about how Jesus turned their lives around. This is the same team that, back in 1977, drew more than 27,000 fans for a "Wet T-Shirt Night" competition. Give me the 1970s, any day.

Most baseball histories and documentaries tend to give short shrift to the decade, remembering only Hank Aaron's 715th home run, the World Series heroics of Carlton Fisk and Reggie Jackson, Pete Rose's 44-game hitting streak, and the introduction of free agency. Perhaps this has something to do with the lack of gaudy offensive numbers put up by players in the '70s, a decade when pitching, speed, and defense dominated the games, when whole teams were built with artificial turf in mind. It was a time when anyone capable of hitting 15 home runs in a single season could be considered a legitimate power threat, and you could win a league home run crown with just over 30 jacks. It wasn't uncommon to see lead-off hitters with .300 on-base percentages stealing 70 or more bases, paunchy starting pitchers throwing 300 or more innings per year, or relievers throwing anywhere from three to six innings per game.

(Speaking of stats, this book is peppered with plenty of 'em. But if you're looking for a serious statistical analysis of the era, or number-crunching comparisons between '70s greats and those of other decades, you'll have to look elsewhere. No offense to my SABR brethren, but I'm much more interested in Oscar Gamble's Afro than in his OBP, and I still think Rollie Fingers's mustache was ultimately more important than his WHIP.)

That '70s baseball still doesn't get much respect is a shame, because the legacy that it's left behind is a rich, complex, and fascinating one. Not only did the era yield some legendary teams, like Oakland's "Mustache Gang," Cincinnati's "Big Red Machine," the "Bronx Zoo" Yankees, and the "We Are Family" Pirates, and bear witness to some of the finest achievements of future Hall of Famers like Rod Carew, Mike Schmidt, George Brett, Johnny Bench, Joe Morgan, Willie Stargell, Nolan Ryan, Tom Seaver, Steve Carlton, Rollie Fingers, and Rich "Goose" Gossage, but it also coughed up a whole mess of colorful characters. What other decade could have produced Bill "the Spaceman" Lee, Mickey "Mick the Quick" Rivers, Dave "King Kong" Kingman, "Stormin'" Gorman Thomas, "Iron Mike" Marshall, Albert "Sparky" Lyle, Ron "the Penguin" Cey, Al "the Mad Hungarian" Hrabosky, or Mark "the Bird" Fidrych? What other decade could have been responsible for the San Diego Chicken, the Cleveland Ten-Cent Beer Night riot, or the Phillies' Hot Pants Patrol?

What other decade, indeed? Pop in a Sister Sledge eight-track, crack open a bottle of Champale, flop down upon your beanbag chair, and prepare to take a trip back in time to an era that was as cool as it was complicated. Just don't forget to close the van door behind you. . . .

Dan Epstein
Palm Springs, California
Summer 2009

CHAPTER 1

1970

After a year marked by the *Apollo 11* moon landing, the Stonewall riots, the Tate-LaBianca murders, the music festival yin/yang of Woodstock and Altamont, and the intensified U.S. bombing of Vietnam, the odds of 1970 being placid and turbulence-free were practically nonexistent. 1969 had witnessed multiple seismic shifts in American culture and consciousness—so many indications that daily reality was growing ever more distant from the idealized Norman Rockwell/*Leave It to Beaver* picture of life in these United States—and sizable aftershocks were all but guaranteed. "I feel alright," growled Iggy Pop on the Stooges' new single, "1970," but hardly anyone else did—which is partially why record buyers rejected the Stooges' apocalyptic celebration in favor of reassuringly palliative 45s from Simon & Garfunkel ("Bridge Over Troubled Water"), the Beatles ("Let It Be"), and Ray Stevens ("Everything Is Beautiful").

Sports had long been a refuge for Americans yearning for the nostalgic, comforting glow of simpler times, but now tremors were occurring in that world, too. "Broadway Joe" Namath, a playboy and raconteur who also happened to play quarterback for the New York Jets, had recently shocked the nation by correctly predicting a Super Bowl victory by his upstart AFL squad over the heavily favored Baltimore Colts of the NFL. Nine months after Namath's career-defining Nostradamus moment, the even less-respected New York Mets—a team that had only been in existence since 1962, and had never finished better than ninth in a 10-team league—capped a miraculous 100-win season with a five-game World Series take-down of the mighty Baltimore Orioles. It didn't take an apoplectic Baltimore sports fan or a busted Vegas oddsmaker to sense that change was in the air.

Anyone paying attention to baseball during 1969 should have recognized that a new era in the sport was rapidly emerging. Four teams joined the majors that year—the Kansas City Royals and Seattle Pilots in the American League, and the San Diego Padres and Montreal Expos in the National League. Not only was major league baseball being played for the first time outside the confines of the 50 states, but both leagues were also now split into Eastern and Western divisions, with a new best-of-five playoff to determine which division winners would represent their league in the World Series.

There were changes happening on the field, as well. Concerned that the low-scoring games which characterized the 1968 season—a.k.a. "the Year of the Pitcher," when only six batters in the major leagues hit .300 or better—were alienating the average baseball fan, commissioner Bowie Kuhn mandated that the regulation height of major league pitcher's mounds should be reduced to 10 inches (down from 15-plus), and that umpires should tighten their strike zones. The adjustments resulted in instant offense: Overall scoring for both leagues increased by an average of nearly a run and a half per game. But these changes, though significant, were nothing compared to what 1970 would bring. . . .

For Kuhn, the first sign that the coming year would be a challenging one arrived on Christmas Eve 1969, in the form of a letter from St. Louis Cardinals outfielder Curt Flood. Two months earlier, Flood—a Gold Glove, three-time All-Star center fielder who had been a mainstay of three pennant-winning Cards teams—received word that he'd been traded to the Philadelphia Phillies as part of a seven-man deal that also sent Cards catcher Tim McCarver to Philadelphia, and brought controversial Phils slugger Dick Allen to St. Louis. And now, in a direct challenge to baseball's reserve clause, Flood was refusing to go to the Phillies.

A relic of the late 19th century, the reserve clause had been invented to keep players from jumping to a new team whenever someone offered more money. Under the reserve clause, a player who signed with a particular ballclub was essentially the property of said ballclub in perpetuity, and could be traded or released at the whim of management. Come contract time, a player could conceivably "hold out" for more money; but if the club refused to meet his salary demands, the player's only options were to sign for whatever pittance the team deemed appropriate, or retire from baseball. Besides a painful lack of leverage in salary negotiations, players under the reserve clause had no say regarding where or when a team might trade them; the "no-trade" and "limited-trade" clauses of today's contracts didn't exist.

An intelligent and dignified man, Flood felt the reserve clause was simply a tool for baseball ownership to keep salaries down and control their players—allowing them, in his tart words, "to play God over other people's lives." After twelve seasons and three World Series with the Cardinals, Flood believed he had the right to be treated better than well-fed livestock, and his letter asked Kuhn to declare him a free agent.

The Major League Baseball Players Association had already attempted several times to get the owners to modify the reserve clause, without any success—so no one was particularly surprised when Kuhn denied Flood's initial request. But on January 16, 1970, Flood shocked the baseball world by filing a $4.1 million civil lawsuit against the commissioner and Major League Baseball; the suit challenged the reserve clause, contending that the rule violated federal antitrust laws.

Though Flood was black, and he certainly caused a stir by likening the reserve clause to slavery, he maintained that *Flood v. Kuhn* had less to do with the Black Power movement of the day than with trying to get rid of an antiquated and inequitable aspect of the game. "I'd be lying if I told you that as a black man in baseball I hadn't gone through worse times than my teammates," he told the Players Association. "I'll also say, yes, I think the change in black consciousness in recent years has made me more sensitive to injustice in every area of my life. But I want you to know that what I'm doing here I'm doing as a ballplayer, a major league ballplayer."

Still, many in the media painted Flood as a militant agitator, a baseball counterpart of Stokely Carmichael and the Black Panthers. In the early '70s, any pairing of the words "black" and "militant" was virtually guaranteed to raise the hackles of white America; unsurprisingly, much of the hate mail that Flood received during the case was racial in nature. Some writers painted a picture of Flood as a greedy, self-centered ballplayer (the fact that Flood was already making $90,000 a year won him little sympathy from fans), or as the unwitting dupe of union negotiator and Players Association executive director Marvin Miller.

In reality, Miller had painstakingly prepared Flood for the disastrous effect that the lawsuit could have upon his career. In order to show that he was serious about the cause, Flood would have to sit out the 1970 season while the case went to court; even if he won the case, Miller told him, it was extremely likely that he would be blackballed from the game for having the temerity to challenge the lords of baseball. Though the Players Association was helping to bankroll Flood's lawsuit, the players themselves were queasy about publicly (or even privately) expressing their support for Flood, because of the damage it might cause their own careers. Once the trial opened in May in New York District Court, Hall of Famers Jackie Robinson and Hank Greenberg (as well as former Indians/Browns/White Sox owner Bill Veeck) testified on Flood's behalf, but the witness stand would be noticeably devoid of Flood's former teammates or current players.

Compounding Kuhn's Flood lawsuit headache, the February 23 issue of *Sports Illustrated* broke a story entitled "Baseball's Big Scandal—Denny McLain and the Mob," which revealed that the Detroit Tigers ace (who'd just won the AL Cy Young Award two seasons running) was deeply enmeshed with a Flint, Michigan, bookmaking operation with ties to organized crime. Most damning was the article's allegation that the mysterious foot injury McLain suffered late in the 1967 season—which caused him to miss six starts, and probably cost the Tigers a pennant—had actually been mob payback for welshing on a bet.

Baseball's public image had been relatively spotless since the 1919 "Black Sox" incident—indeed, since the formation of the baseball commissioner's office itself—and a gambling scandal was about the last thing Kuhn wanted, much less on only the second year of his watch. After grilling McLain, the commissioner announced that he was suspending the pitcher indefinitely while launching a full-scale investigation into the matter.

For all his pitching heroics (most notably a 31-win, 280-K, 1.96-ERA performance in 1968), McLain was anything but a sympathetic figure. A self-proclaimed racist and male chauvinist, McLain was prone to shooting his mouth off at the slightest provocation—a quality that made him a favorite of Detroit sports reporters, but which continually aggravated Tigers management and his teammates. He also seemed willing to do just about anything for money (during the off-season, he had a regular gig at the Riviera Hotel in Vegas, playing a Hammond X-77 organ and telling corny jokes), but had a hard time hanging on to any of it; a month after his suspension began, the IRS raided his home in Detroit and took all his furniture to pay off an outstanding tax debt. The idea that McLain might be involved in an illegal gambling operation hardly seemed far-fetched—and, as investigators eventually concluded, it wasn't.

Following the investigation, McLain received a three-month suspension from the commissioner's office, effective April 1. Kuhn took pains to stress that McLain had not wagered on baseball or tampered with any games, but that his suspension was specifically for "his involvement in bookmaking activities in 1967 and his associations at that time." "Half a season?" snorted Tigers catcher Bill Freehan. "That's like saying he almost did something wrong."

Along with the McLain investigation, Kuhn spent much of the 1970 spring training period monitoring the "X-5" experiment. In his continuing quest to beef up the game's offensive stats, Kuhn asked teams to play some of their spring training contests with a test ball known as the X-5, which was supposedly 5 percent livelier than the regulation orb. After only 22 games, pitchers, umpires, and even American League president Joe Cronin begged Kuhn to put an end to the experiment; the final straws, apparently, were a 19–13 Tigers–White Sox contest that saw four different pitchers get hit by line drives, and a 19–14 victory by the Seattle Pilots over the Cleveland Indians.

For the Pilots, the experiment known as "major league baseball in Seattle" was rapidly coming to an end. After only one season—during which they compiled a dismal 64-98 record while playing at the dilapidated, poorly attended, and picturesquely named Sick's Stadium—the expansion team was already out of cash, and plans to build a new ballpark by the Space Needle had been stalled by an army of petition-waving Seattleites.

Though he would become baseball's commissioner two decades later, in 1970 Bud Selig was merely a Wisconsin car dealer consumed with the idea of bringing major league baseball back to Milwaukee. Once a minority shareholder in the Milwaukee Braves, Selig remained convinced that—despite the defection of the Braves to Atlanta—Milwaukee was still a viable baseball market. Aware of the Seattle franchise's mounting difficulties, he began holding secret off-season talks with Pilots owner Dewey Soriano about buying the team and moving it to the twelfth largest city in the U.S.

But when Selig finally made an official overture, pressure from a variety of sources (including the Washington State attorney general) forced the Pilots ownership to decline his offer and cast about instead for a local buyer. Unfortunately, subsequent offers either fell through or were considered unsatisfactory; and by the time spring training rolled around in 1970, the Pilots players and coaching staff had no idea where they would actually be playing come Opening Day.

On April 1, 1970, the Pilots were officially declared bankrupt by a federal bankruptcy referee, and the team was finally allowed to accept Selig's offer of $10.8 million and make the move to Milwaukee. Six days later, the Milwaukee Brewers played their first Opening Day at County

Stadium, in front of an enthusiastic crowd of 37,237. If the team's uniforms looked suspiciously like those of the Seattle Pilots—several tailors had worked around the clock to remove "Pilots" from the jerseys and replace the lettering with "Brewers"—nobody seemed to mind. As Selig later said, "Andy Messersmith [of the California Angels] beat us, 12–0. It's the only game I didn't give a damn if we won or lost. That first day I looked up at the scoreboard, and it was the greatest thrill of my life."

On April 6, in what would be the last home opener ever played at Cincinnati's Crosley Field, the Reds beat the Expos 5–0, giving new manager George "Sparky" Anderson his first major league win; he would go on to record 862 more victories with the Reds, including a total of 102 in 1970 alone. On April 13 in Oakland, the A's played their opener on a Coliseum diamond that was studded with gold bases—an eye-catching innovation cooked up by A's owner Charlie O. Finley that would shortly be banned by baseball's Rules Committee.

In Chicago, the Cubs' home opener on April 14 turned ugly as a number of drunk and stoned teenagers and college students—many of them out-of-towners who had come to the Windy City for a protest against the Vietnam War—picked fights in the Wrigley Field bleachers and upper deck with Cubs fans, Wrigley ushers, and one another. When the final out of the Cubs' 5–4 victory over the Phillies was recorded, hundreds of fans hurdled the right field wall and invaded the field; Cubs second baseman Glenn Beckert was knocked over in the melee, and one teenage usher had his teeth kicked in.

Though it would become a yuppie haven in the 1980s, Wrigleyville circa 1970 was actually a fairly dicey North Side neighborhood; in May, a group of local Native Americans would stage a monthlong campout across the street from Wrigley Field, erecting tepees and other makeshift shelters in protest of the area's rat-infested housing conditions. (Cubs greats Ernie Banks and Billy Williams supposedly stopped by their campfire one night to express support.) Over 50 police officers had been stationed outside Wrigley on Opening Day, but as the Chicago Police Department was still smarting over bad PR from the 1968 Democratic Convention riots, the assembled officers were leery about entering the privately owned ballpark without an official invitation; they eventually took the field, but only after the worst of the damage had already been done.

The incident instigated a number of security improvements at Wrigley Field, including a ban on beer vendors in the bleachers, the presence of Chicago cops inside the park on weekends and holidays, and—most important—the installation of wire screens that angled out from the top of the outfield walls, which made it far more difficult for crazed Cubs fans to throw things (including themselves) onto the field. From 1970 on, "into-the-basket" homers became as much a part of the Wrigley lexicon as "lost in the ivy" ground-rule doubles.

It didn't take long for the 1970 season to kick into high gear. The Cubs, trying to erase the painful memories of their late-season 1969 collapse, rattled off an 11-game April winning streak, while both the Orioles and Reds took control of their divisions that month and never looked back. (The Reds, in fact, were out of first place for only one game all year, setting an NL record of 178 league-leading days.)

On April 22, just four days after his teammate Nolan Ryan fanned 15 Phillies, Mets ace Tom Seaver tied Steve Carlton's record by striking out 19 Padres, setting another record by striking out 10 in a row to end the game. On April 30, Cubs left fielder Billy Williams ran his NL-record consecutive game streak to 1,000 (it would reach 1,117 before he finally took a day off on September 3); less than two weeks later, indefatigable Atlanta Braves knuckleballer Hoyt Wilhelm became the first pitcher to appear in 1,000 games. On May 12, Williams's teammate Ernie Banks became only the eighth member of the 500-homer club; sadly, Mr. Cub's career was already in decline, thanks to an arthritic left knee, and he would hit only 12 more round-trippers before his retirement at the end of the 1971 season.

On May 17, Hank Aaron—who, unlike Banks, still seemed to have plenty left in the tank—became only the ninth player to cross the 3,000-hit threshold, and also jacked his 570th home run during the game, a

15-inning loss to the Reds. Though Aaron was clearly on pace to pass Babe Ruth's career home run record, he still trailed Willie Mays among active players; many actually expected Mays, who had passed the 600 mark in late 1969, to break the Babe's mark first. On July 18, Mays collected his 3,000th hit, making him and Aaron the only players in history to reach both the 3,000-hit and 500-homer plateaus.

May brought additional migraines for Bowie Kuhn, via an advance excerpt of Jim Bouton's *Ball Four* that appeared in *Look* magazine. A diary of Bouton's 1969 season with the Pilots and Houston Astros, sprinkled with reminiscences from his days with the New York Yankees, *Ball Four* is—at least by today's standards—a highly entertaining if relatively tame read. But back in 1970, Bouton might as well have gone to Cooperstown and smeared the plaques with his own feces.

Though Jim Brosnan, a pitcher for the Cubs and Reds, had published two such memoirs a decade earlier—1959's *The Long Season* and 1961's *Pennant Race*—neither packed the controversial punch of Bouton's book. With its hilarious tales of skirt chasing, drunken benders, and widespread use of amphetamines (or "greenies," as they were known in the dugout), *Ball Four* broke the clubhouse *omerta*, portraying major league baseball players as real human beings, as opposed to idealized paragons of virtue. "Fans are fed a constant stream of bull about these clean-cut, All-America guys," Bouton told *Time* shortly after the book was published. "Let kids start thinking about some real heroes instead of phony heroes."

But for those who still clung to the belief that baseball and its players were an integral part of all that was good and noble and true about America, *Ball Four*'s revelations of a brutally hungover Mickey Mantle, Whitey Ford sneakily doctoring baseballs, and players cheating on their wives (or even French-kissing each other on the team bus in a game called "Pansy") were positively traumatic. Not only was Kuhn—who had spent several idyllic high school summers working as a Washington Senators "scoreboard boy" at Griffith Stadium in the 1940s—profoundly incensed that Bouton would choose to write such a book, but he also simply refused to believe that much of the book's contents were factual. "It struck me as not very credible stuff," Kuhn would later insist in his own autobiography.

On June 1, Kuhn summoned Bouton to his office, where he told the pitcher that he'd done the game "a grave disservice," and tried to pressure him into signing a prepared statement renouncing *Ball Four* and placing the blame for all the book's "falsehoods" on Bouton's editor. When Bouton refused, Kuhn forbade the pitcher (who was still on the Astros' roster) from writing another word about baseball as long as he was playing—and also made Bouton promise to keep their meeting a secret. Instead, Bouton's publisher began promoting *Ball Four* as "the book the commissioner tried to ban"; within weeks, it was on the best-seller list, on its way to becoming the best-selling sports memoir of all time.

In retrospect, Bouton believed that Kuhn's negative reaction to *Ball Four* had more to do with the book's behind-the-scenes look at contract negotiations than with its stories of off-the-field antics. With *Flood v. Kuhn* in the courts, the last thing the commissioner wanted the public to read was detailed accounts of how the owners and their general managers consistently used the reserve clause to their advantage in salary talks; equally damaging was Bouton's assertion that most players had as much difficulty making ends meet as the average American working stiff.

"The owners preached that the reserve clause was necessary [for them] to stay in business," Bouton wrote in a subsequent preface to his book, "and that players were well paid and fairly treated. (Mickey Mantle's $100,000 salary was always announced with great fanfare while all the $9,000 and $12,000 salaries were kept secret.) The owners had always insisted that dealings between players and teams be kept strictly confidential. They knew that if the public ever learned the truth, it would make it more difficult to defend the reserve clause against future challenges."

But most players were too worried about the effect that Bouton's accounts of "beaver shooting" might have upon their own marriages to consider the book's possible long-term labor ramifications. Overnight, Bouton became a pariah, snubbed by teammates past and present, and subjected to all sorts of abuse from other teams. Before a game in San

Diego, the Padres burned a copy of *Ball Four* and left its charred remnants in the visitors' clubhouse for Bouton to discover. When Bouton took the mound against the Reds, Pete Rose berated him from the top step of the Cincinnati dugout, screaming, "Fuck you, Shakespeare!" "Why didn't he write that he is the horniest guy in baseball?" complained Bouton's Astros teammate Joe Pepitone.

Sportswriters were equally peeved about *Ball Four*. Having tacitly agreed for decades to keep the "dirt" on players' personal lives out of their coverage, they realized to their horror that they'd been scooped by one of the very players they'd been protecting. *Ball Four* received many raves from nonsports publications, however; no less a writer than Pulitzer Prize winner David Halberstam compared Bouton's book—and the sporting press's reaction against it—to Sy Hersh's controversial expose of the My Lai massacre.

With its candor, humor, and insightful "regular-guy" attitude, *Ball Four* did indeed move the fences for all subsequent sports autobiographies; over the next decade, the generic, whitewashed, ghostwritten baseball memoir would soon be replaced by such warts-and-all chronicles as Sparky Lyle's *The Bronx Zoo* and Bill Lee's *The Wrong Stuff*. Mickey Mantle and Whitey Ford would both eventually publish tell-alls that went into far greater detail about their personal foibles than Bouton ever did, while Joe Pepitone's sex-drenched *Joe, You Coulda Made Us Proud*—published only five years after *Ball Four*—would make it exceedingly clear that "the horniest guy in baseball" was actually Pepitone himself.

Bowie Kuhn may have been appalled by *Ball Four*'s tales of groupies and greenies, but the commissioner would have suffered a total cardiac if he'd realized what Dock Ellis was up to. With the counterculture still on the rise in the wake of Woodstock, it was only a matter of time before it infiltrated the world between the foul lines—and as befit a man whose name could be written out on a scorecard as "Ellis, D," the 25-year-old Pittsburgh Pirates pitcher loved nothing better than to spend his off-days tripping on acid in his psychedelically decorated basement while cranking

Jimi Hendrix, Black Sabbath, and Iron Butterfly. But on the afternoon of June 12, 1970, just as his latest tab of Purple Haze was beginning to kick in, Ellis realized that he was actually supposed to be pitching in a few hours, in a ballpark 120 miles away.

The strange saga of Dock Ellis's LSD no-hitter actually began two days earlier, on Wednesday, June 10. The Pirates had just finished a series with the Giants in San Francisco and flown down to San Diego, where their four-game series against the Padres was scheduled to commence that Friday. A native of Los Angeles, Ellis decided to take advantage of his day off by dropping acid, renting a car, and driving up to L.A. (apparently in that order) to see some pals. They spent Wednesday night smoking weed and drinking screwdrivers until the sun came up, whereupon Ellis finally crashed. Upon awakening, Ellis dropped another tab of acid; after all, he reasoned, he wasn't slated to pitch again until Friday. Unfortunately, as one of his friends soon informed him, it *was* Friday—Ellis had completely slept through Thursday.

Somehow, Ellis's friend—who also happened to be tripping—managed to get the pitcher to LAX, where he caught a shuttle flight to San Diego. Arriving at the park about 90 minutes before first pitch, he popped several Benzedrine "white crosses" to try to even things out, and went to warm up in the bullpen. Speaking to poet Donald Hall for his book, *Dock Ellis in the Country of Baseball*, Ellis recalled that the ball felt like a "very heavy volleyball," and that he figured he'd be lucky to last an inning.

Things got even weirder once he took the mound. The ball's size and weight kept changing, and at times Ellis couldn't make out his catcher, Jerry May, through the psychedelic fog—but as long as Ellis could still see the reflective tape on May's fingers, he knew more or less where May's mitt would be. For much of the game, Ellis had no idea what the score was, how many outs had been recorded, or how many runners were on base. He was wild, walking eight batters and hitting one, and the Padres—who noticed that Ellis seemed oddly uninterested in holding runners at first—stole three bases off him. All Ellis cared about was throwing the ball "down the multi-colored path" to May.

Baseball superstition dictates that whenever a pitcher is in the process of throwing a no-hitter, his teammates must refrain from speaking to him in the dugout, lest they jinx his effort. Ellis, completely unaware that he was racking up consecutive hitless innings, mistook his teammates' respectful distance for silent disapproval of his acid-fried state. To combat his encroaching paranoia, he concentrated on painstakingly removing the mud from his cleats with a tongue depressor, and avoided any eye contact with the Pirates' players or coaches.

Some sources claim that Pirates rookie Dave Cash committed a major faux pas by blithely informing Ellis halfway through the game that he was working on a no-hitter; others have said Ellis turned to Cash in the seventh and tempted fate with a shout of, "Hey look, I've got a no-no going!" What's certain is that Ellis's concentration grew more laserlike as the game went on; after Willie Stargell put him up 2–0 in the seventh with his second solo shot off Padres pitcher Dave Roberts, Ellis allowed only one more base runner over the three final innings. With two outs in the ninth, Ellis caught Padres pinch hitter Ed Spiezio looking on a 3-2 pitch, and baseball's only LSD-assisted no-hitter was in the bag, man.

If mind-expanding drugs were beyond the comprehension of major league baseball at the time, the sport had equally little clue of how to deal with depression or other mental-health issues. Twelve days after Ellis's no-hitter, in the ninth inning of a 7–2 Indians victory over the Yankees in the Bronx, Cleveland first baseman Tony Horton stepped to the plate and dared New York reliever Steve Hamilton to throw his famous "folly floater," a slow-moving, high-arcing "eephus pitch" that looked easy to hit but mystified most batters. When the 6-foot-7 lefty obliged, Horton fouled it off, then dared the pitcher to throw another. This time, Horton popped the floater back toward the screen, where rookie catcher Thurman Munson made a fine running catch for the out. Horton made a big show of throwing away his helmet and bat, and raising his arms to the crowd in a gesture of helplessness; then, to the amusement of the assembled players and fans, he dropped to his hands and knees and crawled into the dugout.

Horton's "crawl of shame" was done strictly for laughs, but what was actually going on inside his head during 1970 was far less amusing. In 1969, Horton hit 27 homers and drove in 93 runs as one of the few legitimate stars of a terrible Indians squad. When the season ended, Horton asked for a $100,000 contract—nearly three times what he'd been making—but manager Alvin Dark allegedly told him that if he didn't sign for the Indians' offer of $46,000, he'd bench him and play fan favorite Ken "the Hawk" Harrelson at first instead. Horton finally accepted the team's lowball offer in the spring of 1970, then immediately kicked himself for doing so when Harrelson went down with a season-ending injury.

From then on, 1970 was sheer torture for Horton. The Cleveland press portrayed him as a greedy prima donna, and Indians fans booed him mercilessly when he failed to consistently produce as he'd done the year before. He hit three home runs in a May 24 game against the Yankees, then went 21 straight games without hitting another. Already a high-strung, intense individual, Horton was starting to fall apart under the pressure. He was having difficulty eating and sleeping, and the additional batting practice he imposed upon himself only wore him down further.

"You could see it building with him that year," recalled Indians third baseman Graig Nettles. "I think he felt he was letting his folks down, and that pressured him a lot. Then one day he walked into the clubhouse and looked like a zombie with his eyes set back in his head. . . . He was gone."

Finally, during the second half of an August 28 doubleheader against the California Angels, Horton seemed so out of it that several of his teammates prevailed upon Dark to take him out in the fifth inning. "He was deeply troubled, asking me what was wrong with him," Indians hurler Sam McDowell remembered. "He was wandering around the clubhouse in his T-shirt, shorts, and shower slippers, kind of dazed." The next morning, at around 5 a.m., Horton was discovered in his car outside the Blue Grass Motel in Cleveland, where he'd been living at the time; his wrists were slit and bleeding profusely, but motel security was able to call an ambulance before it was too late.

The Indians somehow managed to cover up Horton's suicide attempt, simply announcing that they were putting him on the disabled list for emotional distress. In January 1971, the team finally revealed that their first baseman had been hospitalized since September for a nervous breakdown, and that he would miss spring training and probably the whole 1971 season. "The doctor is talking about Tony playing again next year, and he could even change his opinion about Tony playing this year," Horton's father told the *Sporting News*. (The full extent of Horton's breakdown, including his suicide attempt, wouldn't be known to the public until 1997, when *New York Daily News* sportswriter Bill Madden uncovered the details.)

In reality, Horton's doctors had recommended that he divorce himself completely from the sport, worrying that even watching the game on television could trigger another breakdown. Though Horton would eventually recover from his breakdown, he would never return to baseball.

By the All-Star break, all four of the teams that would make the 1970 postseason—the Pirates, Reds, Orioles, and Twins—were already sitting atop their respective divisions. Of these four, the Reds' success in the first half of the season was by far the most surprising; the Orioles' and Twins' squads were essentially identical to the ones that had met in the first-ever AL Championship Series the year before, while the Pirates were a solid team that still contained a few important links (Roberto Clemente and Bill Mazeroski) to their 1960 world championship roster.

The Reds, however, were piloted by a manager with no prior major league experience, and had several key players (starters Johnny Bench, Dave Concepcion, and Bernie Carbo, and pitchers Gary Nolan, Wayne Simpson, and Pedro Borbon) who were 22 or younger when the season began. And yet, they were beating the tar out of nearly everyone they played.

1970 marked the emergence of the "the Big Red Machine," one of the decade's most dominant and iconic teams. In nine seasons with Sparky Anderson at the helm, they would win the division six times, finishing lower than second place only once. Though the Reds were already 10 games ahead of the second-place Los Angeles Dodgers in the NL West by the All-Star break, the All-Star Game itself officially served notice to the rest of the world that the new-model Reds team was a far different animal from the Cincy squads of the previous decade.

Held at the team's brand-new Riverfront Stadium, the Midsummer Classic featured two Reds in the NL starting lineup—Bench at catcher and Tony Perez at third base—and three others (outfielder Pete Rose and pitchers Jim Merritt and Wayne Simpson) on the bench. 1970 was the first time in over a decade when fans elected the All-Star starters; ironically, the tradition had been suspended following a 1957 ballot-stuffing plot by Cincinnati fans that resulted in seven Reds players making the starting lineup. This time, however, every Red on the squad deserved to be there—and one would even win the game with his trademark hustle.

The National League had taken eight straight and 11 of the last 13 All-Star Games, but in 1970 the American League squad put up a good fight, taking a 4–1 lead into the bottom of the ninth, whereupon the NL tied it up on a Dick Dietz solo shot off of Catfish Hunter, a run-scoring Willie McCovey single off of Fritz Peterson, and a Roberto Clemente sacrifice fly off of Mel Stottlemyre. With the game still tied 4–4 in the bottom of the 12th, Rose stepped to the plate with two outs and no one on, and smacked a Clyde Wright pitch to center for a single. He then took second on a Billy Grabarkewitz single and when Jim Hickman followed with a single of his own, Rose was determined to score. Amos Otis's powerful throw from center looked like it might beat Rose to the plate, but it came in off line; when Indians catcher Ray Fosse moved up the third-base line to flag it down, Rose—who typically slid headfirst—laid the catcher out with a full-body football block, separating Fosse's shoulder in the process. Fosse dropped the ball, Rose was safe, and the National League was again victorious.

Opinion was split on the Rose-Fosse collision; Angels shortstop Jim Fregosi, who was on the AL roster as a reserve, told reporters, "I didn't particularly like the play. All Rose has to do is slide, and nobody gets hurt." But Orioles/AL manager Earl Weaver admitted that he saw nothing wrong with it, saying, "That's the way the game should be played." The hit only enhanced Rose's image as "Charlie Hustle," a guy who would run through a brick wall if the game was on the line—and even if it wasn't. Fosse, a promising young backstop who had been hitting .312 with 16 homers at the time of the All-Star break, was never the same after the collision; altering his swing to compensate for his injured wing, he would hit hit only two homers over the second half of the season.

In addition to Seaver's 19-K game and Ellis's no-hitter, the pitching highlights of the 1970 season included a July 20 no-hitter by Dodger pitcher Bill Singer, who'd recently checked out of the hospital following a three-week stay for hepatitis, and Phillies pitcher Jim Bunning's August 11 victory over the Astros, which made him the first pitcher since Cy Young to win 100 games in both leagues. And on September 21, after taking a no-hitter against the Royals into the eighth inning just ten days earlier, Oakland A's rookie Vida Blue threw a 6–0 no-no against the Twins, walking only one batter in the process.

Blue's mound opponent that night was no less a hurler than Twins ace Jim Perry, whose 24-12, 3.04 record would earn him the 1970 AL Cy Young. Jim's brother, Giants ace Gaylord Perry, would come in second in the NL Cy Young voting behind the Cardinals' Bob Gibson with a 23-13, 3.20 season. It would be the closest two brothers ever came to winning a Cy Young in the same year, and their 47 combined wins for the season were only two fewer than the fraternal record of 49, held since 1934 by Dizzy and Paul Dean.

Blue's dominant performance was both a preview of the greatness he'd achieve the following season, and a harbinger of the A's dynasty to come. In 1970, the team finished second in the AL West to the Twins for the second year in a row, causing owner Charlie O. Finley to fire manager John McNamara and replace him with former Red Sox skipper Dick Williams; from 1971 to 1975, they'd own the division.

If Blue and the A's were on the way up, Denny McLain was on the express elevator down, and he very nearly took the Tigers with him. Already seven games behind the Orioles when their star pitcher returned from his three-month suspension on July 1, the team held out hope that he could help them get back in the race. But while capacity crowds showed up to see him wherever he pitched, McLain proved a pale imitation of his former self. Except, of course, when it came to getting into trouble—in that regard, he was still very much on top of his game.

On August 28, McLain dumped buckets of water on two Detroit sportswriters in the Tigers' locker room; though he claimed it was a practical joke, Tigers GM Jim Campbell suspended McLain for a week. The day before he was scheduled to return to the team, McLain was suspended *again* by Kuhn, who'd gotten word that the pitcher—in total violation of the probationary period following his April 1 suspension—had been packing heat on a road trip to Chicago, where he'd shown off his handgun to several of his teammates during dinner at a Chitown restaurant.

"I'll confess I didn't have a permit to carry a concealed weapon," McLain would later admit, "but thousands of people in Detroit carry guns. After all, Detroit is Murder City and getting bloodier every year." Such logic failed to sway the commissioner, who suspended him for the remainder of the season.

Curt Flood might have had a stronger case than McLain, but he fared no better before the New York District Court than the two-time Cy Young winner had done with the commissioner's office. On August 12, Judge Irving Ben Cooper, who'd displayed a noticeably condescending attitude toward Flood throughout the trial—"This isn't as easy as playing center field, is it?" he asked during one cross-examination—ruled in baseball's favor, forcing Flood, Marvin Miller, and the Players Association to take the case to the U.S. Court of Appeals.

With all four division races already decided by late September—the Orioles, Reds, and Twins won their respective titles with ease; the Cubs and Mets both had a legitimate shot to catch the Pirates in the NL East, but simply ran out of steam—the final day of the season was significant chiefly for Angels outfielder Alex Johnson's edging out Boston's Carl Yastrzemski for the AL batting title, with a .3290 average to Yaz's .3286. (Atlanta's Rico Carty won the NL crown with ease; his .366 average was 41 points higher than those of his nearest challengers—the Cardinals' Joe Torre and the Pirates' Manny Sanguillen—as well the highest major league average recorded since Ted Williams hit .388 in 1957.) The evening of October 1 also witnessed the last game ever played at Philadelphia's Connie Mack Stadium, which Phillies fans observed by staging the season's biggest on-field riot since Opening Day at Wrigley.

With the city's long-delayed, multipurpose Veterans Stadium finally due to open in time for the 1971 season, nearly 32,000 Philadelphians—by far the largest crowd of the year—showed up to bid farewell to the oldest ballpark in the big leagues, which had stood since 1909. Sensing that there might be trouble, the Phillies' management gave away souvenir seat slats to everyone who entered the ballpark, in hopes of discouraging fans from hacking up the stadium's old wooden seats. Which was, of course, exactly what the fans immediately set about doing—only now they had souvenir slats that they could use as hammers. As the *Sporting News* reported, "All through the game, which the Phillies won in 10 innings from the Expos to escape an East Division cellar finish, the sounds of hammering could be heard."

Drunken Phillies fans continually ran onto the field throughout the game, causing the action to be stopped several times. In the top of the ninth, one fan somehow managed to grab Phillies left fielder Ron Stone just as an Expos player hit a soft liner to left, causing Stone to get a late jump on the ball. (For some reason, the hit was allowed to stand.) When the Phillies finally won the game in the bottom of the 10th, team management tried to begin its "fan appreciation" raffle—which included a 1970 Ford Mustang—but despite the presence of 200 of Philadelphia's finest, the fans showed their own appreciation by ransacking the dugouts, the infield tarp, and the outfield-wall billboards for souvenirs; one fan was even spotted carrying off a toilet. Fights broke out over the spoils, and 25 bloodied individuals had to be carted off to local hospitals. When it was all over, the old park looked like a tornado had ripped through it.

In the AL Championship Series, the Baltimore Orioles did a tornado imitation of their own as they blew through the Minnesota Twins in three straight games. The Twins had a strong team led by Jim Perry, third baseman Harmon "the Fat Kid" Killebrew (.271, 41 HRs, 113 RBIs), and outfielder Tony Oliva (.325, 23 HRs, 107 RBIs), but they were no match for an Orioles team anchored by AL MVP Boog Powell (.297, 35 HRs, 114 RBIs), third sacker Brooks Robinson (.276, 18 HRs, 94 RBIs), and right fielder Frank Robinson (.306, 25 HRs, 78 RBIs), and a pitching staff that featured three 20-game winners: Mike Cuellar (24-8, 3.48 ERA, 190 Ks), Dave McNally (24-9, 3.22 ERA, 185 Ks), and Jim Palmer (20-10, 2.71 ERA, 199 Ks). It was essentially all over after the fourth inning of Game 1, when Cuellar smacked a grand slam off of Perry on the way to a 10–6 victory. Sadly for the Twins, the series would also be their last postseason hurrah of the decade; they would finish no higher than third place in the AL West until 1984.

The Reds faced off against the Pirates in the first postseason series ever played on artificial turf, with Pittsburgh's new Three Rivers Stadium— which opened in July, just two and a half weeks after Riverfront—hosting Games 1 and 2, and the series moving to Riverfront for Game 3. The Reds won all three contests, though it turned out to be a far more even matchup between the two teams than their respective won-loss records—102-60 versus 89-73—might have indicated. The Pirates were powered by left fielder Willie Stargell (31 HRs, 85 RBIs) and first baseman Bob Robertson (27 HRs, 82 RBIs), while catcher Manny Sanguillen had tied for second in the NL batting department, and Roberto Clemente (.352, 14 HRs, 60 RBIs) would have qualified for second in the batting race if injuries hadn't limited him to only 412 at bats.

The Reds' offense was even more intimidating. Johnny Bench's production (.293, 45 HRs, 148 RBIs) won him his first NL MVP award, but Tony Perez (.317, 40 HRs, 129 RBIs), first baseman Lee May (34 HRs, 94

RBIs), and rookie outfielder Bernie Carbo (.310, 21 HRs) brought plenty of pop as well, while outfielders Pete Rose and Bobby Tolan had each hit .316 for the year.

And yet, the 1970 NLCS was all about pitching. In Game 1, Dock Ellis (13-10, 3.21 ERA) and Gary Nolan (18-7, 3.27) battled it out for nine scoreless innings before the Reds finally broke through for three runs in the top of the 10th. In Game 2, Tolan single-handedly provided the margin of the Reds' 3–1 victory; in the third, he stole second, went to third on a Sanguillen throwing error, and came home on a wild pitch by Luke Walker (15-6, 3.04); he then hit a solo shot off Walker in the fifth. In Game 3, Bench and Perez hit solo homers off of Bob Moose (11-10, 3.99), but Tolan once again provided the game-winning heroics with an eighth-inning single that drove in Ty Cline to seal the 3–2 victory.

The Orioles, however, proved a much more formidable opponent. Having been embarrassed in the World Series the year before, this Baltimore team would not be denied a championship. Though the Reds were outraged in Game 1 when umpire Ken Burkhart—despite having his back to the play—called Carbo out on a play at the plate, blown calls were the least of their problems. The Cincinnati hitters and pitchers were simply outmatched by the Orioles, and any home-field advantage that the Reds might have enjoyed in Games 1 and 2—the first World Series games ever played on artificial turf—was completely nullified by the stellar Orioles defense. Series MVP Brooks Robinson almost single-handedly dismantled the Reds with his timely hitting (.429 with two homers) and one acrobatic "human vacuum cleaner" fielding play after another. When the Orioles secured the World Championship with a 9–3 blowout in Game 5, Johnny Bench told *Sports Illustrated*, "I hope we can come back and play the Orioles next year. I also hope Brooks Robinson has retired by then."

On October 9, the day before the World Series commenced, Bowie Kuhn called a special press conference to announce that the Tigers had traded Denny McLain to the Washington Senators as part of an eight-player deal. The commissioner didn't usually hold press conferences for trades, but since McLain was still under suspension, he felt he had to put his imprimatur on the transaction. Kuhn also announced that as one of the terms of the deal, McLain had taken (and passed) a psychiatric examination. "I have a piece of paper saying I'm sane," McLain later bragged to reporters. "Do you have the same?" Shortly after the press conference, Tigers GM Jim Campbell was spotted tossing a small package of Tums antacid tablets into the gutter. "I won't be needing these anymore," he said.

His guts still gurgling from the team's fourth-place, 79-83 performance, Campbell also fired manager Mayo Smith at the end of the season, replacing him with Billy Martin—who had managed the Twins to the AL West title the previous year, only to be fired after beating up Twins pitcher Dave Boswell in a bar fight. The Tigers' front office felt that Smith (despite having won the World Series only two years earlier) had "lost" the team with his friendly, low-key style; therefore, it was time to bring in a hard-ass like Martin. The Tigers would show dramatic improvement under their new manager—but as with all of Martin's teams, they would find that the success came at a price.

CHAPTER 2
1971

A platinum year in the middle of the golden age of soul music, 1971 saw the release of Marvin Gaye's *What's Going On*, Sly and the Family Stone's *There's a Riot Goin' On*, Curtis Mayfield's *Roots*, and Funkadelic's *Maggot Brain*, as well as such James Brown hits as "Escape-ism," "Get Up, Get into It, Get Involved," and "Soul Power." All of these records were stunning works of sonic art that pushed the boundaries of soul, funk, and R&B, packed with deeper and more devastating social commentary than most contemporary white recording artists were delivering. And with the exception of Funkadelic, which was a little bit too freaky even for the times, these records all sold in huge numbers; *What's Going On* and *Riot* even spent several weeks at the top of *Billboard*'s pop albums chart.

Though the messages of these records were uncompromising, they found favor with white listeners as well as black ones; living in Nixon's America—especially in the wake of the Kent State shootings in May 1970—it wasn't too difficult for your average Caucasian kid to relate to the sentiments of frustration and disillusionment voiced by Marvin, Sly, et al., or to acknowledge the need for people to stay strong and unified in the ongoing fight against injustice and oppression, as Mayfield and Brown so movingly preached.

1971 was a landmark year for African-Americans in film as well. Shot in guerrilla fashion on a shoestring budget, Melvin Van Peebles's *Sweet Sweetback's Baadasssss Song* grossed over $4 million upon its release, demonstrating to the Hollywood establishment that there was an untapped market among black audiences (and white audiences, too) for movies featuring ass-kicking black heroes socking it to The Man. The first true salvo of the ensuing "blaxploitation" boom—which would produce works as brilliant as *Across 110th Street*, and as regrettable as *Blackenstein*—was 1971's *Shaft*, an action film directed by renowned black photographer-journalist Gordon Parks Sr., and starring Richard Roundtree as a black private detective who goes up against the New York mob. Made for just over $1 million, *Shaft* grossed over 12 times that amount, and the film won an Academy Award for Isaac Hayes's percussive, wah-wah-driven sound track.

But while blacks were increasingly making their presence felt in the mainstream entertainment industry, African-American progress in major league baseball was moving at a slower pace. It had been nearly a quarter century since Jackie Robinson and Larry Doby had integrated their respective leagues; and while the number of players of color in the sport had steadily increased in recent years, especially in the National League, there still weren't many positions for blacks outside the foul lines in the early 1970s. A black man could direct a Hollywood film or run his own record label—yet major league teams were still too squeamish to hire a black manager, put a black man in their front office, or in most cases even include one on their coaching staff.

Nevertheless, the 1971 baseball season saw several important advances that pointed to the continuing integration of the sport, advances as significant in their own way as *Sweet Sweetback's* box-office profits or Isaac Hayes's Oscar. In February, the Hall of Fame's new Special Committee on the Negro Leagues recommended the legendary Satchel Paige for induction at Cooperstown; the very existence of a Negro Leagues committee, formed at the urging of the Baseball Writers' Association of America, was a long overdue acknowledgment of the excellence of black ballplayers who played during the "color-line" era. It was also a tacit admission that in more enlightened times, Paige and his fellow Negro League stars—including Josh Gibson, Buck Leonard, Judy Johnson, Cool Papa Bell, Pop Lloyd, Oscar Charleston, and Martin Dihigo—would have been fit to compete against or play alongside the likes of Ruth, Cobb, et al.

In July, Vida Blue and Dock Ellis would take the mound as the respective AL and NL starters for the 1971 All-Star Game, marking the first time that two black pitchers had been tapped to start the same Midsummer Classic. At the end of the season, Blue would take home the AL Cy Young Award, while Cubs ace Fergie Jenkins would get the Cy nod in the NL—the first time two black hurlers won pitching's top honor in the same season. And in September, on their way to their first World Series championship since 1960, the Pittsburgh Pirates would become the first team to field a starting nine made up entirely of black and Latino players.

But even amid these signs of progress, Curt Flood's historic battle seemed to be going nowhere. Major league owners were absolutely petrified by the prospect of Flood winning his case, and the ramifications it might have upon both player salaries and baseball's antitrust exemption; on several occasions in late 1970 and early 1971, their lawyers had approached Flood's attorneys about settling the case before the U.S. Circuit Court of Appeals had a chance to rule upon it. But they breathed a collective sigh of relief on April 7, 1971, when the court of appeals upheld the district court's original dismissal of *Flood v. Kuhn*.

In the months leading up to the appeals court's ruling, Carl Yastrzemski had signed a three-year deal with the Boston Red Sox that totaled $500,000 (to date, the heftiest contract ever signed), and the San Francisco Giants had made Willie Mays the highest-paid player in the game with a $165,000-per-year deal that would last through the 1972 season. Though the average baseball salary at the time was just a little over $31,000—and many players were making the minimum of $12,750—the announcement of Yaz's and Mays's new big-bucks contracts didn't exactly bolster Flood's case before the appeals court, or in the court of public opinion.

Left with the choice of dropping the case or filing an appeal with the U.S. Supreme Court, Flood, Marvin Miller, and their attorneys opted for the latter; meanwhile, Flood tried to resume his stalled baseball career. He'd been traded over the winter by the Phillies—for whom he never played a game—to the Washington Senators in exchange for three minor league players. Flood signed a deal with Washington owner Bob Short, under the conditions that Short not trade him without his consent, that Flood would be paid his full salary ($110,000) if he was cut from the team before the end of the season, that he would be unconditionally released if they couldn't agree on the terms of a new contract for 1972, and that major league owners wouldn't argue in court that Flood had invalidated his lawsuit by donning a Senators uniform.

Short agreed to all of Flood's conditions; unfortunately, the former All-Star's body was less cooperative. He hadn't kept up a rigorous training schedule during his hiatus; and the 34-year-old's speed, stamina, and batting eye weren't what they used to be. Two days before the court of appeals handed down its ruling, Flood went 1-for-3 with two walks and two runs scored in the Senators' 8–0 Opening Day victory against the A's and Vida Blue; but over the next 12 games, Flood would manage only six singles in 32 at bats. Humiliated by his poor on-field performance, and beset by a number of personal and financial issues, Flood abruptly jumped the team on April 25 and caught a jet to Europe, never to play another game in the major leagues. His telegram to Short read, in part: "I tried. A year and a half is too much. Very serious problems mounting every day. Thanks for your confidence and understanding." As Bowie Kuhn would wryly note in his autobiography, "Short . . . would have probably preferred a money order for the unearned salary."

Flood's impromptu defection was actually the least of Short's worries. When Short originally purchased the Washington franchise for $9.4 million in December 1968, the Senators were coming off a last-place finish; it was their eighth straight losing season since joining the American League as an expansion replacement for the original, Calvin Griffith–owned Senators, who had become the Minnesota Twins after the 1960 season. Short's honeymoon period was exciting—under new manager Ted Williams, the new Senators franchise finished fourth in 1969, its first-ever winning season, drawing a franchise-record 918,106 fans in the process. But attendance and team performance began to slide again in 1970, leaving Short with $1 million in operating losses for that season alone; and even though the Senators were still only a game out of first when Flood's apologetic telegram arrived, it was rapidly becoming clear to Short that it would take more than the charismatic presence of Denny McLain, Short's other high-profile reclamation project, to make the Senators a profitable enterprise.

Griffith had often complained that the nation's capital was incapable of supporting a major league team, and now—with the D.C. Armory Board threatening to cut off RFK Stadium's lights if it didn't immediately receive back rent for 1970—Short was beginning to agree. Outside of the Beltway, the capital was becoming an increasingly dangerous city; more and more middle-class residents were moving to the suburbs, and the Senators' shoddy brand of baseball wasn't exactly luring them back.

"No place in Washington is safe at night, and [President] Nixon can't do anything about it," Short complained to Bowie Kuhn, who adamantly opposed the idea of a Senators move. "Ted [Williams] says Washington is a horseshit town and I've gotta get out. I'll go elsewhere before I'm forced into bankruptcy like Seattle." With Short dropping hints that Dallas would be a better fit for the team, few would be surprised when 1971 turned out to be the Senators' final season in D.C.

Along with the Flood saga, the big story of the spring was Oakland A's pitcher Chuck Dobson's public admission that he'd taken "greenies"— the prescription Dexamyl pills Jim Bouton had mentioned in *Ball Four*— on several occasions. "I don't see anything wrong with it," Dobson told an Oakland beat writer, adding that he'd pitched a greenie-assisted shutout the previous year. Bowie Kuhn blew a fuse upon hearing this, and promptly sent out a warning to players that they were expected to comply with state and federal drug laws. "If the commissioner says we can't use [greenies] anymore," retorted the loquacious pitcher to a reporter, "then the next time someone asks me whether I use them, I'll say no, go around the corner and pop."

Dobson's "What me worry?" attitude toward amphetamine use was shared by a number of big leaguers, as well as countless average Americans; by the late 1960s, businessmen and housewives were now consuming more "diet aids" and "pep pills" than ever before, while soldiers (whom the U.S. government thoughtfully provided with an estimated 225 million doses of amphetamine during the Vietnam War) were returning from 'Nam with a definite taste for the stuff. Amphetamine use had also become prevalent in the counterculture—not just among musicians who used speed as a way to combat the exhausting rigors of touring, but also among hippies and other recreational drug users who wanted to balance out the lows brought about by barbiturate and opiate abuse. In 1970, the Food and Drug Administration had reclassified amphetamines as a Schedule III drug, banning their use without a prescription.

For Kuhn, having a ballplayer loudly extolling the virtues of greenies, especially so soon after the publication of *Ball Four*, was a public-relations nightmare. Dobson—presumably after a stern talking-to from the commish—soon recanted his initial pro-amphetamine statement, issuing a press release that downgraded his career greenie use to a single occasion in 1970, when he popped one "prior to pitching a game after I'd had a bout with the flu." Dobson went on to note penitently that he was "strongly against anyone using drugs in any form."

While the Dobson flap was running its course, A's owner Charlie O. Finley briefly fiddled with an experiment that seemed calculated to drive any pitcher to drug use—namely, the three-ball walk. Designed to increase scoring and speed up the game, Finley's latest "innovation" was showcased in the A's March 6 exhibition contest against the Milwaukee Brewers, wherein the respective staffs combined for a whopping 19 walks over the course of a 13–9 A's victory. Needless to say, Finley's three-ball concept failed to excite the imagination of his fellow owners.

The 1971 season literally started off with a bang, as Willie Mays—just a month away from turning 40—set a major league record by homering for the San Francisco Giants in each of the team's first four games. It was a good omen for the Giants' fortunes; led by Mays and the other three re-maining veterans of the 1962 National League champions squad (Willie McCovey, Juan Marichal, and Gaylord Perry), and bolstered by young slugger Bobby Bonds, the team moved into first place in the NL West on April 12 and stayed there for the rest of the year. Across the Bay, the Oakland A's claimed the AL West top spot just eight days later. While the Giants would have to fight off a late-breaking challenge by the Los Angeles Dodgers in order to make the playoffs, the A's lead over the California Angels just grew more insurmountable as the season went on, thanks in part to the mound heroics of Vida Blue. Blue, who got knocked out of the box by the Senators on Opening Day after only $1\frac{2}{3}$ innings, suddenly became damn near unhittable; by May 23, the 21-year-old lefty with the dramatic windup was already 10-1, and the A's were $7\frac{1}{2}$ games in front of the Angels with a 30-15 record.

Over in the AL East, the defending World Champion Orioles spent most of April in first, then briefly squandered the lead to a surging Bos-ton Red Sox squad before finally taking it back for good in early June. Of the four divisions, the NL East was the one most up for grabs, with every-one except the lowly Philadelphia Phillies taking turns at the top in the first two months of the season, until the Pittsburgh Pirates finally took con-trol on June 10. Pirates first baseman Willie Stargell virtually carried the team through April all by himself, setting a major league record for the month with 11 homers. (Stargell would finish the season with 48 jacks and 125 RBIs, eventually coming in second in the NL MVP voting to Joe Torre of the St. Louis Cardinals, who would lead the NL with a .363 av-erage and 137 RBIs.) Stargell poled his 11th on April 27, but his thunder was stolen somewhat by the Atlanta Braves' Hank Aaron, who homered that day off of Gaylord Perry to become just the third player (behind Mays and Babe Ruth) to hit 600 career round-trippers.

The defending NL champion Cincinnati Reds, off to a lousy start, were already 16 games behind the Giants by the end of May. (They would end up with a 79-83 record, their only losing season under skipper Sparky Anderson; it would also be Anderson's last losing season with any team until 1989.) Bobby Tolan, the fleet-footed center fielder who had hit .316, stolen 57 bases, and scored 112 times for the team in 1970, was out for the season, having ruptured an Achilles tendon while playing for the Reds' off-season basketball team. The Reds' front office summarily disbanded the hoops squad—not exactly a brilliant concept in the first place—but couldn't do anything about its team suffering the indignity of being no-hit twice in three weeks, first on June 3 by the Cubs' Ken Holtzman, then on June 23 by the Phillies' Rick Wise. Holtzman, who had already pitched a hitless gem in 1969, became the only Jewish pitcher besides Sandy Koufax to throw multiple no-nos. (He would go on to become the winningest Jewish pitcher of all time, with 174 victories to Koufax's 165.) Wise homered twice and drove in three runs in his 4–0 no-hit victory over the Reds, becoming the first hurler to homer in his own no-hitter. One of the best hitting pitchers of his era, Wise would finish the season with six round-trippers, including a grand slam against the Giants in August.

The Angels, coming off a 1970 season in which they'd tied a franchise record for victories with 86, never really got it together in '71. The team was beset by injuries to a number of players, but the dark cloud that hovered over defending AL batting champ Alex Johnson seemed to take an even greater toll on the Halos' season.

An enigmatic figure prone to brooding silences, the physically imposing Johnson had been accused in the past of "intimidating" umpires and reporters, but his skill with the bat usually earned him slack (if not exactly affection) from his teammates. But now, Johnson had suddenly begun to "dog it" between the lines. Angels manager Lefty Phillips, upset and mystified by Johnson's lack of hustle, benched his star player five times and fined him on 29 separate occasions, all to no avail; if anything, Johnson became more recalcitrant with each disciplinary action. Though he willingly discussed the benchings and finings with reporters, Johnson seemed unable to explain his lack of motivation in anything but the most oblique terms possible.

"I didn't consciously decide to do this," Johnson told *Sports Illustrated*. "But things are just so disgusting [with the club], it drills on my mind, drills on my mind. . . . I'm not playing any part of the game up to par. I can't. I can't get my mind to want to play the game the way others do."

The difficult situation took a bizarre turn on June 13, when Johnson accused Angels utility man Chico Ruiz of pulling a gun on him in the California locker room during a game against the Senators. Ruiz denied doing anything of the sort, but by now it was obvious that things with Johnson and the Angels were not going to end well. On June 26, the Angels suspended him without pay "for failure to give his best efforts to the winning of games." The Players Association filed a grievance over the suspension; three months later, arbitrator Lewis Gill ruled that Johnson was "emotionally incapacitated" during the 1971 season, and should have been treated the same as a physically disabled player. The Angels, forced to pay Johnson nearly $30,000 in back salary, shipped him off to the Cleveland Indians at the end of the season.

Like Alex Johnson, Dock Ellis was a black man who spoke his mind—only Ellis did it in a far less elliptical fashion. "I'm never sorry for anything I say," he once told a reporter. "If you [can't] say what you want in so-called America, I might as well go to Russia." Of course, such brashness went down easier with a steady string of wins, and the Pirates pitcher was having the season of his life in 1971; by the time the All-Star Game rolled around in July, Ellis had posted a 14-3 record with a 2.11 ERA, and was an obvious shoo-in for inclusion on the NL All-Star roster. But that wasn't enough for Ellis, who felt he deserved to be named as the NL starter against the A's Vida Blue—who, off to an even better start to the year than Ellis (17-3 with a 1.42 ERA), was expected get the ball for the AL. But since both Ellis and Blue were African-American, and the All-Star Game had never previously featured a pair of black starting pitchers, Ellis figured he was fated to start the game on the NL bench.

"I doubt very seriously if they'll start a brother from the American League and a brother from the National," Ellis told the Associated Press, effectively daring NL manager Sparky Anderson to start him—and setting off a firestorm of angry letters and editorials railing against the temerity of this uppity Negro to suggest that baseball (and, by extension, America) didn't always reward the most deserving individuals. Anderson, actually one of the more "color-blind" skippers in the game, surprised Ellis (and defused the controversy) by naming him as the NL starter. The Reds manager insisted on the day of the contest that "what Ellis said didn't influence me. His 14-3 record did—that and the fact that he has had six days' rest."

Blue, a 21-year-old lefty pitching in his first full season, already seemed on the verge of becoming the most dominant hurler in baseball. With his unusual name, flamboyant windup, and dazzling fastball, Blue definitely captured the public imagination. Albert Jones, a Detroit soul singer, even cut a funky single called "Vida Blue": "Killebrew, Yastrzemski, and Gates Brown too," Jones sang, "they can't buy a hit off of Vida Blue." (No disrespect to Brown, one of the great pinch hitters in baseball history, but Jones's song was surely one of the few instances where the Tigers outfielder was ever mentioned in the same breath as Hall of Famers Harmon Killebrew and Carl Yastrzemski.)

Though the Blue-Ellis All-Star pairing was certainly historic, the game—held July 13 at Detroit's venerable Tiger Stadium—would be defined not by ace pitching, or by Jose Feliciano's rocking game-opening rendition of "The Star-Spangled Banner," but by mammoth home runs. Blue, who just four days earlier had thrown an 11-inning shutout against the White Sox, was in far from top form, giving up home runs to Johnny Bench and Hank Aaron in the second and third innings, respectively; Ellis, who managed to get through the first two innings unscathed, melted down in the third, giving up two-run blasts to Reggie Jackson and Frank Robinson (the latter becoming the first player to homer for both leagues as an All-Star). Jackson, pinch-hitting for Blue, rocketed a tremendous shot off the light tower on the right-field roof; the blast was variously estimated as traveling between 520 and 550 feet, but would have sailed even farther if the lights hadn't blocked its trajectory. Jackson stood at the plate and admired his handiwork, then trotted triumphantly around the bases while Ellis fumed on the mound.

Harmon Killebrew added a two-run dinger in the sixth off of the

Cubs' Fergie Jenkins; Roberto Clemente hit a solo shot in the ninth off of Detroit's Mickey Lolich, but the game ended 6–4 in favor of the American League—the first AL victory since 1962, and the last for another 12 years. Blue got the victory, Ellis was tagged with the loss; with all 10 runs coming as a result of home runs by six different future Hall of Famers, the '71 All-Star Game was easily the most memorable NL-AL showdown of the decade, if not the entire post–World War II era.

Both Ellis and Blue slowed down somewhat in the second half of the 1971 season; the former ended the year 19-9 with a 3.06 ERA, while Blue finished with a still-outstanding record of 24-8 and a league-leading 1.82 ERA, along with 301 strikeouts. (He came in second in wins and Ks behind Detroit's Mickey Lolich, who notched 25 and 308, respectively.) On August 7, Blue became the first 20-game winner in the majors. Three days later, Killebrew went yard twice against the Orioles, becoming only the 10th player to pass the 500-homer mark. (Frank Robinson would follow him into the "500 Club" a month later.) And on August 14, the St. Louis Cardinals' Bob Gibson, one of the most dominant pitchers of the 1960s, finally notched his first career no-hitter, striking out 10 and driving in three runs while beating the Pirates 11–0 at Pittsburgh. "This was the greatest game I've ever pitched anywhere," exulted Gibson, whose victory pulled the suddenly resurgent Cardinals within five games of the first-place Bucs.

The Cubs were beginning to make a move in the NL East as well; 10½ games back on July 31, they went on a tear and pulled within 4½ on August 20, when staff ace Fergie Jenkins notched his 20th win of the season versus the Houston Astros. Jenkins would beat out Tom Seaver for the NL Cy Young with a 24-13, 2.77-ERA, 263-strikeout season—his fifth straight 20-W, 200-plus-K season for the Cubs.

On August 24, Ernie Banks hit his 512th homer against the Reds at Wrigley Field, but Mr. Cub's final career four-bagger was also one of the last highlights of the Cubs' season. Distracted by increasing animosity between Cubs players (especially Joe Pepitone and Ron Santo) and manager

Leo Durocher, the team blew 10 of its next 12 games, and finished up the season 14 games back of the Pirates. The Cubs did, however, manage to inadvertently help make baseball history on September 29, when hurler Milt Pappas hit Expos second baseman Ron Hunt with a pitch; it was the 50th time that Hunt had been nailed over the course of 1971, breaking a single-season record set back in 1896 by Hughie Jennings. A scrappy hitter with zero power, Hunt would choke up on his bat just short of the trademark and lean precariously over the plate. "Some people give their bodies to science," he'd later joke. "I gave mine to baseball."

Despite the late challenges being mounted by St. Louis and Chicago, the Pirates never stumbled; after August 15, when the Cardinals cut their lead to a mere 3½ games, the Bucs waltzed to the pennant by playing 26-15 ball. Lost in the excitement of their final surge was the fact that on September 1, Pirates manager Danny Murtaugh fielded the first all-black lineup (albeit including several dark-skinned Latinos) in major league history. Starting that day at Three Rivers against the Phillies were Rennie Stennett (2B), Gene Clines (CF), Roberto Clemente (RF), Willie Stargell (LF), Manny Sanguillen (C), Dave Cash (3B), Al Oliver (1B), and Jackie Hernandez (SS), with the ubiquitous Dock Ellis on the mound.

While most of the 11,278 fans in attendance probably failed to recognize the lineup's significance, the majority of the players in the Pirates' clubhouse were well aware of it—though, in testament to the team's impressive interracial harmony, it was seen as an occasion for mirth rather than resentment or payback. "We had a loose group, [so] we were all laughing about it and teasing each other," remembered Steve Blass, a white pitcher who went 15-8 with a 2.85 ERA for the Bucs in '71. Richie Hebner, the Pirates' white regular third baseman, who was then riding the bench with an injury, recalled that "some of the guys joked around the clubhouse, saying, 'Hey, you white guys, you can take it easy tonight.'"

The Pirates won the historic game 10–7, Sanguillen providing the game-winning RBIs with a two-run homer. Murtaugh insisted afterward that his lineup decisions were motivated by the desire to win, not the desire to make social statements. "I put the nine best athletes out there," he told reporters. "The best nine I put out there happened to be black. No big deal. Next question."

The A's and Orioles cruised to their AL division titles, the latter behind the stunning pitching of their "Big Four": Mike Cuellar (20-9, 3.08 ERA), Pat Dobson (20-8, 2.90), Jim Palmer (20-9, 2.68), and Dave McNally (21-5, 2.89), who boasted 12 shutouts and a whopping 70 complete games among them. There hadn't been a team with four 20-game winners since the 1920 White Sox, and the O's seemed like a good bet to repeat as World Champs.

Over in the NL West, the Giants nearly blew an eight-game lead over Los Angeles by losing 11 of 12 over the first two weeks of September. The Dodgers, still in transition between the Koufax-Drysdale glory years and what would become known as the Garvey-Lopes-Russell-Cey era, stayed in the race despite a mediocre lineup, thanks mostly to the strong pitching of Al Downing (20-9, 2.68 ERA), Don Sutton (17-12, 2.54), and closer Jim Brewer (6-5, 1.88, 22 saves). Dick Allen, who hit 23 homers and drove in 90 runs his lone year in Los Angeles, was the only Dodger with more than 12 HRs and 74 RBIs. Allen later opined that the Dodgers could have won the West, but "the problem was all that Dodger Blue jive. [The organization puts] a lot of pressure on players to sign autographs and have their picture taken. They want you to visit with celebs in the clubhouse before games. Have a laugh with Don Rickles. Eat spaghetti with Sinatra. . . . It distracts from the team's mission to win ballgames." In the end, the Giants won the NL West by a single game, and Allen—who quite obviously did not bleed Dodger Blue—was shipped to the White Sox for pitcher Tommy John.

On the night of September 30, the Senators played their final game in Washington, D.C. It had been an awful season, with the Ted Williams–managed team going 63-95—Denny McLain, the Senators' star attraction, was personally responsible for 22 of those losses—and drawing just over 640,000 fans to RFK Stadium. On September 21, American League

owners had voted 10–2 to allow Bob Short to relocate his team to Arlington, Texas, where they would start a new life as the Texas Rangers. (Ironically, one of the no votes came from the Baltimore Orioles, the Senators'
local competition, who were afraid that the National League would move
a better team into the D.C. void.) Now, some 18,000 Senators fans (included an estimated 4,000 gate crashers) showed up to say good-bye to
their team and bay for Short's blood—and not necessarily in that order.

Throughout the Senators' last contest, played against the Yankees, the
crowd expressed its collective displeasure at the team's impending departure by unfurling various homemade signs, most of them reading along
the lines of "Short Stinks," "How Dare You Sell Us Short," and "Fuck
You, Short." In the top of the ninth, with the Senators leading 7–5, the
fans began flocking toward the rails along the field and chanting, "We
want Short!" Some patrons briefly interrupted the game by running onto
the field near first base; as the police escorted them back to their seats, 50
more vaulted over the left-field fence, causing another delay. The Senators'
PA announcer repeatedly asked the crowd to stay in the stands, warning
them that their presence on the field could lead to a forfeit of the game;
but with two out, and the Yankees' Horace Clarke at the plate, one fan
managed to elude the police and promptly set about pulling up first base.
A full-scale riot ensued, with the fans overrunning the field and looting
anything they could get their hands on, including the numbers and light-
bulbs from the scoreboard. The Yankees were awarded a 9–0 forfeit, and
the long (if not exactly glorious) history of Washington, D.C., baseball
came to an ignominious end.

The defending World Champion Orioles took the A's out three games to
nothing in the American League Championship Series, making it look
fairly easy. The young Oakland squad was simply no match for Baltimore's veteran rotation and lineup; Dave McNally beat Vida Blue 5–3 in
the opening contest, and then Mike Cuellar and Jim Palmer followed with
complete-game victories against Catfish Hunter and Diego Segui. Charlie Finley's dream of bringing a championship to Oakland would have to

wait another year, while the Orioles advanced to the World Series for the third straight season.

Over in the NLCS, the Giants won Game 1 5–4, thanks to two-run homers by second baseman Tito Fuentes and first baseman Willie McCovey. Pirates first baseman Bob Robertson single-handedly dismantled the Giants in Game 2, homering three times and driving in five runs in an easy 9–4 win. Giants pitching legend Juan Marichal battled it out with the Bucs' Bob Johnson in Game 3, but came out on the losing end of a 2–1 score thanks to a Richie Hebner solo homer in the eighth. Hebner hit another one in Game 4, but it was Roberto Clemente who broke a 4–4 tie in the bottom of the sixth with a run-scoring single; Clemente then took second on a passed ball, Willie Stargell walked, and Al Oliver put the game out of reach with a three-run blast. For the first time since 1960, the Pirates were going to the World Series, and Clemente's go-ahead RBI was just a taste of the heroics to come.

An intensely proud individual, Clemente had labored in relative obscurity for 16 seasons with the Pirates, often as the lone star of undistinguished teams. Clemente rarely batted below .300, and often hit much higher—his averages for the 1969 through 1971 seasons were .345, .352, and .341, respectively. But because he was a natural line-drive hitter who played most of his career in spacious Forbes Field, his home run and RBI totals were significantly lower than those of Mantle, Mays, and Aaron, so he was generally excluded from the "Who's the greatest outfielder?" debates that continually raged in the papers and the schoolyards.

A far worse indignity, in Clemente's mind, was that the press had long ago branded him a hypochondriac, thanks to a series of chronic physical ailments (some dating back to a childhood car accident) that occasionally required him to sit out two or three games at a time. Bad health continued to dog him in the '71 postseason: Clemente came down with a vicious case of food poisoning on the eve of the World Series, and grew so dehydrated that the team doctor had to hook him up to an IV drip. But it would take a lot more than severe intestinal distress to keep Clemente out of the October Classic. . . .

The 1971 World Series opened in Baltimore, and the Orioles looked every bit the heavily favored returning champions in the first two games, with McNally and Palmer handily keeping the Pirates at bay in 5–3 and 11–3 victories. Frank Robinson and Brooks Robinson both caused significant damage at the plate—the former with a home run and five hits in the first two games, and the latter tying a Series record by reaching base five times in Game 2.

Festivities moved to Pittsburgh for Game 3, where Steve Blass punctured the Orioles' hopes for a Series sweep with a three-hit, complete-game 5–1 Pirates' victory. Frank Robinson homered for the O's in the seventh, and briefly kept the team's hopes alive with a single in the ninth; they would turn out to be the future Hall of Famer's last hits of the Series. Clemente, however, was just getting started. After Robinson's homer cut the Pirates' lead to 2–1, the 37-year-old right fielder led off the bottom of the seventh with a high chopper back to the mound. It looked like a routine out, the sort of play where most batters would have taken a few perfunctory steps toward first before giving up and heading back to the dugout. But as Mike Cuellar nonchalantly waited for the ball to come back to earth, Clemente surprised everyone by actually trying to beat out the hit. A shocked Cuellar threw wide of the bag, and Clemente was safe at first. The play, which Orioles manager Earl Weaver would later call "the key to the Series," unnerved Cuellar enough that he walked Willie Stargell on four pitches, then gave up a three-run Bob Robertson blast to right center, icing the game.

Back in May, Bowie Kuhn—ever mindful of the growing commercial potential of televised baseball—had signed Major League Baseball to a $72 million contract with NBC. As an experiment, Kuhn decided that Game 4, which fell on a Wednesday, would be played at night and broadcast during prime time, making it the first night game in the history of the World Series. In addition to a record-setting Three Rivers crowd of 51,378, the October 13 game attracted a phenomenal 61 million viewers, a significantly larger audience than would have tuned in for a day game. And while Pirates pitcher Bruce Kison earned the 4–3 win with 6⅓ innings of relief work, everyone was talking about Clemente—how he seemed able to hit or catch any ball that came near him, and was running the bases like a man half his age. Each time he came to the plate in Game 4, the Three Rivers organist played "Jesus Christ Superstar," the hit title theme from the Andrew Lloyd Webber/Tim Rice musical that had just opened on Broadway.

In Game 5, veteran Pirates pitcher Nelson Briles shut down the Orioles 4–0 on two measly singles, with Clemente and Robertson (who hit another bomb) driving in key runs for the Bucs. Both players went 2-for-4 in Game 6, with Clemente hitting his first home run of the Series off of Palmer, but the Orioles held on to win it 3–2 in 10 innings on a Brooks Robinson sacrifice fly. The Series was tied at three games apiece, with the home team winning in each contest; despite the Pirates' heroic performances (Clemente's chief among them), conventional wisdom favored the Orioles in Game 7. Clemente, however, wouldn't hear of it. "Don't worry," he told each of his teammates beforehand. "We are gonna win this game. No problem."

Game 7 saw Blass and Cuellar matching up in a scoreless duel for the first three innings. Cuellar, a crafty Cuban lefty who'd perfected a particularly nasty "palmball," had already set 11 Pirates down in order when Clemente stepped to the plate in the top of the fourth—and promptly whacked Cuellar's inside pitch 390 feet into Memorial Stadium's left-field seats. Cuellar refused to be rattled by the blast, however, and kept the Pirates from scoring again until the top of the eighth, when Clemente's fellow countryman Jose Pagan drove in Willie Stargell with a double. The Orioles finally touched Blass for a run in the bottom of the eighth on a fielder's choice, but were unable to gain additional traction. Blass set three straight O's down in the bottom of the ninth, and the Pirates were World Series Champions. Clemente, who had led the team with 12 hits and a .414 average, was named the Series MVP, receiving a new Dodge Charger from *Sport* magazine for his efforts.

Earl Weaver, though impressed with Clemente's performance, crustily refused to concede that the Orioles had been beaten by a better team. "I still think we're the best team in baseball, even though we lost the seventh game to the Pirates," the O's skipper told reporters. "We'll be back here again. We'll win 100 games next year." Though unquestionably a great manager, Weaver would have made a terrible psychic; Baltimore wouldn't win 100 games or return to the World Series until 1979—when they would once again face the Pirates.

Over in the Pirates' clubhouse, Clemente spoke to the TV cameras in Spanish before exulting in English, "Now people in the whole world know the way I play." He then launched into an extended monologue rebutting, once and for all, the years of erroneous talk about him being a hypochondriac, an incomplete player, or too aloof to be a true team leader. "Everything he's saying is true, you know," commented Bucs catcher Manny Sanguillen, who had turned in an impressive 11-hit, .379 batting performance in the Series. "It's strange that he would have to remind people. Everyone should know it."

Now, everyone would. In 1974, singer Tony Orlando and comedian Freddie Prinze would make television history as the first men of Puerto Rican descent to get their own network TV shows, with CBS's *Tony Orlando and Dawn* and NBC's *Chico and the Man*, respectively. But the World Series had already turned Roberto Clemente into America's first true Puerto Rican TV star.

CHAPTER 3
ASHTRAYS AND ASTROTURF

In a decade bookended by *2001: A Space Odyssey* and *The Empire Strikes Back*, it was somehow appropriate that over half of major league baseball's teams played their home games in stadiums that resembled spaceships. In the cultural shorthand of the American 1960s and '70s, space signified the future, the future represented progress, and the civic architecture of the day did its best to reflect this futuristic impulse. While clubs like the Red Sox, Tigers, and Cubs held fast to their charming but ancient bandboxes, a number of organizations would choose to move their operations into larger, publicly funded, multiuse, poured-concrete "state-of-the-art" facilities— many of which looked like crosses between the brutalist concrete structures of Brasilia and sets from *Logan's Run*.

But like *Skylab*, the U.S.-launched space station that fell prematurely out of orbit during the summer of 1979, these "modern" stadiums ultimately failed to stand the test of time. Though they offered welcome improvements like additional restrooms, wider seats, and better sight lines for the fans—the latter thanks to the lack of view-obstructing steel girders—the circular layout of parks like Pittsburgh's Three Rivers Stadium and Philadelphia's Veterans Stadium put a much greater distance between the fans and the field. Along with the physical intimacy of the older parks, the new stadiums also dispensed with quirky angles and visual characteristics in favor of an aesthetic of soulless uniformity; on TV broadcasts, it was often difficult to identify where a game was actually being played. Some players felt the same way, even *on* the field: "I stand at the plate in the Vet and I don't honestly know whether I'm in Pittsburgh, Cincinnati, St. Louis, or Philly," complained Richie Hebner, who spent most of the '70s with the Pirates and Phillies. "They all look alike."

Several of these new parks were situated in isolated, highway-adjacent suburban areas, which further added to the overall sense of anonymity and dislocation. And once age and the elements began to take their combined toll, these stained and cracked sporting palaces looked about as inviting as your average high-rise housing project.

But if baseball purists despised these "ashtray" or "cookie-cutter" stadiums, they were even less enthusiastic about the artificial playing surfaces that proliferated during the 1970s. The concept of a low-maintenance plastic lawn—laid over a concrete base—that could be quickly vacuumed and dried after a rainstorm greatly appealed to cost-conscious owners; ditto for the fact that the carpet could easily be rolled up and replaced by a football gridiron, a feature which made AstroTurf (and its various competitors) ideal for multiuse stadiums.

Ashtray stadiums and artificial turf are typically associated with the 1970s, but both actually began popping up a decade earlier. Opened in 1961, and shared by the Washington Senators and Redskins, D.C. Stadium (renamed RFK Stadium in 1969) was the first of the multipurpose "concrete doughnuts," followed in 1964 by New York's Shea Stadium, and Atlanta–Fulton County Stadium and the Houston Astrodome a year later.

The most influential and emblematic stadium of the ashtray era, the Houston Astrodome—dubbed the "Eighth Wonder of the World" by Astros owner Judge Roy Hofheinz—was a salute to the Texas city's booming space industry; everything about the circular, multipurpose domed stadium, from its air-conditioned climate to its 474-foot animated "exploding" scoreboard to its plush orange and red airplane-style seats, seemed designed to radiate futuristic luxury.

The world's first indoor baseball stadium was not without its unplanned idiosyncrasies, however. Early on, the Astros were accused of monkeying with the air-conditioning to achieve a "wind-blowing-in" effect while their opponents were at the plate; in truth, the stadium's dead air and extremely spacious outfield (340 down the lines, 390 to the power alleys, and 406 to straightaway center) conspired to give pitchers on both sides a distinct advantage. Even feared hitters like the Cubs' Billy Williams and the Phillies' Mike Schmidt were humbled by the Astrodome: On July 16, 1970, Williams lost his bid for a game-tying ninth-inning homer when his shot struck a hanging speaker and landed in foul territory. Nearly four years later, on June 10, 1974, Schmidt blasted a Claude Osteen pitch off the dome's main PA system, which hung suspended from the ceiling 117 feet above the field. The ball's rocketlike trajectory had onlookers estimating that it could have been a 500-foot homer in any other park; in the Astrodome, however, the ball just dropped meekly into center field for a single.

But it was the Astrodome's most glaring defect that led to its most influential innovation. The stadium was built with 4,796 clear Lucite tiles set into the dome's ceiling, in order to allow the entry of natural light. Unfortunately, no one gave much advance thought to the blinding effect that the sun, when magnified through the Lucite, would have upon the upturned eyes of backpedaling outfielders; nor did anyone consider how quickly the playing field's lush Bermuda grass covering would die once the team tried to compensate for the glare by painting the roof panels a translucent white.

The solution to the Astros' space-age groundskeeping conundrum came via Monsanto Industries, an American chemical company that had already been experimenting with synthetic grass for nearly a decade. (The folks at Monsanto also knew a thing or two about destroying the real stuff—the company was a major manufacturer of the defoliant Agent Orange, which was used extensively by the U.S. military in Vietnam during the 1960s and '70s.) Hofheinz arranged to have the company cover the Astrodome's playing surface with its new ChemGrass product, and on July 19, 1966, the first major league baseball game was finally played on an all-artificial-turf field.

For the Astros players and their opponents, the new surface (soon renamed AstroTurf in honor of its high-profile home) took a little getting used to. Hot grounders seemed to skid instead of bounce on the hard and slippery surface, and a ball that hit a "seam" in the turf might ricochet off in any imaginable direction. "The AstroTurf was terrible . . . like running on a carpet," Astros slugger Rusty Staub would later recall. "I wore a spike on my back foot when I hit, and a soccer cleat on the front foot. If I got on base, they'd toss me another soccer cleat real quick and I'd make the switch."

Other players dealt with the new surface by wearing flat-bottomed shoes, or filing down their spikes to keep them from ripping up or catching on the synthetic grass. When Pete Rose donned a pair of "soccer-type shoes with rubber cleats for better traction" during the 1970 All-Star Game—which was held at the newly opened, freshly AstroTurfed Riverfront Stadium—his footwear choice was unusual enough that it warranted a special mention in the *Sporting News*. Within just a few years, however, rubber cleats would become practically de rigueur for ballplayers playing on artificial turf.

The St. Louis Cardinals played in one of the more visually distinctive "ashtray" stadiums, thanks to architect Edward Durell Stone, who crowned Busch Stadium—which was finished in 1966—with a ring of arch-shaped roof supports that mirrored the shape of the nearby Gateway Arch. The A's and Padres teams of the '70s played at Oakland–Alameda County Coliseum and San Diego Stadium, two multipurpose ashtrays built specifically for professional football teams—the AFL's Raiders and Chargers, respectively. Built in 1966, the Oakland ballpark was a chilly concrete space softened only by the green, sloping hills beyond the outfield walls.

The Padres' brutalist concrete home, on the other hand, was anything but chilly; the giant electronic scoreboard behind the right-field bleachers generated so much heat, Padres fans in the back rows were often afraid they might spontaneously combust.

Ashtray stadiums and AstroTurf first emerged in the 1960s, but their true MLB coming of age occurred in the summer of 1970, with the opening of Riverfront Stadium in Cincinnati and Three Rivers Stadium in Pittsburgh. Both the Reds' and the Pirates' new homes were quintessential ashtrays—circular, symmetrical multiuse concrete stadiums utterly devoid of ornamentation or character. *New Yorker* sportswriter Roger Angell referred to the former as a "cheerless, circular, Monsantoed close," and bemoaned how the stadium's press box was "glassed-in and air-conditioned, utterly cut off from the sounds of baseball action and baseball cheering. After an inning or two, I began to feel as if I were suffering from the effects of a mild stroke."

Reds general manager Bob Howsam had briefly explored the novel idea of artificially spraying the scent of freshly baked bread throughout Riverfront Stadium, theorizing that the homey smell would (a) create a more pleasant environment for the fans, and (b) encourage fans to buy more food. Though it was ultimately found to be unfeasible, this innovation would certainly have lent some personality to Riverfront's rather generic confines.

Four years after the initial carpeting of the Astrodome, Busch (which switched over to plastic grass at the beginning of the 1970 season), Three Rivers (which used Tartan Turf, an AstroTurf competitor), and Riverfront became the first outdoor major league ballparks to entirely forsake natural grass in favor of "mod sod," as some wags in the press dubbed artificial turf. San Francisco's Candlestick Park would follow suit in 1971, as would nearly every other stadium that opened during the decade.

The fact that both the Reds and the Pirates won their divisions in 1970, thus setting up the first all-turf playoff series, probably helped popularize baseball's use of artificial turf. Riverfront established an additional trend—one eventually adopted by every other major league park with artificial turf—by fully carpeting the baselines and leaving only small dirt "sliding pits" around the bases. Instead of becoming muddy trenches during rain showers, these synthetic baselines could simply be vacuumed of moisture like the rest of the field.

But if artificial turf was a godsend in cases of inclement weather, it could be absolutely murderous on a hot summer day. The turf at Philadelphia's Veterans Stadium, which opened in 1971, was infamous not only for its patchy surface and its magical ability to make a batted baseball bounce like a rubber Super Ball—the Vet's outfield walls were given six-foot Plexiglas extensions in 1972 in order to combat the constant barrage of ground-rule doubles—but also for the way it retained and reflected heat. In the dead of a Philadelphia summer, on-field day-game temps at the Vet were said to occasionally rise as high as 140 degrees. (After the installation of artificial turf, the Cardinals' home field became similarly uncomfortable during the summer months.)

Built in an "octorad" shape similar to San Diego Stadium, the Vet was one of the largest ballparks in the majors at the time, able to accommodate nearly 60,000 people in comfortable theater-type seating—each level of which was colored in "autumn shades" of yellow, orange, and brown. And since the Phillies of the early '70s were absolutely horrible, the Vet provided its own entertainment: Whenever a Phillies player hit a round-tripper, a "home run spectacular" involving an animated Liberty Bell would play out across a gigantic pair of electronic scoreboards; a colonial flag would then unfurl from the press box, followed by the eruption of a "dancing waters" display behind the fence in center field. On May 16, 1972, Greg "the Bull" Luzinski delivered a home run spectacular of his own when he smacked a ball off the replica Liberty Bell that hung from the fourth-level roof in deep center field, an estimated 475 feet from home plate. Luzinski-launched long balls would become a regular occurrence at the Vet during the rest of the decade, but neither the Bull nor anyone else would manage to ring the Liberty Bell again.

On April 10, 1973, the most unique, attractive, and fan-friendly ballpark of the AstroTurf era opened in Kansas City, Missouri. Unlike most of its concrete cousins, Royals Stadium was never intended as a multiuse facility, since the NFL Chiefs played ball just across the parking lot at Arrowhead Stadium. Thus, the architects (Kansas City firm HNTB) were able to keep the park's dimensions relatively intimate—the seating capacity of 40,625 was the smallest of any modern major league park— and add a number of alluring visual flourishes, including the gracefully swooping upper deck and the 12-story, crown-shaped scoreboard in center field. The most inspired touch of all was the 322-foot water display beyond the outfield walls; the colorfully illuminated fountains (which could send jets of water shooting as high as 70 feet in the air) looked like Liberace's Vegas stage on steroids, but they quickly became some of the best-loved attributes of the stadium. For Royals fans who had endured the obstructed views of decrepit old Municipal Stadium, Royals Stadium was truly a gift.

Fans of the Montreal Expos, on the other hand, got a completely raw deal. From 1969 to 1976, the Expos played their home games at Jarry Park—a.k.a. Parc Jarry—a 3,000-seat municipal ballpark that had been expanded to fit over 28,000 French-Canadian backsides just in time for the Expos' expansion entry into the National League. Though cozy and not without its appealing quirks (like the public swimming pool located just beyond the right-field fence), Parc Jarry was a no-frills ballpark that offered fans little shelter from the sunshine or—more pertinently for Montreal—the cold and damp. But since the park was intended only as a four-year stopgap until Olympic Stadium was completed, no attempt was made to improve Jarry Park beyond its rudimentary amenities. Unfortunately, a strike by local construction workers halted the new stadium's progress, eventually dooming the Expos and their fans to eight seasons at Parc Jarry.

When Olympic Stadium opened for the 1976 Summer Olympics, it was barely half completed; the retractable roof wouldn't actually work for another 13 years, forcing the Expos (and the Montreal Alouettes of the Canadian Football League, who shared the multiuse facility) to play under an open-air hole in the ceiling roughly the same size as the AstroTurf-covered field. But even on the sunniest days, Stade Olympique had a dreary atmosphere; though Expos attendance more than doubled during the team's first season in the new stadium—up from just under 8,000 per game to nearly 18,000—the place's strange acoustics seemed to muffle the noise of even the most rambunctious crowds, and the oblong seating layout meant that most fans were kept farther from the action than they'd ever been at Jarry. "Olympic Stadium was one of the worst stadiums I ever played in, from a fan's standpoint and from the feeling a player has on the field," Tom Seaver would recall. "The service of the field was far less than adequate—it was so bumpy and there were ridges in the outfield. Players sometimes got hurt."

Canada's other major league franchise, the Toronto Blue Jays, was also forced to make do with temporary lodgings while its city cast about for funds to build a proper stadium. (The team would finally move to the $578 million SkyDome in 1989.) But while the Expos had Parc Jarry, which had at least been built for baseball, the Blue Jays set up shop at Exhibition Stadium, home of the CFL's Toronto Argonauts. With the football grandstand (the only covered seating in the park) serving as the left-field bleachers, some seats were as far as 300 feet from the field, and others faced the field at awkward angles. The park's location on the Lake Ontario waterfront meant that the Jays and their fans enjoyed football-like weather conditions even during baseball season: On April 7, 1977, the team's inaugural Opening Day game was played on a snow-covered field.

Completed in 1976, Seattle's Kingdome became the AL's first domed stadium in 1977, when the expansion Mariners moved in. A cavernous, multiuse, AstroTurf-carpeted concrete dome that also housed the NFL's Seattle Seahawks, the Kingdome lacked the giddy space-age charm of its predecessor in Houston, though it still had a few interesting quirks. Only 316 feet down the lines and 357 to the power alleys, the Kingdome should have been a hitter's dream; but the potential for home run derbies was greatly minimized by the strategic placement of 42 air-conditioning units, all of which blew air toward the field. (A 23-foot mini–Green Monster wall in right and right-center field, known as "the Walla Walla," also helped to keep quite a number of potential homers in play.) During a game on August 4, 1979, Mariners fan favorite Ruppert Jones popped a foul over first base; it should have been a sure out, but the ball somehow lodged itself in a PA speaker suspended above the dugout. The home plate ump ruled it a strike.

By 1977, with the addition of the Mariners and Blue Jays, 10 out of 26 major league teams were using synthetic turf instead of grass. (It would have been 11, but White Sox owner Bill Veeck ripped up Comiskey's fake infield as soon as he took over in 1976.) Rusty Staub wasn't the only player to express his distaste for the now-fashionable pseudosod; "If horses don't eat it, I don't want to play on it," was Dick Allen's memorable quip on the matter. But like polyester uniforms, artificial turf had become a fact of life in the bigs—especially in the NL, where seven out of 12 stadiums made use of the stuff—and players had no choice but to adjust accordingly. Savvy infielders like Reds shortstop Dave Concepcion and Phillies shortstop Larry Bowa played deeper on turf, realizing that the density of the infield fabric meant there was little chance of the ball taking a "bad hop," and that they could make up the additional distance on a throw to first with a well-placed bounce.

Outfielders had a more difficult time on artificial turf, where a misjudged fly ball or line drive could easily turn into a triple or inside-the-park home run. Guardians of the artificially green pastures began playing deeper to keep balls from getting past them, and tended to eschew heroic diving catches unless absolutely necessary—sliding across the plastic-covered concrete could result in some nasty rug burns, if not worse. "Artificial turf limits my defense," complained Red Sox center fielder Fred Lynn, who typically went after fly balls with all the fearless intensity of Evel Knievel going up a motorcycle ramp. "I have to play deeper because the ball bounces so much higher and faster, and I can't dive for a ball the way I do on grass because of the danger of getting hurt. . . . I don't think that's the way baseball was meant to be played."

Still, there was no denying that artificial turf lent additional excitement to the game. Once they got used to running the bases with rubber cleats, players realized that turf gave them exceptional traction—a handy thing when trying to steal, or when taking the extra base on a hit to the outfield. Stolen-base totals exploded in the '70s, with players in both leagues committing larceny at a pace not seen since the deadball era. From 1970 through 1979, 49 players stole 50 or more bases in a season, compared to a mere 20 who had accomplished the same feat the decade before. Out of those 49 players, 30—including Lou Brock, who swiped a then-record 118 in 1974—played their home games on artificial turf.

The symmetrical dimensions of the ashtray stadiums generally meant that most of them contained more outfield and foul-territory real estate than their predecessors, which put free swingers at a disadvantage. Contact hitters, however, thrived in these surroundings—especially ones with enough speed to stretch a double into a triple (or even an inside-the-park home run) while their hit rattled around in the corner like an oversized pinball. Between the more spacious playing areas and the harder playing surfaces, teams with a surplus of speed, defensive range, and excellent contact hitting had a decided advantage in ashtray stadiums over slower, power-based squads.

Indeed, the most successful "turf teams" of the 1970s were the Cincinnati Reds, the Pittsburgh Pirates, the Philadelphia Phillies, and the Kansas City Royals, all of whom were assembled (or at least managed) with their ashtray homes in mind. While each team contained a formidable slugger or two—Johnny Bench and George Foster on the Reds, Willie Stargell and Dave Parker on the Bucs, John Mayberry on the Royals, Mike Schmidt and Greg Luzinski on the Phillies—the rest of the starting lineups were packed with guys like Ken Griffey, Omar Moreno, Frank White, and Garry Maddox, who could slap a hot grounder through an AstroTurf infield seemingly at will, and who fielded their positions with the impressive speed and range demanded by the artificial surface. Maddox, whose nickname was "the Secretary of Defense," was perhaps the archetypal AstroTurf outfielder. "Two-thirds of the earth is covered by water—the rest is covered by Garry Maddox," testified Mets announcer Ralph Kiner.

While one could certainly argue that the Big Red Machine possessed enough talent to win on any surface, there's no question that the fortunes of the Royals changed drastically once new manager Whitey Herzog came aboard in July 1975. Seeking to turn Royals Stadium's expansive outfield and ball-rocketing playing surface to the team's advantage, Herzog preached patience at the plate and aggression on the base paths; with crucial assistance from hitting coach Charlie Lau, who advocated hitting line shots and hard grounders instead of swinging for the fences, Herzog led the Royals to the AL playoffs for the first time in 1976—when the team made up for a noticeable lack of slugging (only 65 home runs all season) with 218 steals and a very respectable .269 team batting average—and back again in 1977 and 1978. Herzog's signature strategy would become known as "Whiteyball" in the 1980s, when he moved across the state to manage the Cardinals, but Kansas City was where Whiteyball was invented.

In 1980, the Royals squared off against the Phillies in the first all-AstroTurf World Series, signifying that artificial turf was no longer a controversial novelty, but an established part of the game. It would remain so until the mid-'90s, when the trend toward smaller, retro-styled bandboxes—spearheaded by the opening of Baltimore's Camden Yards in 1992—rang the death knell for ashtrays and AstroTurf. (As of this writing, only two teams in the majors still play their home games on artificial surfaces.)

Ultimately, fans and players shed few tears over the demise of the drab concrete doughnuts and their rock-hard unnatural surfaces, even though the combination of the two produced a flashy, speed-driven brand of baseball that's rarely seen in today's game. For fans who were there "back in the day," it's almost impossible to imagine the Big Red Machine or the "We Are Family" Pirates in any other setting. If ashtrays and artificial turf were good enough for those teams, and gave birth to a squad as thrilling as the '76–'78 Royals, perhaps they weren't entirely without redeeming value.

CHAPTER 4

1972

"You don't assign him to murder cases," read the tagline for *Dirty Harry*, the gritty Clint Eastwood cop flick that opened in U.S. theaters shortly before Christmas 1971. "You just turn him loose." You could pretty much say the same thing about Dick Allen—only, instead of murder cases, Allen's beat was the territory between the foul lines. In 1972, the White Sox first baseman patrolled that beat like no one else in baseball, racking up some of the best numbers of his career, winning the American League MVP Award, and almost single-handedly carrying the White Sox (a team charitably described during spring training by a Chicago journalist as an aggregation of "has beens and also rans") to within sniffing distance of the AL West pennant. But much like Eastwood's character, Allen just wanted to be left alone to do his thing. If you questioned his methods, asked him to conform, or attempted to put the squeeze on him in any way . . . neither of you would be particularly happy with the outcome.

Loners and antiheroes were a staple of American film in the early 1970s, and they seemed to dominate the 1972 baseball season as well. Like mysterious cowboys riding in from the plains to aid the defenseless populaces of besieged frontier towns, veteran hurlers Steve Carlton and Gaylord Perry won Cy Youngs in their debut seasons with terrible teams in Philadelphia and Cleveland. Detroit Tigers manager Billy Martin, who pursued victory with the sociopathic intensity of Al Pacino settling "family business" in *The Godfather*, nearly made it to the World Series with a motley crew of aging vets and untested youngsters, none of whom managed to drive in more than 61 runs during the season. And then there were the newly hirsute Oakland A's—a team as unruly (both temperamentally and follicularly) as the gang of Civil War deserters in the 1972 "acid western" *Bad Company*—who would battle one another, manager Dick Williams, A's owner Charlie O. Finley, and everyone else all the way to a World Series crown.

As if the antics and achievements of the above individuals weren't enough to put baseball traditionalists in a cold sweat, the rebellious, antiauthoritarian spirit that had been so palpable on college campuses since the late 1960s seemed to have finally infected the sport. At the end of spring training, for the first time in baseball history, major league players walked out en masse, in a strike that would delay Opening Day for two weeks.

At issue, ostensibly, was the players' pension fund—the amount that the 24 team owners paid into it, and how the fund's profits were to be additionally invested—but there were greater subtexts at work. "A last minute modicum of patience on both sides might have averted the whole thing," wrote *New Yorker* columnist Roger Angell. "It is clear that some of the more dedicated Cro-Magnons among the owners (including the Cardinals' Gussie Busch, the Reds' Frank Dale, the Mets' Donald Grant, and the Royals' Ewing Kauffman) saw the strike as a precious opportunity to strain, and perhaps crack, the labor union of their upstart, ungrateful young employees and, above all, to discredit its executive director, Marvin Miller." For Miller and the Players Association, the strike was an opportunity to demonstrate that even though they'd lost the Curt Flood battle, the war over player servitude was far from finished.

Over in Oakland, A's phenom Vida Blue was staging a rebellion of his own. Having earned only $14,750 the year before while pitching well enough to win both the AL Cy Young *and* MVP awards—and drawing thousands of extra fans, at home or on the road, whenever he pitched— Blue now demanded compensation from Finley along the lines of

$100,000 per season. (The average player in 1972 made a little over $34,000, but star players were making significantly more. Fergie Jenkins, Blue's Cy Young counterpart, was making $125,000 a year with the Cubs, and Hank Aaron would shortly sign a three-year deal with the Atlanta Braves guaranteeing him $200,000 per season.)

This wasn't the first time Blue had locked horns with Finley. Having already convinced his pitchers Jim Hunter and John Odom to go by the nicknames "Catfish" and "Blue Moon," respectively, Finley had lobbied Blue to go by the moniker "True Blue." Blue declined somewhat testily— "Why don't you call yourself True Finley?" he asked—and the matter was dropped. This time, when Finley countered with an offer of $50,000, an insulted Blue began exploring other options, including jumping to the Japanese leagues. There was also talk of Blue becoming a movie star; though he had no prior screen experience, the charismatic pitcher reportedly signed a deal with MGM to costar with Richard Roundtree in *Shaft's Big Score*. (Sadly, at least for fans of the blaxploitation genre, this all-star action pairing never happened.) When Finley refused to budge— and caused further uproar in the Bay Area by spending the fifty grand earmarked for Blue on the purchase of the volatile, washed-up Denny McLain from the Texas Rangers—Blue announced that he was retiring from baseball to serve as the vice president of public relations for Dura Steel Products, a company that manufactured plumbing fixtures.

The rest of the A's, though united in their support for the players' strike, were oddly less than sympathetic to Blue's holdout. Some blamed Blue's agent, Bob Gerst, for putting grandiose notions in his head; others thought Blue was merely being stupid. "He's foolish for giving up $50,000," Curt Blefary opined to the press. "He could have made it $100,000 with endorsements." Sal Bando was equally unsupportive. "I'm for a guy getting all he can, but Charlie has offered Vida a fair contract," said the A's team captain, who had placed second behind Blue in the previous year's MVP voting. "We can win without Vida Blue. It would be harder, but we can."

As if the prospect of an April without baseball weren't bad enough, a further pall was cast over the spring by the sudden death of Mets manager Gil Hodges, who succumbed to a heart attack on a West Palm

Beach golf course on April 2, two days short of his 48th birthday. The unexpected demise of their popular skipper (who'd guided the team to their "miracle" World Series championship in 1969) hit the Mets players hard. Mets coach Yogi Berra was named as the club's new manager; and while Yogi would lead the team back to the World Series in 1973, Hodges's death was, in retrospect, one of many sorry events that would lead to the Mets becoming NL laughingstocks before the decade was out. Not least among these was the team's late-1971 decision to trade right-hander Nolan Ryan to the California Angels for infielder Jim Fregosi.

Already pitching-rich—what with a rotation that included Tom Seaver, Jerry Koosman, Gary Gentry, and hot prospect Jon Matlack—the Mets' front office had no reservations about swapping their wild fastballer for the Angels' six-time All-Star shortstop, who they felt sure could fill their gaping hole at third base. But once in the American League, Ryan would transform himself into one of the most feared strikeout artists in the history of the game, while Fregosi (who had batted .278 with 22 homers in 1970) would hit only .233 with a measly six round-trippers over the next season and a half with New York, while knee injuries curtailed his playing time and hampered his range at third.

The Ryan-for-Fregosi transaction would go down as one of the most notoriously one-sided trades in baseball history—even more so than the deal between the '71 and '72 seasons that sent Red Sox reliever Sparky Lyle over to the Yankees for infielder Danny Cater. Lyle would become one of baseball's top closers, saving more than 140 games (including several key ones against the Red Sox) in seven seasons with the Bronx Bombers. Cater, who would never be more than a parttime player for Boston, eventually retired in 1975.

The players' strike, which began on April Fools' Day, lasted 13 days; in the end, the owners compromised by agreeing to contribute an additional $490,000 to the pension fund for the 1972 season, with $500,000 of the fund's profits going toward additional benefits. Rather than push the end of the season all the way into mid-October, it was decreed that the season would officially start on April 15, and that there would be no makeup games for the 86 scheduled contests that had been preempted by the strike. This decision resulted in an imbalanced schedule for the rest of the season, one that would influence the outcome of at least one division race.

At this point in history, the idea of a players' strike was still completely alien to baseball fans, and the reasons (both stated and unstated) behind the walkout were too obscure and convoluted for most of them to understand, much less sympathize with. Instead of the customary Monday or Tuesday, 1972's Opening Day landed on a Saturday; even so, fans demonstrated their displeasure by staying away in droves. The Cincinnati Reds did draw nearly 38,000 fans for their home opener against the Los Angeles Dodgers, while a crowd of 31,510 showed up at Fenway to see the Red Sox take on the Tigers. But at Wrigley Field, usually a near sellout or better on Opening Day, the Cubs sold only 17,401 seats; and St. Louis, Kansas City, and Minneapolis all drew fewer than 10,000 to their home openers. The fans would return as the season progressed, but the initially chilly reception did not go unnoticed by the players, owners, or Bowie Kuhn—the latter of whom was booed mercilessly when he showed up at Shea Stadium for the Mets' opener.

The day after the Cubs' less-than-ecstatic home opener, rookie Burt Hooton—making only his fourth major league start—gave a meager Sunday afternoon Wrigley crowd of 9,583 something to cheer about with a 4–0 no-hitter over the Phillies. Hooton struck out seven batters with his patented "knuckle curve," though the fact that he also walked seven showed that he hadn't quite figured out how to control the pitch. It would take a few years and a trade to the Dodgers before "Happy" (as he was jokingly nicknamed due to his perpetually glum visage) would really come into his own.

On the same day as Hooton's no-no, young Giants slugger Dave Kingman practically dismantled the Astros single-handedly, hitting for the cycle with six RBIs in a 10–6 Giants victory at the Houston Astrodome. Kingman, a 6-foot-6 USC grad playing his first full season in the majors, could hit (and throw) the ball a country mile; but his strikeout-prone uppercut and stone glove would give more than a few of his managers conniption fits over the course of his 16-season career. In 1972, Kingman would lead the lowly Giants with 29 home runs and 83 RBIs, despite amassing only 472 at bats; unfortunately, he also struck out 140 times.

It took less than a month into the 1972 season for the Giants to decide that they no longer had room on the roster for Willie Mays. The last remaining player from the Giants team that had moved to San Francisco from New York City in 1958, Mays had hit .271 with 18 HRs and a league-leading 112 walks the year before—not the superstar numbers of his 1950s and '60s seasons, perhaps, but hardly shabby. Now, however, the center fielder appeared to be in rapid decline, hitting only .184 in his first 19 games of the season; and on May 11, the Giants sent him back to the Big Apple, trading him to the first-place Mets for minor league pitcher Charlie Williams and $50,000. Three days later, Mays made his first appearance in a Met uniform, hitting the game-winning home run in a 5–4 victory over the Giants at Shea. It was a sweet return for a beloved New York icon.

Vida Blue finally ended his long holdout from the A's on May 2, signing a contract for $63,000—the $50,000 that Finley had originally offered, plus a $5,000 "retroactive bonus" and $8,000 in a "reserve scholarship fund," the latter to be used whenever Blue decided to go back to college. By the time Blue pitched his first game of the season for the A's (a one-inning relief stint in a loss to the Angels on May 24), Sal Bando's earlier words seemed prophetic. The A's had played 19-10 ball in Blue's absence; but though they were winning without him, they were only in second place in the AL West, 1½ games behind the newly rejuvenated White Sox, whose off-season acquisition of Dick Allen was quickly proving a blessing for both Allen and the team.

Allen hadn't vibed too well with his previous managers—the Phillies' Gene Mauch, Red Schoendienst of the Cardinals, and Dodgers skipper Walter Alston—but he and Sox skipper Chuck Tanner were definitely on the same wavelength. Tanner, who was from the same part of western

Pennsylvania as Allen, had played basketball in high school with one of Allen's older brothers; and despite the slugger's reputation for refusing to abide by team rules, Tanner was inclined to give his new first baseman the benefit of the doubt. If Allen didn't feel he needed to take batting practice before a particular game, Tanner merely shrugged and left him alone, figuring that no one knew Allen's abilities and limitations better than Allen himself.

"Guys [in the Chicago papers] would write that I had one set of rules for twenty-four players and a different set of rules for Dick Allen," Tanner would say later. "Not true. I had twenty-five sets of rules. I took every player case by case. . . . My managing philosophy was a simple one—communication, not regimentation." Tanner also put great stock in Allen's ability to analyze the game; the first baseman would make tactical suggestions to Tanner, who acted on them more often than not. "In 1972, Dick Allen piloted the Chicago White Sox club as much as I did," Tanner claimed. "We were co-managers."

Allen appreciated Tanner's modern (at least by baseball standards) managerial philosophy and responded extremely well, doing significant damage to opponents with his mammoth 41-ounce bat. After finishing the 1971 season 22½ games behind the A's, the White Sox now suddenly looked like contenders. With third baseman Bill Melton, who had led the AL the previous year with 33 homers, on the disabled list for most of the season, Allen—who would lead the league in '72 with 37 homers and 113 RBIs, and tie for third with a .308 batting average—and left fielder Carlos May (.308, 12 HRs, 68 RBIs) were the only guys who could be counted on to put up some runs on a regular basis.

Luckily for the Sox hitters, their pitching staff—anchored by Wilbur Wood, Stan Bahnsen, and 20-year-old closer Terry Forster—was generally able to hold opponents to three runs or fewer. Bahnsen, picked up in the off-season from the Yankees, would win a career-high 21 games in '72; Wood, a workhorse knuckleballer who at Tanner's behest had been converted to a full-time starter only the year before (winning 22 games in the process), would notch 24 victories before the season ended, often pitching on no more than two games' rest. A throwback to the deadball era,

Wood threw 376⅔ innings in 1972, and his 49 starts were only two shy of the modern record, set in 1904 by Jack Chesbro.

Impressive as Wood's 1972 numbers were, he ultimately lost out in the year's Cy Young voting to Gaylord Perry. In his first year with Cleveland, the veteran spitballer became the first pitcher in 48 years to win 20 games in both leagues, racking up 24 wins and 234 strikeouts for a 72-84 Indians team while posting a 1.92 ERA in 342⅔ innings. Steve Carlton, the NL Cy Young winner, put together an even more phenomenal season, going 27-10 with 310 Ks and a 1.97 ERA in 346 innings for an absolutely awful Phillies squad. Carlton accounted for a record 45.8 percent of his team's 59 victories—reliever Bucky Brandon had the second-most wins on the staff, with seven. At one point, Carlton even rattled off a 15-game winning streak, and his eight shutouts were the most for a Phillies pitcher since Grover Cleveland Alexander in 1917.

Somewhat overshadowed by Carlton, Perry, and Wood was the year had by Angels starter Nolan Ryan. After four straight mediocre seasons with the Mets, the (really) hard-throwing right-hander won 19 games while posting a 2.28 ERA, whiffing 329 AL batters—the fourth-highest total in major league history—and setting a major league record by allowing only 5.26 hits per nine innings. Over the course of the season, Ryan struck out 15 or more batters on four different occasions, including a one-hit shutout against the Red Sox on July 9 wherein he struck out an AL record eight batters in a row. Ironically, Ryan had seriously considered leaving baseball for good during the players' strike. "If it had gone on for another week, I would have quit and gone back to Alvin, [Texas]," he later admitted. "I would have gotten a job as a laborer, and that would have been it."

San Diego's Steve Arlin probably considered packing it in a few times during the year as well. Having already led the NL in losses the previous season with 19, Arlin went 10-21 for the Padres in 1972, despite pitching three two-hitters, a one-hitter, and a 10-inning one-hit no-decision at various points in the season. During a July 18 contest against Philadelphia, Arlin actually took a no-hitter into the ninth inning with two outs; but when new Padres manager Don Zimmer signaled third baseman

Dave Roberts to play in on batter Denny Doyle, Doyle promptly blooped a single over Roberts's head, breaking up the no-no.

Milt Pappas, who had his best season with the Cubs in 1972, going 17-7 (including an 11-game winning streak) with a 2.77 ERA, experienced similar frustrations in a September 2 game against the Padres at Wrigley Field. Pappas, who had pitched 8⅔ innings without allowing a runner on base, lost his bid for a perfect game when he walked pinch hitter Larry Stahl on a very close pitch after running the count to 3-and-2. Pappas then retired Garry Jestadt to clinch the no-hitter; but having come so near to perfection, he complained vociferously about plate umpire Bruce Froemming's ball-four call on Stahl. "He had a chance to become famous as the umpire in the twelfth perfect game in baseball history, but he blew it," Pappas groused. The next day, when Froemming asked Pappas to autograph a ball for him, the pitcher allegedly replied, "I'd be happy to—and you know where to stick it after I sign it."

There was certainly no shortage of pitching heroics in 1972: Pappas's rotation mate Fergie Jenkins hit the 20-victory mark for the sixth straight season; Expos pitcher Bill Stoneman threw the second no-hitter of his career; Mickey Lolich won 22 games for the Tigers; Don Sutton went 19-9 with a minuscule 2.08 ERA for the Dodgers; Bob Gibson had his last great season for the Cardinals, going 19-11 with a 2.46 ERA and 208 Ks; Tom Seaver posted his third 20-win season in four years for the Mets, while his teammate Jon Matlack won the NL Rookie of the Year Award for a 15-10, 2.32 ERA performance; and the Reds' Clay Carroll and the Yankees' Sparky Lyle led their respective leagues with 37 and 35 saves apiece. Indeed, if 1968 was dubbed "the Year of the Pitcher," 1972 seemed kind of like the sequel—at least in the AL, where the league batting average dropped to .239 from the previous season's .247, and the league ERA went from 3.46 in 1971 to a stingy 3.06. Rod Carew, who led the AL in batting with a .318 average, became the first player to win a major league batting title without hitting a single homer. These weak power numbers, along with the general attendance drop, would influence the AL's adoption of the designated hitter for 1973.

Reds catcher Johnny Bench was one of the few hitters who seemed entirely unaffected by 1972's dominant pitching, leading the NL with 40 home runs and 125 RBIs and winning his second MVP Award in three years. The Cubs' sweet-swinging Billy Williams placed second in the MVP balloting, thanks to league-leading numbers in batting average (.333) and slugging percentage (.606), on top of 37 homers and 122 RBIs. Though San Diego first baseman Nate Colbert finished only eighth in the voting, he did smack a record-tying five home runs with a record-breaking 13 RBIs in an August 1 doubleheader against the Braves. The lone offensive bright spot on a Padres squad that hit a collective .227, Colbert finished the season with 38 HRs and 111 RBIs, setting a major league record by driving in 22.75 percent of his team's runs.

Even without Vida Blue (or Denny McLain, who was shipped to Atlanta for former NL MVP Orlando Cepeda in June, after going 2-3 with a 6.04 ERA for Oakland), the A's were blessed with strong pitching. Catfish Hunter had gone 21-11 in 1971 with a 2.96 ERA; in 1972, he bettered those numbers with a 21-7 record and a 2.04 ERA. Kenny Holtzman, who'd come over from the Cubs in the off-season, chipped in with 19 wins and a 2.51 ERA, while Blue Moon Odom had one of the best seasons of his career with a 15-6, 2.50 performance. Rollie Fingers led the bullpen with 11 wins and 21 saves, but the A's relief corps was additionally bolstered by Bob Locker and Darold Knowles, who won an additional 11 games and saved 21 more between them.

The '72 A's didn't put up spectacular offensive numbers, but the core of the lineup—center fielder Reggie Jackson (.265, 25 HRs, 75 RBIs), left fielder Joe Rudi (.305, 19 HRs, 75 RBIs), first baseman Mike "Super Jew" Epstein (.270, 26 HRs, 70 RBIs)—was reliably solid. (Along with Epstein and Holtzman, the acquisition of veteran first baseman Art Shamsky—who would play only eight games for Oakland—briefly gave the team three Jewish players. When a reporter pointed out the relative abundance of Chosen People on the A's, Holtzman cracked, "I hear we're going to have Golda Meir as a shortstop.") Third baseman Sal Bando had an off year in '72, hitting only .236 with 15 HRs, but still led the team with 77

RBIs. Catcher Dave Duncan, though he hit a measly .218, still managed to contribute 19 homers, while scrappy shortstop Bert Campaneris made up for his .240 stroke with a league-leading 52 stolen bases, not to mention a fiery attitude that rubbed off on those around him. "This is my MVP," Cepeda remembered A's manager Dick Williams saying about Campaneris. "If we don't have this guy on this ballclub, no way we're gonna win no pennant."

But it wasn't pitching, power, or speed that gave the '72 Oakland team its lasting identity—it was the hair. Many of the players on the team already sported longer locks than most of their contemporaries around the league, but the A's rampant facial hair really set them apart. But while the A's "Mustache Gang" might have looked like hippies, their agenda had nothing to do with peace and love. They weren't shy about brawling with other teams, as in the case of massive dustups with the Brewers in July and the Royals in August, the latter of which resulted in a rib cage injury to Jackson that caused him to miss three weeks' worth of games in a critical pennant stretch. They also weren't afraid to square off against one another; though the level of tension between players in the Oakland clubhouse would increase considerably in the coming seasons, Fingers's constant ribbing of his teammates, Bando's in-your-face attitude, and Jackson's constant desire to be the center of attention all raised occasional hackles.

Epstein, who carried as much of the team's left-handed power load as Jackson, resented the latter's habit of referring to himself as "Mr. B and B," as in "Mr. Bread and Butter." On one occasion, the two men got into a heated shouting match over Epstein's use of complimentary game tickets, and the beefy Epstein settled the dispute by decking Jackson with a single punch. But the pair put their differences aside in September when, in tribute to the Israeli athletes murdered at the Munich Olympics, Epstein and Jackson—along with Holtzman—took the field with black armbands on their uniforms.

Mostly, however, the A's players were bonded together by their mutual dislike of Finley. Many of them had gone through difficult salary negotiations with the A's owner, but they also despised him for his harassment of Williams, and his propensity for monkeying around with the

A's roster—during one three-week period in May, Finley completed six different transactions involving 12 players in all. But mostly they hated him for his cheapness.

"The A's were talented but unhappy," remembered Dick Allen years afterward. "That's why I felt we could beat their ass, even though we were just a bunch of scrappers. When we'd play the A's and one of their guys would reach first base, I'd get an earful about Finley. Especially from Reggie. He'd start talking about how cheap Charlie Finley was—the cattle car flights, no meal money, no food in the clubhouse. . . . For a while that worked in our favor, but by September the A's were united in their loathing of Finley. Once they were all united, they began playing for each other, not for their owner."

Though the White Sox ultimately weren't able to keep pace with the A's in the division race, they put on quite a show down on Chicago's South Side, drawing nearly 300,000 more fans than in 1971, and more than doubling the abysmal Comiskey Park attendance figures from 1970. The same team that, just three years earlier, had been relegated to playing occasional "home" games in Milwaukee in a desperate attempt to improve cash flow, now ranked third in the AL in attendance. "Dick Allen," Sox GM Roland Hemond would later testify, "is responsible for saving the Sox franchise. Period."

But despite the valiant efforts of Allen and the team's starting rotation, the White Sox ended the season 5½ games short of the A's, whose 93-62 record was good enough for their second straight division title.

While Oakland and Chicago fought it out all summer in the AL West, the AL East witnessed an insanely tight four-way race between the New York Yankees, the Boston Red Sox, the Detroit Tigers, and the defending AL champs from Baltimore. The Yankees, though paced by the 33 home runs and 96 RBIs of center fielder Bobby Murcer and Sparky Lyle's 35-save, 1.92-ERA season out of the bullpen, simply didn't have sufficient hitting or pitching to compete effectively with the other teams; the Yanks faded in September and ended up in fourth place, 6½ games out of first.

The Orioles, now without Frank Robinson (who had been traded to the Dodgers during the off-season), experienced an unexpected power outage: After hitting .261 with 158 home runs in 1971, the aging O's hit only .229 with 100 homers in '72; Boog Powell was the only player to hit 20 or more round-trippers, and young infielder Bobby Grich led the team with a .278 batting average. Though the team's "Big Four" starting rotation of Mike Cuellar, Pat Dobson, Dave McNally, and Jim Palmer was as sharp as ever, the diminished offense kept all but Palmer from winning 20 games.

The Red Sox, who hadn't finished higher than third since winning the AL pennant in 1967, were visibly revitalized by the addition of two players who would play significant roles with the team for several seasons to come—Carlton Fisk and Luis Tiant. Fisk, a catcher who'd been the top Red Sox pick in the 1967 amateur draft, arrived in the big leagues in 1972, and wasted no time in establishing himself as one of the top catchers in the game. Fisk hit .293 with 22 homers (and, unusual for a catcher, nine triples), was named to the AL All-Star team, won a Gold Glove for his defense, and racked up unanimous Rookie of the Year honors.

Tiant, a crafty Cuban twirler who looked a good 10 years older than his stated age of 31, had parlayed his patented "pirouette" delivery into a league-leading 1.60 ERA (as well as 21 wins and 264 Ks) with the Indians in 1968, before falling on hard times. A 20-loss season in 1969, followed by a long and rocky recovery from a broken shoulder blade, left most of baseball convinced that "El Tiante" was finished. The Red Sox picked him up in 1971 but relegated him to the bullpen after he went 0-6 as a starter. He spent much of 1972 as a reliever, occasionally serving as a spot starter; but once manager Eddie Kasko returned him to the rotation in early August, Tiant went on a 10-2 tear, throwing six shutouts along the way (including, at one point, four in a row). He finished the year with a 15-6 record and a league-leading 1.91 ERA, and single-handedly kept the Red Sox in the pennant race until the second-to-last day of the season, when he lost a 3–1 heartbreaker to the pennant-winning Detroit Tigers. Billy Martin's team finished the season 86-70, a mere half game ahead of the 85-70 Red Sox; if the strike hadn't caused the Red Sox to wipe seven games from their schedule, as opposed to the Tigers' six, the outcome of the AL East race might have been different.

Like their city, the Tigers had been in a state of severe decline when Martin took over as manager. The nucleus of the 1968 World Championship lineup—Al Kaline, Norm Cash, Willie Horton, Mickey Stanley, Dick McAuliffe, Bill Freehan—was still there, as was pitcher Mickey Lolich; but with the exception of the portly Lolich, who had emerged from the shadow of Denny McLain and transformed himself into one of the game's top starters, these aging veterans were fast becoming pale shadows of their former selves. Faced with his players' declining power and lack of mobility on the base paths (they nabbed only 17 stolen bases all season, while being caught 21 times), and with no real help in sight from the Tigers' farm system, Martin managed the Tigers with a decided emphasis on pitching and defense. Eddie Brinkman, the team's all-field, no-hit shortstop, set a major league record in 1972, going 72 straight games and 331 consecutive chances without committing an error.

As per Martin's preferred modus operandi, the '72 Tigers also put a decided emphasis on cheating and intimidation. Under the tutelage of Martin and his pitching coach, Art Fowler, several Tiger hurlers mastered two key pitches: the spitball and the brushback. "Billy had contempt for pitchers who wouldn't throw at hitters," remembered pitcher Bill Denehy, who served as Martin's main "enforcer" out of the bullpen during the 1971 season.

In January 1972, Tigers owner John Fetzer announced that the Tigers had signed a lease with the city to move into a domed stadium along the river in downtown Detroit, which would be constructed with a $126 million bond issue to be paid back over 40 years. Local politicians and business leaders had been dreaming of this sort of development for years, believing that a new, all-weather home for the Tigers, the NFL's Lions, and possibly even the NHL's Red Wings would help revitalize the city's decrepit downtown. The 12th Street Riot of July 1967 had decimated urban Detroit and triggered a massive wave of white flight that seemed to get worse with each passing year; now, the domed sports complex—along with the "city within a city" of the Ford-bankrolled Renaissance Center, plans for which had been unveiled in 1971—was going to lure upscale whites out of the suburbs and back to the Motor City, at least on evenings and weekends.

Or, at least, that was the idea. Hampered by lawsuits and various economic stumbling blocks, the Tigers' new domed home would never be constructed. The Lions would follow their fans to the suburbs in 1975, with a move into the newly built Pontiac Silverdome, but Detroit baseball would continue to be played at Michigan Avenue and Trumbull Boulevard for the foreseeable future. Ironically, even as other downtown businesses felt the crunch of a worsening local economy, the '72 Tigers had no trouble attracting paying customers: Even in a strike-shortened season, the team drew over 300,000 more fans than they had in 1971, and finished at the top of the year-end AL attendance figures with 1,892,386 tickets sold; only the Mets, who drew 2,134,185 fans to Shea Stadium, had a higher attendance mark. The reason, of course, was winning baseball—and Martin's pugilistic managerial style. (Martin's baseball card photo for 1972 offered a rather candid glimpse of his personality, showing him giving "the finger" to the camera in an underhanded manner. How this got past Topps's quality control department, we'll never know.)

On August 22, more than 30,000 Detroit fans turned up at Tiger Stadium on a Tuesday night to see Mickey Lolich try to notch his 20th victory of the season against the Oakland A's. Lolich, roughed up by three A's home runs (including one by opposing pitcher Blue Moon Odom), didn't make it past the fifth, but the crowd still got its money's worth, thanks to a particularly cinematic brawl in the seventh. Martin, who believed that Latino ballplayers were easily intimidated by brushback pitches, instructed Tiger reliever Bill Slayback to throw at the heads of Bert Campaneris and A's outfielder Angel Mangual in rapid succession; when Mangual took offense and punched Slayback, the dugouts emptied, and the assembled multitudes made their appreciation of the spectacle known by hurling garbage onto the field. The animosity from this night would still linger over a month later, when the two teams faced off in the AL playoffs.

By far the most well-rounded teams in the National League, the Reds and Pirates, both moved into first place in their divisions by late June, and never really looked back. The defending World Champion Pirates batted a league-leading .274, with five regulars hitting .300 or better—Vic Davalillo (.318), Al Oliver (.312), Roberto Clemente (.312), Gene Clines (.334, though he lacked enough at bats to take the batting crown from Billy Williams), and Richie Hebner (.300)—catcher Manny Sanguillen lagging just slightly behind at .298, and Willie Stargell placing third in the NL MVP voting with a .293, 33-HR, 112-RBI season. Steve Blass carried his momentum from the 1971 World Series into the new year, winning 19 and losing just eight games while posting a 2.49 ERA; his fellow starting pitchers Dock Ellis (15-7, 2.70), Nelson Briles (14-11, 3.08), and Bob Moose (13-10, 2.91) all delivered solid seasons as well, while relievers Dave Giusti (7-4, 1.93, 22 saves) and Ramon Hernandez (5-0, 1.67, 14 saves) made facing the starters seem almost preferable to opposing batters.

Pirates manager Danny Murtaugh had retired after the '71 World Series, but the clubhouse vibe under new skipper Bill Virdon was as congenial—if not more so—than it had been the previous year. Hebner, who earned his crust in the off-season digging graves, knew Clemente was unnerved by his chosen sideline; the infielder constantly needled him about it, and once jokingly informed the Pirates star that he was measuring him up for a casket. But Clemente, who in his last at bat of the season collected career hit number 3,000 with a double to left off of the Mets' Jon Matlack, hardly seemed a likely candidate for retirement, much less a pine box. His Bucs handily won their division with a 96-59 record, finishing 11 games over the second-place Cubs.

The Reds, who had finished a disappointing fourth in the NL West in 1971, played like they had something to prove in '72, winning the NL West with a 95-59 record and finishing 10½ games above the second-place

Dodgers and Astros. Bobby Tolan, who had missed the entire previous season with a torn Achilles tendon, returned to hit .283 and steal 42 bases, while longtime Reds stars Pete Rose (.307) and Tony Perez (.283, 21 HRs, 90 RBIs) put up typically solid numbers. But the spark plug of the Reds' offense was second baseman Joe Morgan, who came over from Houston in the off-season as part of an eight-player deal. In his debut Cincinnati season, the 5-foot-7 Morgan hit .292 with 16 HRs and 73 RBIs, stole 58 bases, walked a league-leading 115 times, and made only eight errors in 149 games.

In addition to Clay Carroll, the NL's top fireman, the star of the Reds' pitching staff was Gary Nolan. The 24-year-old right-hander seemed a sure bet to win 20 or more games before various neck and shoulder issues benched him for most of the second half of the season; he still finished with a stellar 15-5 record and a 1.99 ERA. Jack Billingham (12-12, 3.18) was the only Reds pitcher to throw more than 200 innings all year, but Sparky Anderson was able to get solid efforts out of most of his staff, especially from Ross Grimsley (14-8, 3.05) and Tom Hall (10-1, 2.61). Though the Pirates were tough, the Reds had won eight out of 12 games against them during the season, and were certain that they could take them in the playoffs as well.

The NLCS began in Pittsburgh, with Pirates outfielder Al Oliver hitting a triple, then a homer, and driving in three runs as Steve Blass cruised to a 5–1 Game 1 victory at Three Rivers Stadium. But in Game 2, the Reds drove Bob Moose from the mound in the first inning, smacking five consecutive hits and plating four runs before the Pirates starter could even record an out, then hung on to win 5–3. The playoffs then moved to Riverfront Stadium, where Manny Sanguillen struck back for the Pirates, homering and driving in two runs in a 3–2 nailbiter. The Reds evened it up again with a 7–1 blowout in Game 4, with the Pirates managing only two hits in that contest against Grimsley, one of them a meaningless solo homer by Roberto Clemente.

Steve Blass managed to hold the Reds at bay in Game 5, leaving in the bottom of the eighth inning with his team up 3–2. The Pirates failed to make anything happen against Clay Caroll in the top of the ninth, and brought Dave Giusti in to face the Reds in the bottom of the frame. Giusti promptly gave up a rare opposite-field home run to Johnny Bench; and after consecutive singles from Tony Perez and third baseman Denis Menke, Bill Virdon yanked Giusti and sent in Bob Moose, the goat of Game 2. Cesar Geronimo's fly to right advanced George Foster—pinch-running for Perez—to third, but shortstop Darrel Chaney popped out to short. Then, with Hal McRae pinch-hitting for Carroll, Moose uncorked a wild slider that bounced over the head of the normally sure-handed Sanguillen, and sent Foster scampering home. The catcher, in anguish and frustration, retrieved the ball and whipped it into center field while the Reds jubilantly celebrated around home plate. They were going to the World Series for the second time in three years.

The AL playoffs also went to five games, and—not unpredictably, given the teams involved—were even harder-fought than the NL's. In the opener, the A's and Tigers went into extra innings, tied 1–1; Tigers great Al Kaline looked to be the hero of the game when he broke the tie in the top of the 11th with a home run off Rollie Fingers, then became its goat in the bottom of the inning when his errant throw from right allowed A's catcher Gene Tenace to cross the plate for the game-winning run. Game 2 was even uglier for Detroit, with Blue Moon Odom shutting out the Tigers on three singles. Frustrated by his team's performance, and enraged by the uncanny ease with which Bert Campaneris stole two bases against them, Billy Martin ordered reliever Larrin LaGrow to dust off the A's shortstop when he came to the plate in the bottom of the seventh. When LaGrow plunked Campaneris on the ankle, Campy responded by whipping his bat toward the mound; thankfully, LaGrow managed to duck just in time. Campaneris and LaGrow were both thrown out of the game, and Campaneris was suspended for the rest of the series.

It should have all ended for the Tigers in Game 3, but no one apparently told Joe Coleman. The veteran righty, who had struck out 222 hitters in 280 innings while winning 19 games during the season, won one more with a dominant 14-K shutout. The Tigers won again in Game 4, scoring three runs in the bottom of the 10th for a 4–3 victory that evened the series at two games apiece, and appeared poised to return to the World Series for the second time in five years.

Alas for Tigers fans, 1972 wasn't fated to be a repeat of '68. Though the Tigers took a 1–0 lead in the first inning of Game 5 on a fielder's choice, the A's tied it in the second on a Reggie Jackson–Mike Epstein double steal. (Unfortunately for the A's, Jackson ruptured his hamstring on the play, rendering him useless for the coming World Series.) Oakland scored again in the fourth on a Tenace RBI single, and then let the deadly combo of Odom and Vida Blue hold the fort the rest of the way. The mood at Tiger Stadium turned increasingly foul as the game went on, and fans pelted the field with smoke bombs, rolls of toilet paper, and whatever garbage they could get their hands on. "When [George] Hendrick went back to center field to catch the ball for the final out," reported Detroit sportswriter Joe Falls, "he almost stepped on a wine bottle. It was, of course, empty."

In the Oakland clubhouse afterward, the postgame celebration briefly turned equally ugly, when Blue made a "choke" sign at Odom and ribbed him for not being able to pitch the full nine innings. Odom jumped up with the intention of decking Blue, but the two were separated by their teammates before anything more serious could occur. A contrite Blue apologized to Odom a few minutes later, then started ranting in front of the assembled press about Finley (who had tried "to destroy my career") and Williams, who hadn't used Blue as a starter in the playoffs. Reaching for a bottle of champagne, Blue was waved off by a clubhouse attendant, who told him the bubbly was reserved for Finley's wife. "What did *she* do?" Blue barked back.

Thus, the stage was set for the "Hair vs. Square" World Series, pitting Sparky Anderson's clean-cut, old-school Reds (whose team rules forbade players to have longer-than-collar-length hair) against Dick Williams's gold-and-green-suited band of mustachioed ruffians. The Reds, already widely favored, received additional support from numerous baseball and political columnists, who talked the Series up as a microcosm of the cultural and generational wars then being waged across the country between the "longhairs" and the "silent majority." Joe Trimble of the *New York Daily News* went so far as to refer to the A's as the "bad guys" and their opponents as "the good guys, the clean-shaven Cincys." The A's players, however, brought no such social agenda with them to the World Series—they just wanted to win.

Coming in without their most feared hitter—thanks to Jackson's ruptured hammy—the A's caught a break when Bowie Kuhn announced that Bert Campaneris would be allowed to play in the Series. But Campy, who went 2-for-3 in Game 1—only to be erased from the base paths twice by Bench's deadly throwing arm—wouldn't be the Athletics' hero of the Series; nor, despite a key home run and an amazing backhanded catch in Game 2, would Joe Rudi, or any of the team's other stars. That honor would belong to Gene Tenace, the A's part-time catcher, who had hit only .225 with five home runs during the regular season, and who had just gone a pathetic 1-for-17 in the playoffs against the Tigers. In Game 1, Tenace became the first player in history to homer in each of his first two World Series plate appearances, driving in all three A's runs in their 3–2 victory at Riverfront Stadium.

Game 2 opened with a special pregame salute to Jackie Robinson, who had played in his first World Series a quarter century earlier. Before throwing out the ceremonial first pitch, Robinson spoke passionately and eloquently to the Cincinnati crowd, saying that major league baseball wouldn't be truly integrated until there were black managers as well as black players in the dugout. It would be another two and a half years before Robinson got his wish; sadly, he wouldn't live to see it happen. Only nine days after being honored at the World Series, Robinson—already nearly blind, and in shaky health—died of a heart attack at the age of 53.

The Reds' staff was able to shut down Tenace in Game 2, but not Rudi, whose third-inning homer off Ross Grimsley made the difference in the 2–1 final score. Rudi also saved the A's victory with a stunning backhanded ninth-inning catch off the bat of Denis Menke: With Tony Perez on first and nobody out, and the A's up 2–0, Menke drove a Catfish Hunter pitch on a line to left field; it looked like it had the power and the distance to clear the fence, but Rudi, leaping high while bracing himself against the wall with his right hand, managed to snag Menke's liner in the upper web of his glove. Perez eventually came home on a Hal McRae single, but Rollie Fingers shut the door on the Reds before they could score again.

For the Reds, who hadn't won a World Series since the infamous "Black Sox" Series of 1919, things looked unexpectedly bleak; no team had ever won a World Series after losing the first two games at home. The A's, who should have been in high spirits, had more bad vibes to deal with—this time in the form of a drunken argument on the plane home between Dick Williams and Mike Epstein, who objected to being taken out of Game 2 for a pinch runner.

Remembering the ratings success of the previous year's World Series night game, Bowie Kuhn decreed that all of the games at the Oakland Coliseum would begin at 5:15 p.m. local time, enabling NBC to broadcast them during prime time to viewers in the eastern and central time zones—but also forcing the games to be played in the strange shadows thrown up by the Oakland twilight. In Game 3, Jack Billingham kept the Reds' hopes alive, emerging the victor in a 1–0 pitchers' duel against Blue Moon Odom. Tenace did more damage against the Reds in Game 4, homering off Don Gullett in the fifth, but a two-out double by Bobby Tolan had the Reds up 2–1 going into the ninth. After getting A's backup first baseman Mike Hegan to ground out to third, Reds reliever Pedro Borbon melted down, giving up four A's singles in a row; the last one, by pinch hitter Angel Mangual, scored Tenace for the game-winning run.

Tenace homered again in Game 5, a three-run shot off Jim McGlothlin, which gave him a record-tying total of four homers for a single Fall Classic. But the Reds—who began the game with a Pete Rose round-tripper off Hunter—battled back throughout the game, stealing three bases off of Tenace, and eventually going ahead 5–4 on Pete Rose's run-scoring single in the top of the ninth. With men on first and third and only one out, the A's had a chance to wrap the Series up in the bottom of the ninth; unfortunately, Odom—in the game for Tenace, who'd walked to open the inning—tried to tag up and score from third when Campaneris popped out to Joe Morgan in foul territory. He was out by a mile.

And so it was back to Cincinnati for Game 6, where—in the lone blow-out of the Series—the Reds hammered Vida Blue and three other A's pitchers for eight runs and 10 hits, while the A's managed only one run off of Ross Grimsley. After the game, it was revealed that local authorities had arrested a man at Riverfront who had been overheard making threatening remarks about Tenace; the 32-year-old Louisville suspect had a loaded pistol and a bottle of whiskey in his pockets when he was apprehended. "If you got to go, Gene," Reggie Jackson joked, "at least it will be on national television."

Death threats or no, Tenace was determined to play in Game 7, and Dick Williams was determined to keep his hot bat in the lineup. But with the Reds having already stolen 11 bases off of the weak-armed Tenace—and with Epstein having completely alienated the A's manager with his attitude and his 0-for-16 performance in the first six games—Williams moved his catcher to first base for the final contest, and brought Dave Duncan in behind the plate. The move proved a prescient one; not only did Duncan gun down Morgan in the fourth inning trying to steal second, but Tenace drove in two key runs—one with a first-inning single that put the A's up 1–0, then another in the sixth with a double that made the score 2–1 in their favor. Williams then sent Allan Lewis in to pinch-run for Tenace, and Lewis made it 3–1 when he scored on a Sal Bando double.

In the bottom of the eighth, the Reds scored a run on a sacrifice fly by Tony Perez, who led the Series with 10 hits and a .435 average; but with two on and two outs, the handlebar-mustached Rollie Fingers got Denis Menke to fly out to end the inning. In the ninth, with two out, Fingers briefly rekindled the hope of the Cincy faithful when he plunked weak-hitting pinch hitter Darrel Chaney, bringing the perpetually clutch Pete Rose to the plate. Rose hit a long drive to left, which briefly looked like it might fall for a game-tying double until Joe Rudi tracked it down. "Hair" had officially beaten "Square," and Charlie Finley—or, rather, Series MVP Gene Tenace and his teammates—had brought the Bay

Area its first sports championship. The battling A's, who averaged fewer than 12,000 fans per game during the year, celebrated their victory with a 15-block parade through downtown Oakland in front of an ecstatic crowd of more than 150,000 revelers.

Just over two months later, a far more somber crowd lined the streets of Carolina, Puerto Rico, as two buses filled with Pittsburgh Pirates players and officials and their families drove slowly toward the town's San Fernando Roman Catholic Church, where a memorial mass was scheduled for Roberto Clemente.

On New Year's Eve, the Pirate great had taken off from San Juan in a DC-7 loaded with supplies intended for victims of the massive earthquake that had recently destroyed much of Managua, Nicaragua. Sadly, Clemente's humanitarian mission was never completed; just two minutes after takeoff, the plane—which was later determined to have been carrying at least 4,193 pounds over maximum allowable gross weight—went down in the Atlantic Ocean. Other than his briefcase and a single sock, no trace of Clemente was ever found.

On March 20, the proud outfielder who had done so much for the Pirates—and for Latin American players, and for the game of baseball in general—became the first player elected to the Hall of Fame without a five-year wait. Appropriately enough, Clemente's induction also made him the first Latin American to be enshrined in the hall.

CHAPTER 5

1973

By the early 1970s, the sexual revolution was in high gear, and "free love"—a concept once limited to the bohemian enclaves of the Bay Area—had fully spread to the American suburbs. Key parties and other "wife-swapping" festivities involving swinging couples had become, if not as common as Tupperware parties, at least familiar to the mainstream consciousness, thanks in part to the hit 1969 film *Bob & Carol & Ted & Alice*, which followed the wife-swapping adventures of two Los Angeles couples. ("Consider the possibilities," read the movie's lascivious advertising tagline.) In 1973, the New York Yankees produced their own sequel, which, had it ever actually been immortalized on celluloid, could have been titled *Mike & Susan & Fritz & Marilyn*.

Fritz Peterson and Mike Kekich had been Yankees teammates since 1968. For the last four seasons, Peterson had been one of the mainstays of the Yanks' pitching staff, averaging more than 17 wins a year, while Kekich had worked his way into the back end of the Bronx rotation. Both lefties lived in the same part of New Jersey, with kids about the same age, and they and their wives quickly became close friends. But it wasn't until 1972, after they went on a double date to see *The Godfather*, that the idea of becoming *more* than close friends first came up. That evening, over several beers, the couples giddily discussed the idea of wife swapping, though nothing initially came of it; but after a party that August at the home of New York sportswriter Maury Allen, Marilyn Peterson and Susan Kekich agreed to go home with each other's husband. When all of the parties involved agreed that they had enjoyed the one-night experiment, it became a semiregular thing: "Some nights I would go home with Fritz, and some nights I would go home with Mike," said Susan.

Given the liberal sexual atmosphere of the era, it's unlikely that the Petersons and Kekiches were the only major league couples to take a walk on the wife-swapping side; it's just that the others managed to be discreet about it. When the 1972 baseball season ended, and the two couples decided to make their swaps permanent—Peterson moved into the Kekich household with Susan and her two daughters, and Kekich moved into the Peterson residence with Marilyn and her two sons—it was only a matter of time before word of their unorthodox arrangement got out. And once it did, during spring training in March 1973, the Yankees found themselves with a public-relations nightmare on their hands.

At first, the Yankees thought it was some kind of practical joke. Peterson and Kekich, in the grand baseball tradition of eccentric lefties, were the biggest pranksters on the team, and this wife-swapping thing seemed like just the sort of outlandish goof the pair might cook up—only, much to the organization's utter shock and mortification, they weren't joking. "In all my years in baseball," Yankees manager Ralph Houk later lamented, "that was the biggest surprise that ever happened to me."

The press, of course, totally ate up the story, printing headlines like "Yankee Panky" and trying to dig up every sordid detail of the swap. Peterson and Kekich, both presumably under "clam-up" orders from new Yankees owner George Steinbrenner—whose group of investors had just purchased the team for $10 million from the CBS organization—said nothing, and Marilyn Peterson briefly went into seclusion at her parents' home in the Chicago area. Susan Kekich, however, tried to explain the situation to the media. "A lot of people get divorces," she insisted. "We didn't do anything sneaky or lecherous. There isn't anything smutty about this. We were all attracted to each other and we fell in love."

Bowie Kuhn, confronted with a trade that even he was powerless to overturn, issued a stern statement to the press: "I deplore what happened and am appalled at its effect on young people," thundered the commissioner, apparently under the misguided impression that the Peterson-Kekich domestic swap had triggered a massive wave of licentious behavior among teens everywhere. "It's a most regrettable situation that does no good for sports in general." Religious groups and other self-appointed guardians of the public morality threatened to boycott the team. Meanwhile, Yankees general manager Lee MacPhail attempted to find some humor in the situation. "We may have to call off Family Day," he sniggered.

Like so many American couples of the era who tried to "get with it" and cast off their sexual inhibitions, the Petersons and the Kekiches were completely unprepared for the emotional and professional fallout that their swap created. Mike Kekich and Marilyn Peterson realized soon after the scandal broke that they actually weren't that into each other; unfortunately for them, their former spouses had fallen completely in love. "All four of us had agreed in the beginning that if anyone wasn't happy, the thing would be called off," mourned Kekich later. "But when Marilyn and I decided to call it off, the other couple already had gone off with each other."

With his marriage and his friendship with Peterson now both on the rocks, Kekich had difficulty focusing on baseball once the season started. After he got knocked around in five appearances and went 1-1 with a 9.20 ERA, the Yankees—desperate to put the whole wife-swapping incident behind them—exiled Kekich to the Indians in June. Peterson would finish the 1973 season with the Yankees, but his pitching also suffered. "Fritz was never the same after the swap," said Yankee reliever Fred Beene. "He was practically destroyed by all the negative reaction." After pitching only a few games for New York in 1974, Peterson would be shipped to Cleveland as well. As Kekich had already moved on to the Texas Rangers by then, he was at least spared the awkwardness of having to share the clubhouse with his former best friend, his wife's ex-husband, and the father of his stepkids. "Imagine the possibilities," indeed.

Compared to the Peterson-Kekich scandal, this year's Charlie Finley spring training experiment—the use of orange-colored baseballs in a March 29 exhibition game between the A's and Indians—seemed downright quaint. Finley's orange-baseball concept found no takers, but there were several other changes afoot for 1973, one of which would enrage baseball purists even more than the idea of a Yankees love quadrangle.

Over the winter, in a move that acknowledged the standout seasons of relievers Clay Carroll and Sparky Lyle and reflected the growing importance of the closer, the major league Rules Committee voted to make the save an official statistic. Any relief pitcher who entered the game with the tying run on base or at the plate, and preserved the lead, would now be credited with a save; ditto for a reliever who pitched three effective innings and preserved the lead. From here on out, saves—as well as blown save opportunities—would become the popular (if not exactly scientific) stat for determining a closer's worth, just as wins and ERA were for a starter.

In March, the owners and Players Association hammered out a three-year "Basic Agreement," which attempted to address several of the underlying issues behind the previous year's players' strike. According to the pact, major league ballplayers were guaranteed a $15,000 minimum salary and the right to salary arbitration; also included in the agreement was the "10 and 5" trade rule, which stipulated that any player who had accrued at least 10 years of major league service—and who had spent at least five years with his current team—had the right to veto any trade involving him. The owners hoped that the Basic Agreement would sufficiently mollify the players and help avoid further labor disputes; in reality, it would turn out to be a major blow against the owners' beloved reserve clause, as well as a major step toward widespread free agency.

But the most controversial off-season decision was the American League's 8–4 vote to adopt the designated hitter on a three-year experimental basis. Though the National League wanted nothing to do with this particular "innovation," the junior circuit's decision to use it was directly motivated by the decline in offensive stats and attendance figures during the 1972 season—as well as the fact that the AL had been outhit by the NL for the last nine years. By substituting a DH for a weak-hitting pitcher, the theory went, more sock would be added to the lineup; and wherever bats were booming, attendance would surely boom as well. It would also save a lot of wear and tear on pitchers, who could now devote themselves entirely to pitching without having to expend any thought or energy on swinging a bat or running the bases.

A large percentage of players, managers, writers, and fans remained unconvinced. If the pitcher did not bat, they argued, then much of the game's basic strategy—including deciding when to bunt, pinch-hit, or double-switch, or whether or not to pull a struggling pitcher who was due up in the next inning—would go out the window. And if pitchers didn't have to face the wrath of opposing hurlers, what was to stop, say, Billy Martin's beanball brigade from headhunting at will? "It's legalized manslaughter," Carl Yastrzemski complained. "The only thing preventing pitchers from throwing at hitters now is that they must come to bat themselves."

Others, like Orioles manager Earl Weaver, simply objected to tampering with the sport. "I think baseball is a very good game and has been very successful, and I don't think it has to have any changes," Weaver opined. "I might be from the old school, but I don't think baseball needs saving." Major league baseball had been played without a DH for nearly a century—so why start now?

Like so many other baseball arguments, the DH question would never be resolved to everyone's satisfaction. Both sides, in fact, would be proved correct: The presence of the DH did indeed diminish the strategic aspects of managing a lineup, while driving the sacrifice bunt closer to extinction—in 1973, the first season that the DH ruling went into effect, NL teams successfully sacrificed nearly twice as often as AL teams. At the same time, the AL immediately saw a much-hoped-for boost in its offensive numbers; not only did the league batting average jump by 20 points, from .239 in 1972 to .259 in 1973, but AL hitters also smacked 1,552 home runs, up from 1,175 the previous year.

One somewhat unforeseen by-product of the designated hitter ruling was that it extended the careers of veteran players who could no longer run, field, or throw but could still knock a pitch into the seats. The Yankees' Ron Blomberg, who on Opening Day became the first DH to come to the plate in an official game (he drew a walk), was only 24 at the time; but in 1973, the average age of regular DHs around the league was closer to 31. Frank Robinson, recently put out to pasture by the Dodgers at age 37, led the 1973 Angels with 30 home runs and 97 RBIs. Thirty-five-year-old Orlando Cepeda, whose ailing knees had limited him to a mere three at bats in 1972, found new life as a Red Sox DH, batting .289, with 20 HRs and 86 RBIs. In Minnesota, 34-year-old two-time batting champ Tony Oliva, who had played in only 10 games a year earlier, hit 16 homers and drove in 92 runs while batting .291 for the Twins. Tommy Davis, who had been one of the NL's most feared batters before an ankle injury reduced him to a journeyman part-timer, was now comfortably ensconced as the Orioles' DH—and at the age of 34, he was able to play a full season with one team for the first time since 1968, hitting .306 with a team-leading 89 RBIs. Even the much-maligned Alex Johnson, who had hit just .239 the previous season with the Indians, found new life as the DH for the Texas Rangers, hitting .287 and driving in 68 runs.

And yet, for all the AL's renewed offensive pop, the biggest story in the league during the 1973 season was Nolan Ryan's arm. Pitching in a career-high 326 innings, the Angels hurler proved that his exceptional 1972 season was no fluke. In addition to winning 21 games in 1973, Ryan pitched the first two no-hitters of his career: one on May 15 against the Kansas City Royals at their spanking new Royals Stadium, and another exactly two months later against the Detroit Tigers at Tiger Stadium. Ryan was so dominant in the second contest, fanning 17 hitters while walking only four, that when veteran Tiger first baseman Norm Cash (who had struck out three times already) came to the plate with two out in the bottom of the ninth, he jokingly brandished a piano leg instead of a bat. Umpire Ron Luciano, reluctantly citing league regulations, made Cash return to the dugout for his real bat. Cash then popped out and ended the game.

Amazingly, Ryan almost pitched a *third* no-hitter on August 29, against the Yankees at Anaheim Stadium. In the first inning, Yankees catcher Thurman Munson popped a Ryan fastball off the fists toward second base. Angels shortstop Rudi Meoli and second baseman Sandy Alomar both assumed that the other would field the ball, which dropped untouched into the infield dirt. Munson was safe at first and since neither player had actually touched the ball, the play was officially scored a hit. Thereafter, Ryan set the rest of the Yankees down without a hit, allowing only three more base runners (two walks and an error) the rest of the way.

As if all those achievements weren't impressive enough, Ryan also broke Sandy Koufax's single-season strikeout record of 382, notching number 383 against the Twins' Rich Reese on his last pitch of the season. Since the Angels still had three games left to play, Ryan could conceivably have pitched the final game of the season in a quest for 400 Ks; but with his team well out of contention by this point and the division races already sewn up, he declined the opportunity. Still, the mind boggles at the prospect of how many batters Ryan might have fanned in 1973, had he faced other pitchers several times a game instead of designated hitters.

For all his mound heroics, Ryan still came in second in the year's Cy Young balloting to Jim Palmer of the Orioles. For the second season in a row, Ryan led the AL in bases on balls, with 162 (Halos manager Bobby Winkles bet Ryan $100 that he couldn't pitch a complete game without walking anyone; he never had to pay up), and his 16 losses—despite the fact that the Angels had one of the weakest offenses in the league— obviously didn't look too good to some of the voters. But Palmer, whose 22 wins in 1973 gave him four straight seasons of 20 victories or more, also posted an ERA significantly lower than Ryan's (a league-leading 2.40 to Ryan's 2.87), and his 10-game winning streak between July 14 and August 26 (which included six straight complete-game victories) had played a significant role in helping the Orioles emerge as the front-runners on their way to winning the AL East pennant.

As fearsome as Ryan's fastball was (it would be clocked the next year at a *Guiness Book of World Records*–worthy 100.8 mph), the case was often made by sportswriters of the day that the Orioles ace was the superior pitcher of the two. Palmer certainly shared that belief. As Ryan noted in his 1977 biography, "The only thing that bothered me about not winning [the 1973 Cy Young] was that Palmer told the press he deserved it because he pitched for putouts while I went for strikeouts. I thought they amounted to the same thing."

After their limp showing in 1972, Palmer's Orioles came back stronger in '73. Though their 30-something stars Brooks Robinson and Boog Powell still seemed in decline, their diminished offensive contributions were off-set by what appeared to be a legitimate O's youth movement: 24-year-old starting catcher Earl Williams led the team with 22 homers, while 24-year-old outfielder Don Baylor racked up a team-leading 32 stolen bases; Bobby Grich, also 24, became a permanent fixture at second, while 26-year-old rookie Al Bumbry—who had served as a platoon leader in the Vietnam War before making his O's debut—led the team with a .337 average, winning the AL Rookie of the Year Award.

As with the year before, the AL East came down a four-way dogfight between Baltimore, Boston, Detroit, and New York. (In some cases, the fight was quite literal, such as the August 1 game at Fenway when Thurman Munson collided with bitter rival Carlton Fisk at the plate, setting off a vicious brawl.) The Tigers and Yankees both logged significant time at the top of the division before mid-August, whereupon the Orioles went on a 14-game winning streak that put them in first place for keeps.

Though the Tigers got 23 wins out of starter Joe Coleman, and 38 saves, 10 wins, and a 1.44 ERA from closer John Hiller—who was bouncing back impressively after suffering a massive heart attack during the 1971 season—Billy Martin grew increasingly frustrated by the Tigers' lack of run production. He openly feuded with Detroit fan favorites Willie Horton and Jim Northrup, both of whom were unhappy with being platooned in the outfield; he also locked horns with the Tigers brass, whom he accused of letting the team get too old and too slow, with no real rebuilding plan for the future. The Tigers' conservative GM, John Campbell, on the other hand, was appalled by the still-married Martin's flagrant womanizing, not least because he suspected that Martin's affair with a Kansas City flight attendant was causing him to miss team flights and show up late for ball games.

But ultimately, it was Martin's temper that prematurely ended his tenure with the Tigers. On August 30, Gaylord Perry pitched a six-hit shutout against the team at Tiger Stadium; after the game, Martin angrily told reporters that he had ordered Tigers pitchers Joe Coleman and Fred Scherman to throw spitters because Perry had been throwing them all game and the umpires hadn't done anything about it. He then doubled down by calling Bowie Kuhn and AL president Joe Cronin "gutless" for refusing to hold Perry to the same rules as everyone else. Campbell, deeply embarrassed by the incident, fired Martin on September 2 "for the good of the organization." Just a few days later, Martin signed on with the Texas Rangers, who'd canned manager Whitey Herzog after the team had gone 6-24 in August.

The World Champion A's had started the season slowly, hovering around the .500 mark for the first two months while the White Sox and the surprisingly tough Royals duked it out at the top of the division. The Sox, buttressed by the return of power-hitting third baseman Bill Melton, seemed poised to finish what they'd started in 1972. Then, on June 28, in a game against the Angels, Dick Allen (who was hitting .316 with 16 homers and 41 RBIs) collided with the equally massive Mike Epstein, resulting in a fractured leg that would effectively end Allen's season—and with it, Chicago's pennant hopes.

Wilbur Wood, as always, stoutly tried to carry the load for the Sox, starting 48 games for the team, including both ends of a July 20 doubleheader against the Yankees. (Sadly, he lost both contests; no one has attempted the foolhardy feat since.) Already 13-3 by the end of May, Wood became the first pitcher of the season to hit the 20-win mark, with a victory over the Twins on July 29. Unfortunately, Wood's record took a dive in the second half of the season, and the tireless knuckleballer finished with a 24-20 record—the first time anyone had won *and* lost 20 games in the same season since Walter Johnson posted a 25-20 record in 1916.

The Royals, enjoying their first year in their new, ultramodern stadium, shocked everyone by hanging tough throughout the season. John Mayberry enjoyed his second straight 100-RBI performance and upped his home run total to 26, while center fielder Amos Otis added another 26 of his own, and led the team with a .300 average. Rookie hurler Steve Busby, who threw a no-hitter against the Tigers on April 27, won 16 games in all, while lefty starter Paul Splittorff became the first pitcher in Royals history to win 20 games. Managed by first-year skipper Jack McKeon, the team finished second in the West with an impressive 88-74 record, though it was clear that they would need a few more bats before they could truly challenge the A's Western supremacy.

At the bottom of the division sat the Texas Rangers, whose move from Washington to Arlington had so far been something less than an inspiring success story. The team was drawing only a fraction more paying customers than it had in D.C., and was playing even worse: After going 54-100 in the strike-shortened '72 season, the Rangers would finish '73 with a 57-105 record.

Desperate to drum up some excitement (and some extra gate receipts), Rangers owner Bob Short played the "local hero" card. On June 7, in the same amateur draft that saw future Hall of Famers Dave Winfield and Robin Yount get picked by the Padres and Brewers, the Rangers signed high school pitching phenom David Clyde, offering him a $125,000 signing bonus—the largest ever given to a draft pick. Clyde was already quite renowned throughout the state of Texas, having just gone 18-0 with a 0.18 ERA for Houston's Westchester High. Rather than send his new prospect to the minors for seasoning, Short insisted that manager Whitey Herzog put Clyde in the Rangers' starting rotation; and on June 27, less than three weeks after signing a contract with the team, Clyde made his first major league start. The biggest Arlington Stadium crowd in the team's short history—35,698—showed up to see the heavily hyped youngster face Rod Carew and the Minnesota Twins.

Clyde performed surprisingly well that night, striking out eight batters in five innings (as well as walking seven) and giving up only one hit—a two-run homer by Twins outfielder Mike Adams—on the way to his first major league victory. Unfortunately, it would all be downhill from there for the Rangers' bonus baby. Now expected to single-handedly pitch the team into contention, the wide-eyed kid buckled under the pressure; he also fell in with some of the team's harder-partying veterans, with predictably destructive results. Clyde finished his rookie year with a 4-8 record and a 5.01 ERA. He would win only 14 more games over the rest of his career, and would be out of the majors for good by the end of 1979.

Though it took a while for the A's to get into gear, the 1973 Oakland squad actually turned out to be even stronger than the 1972 edition. Having gotten rid of Mike Epstein in the off-season and picked up excellent defensive catcher Ray Fosse, the team was free to move World Series hero Gene Tenace out from behind the plate—where he was a decided liability—and put him at first base; "Tenacci," as he liked to call himself, responded by hitting 24 homers and driving in 84 runs. Sal Bando bounced back after a disappointing '72, hitting .287 with 29 homers and 98 RBIs; and Reggie Jackson's .293 average, 32 dingers, and 117 RBIs (along with 99 runs and 22 stolen bases) were good enough to win him the lone AL MVP Award of his career.

Many of Jackson's and Bando's extra RBIs this season were the result of having speedy new center fielder Billy North hitting in front of them. A scrappy switch-hitter who'd come over from the Cubs, North had one of the best seasons of his career with the '73 A's, hitting .285, stealing 53 bases, and scoring 98 runs. North fit in well with his new team, not just because of his mod sideburns, but also because of his willingness to mix it up with anyone at any time. In a May game against the Royals, North charged the mound to deliver a beatdown to pitcher Doug Bird, in retaliation for Bird's beaning him in the minors three years earlier.

The Oakland pitching staff was even more formidable than in 1972. Vida Blue bounced back from his 6-10 1972 record with a 20-9 season, while Ken Holtzman and Catfish Hunter both won 21 games; Rollie Fingers once again ruled the bullpen, delivering 22 saves while striking out 110 men in 126⅔ innings. On June 28, the A's moved into first place in the AL West with a 3–2 Vida Blue victory over Steve Busby and the Royals. With the exception of a brief slump in early August, when they slipped into second behind Kansas City, the A's controlled the division the rest of the way, finally clinching on September 23 with a 10–5 bludgeoning of the White Sox that tagged Wilbur Wood with his 20th loss of the season.

In the National League West, the defending NL champion Reds spent much of the season looking up at the Dodgers, who—though they would ultimately finish in second place for the fourth straight year—put together their best season since the Koufax-Drysdale era. With Don Sutton (18-10, 2.42 ERA), Claude Osteen (16-11, 3.31), Tommy John (16-7, 3.10), and Andy Messersmith (14-10, 2.70) all in the rotation, manager Walter Alston had possibly the strongest pitching staff in the NL, which was ably handled by slugging catcher Joe Ferguson. In his first full season as the Dodger backstop, Ferguson led the team in homers (25) and RBIs (88), all while committing only three errors in 122 games behind the plate.

June 23 marked the debut of the long-running Dodgers infield of third baseman Ron Cey, shortstop Bill Russell, second baseman Davey Lopes, and first baseman Steve Garvey. The clean-cut Garvey, who had played third base for the previous two seasons, was moved to first to make room for the more capable Cey, whose squat build and strange waddling gait earned him the nickname "the Penguin." Lopes and Russell had both been highly touted center fielders in the Dodgers' farm system; but with Willie Davis still holding down that position, they were slotted into second and short, respectively. With Lopes hitting at the top of the lineup, the Dodgers finally had another base-stealing threat worthy of Maury Wills's legacy; he stole 36 bases in '73, and would ramp up his thefts significantly over the next few seasons. Thanks to the team's new "mod squad," the Dodgers won 95 games in '73, and looked set to contend for years to come.

But even with youth and great pitching on their side, the Dodgers still couldn't stop the Reds, who topped the NL West with 99 victories. Once again, the Cincy core of Johnny Bench (25 HRs, 104 RBIs), Tony Perez (.314, 27 HRs, 101 RBIs), Joe Morgan (.290, 26 HRs, 82 RBIs, 116 Rs), and Pete Rose (who hit .338 with 230 hits and scored 115 runs—good enough to beat out Willie Stargell for NL MVP) proved too potent to be contained, and Sparky Anderson got some solid performances out of a fairly unspectacular pitching staff, whose leading lights included Jack Billingham (19-10, 3.04 ERA), Don Gullett (18-8, 3.51), and new closer Pedro Borbon (11-4, 2.16, 14 saves), who stepped into the breach when Clay Carroll failed to dominate as he had the previous season. The team wrapped up its third division pennant on September 24, with a 2–1 victory over the last-place Padres.

The Atlanta Braves, who sank into fifth place in the NL West on April 25 and pretty much never left, were probably 1973's most unbalanced team. Armed with the first trio of teammates ever to hit 40 or more home runs in the same season—second baseman Davey Johnson (who had never before hit more than 18) somehow banged 43, third baseman Darrell Evans smashed 41, and Hank Aaron poled 40—the Braves led the league in offense. But aside from starting hurlers Carl Morton (15-10, 3.41) and Phil Niekro (13-10, 3.31, with a no-hitter against the Padres on August 5), the team's pitching staff was easily the worst in the senior circuit.

Having passed Willie Mays on the all-time home run list the previous year, Aaron began the 1973 season with 673 career round-trippers, putting him within reach of Babe Ruth's hallowed 714. Though Aaron was cut from a far more conservative cloth than such African-American sports icons as Muhammad Ali and Kareem Abdul-Jabbar, the idea of any black man overtaking Ruth's record didn't sit well with the many Americans who took the racist comments of *All in the Family*'s Archie Bunker as hilarious affirmations. While Aaron did receive a ton of mail from fans who were genuinely supportive of his progress, he also found himself opening a number of letters that, in the words of *Sports Illustrated*'s William Leggett, "Start with 'Dear Nigger' and go downhill from there." Several death threats were deemed sufficiently realistic as to require FBI protection for Aaron and his family.

Still, despite all the stress and media scrutiny—and the fact that his 39-year-old body could no longer handle the strain of playing in 150-plus contests a season—Aaron showed up at the ballpark every day without complaint, finishing 1973 with 713 career homers, one short of Ruth's record. "Hank was kind of like your dad," Dusty Baker, then a 24-year-old outfielder on the Braves, would recall decades later. "[He] goes to work and you know work's not always rosy, but Dad never tells you about it."

After four straight years of contending—but never quite making it to the postseason—under Leo Durocher, the Cubs came out roaring in their first full season with manager Whitey Lockman, jumping into first place on April 28 and staying there for nearly two straight months. But with the exception of 27-year-old centerfielder Rick Monday, who led the team with 26 home runs, and the flaky, voluminously Afroed 29-year-old right fielder Jose Cardenal (who topped the team with a .303 average and 19 stolen bases), the Cubbies' regular lineup was over 30 and aging fast, a fact that would become painfully obvious as the season progressed.

The great Ernie Banks, now retired from active duty, was still in the dugout as a member of the Cubs' coaching staff; and on May 8, he briefly became the first black man to manage a major league team. The historic event, which went largely unnoticed by the press, occurred when Lockman was thrown out of the game in the third inning; Banks, who was coaching first base at the time, took over the managerial reins for the remainder of the contest, guiding the team to a 3–2 extra-inning victory over the Padres in San Diego. Of course, Lockman was back in the saddle the following day, and it would be another two seasons before Frank Robinson became the first black full-time major league skipper.

The Cubs went into complete free fall in July, setting in motion one of the strangest pennant races in history, in which five NL East teams—all except the Phillies, who never managed to rise above fifth place—jockeyed for first while simultaneously struggling to stay above (or even reach) the .500 mark. The division had come to resemble, in Roger Angell's immortal words, "a crowded and dangerous tenement."

The Pittsburgh Pirates, reigning champs of the NL East for the last three seasons running, had been favored at the beginning of the season to take the division easily. But even with a .299, 44-HR, 119-RBI season from Willie Stargell, the post-Clemente Bucs never caught fire like they were supposed to. Steve Blass, the ace of the staff the year before, suddenly found it difficult to throw strikes; he would finish the season with a 3-9 record and a horrific 9.85 ERA, having walked 84 batters in 88⅔ innings. On September 6, with the team at 67-69—yet still in second place, only three games behind the sputtering Cardinals—the Pirates fired manager Bill Virdon and pulled Danny Murtaugh out of retirement to replace him for the pennant stretch.

On the day Virdon was fired, the Pirates were only half a game up on the Montreal Expos, who—though hardly tipped to be a competitive team—were still alive and kicking, thanks in part to a breakout season by right fielder Ken Singleton (.302, 23 HRs, 103 RBIs) and some stand-out pitching from Steve Renko (15-11, 2.81 ERA), indefatigable closer Mike Marshall (who appeared in 92 games and pitched 179 innings—both major league records for relievers—and went 14-11 with a 2.66 ERA and 31 saves), and rookie Steve Rogers, who went 10-5 with a 1.54 ERA after being called up in July. The Cubs, despite having seemingly flushed the season down the toilet during the summer, were still only 5½ back of the Cardinals, who were running out of gas even while their star out-fielder, Lou Brock, was getting hotter; over the last month the St. Louis speedster would hit .322 with 18 stolen bases, bringing his seasonal marks up to .297 and 70, respectively.

Tied with the Cubs were the New York Mets, who, frankly, didn't seem to have a chance. Tom Seaver was having another terrific season (he would finish at 19-10 with 251 strikeouts and a 2.08 ERA, and become the first pitcher to bag a Cy Young Award without winning 20 games or more—despite the fact that Ron Bryant rang up a league-leading 24 wins for the San Francisco Giants), while his three lefty pals in the rotation—Jerry Koosman (14-15, 2.84 ERA), George Stone (12-3, 2.80 ERA), and Jon Matlack (14-16, 3.20 ERA, 205 Ks)—could be counted on to keep the Mets in nearly every game. Unfortunately, the Mets' injury-riddled lineup was rarely up to the task of winning ball games. The '73 Mets squad featured the second-weakest offense in the league; second baseman Felix Millan led the team in batting with a .290 average, while first baseman John Milner (23), third baseman Wayne Garrett (16), and right fielder Rusty Staub (15) were responsible for nearly two-thirds of the team's 85 homers. Staub also led the team with a rather unimpressive 76 RBIs.

And yet, insisted the irrepressible Tug McGraw, "You gotta believe!" McGraw, a veteran closer who had been a crucial member of the Mets' 1969 World Champion squad, seized upon the phrase during a team meeting following a frustrating 2–1 extra-inning loss to the Reds on August 17. Team chairman M. Donald Grant, a stiff and uncharismatic gentleman not known for his oratorical abilities, had taken it upon himself to deliver a postgame pep talk. "I told them they had to have faith," Grant would later explain. "I told them they had to believe in themselves."

Like wise-ass *M*A*S*H** doctor Hawkeye Pierce ridiculing the uptight Major Burns, McGraw began mimicking Grant's speech once he thought the Mets chairman had left the clubhouse, chanting, "You gotta believe!" Grant—still in the clubhouse, but completely oblivious of the fact that McGraw was mocking him—returned to the locker room and commended McGraw on his positive attitude. From that point on, "You gotta believe!" became McGraw's battle cry; and no one seemed to benefit more from the advice—born of sarcasm though it may have been—than the reliever himself. Having been knocked around all season (at the All-Star break he was 0-4 with a 6.17 ERA), McGraw suddenly became unhittable; of the 14 games McGraw appeared in during the last month of the season, he won three and saved 10, while holding opponents to a .183 batting average and allowing only two runs to cross the plate. His team, meanwhile, went 20-8 over the same period. "It ain't over 'til it's over," Yogi Berra had insisted to reporters earlier in the year, and now his team was proving him right.

On September 21, the "Miracle Mets"—who had been in last place and 10 games under .500 on August 30—reached the .500 mark and the top of the division in the same day with a 10–2 thrashing of the Pirates, who would finish the season in third place with an 80-82 record. Though a five-way end-of-the-season tie for first was still possible as late as September 30, Tug's boys held on and clinched the division title on the final day of the season, with a 6–4 win over the Cubs in front of fewer than 2,000 dejected fans at Wrigley. The Mets finished at 82-79, giving them the lowest winning percentage—.509—of any team to appear in the postseason.

Of course, even with their hot September, most observers believed that the Mets would be eaten alive in the NL playoffs by the Reds, who were coming off a sizzling final stretch of their own. Even if the Cincinnati lineup wasn't quite as daunting as it had been the year before, the Reds still had Bench, Rose, Morgan, and Perez, while the Mets' best four position players were named Staub, Milner, Millan, and Garrett. But the Mets had the edge when it came to pitching; and though the Reds won Game 1, they didn't lead in the contest until a Bench home run off Seaver in the bottom of the ninth gave them a narrow 2–1 victory. Jon Matlack evened the series in Game 2 by blanking the Reds with a two-hit, 5–0 shutout. Asked in the clubhouse what he thought of the Big Red Machine's overall performance against Matlack, Mets shortstop Bud Harrelson—whose '73 stats included a career-high batting average of .258 and zero homers—cracked to reporters that "they looked like me hitting."

Though Harrelson hadn't called out any of the Reds by name, word quickly got back to the Cincy clubhouse that he'd insulted Pete Rose and Joe Morgan, both of whom became completely livid when they heard about the weak-hitting shortstop's remarks. The general consensus was that the Reds, fueled by Harrelson's put-down, would be so psyched up as to be unstoppable when the series moved to Shea for Game 3. But Staub—the flame-haired right fielder who had become one of the Mets' most popular players since coming over from Montreal in the spring of '72—trashed the script by cracking two home runs in that game off Ross Grimsley. By the time Rose came to the plate in the top of the fifth, his team was down 9–2, and he was clearly unhappy about the situation. After Rose singled to center off Jerry Koosman, Morgan hit a grounder to first, which Milner fielded and threw to Harrelson for the out at second; Harrelson was able to make the return relay to first to double up Morgan just as Rose laid him out with a pop-up slide. Harrelson swore at Rose, Rose grabbed Harrelson, and suddenly players came streaming out of both dugouts and bullpens to join the fun.

Ironically, despite the 40-pound weight differential between Rose and the skinny Mets shortstop, Harrelson wasn't the Met who got the worst of the fight. That honor went to pitcher Buzz Capra, who was sucker punched by Pedro Borbon right as the scuffle was being broken up. After landing a few return blows on Borbon, Capra tripped and fell to the ground, and had to be extricated from the fray by Willie Mays, the lone Met that the Reds respected too much to punch. Borbon accidentally picked up Capra's Mets cap and, thinking it was his own, put it on his head while being led back to the Reds' dugout. Upon realizing his mistake, Borbon—still pumped up from the fight—pulled it off his head and proceeded to tear into it with his teeth.

The fans at Shea, outraged by (or more likely, wishing they could have joined in) the fracas, pelted Rose with trash when he returned to his position in left field in the bottom of the fifth. When a whiskey bottle landed near Rose, he and the rest of the Reds fielders were waved back to the dugout by Sparky Anderson, and National League president Chub Feeney sent word that if the fans didn't behave, the Mets would have to forfeit the game. When repeated public address announcements to that effect failed to calm the natives, a diplomatic party made up of Staub, Seaver, Mays, outfielder Cleon Jones, and manager Yogi Berra trotted out to left field to flash peace signs and beg the fans to end their rain of garbage. Their mission successful, play resumed, and the Mets were able to hold on to a 9–2 victory.

When the Reds returned to Shea for Game 4, they were greeted by the sight of several large banners hanging from the upper deck, with "Rose Is a Weed" and "This Rose Smells" being some of the less offensive messages. Rose answered back in the top of the 12th inning, breaking a 1–1 tie with a solo shot off reliever Harry Parker; circling the bases with his right fist raised in a victorious salute, Rose doubtless considered raising his middle finger as well. In Game 5, the Mets took an early lead

when Ed Kranepool—the last remaining alum from the legendarily terrible '62 Mets team, now filling in for an injured Staub—rapped a two-
run single in the first off of Jack Billingham. The Reds tied it up in the
top of the fifth, when Perez drove Rose home with a single, but the Mets
broke it open with four more runs in the bottom of the inning. The Mets
plated one more in the sixth, and Seaver held the Reds at bay until the
ninth, whereupon McGraw loaded the bases before finishing them off.

Fearing for their safety, Shea security led the Reds' wives down to the
visitors' dugout before the final out, and several Reds players grabbed
bats for added protection. As soon as Dan Dreissen grounded out to end
the game, Mets fans surged onto the field, lighting celebratory firecrackers and pulling up anything they could get their hands on, while the
players ran for their lives. "The fastest I've ever run on a ball field was
from second base to the third-base dugout that day at Shea Stadium,"
said Rose, who had been on second when Driessen came to the plate.
"The sad part is that these fans would have done this to the field even if
we had lost," lamented Tom Seaver. "I think a lot of them didn't care
whether we won or not." Gazing forlornly out at the orgy of mayhem
happening on the field, Sparky Anderson sighed and asked a reporter,
"Can you imagine this happening in America?"

The AL playoff meeting between the A's and the Orioles—the second in
three years—was less combative than the NL series, but no less competitive. Jim Palmer's 6–0 shutout in Game 1 was followed by a 6–3 Catfish
Hunter win in Game 2, the margin of victory provided by two Sal Bando
homers and another by Bert Campaneris. Campy, who had hit only four
jacks all year, won Game 3 in the bottom of the 11th with another solo shot.
In Game 4, Vida Blue took a 4–0 lead into the top of the seventh, only to
exit after a three-run homer by O's catcher Andy Etchebarren tied the
game. Rollie Fingers gave up a go-ahead solo shot to Bobby Grich in the
eighth, and the series went to the fifth and final game.

Having made its debut during the season, the designated hitter was
used in the AL playoff for the first time in 1973 as well. For the first four

games, Orioles DH Tommy Davis thoroughly outhit his A's counterpart, Deron Johnson, .353 to .100; but in Game 5, Hunter shut Davis (and most of his teammates) down completely, scattering five hits on the way to a 3–0, pennant-clinching shutout. Having avenged their sweep by the O's in the 1971 playoffs, the A's were returning to the World Series to defend their crown.

While still widely favored to beat the Mets, the A's were now slightly less than a sure thing to repeat as World Champs. For one thing, the green-and-gold gang had batted only a cumulative .200 in its five games against the Orioles—the team's key sluggers, Sal Bando and Reggie Jackson, had hit .167 and .143, respectively—and many believed that the Mets' pitching staff was superior to the Orioles'. For another, the A's were playing without Billy North, who had suffered a severely sprained ankle in September and was unavailable for the Series. And finally, with the NL refusing to recognize the DH as a legitimate position, the A's pitchers would have to bat in the World Series, something they hadn't done all season.

Ken Holtzman, who started Game 1 of the Series for Oakland, immediately proved that the last of the above concerns was a nonissue: Coming to the plate for the first time in the third inning, he promptly stroked a double off Jon Matlack that started a two-run A's outburst—all the runs the team would need in its 2–1 victory.

Game 2 was a far messier affair, a bizarre 12-inning epic at the Oakland Coliseum that, at four hours and 13 minutes, would set a World Series record for longest game. Sloppy A's fielding and some ineffective pitching by Vida Blue and reliever Horacio Pina gave the Mets a 6–3 lead in the top of the sixth; the A's cut it to 6–4 with a Reggie Jackson double off Tug McGraw in the seventh, and then tied things with two outs in the bottom of the ninth with back-to-back RBI singles by Jackson and Gene Tenace off McGraw. In the 10th, with one out and Harrelson on third, Felix Millan hit a short fly to Joe Rudi in left; the speedy Harrelson tagged up and tried to score, only to be called out at the plate in a controversial ruling by home plate ump Augie Donatelli, who claimed that A's catcher Ray Fosse had tagged Harrelson's hip. Subsequent replays showed that Fosse had missed Harrelson entirely; Willie Mays, who was in the on-deck circle and had a better view of the plate than Donatelli, dropped to his knees in disbelief.

Harrelson returned to the plate in the top of the 12th with the score still tied 6–6 and whacked a Rollie Fingers pitch into right-center for a double. He then advanced to third on a bunt single by McGraw (who, amazingly, was still pitching); Mays, who had looked old and lost in center field all day—even falling down on one play—redeemed himself by driving in Harrelson with a two-out single off Fingers, a tie-breaking blow that would turn out to be the final hit in the long and storied career of the "Say Hey Kid." Cleon Jones then singled to load the bases, bringing John "the Hammer" Milner to the plate.

Rather than live up to his nickname, Milner hit a bounding ball to the right side that should have ended the inning. But A's second baseman Mike Andrews, who had come into the game in the eighth as a defensive substitute, somehow let the ball squirt through his legs; when the dust cleared, two runs had scored, and Milner and Jones were perched at second and third. Mets catcher Jerry Grote then hit another apparent inning ender to Andrews; the second baseman fielded the ball cleanly enough, but his throw pulled Gene Tenace off the bag at first, giving Andrews his second error of the inning, and the Mets another run. Down 10–6, the A's battled back in the bottom of the 12th, scoring a run and loading the bases with one out, before George Stone (pitching in relief of McGraw, who had hung in there for six innings) finally shut the door.

A's owner Charlie Finley, apoplectic over Andrews's errors, wanted to "fire" Andrews and replace him on the team's World Series roster with rookie infielder Manny Trillo, who had played in only 17 games with the club during the regular season. Bowie Kuhn initially okayed the switch, pending approval from the Mets; but when Mets GM Bob Scheffing refused to grant permission, Finley hit upon a more devious solution, haranguing Andrews into signing a physician's statement that pronounced him "disabled for the rest of the year" due to "bicep groove tenosynoritis of the right shoulder."

When the news broke about Andrews's imminent medical release from the team, the A's players were furious. Reporting to Shea Stadium for a mandatory team workout before Game 3, each A's player showed up sporting a black armband emblazoned with "19"—Andrews's number—on his uniform sleeve. "Charlie just went absolutely berserk when he saw that," remembered Ray Fosse several decades later.

The New York media, predictably, sank their fangs into the story, which got even juicier when several A's players revealed that they were considering boycotting the rest of the World Series in protest. "There is a possibility of refusing to play," Jackson told the *New York Daily News*. "There are a bunch of guys who are close to that point."

Meanwhile, Kuhn met with Andrews in New York and determined that—since Andrews had actually been playing with his "medical condition" all year—he would have to be reinstated on the A's roster in time for Game 3. After admonishing Finley for "unfairly embarrassing a player who has given many years of able service to professional baseball," Kuhn fined the A's owner $5,000 for attempting to circumvent the World Series roster rules with his medical ruse.

A's manager Dick Williams, utterly fed up with all the Finley-related drama, called his team together for a clubhouse meeting before Game 3. If the players thought their skipper intended to give them a "Let's put this behind us and go beat the Mets" kind of pep talk, they were in for a shock. "I'm going to deny this if it leaks out from this room," Williams told them, "but I'm resigning at the end of this World Series, win, lose, or draw."

It wasn't much of a motivational speech, but the A's managed to pull out a 3–2 victory in an 11-inning Game 3, the second-straight extra-inning contest of the Series. Game 4's 6–1 Mets victory was spearheaded by Rusty Staub's four-hit, five-RBI performance, which included a three-run shot off of Ken Holtzman in the first inning. Staub had badly hurt his shoulder running into a wall in Game 4 of the NLCS, an injury that forced him to throw underhand from right field for the rest of the Series; however, his bat obviously still worked fine.

The fans at Shea cheered every Mets run in Game 4 not just as a step toward a World Series victory, but also as a personal insult to Finley; the "Folding Sign Man," a fixture at Shea since the ballpark opened, received thunderous applause for flashing the message "SIT DOWN, YA BUM!"

when Finley stood for the ritual seventh-inning stretch. And in the top of the eighth, when Williams sent Andrews to the plate to pinch-hit for Horacio Pina, the Mets faithful gave him a standing ovation. Finley just stared ahead blankly and waved his green-and-gold A's flag.

Game 5 saw Koosman and McGraw combine for a masterful three-hit, 2–0 shutout, which meant that the Mets had to win only one of the next two games in Oakland to take the Series. But it wasn't to be; Catfish Hunter outdueled Tom Seaver for a 3–1 victory in Game 6, and then Bert Campaneris and Reggie Jackson ganged up on Jon Matlack with a pair of two-run blasts in the fourth inning of Game 7. The A's added another run in the fifth on a Joe Rudi single, then coasted to a 5–2 victory.

For the second year in a row, the A's were the champions of the world; but this October, the celebration in the Oakland clubhouse was muted. Williams, as promised, announced his resignation to the press while the corks were still popping; though he insisted that he wanted to spend more time with his family in Florida, the truth was that Williams had already notified the New York Yankees of his availability. (The Yankees had just bid adieu to Ralph Houk, who told his players that he had to quit, lest he wind up punching out George Steinbrenner.)

Unfortunately for the Yankees, Williams was still under contract to Finley through the 1974 season, and Finley made it clear that he had no intention of releasing Williams to another team without receiving "adequate compensation" in return. In a typically Finleyan move, the A's owner made a big show of sending Williams a paycheck on the first and 15th of every month, just to demonstrate that he still considered Williams "his" manager. (Williams kept the checks but never cashed them.) The Yankees would be forced to look elsewhere for a new manager for the 1974 season; but with Williams refusing to return to Oakland, Finley would have to find someone else to torment.

CHAPTER 6
THE POLYESTER PROLIFERATION

"Pirates and Rawlings Spark Mod Revolution in Athletic Clothing," trumpeted an ad in the January 16, 1971, issue of the *Sporting News* for the Rawlings Sporting Goods Company. Mod? *Revolution?* As overused as those two buzzwords were during the late '60s and early '70s, applying them to something so mundane (and frankly, *square*) as athletic clothing seemed an exceptional stretch.

And yet, seven months earlier, when the Pittsburgh Pirates took the field for the first time at the new Three Rivers Stadium, the dapper, form-fitting new uniforms sported by Roberto Clemente, Willie Stargell, and their teammates were indeed eye-catching, stylish, and tailored to flatter a man with a lean and muscular build—not unlike the "mod" styles then favored by 20-something males who had a bit of extra cash in their pocket. The "Pirates" lettering and gold-and-black trim were held over from uniforms the team had worn up until the 1970 All-Star break, but the jerseys were now button-free pullovers, and the skintight white pants were now held up not by a belt, but by a striped elastic waistband.

With their slim silhouettes and lightweight, double-knit fabric (a stretchable blend of cotton and nylon), the Pirates' new uniforms were as much of a departure from the baggy wool flannels of yore as Three Rivers was from the team's old Forbes Field home. According to the Rawlings ad copy, "[Pirates] officials wanted a modern image to go with their new stadium," and these new ensembles definitely fit the bill. If anything, they looked a little like what William Shatner and the cast of TV's *Star Trek* might don for a baseball showdown with the Klingons. The ad wasn't wrong on the "revolution" front, either: Within just a few years of Three Rivers' Opening Day, every team in the major leagues would abandon its old-style wool-blend uniform for pants and jerseys made from double-knit fabrics—some of them in retina-searing color combinations that would've made Ty Cobb choke on his chaw.

The basic baseball uniform had already been subjected to numerous changes since 1876, when the National League first came into existence. But with the possible exception of the reflective, brightly colored satin jerseys that teams like the Brooklyn Dodgers briefly experimented with during the early years of night baseball, the double-knit uniforms of the 1970s were easily the most radical that the sport had ever seen.

Less than a decade earlier, Joe Pepitone had been widely ridiculed (and often had his masculinity questioned) for tailoring his Yankee uniforms to accent his physique; and now, suddenly, everyone was wearing body-hugging uniforms that looked great on lean, athletic dudes like Amos Otis and Garry Maddox, but looked fairly ridiculous on beefy lugs like Mickey Lolich and Boog Powell. (When the 6-foot-4, 270-plus-pound Powell was shipped to Cleveland from Baltimore in 1975, he supposedly took one look at himself in the Indians' all-red road uni and lamented, "I look like the world's biggest Bloody Mary!")

While it's unlikely that the folks at Rawlings or the teams themselves were directly inspired by, say, the contemporary designs of Oleg Cassini or Yves Saint Laurent, there's no question that men's fashion had become considerably less conservative since the mid-'60s, when Pepitone (a noted fashion plate off the field) first modded out his pinstripes. Ties, collars, and lapels were wider than ever; shirts and trousers fit more snugly, even while the latter flared ridiculously wide below the knee. Synthetic, chemically concocted fabrics like Rayon, Dacron, and Qiana were finding favor over cotton and wool, since they were easier to clean and often didn't require an iron. Bold floral, psychedelic, and even op-art patterns were no longer limited to the domain of urban hipsters, but had effectively infiltrated both the swinging-singles and the straitlaced nine-to-five scenes as well. A 1971 *Time* magazine profile described Pepitone as "favor[ing] lavender suede sashes and see-through paisley shirts off duty," but even Pepitone's squarer Cubs teammates like Ron Santo and Randy Hundley were beginning to sport funkier clothes off the field. In that context, and within the visual environment of the new AstroTurf-carpeted stadiums, the new uniforms—some of which looked as funky and bold as anything sold by such urban '70s clothiers as Flagg Bros. and Eleganza—made perfect aesthetic sense.

They also made good sense from a practical standpoint. The new fabrics (which soon morphed again from cotton-nylon blends to polyester) were cooler on the skin, harder to rip, and stood up to repeated launderings; and the stretchier fabric meant that the players enjoyed more freedom of movement. Juan Marichal, possessor of one of baseball's most extravagant windups, sang the praises of the new uniform material in 1972: "The double knits will stretch and make it easier when I kick high," the aging San Francisco Giants ace explained. "That's very important. I've sometimes worn pants that were too tight and interfered with my windup." Sadly, Marichal would get to play only a little more than three seasons in double knits; he retired in 1975 with 243 wins. Could he have reached the 300-victory mark if he'd pitched his whole career in pants with a little more "give"? We can only speculate. . . .

Fit and fabric aside, the most memorable aspect of '70s baseball uniforms was the vivid color schemes. In the post–World War II era, major league uniforms had typically been understated affairs—white (or white with pinstripes) at home, gray on the road, and maybe a bit of colored piping on the sleeve and the placket. The only solid blocks of visible color were displayed on the caps, the stirrups, and the sleeves of the undershirt; and the tints themselves were rarely much more exotic than basic variations on blue and red. The only real flash came, if at all, from the team insignia on the cap, a cartoonish patch on the sleeve (like the Indians' maniacally grinning "Chief Wahoo"), or the cursive flourish of the team name on the front of the jersey. That is, of course, until Charlie Finley took it upon himself to lob a Technicolor bomb onto the playing field.

Whatever one might say about the controversial A's owner, it can't be denied that the man had an eye for color. While Finley's push for orange-colored baseballs and gold bases never gained much support from fellow owners, he was free to dress his players however he pleased. In 1963, Finley caused a major stir by sending his Kansas City players onto the field in matching vests and pants of "Tulane gold," with undershirts and caps of "Kelly green," then further enraged baseball traditionalists by adding white shoes and gold socks to the equation.

After moving the A's Oakland in 1968, Finley continued to tinker with this color combination, adding a gold bill to the team's green cap— the A's coaching staff would eventually adopt caps with white crowns and green bills—and concocting multiple "alternate" uniforms for both home and road games. In 1972, with polyester double knits all the rage, Finley swapped the vests for V-neck pullovers (worn variously in white, green, or gold) and bright white pants with green-and-gold-striped elastic waistbands; over the next two years, Finley would also toss green- and gold-colored pants into the mix.

One could never be entirely sure which eye-popping combination of jerseys and pants the A's would take the field in, and sometimes the myriad possibilities confused the players themselves. At the 1975 All-Star Game, A's players Rollie Fingers, Reggie Jackson, and Joe Rudi wore green jerseys and white pants; Gene Tenace and Bert Campaneris wore gold jerseys and white pants; Vida Blue sported a gold jersey and gold pants; and Claudell Washington showed up in an all-white ensemble. Considering that Jackson, Rudi, Campaneris, Tenace, and Blue were all starters, and therefore all on the field together for the first few innings, it's possible that they just wanted to add an extra element of visual interest for the fans. But it's more likely that their other uniforms were still at the cleaners; for despite Finley's penchant for multiple color combinations, he was too stingy to supply his players with more than one of each jersey, cap, or pair of pants at a time. "There were no new uniforms from one season to the next," Reggie Jackson recalled in his autobiography. "I remember starting 1975 with 1972 pants. And a jersey from 1974. That was the season after we'd won our third World Series in a row."

With their long hair, wild mustaches, and colorful uniform options, the A's were the sartorial pioneers of '70s baseball—and rather telegenic ones, at that. "When I first outfitted the Athletics in gold and green uniform combinations, they said we looked like monkeys," Finley bragged to the *Sporting News*. "The Athletics led the way, and today you see most teams in attractive uniforms that lend more to color TV."

Ah, yes—color TV. The explosion of color in major league uniforms was certainly related to the rise in popularity (and the decline in cost) of color televisions in the U.S. 1972 was the first year that color TVs outsold their black-and-white counterparts; it was also the first year that color sets outnumbered black-and-whites in American households. Baseball purists might have grumbled; but for many fans, watching the '72 World Series on a color TV—with the golds, greens, and whites of the A's uniforms and the (more conservative, but equally striking) whites and reds of the Cincinnati team set against the unnaturally green AstroTurf of the Reds' Riverfront Stadium—was a glorious, almost psychedelic experience, especially when compared to the drab palettes of Fall Classics past.

Over the next few seasons, as most major league teams clambered aboard the Technicolor bandwagon, "road grays" would became all but extinct, as bright powder blue became the basic road color of choice. Even the conservative Detroit Tigers, who remained true to their classic white button-up home uniforms, hot-rodded the accents on their gray V-neck road pullovers with a fluorescent shade of orange, and applied the same color to the Old English D on their road caps.

During the 1970s, the teams that altered their uniforms the least were the New York Yankees and the Los Angeles Dodgers, both of whom switched to double-knit materials but otherwise stubbornly stuck with the classic belted and buttoned-up look that they'd worn in decades past.

The Montreal Expos likewise stayed with the same white home/blue road uniforms (and the red, white, and blue M logo) they'd worn since they'd entered the big leagues in 1969. The New York Mets made only minor adjustments, affixing the "Mets" name to their road jerseys in '74, and adopting a "sporty" two-button road jersey for '78 and '79.

Everyone else, though, took the color explosion of the 1970s as a license to break free from the bonds of sartorial tradition, even if it only meant adopting a V-neck, elastic-waist variation of their previous uniforms (Boston Red Sox, Cincinnati Reds, California Angels), adding "road blues" to their wardrobe (Philadelphia Phillies), or doing both (Minnesota Twins, Texas Rangers, Kansas City Royals, St. Louis Cardinals). The Toronto Blue Jays and Seattle Mariners, the two expansion teams of the '70s, also adhered to the then-popular V-neck, road-blues combination when they joined the AL in 1977, though the Mariners' clever incorporation of a trident-shaped M worked much better—from a design standpoint, at least—than the Blue Jays' bird logo, which was awkwardly placed in the very center of the jersey, right over the player's gut.

With some teams, the fun was in the smaller details, like the Milwaukee Brewers' groovy baseball-glove-shaped MB cap insignia, the Phillies' stylized P, and the feather motifs on the sleeves of the Atlanta Braves. (Though the less said about the clownish red pinstripes that Ted Turner's team wore at home from 1976 to 1979, the better.) For others, it was garish, solid-colored road (and sometimes home) ensembles, like the kind that bummed Boog Powell out when he joined the Indians.

The San Francisco Giants and Baltimore Orioles (Powell's old team) each donned some fairly diabolical shades of orange during the decade. In 1971, Orioles third bagger Brooks Robinson—who supplemented his baseball salary by running a sporting goods operation—convinced his team to buy an all-orange double-knit uniform from the Brooks Robinson Sporting Goods Company. That outfit surely must have made Powell look like the world's biggest pumpkin; and, in fact, it was rumored that the first baseman's objections were one of the main reasons that the team dumped the all-orange uni after only a few wearings in 1971 and 1972.

No team sported more drastically different looks over the course of the 1970s than the Chicago White Sox. The team started the decade wearing a royal blue, white, and gray color scheme that was actually quite conservative looking, but which ran afoul of many South Side fans who decried the lack of dark pinstripes, which had been a part of the Sox' home uniform since 1951. After a 106-loss season in 1970, new owner John Allyn was desperate to create some excitement at Comiskey, so he brought the pinstripes back—although this time, they (along with the team's caps, undersleeves, stirrups, and shoes) were bright scarlet, while the Sox' road uniforms were now powder blue with scarlet lettering. Both home and road jerseys also featured an old-fashioned zip-up front, something that hadn't been seen in baseball since the late '50s.

Five years later, when Bill Veeck took over the team, the Sox made an even more radical change, donning wide-collared tunics that made their previous zip-up jerseys look like spacesuits by comparison. These old-timey jerseys—white with stand-up navy blue collars for home games, solid navy blue for the road, both emblazoned with "Chicago" across the chest—were worn untucked over matching, stirrupless pants, a look that resembled nothing else worn on a baseball diamond in the 20th century.

And when the 1976 Chisox squad paired those tunics with blue Bermuda shorts and striped kneesocks, the results were simply unforgettable—and, in the eyes of long-suffering White Sox fans, totally unforgivable. The idea for the shorts was originally hatched by Veeck's wife, Mary Frances, and Veeck—always game for a novel concept—was already off and running with it by the time his new team arrived at spring training. In March, the *Sporting News* reported that Veeck was "kicking around" the idea of having his players wear shorts during hot and humid summer day games, and claiming that several of his players had actually expressed interest in the idea.

The infamous White Sox shorts finally made their regular-season debut on August 8, 1976, when the team wore them for the first half of a doubleheader against the highly amused Royals. "You guys are the sweetest team we've seen," cackled Royals first baseman John Mayberry, while the rest of his teammates snickered into their mitts. "Hey, Ralph," Big John called out to Sox speedster Ralph Garr. "You get over to first and

I'm going to kiss you!" Chicago manager Paul Richards took pity on his humiliated squad, allowing them to change back into their regulation uniform trousers for the second game.

The Sox wore shorts twice more that August before mercifully shelving them for good. ("Now we'll wait to see if any other teams try them," cackled Veeck to reporters. We're still waiting.) And yet, decades after their brief appearance, the memory of the shorts continues to haunt the Sox and their fans; to this day, many still believe that the Sox sported the shorts repeatedly throughout the Veeck era—even for whole seasons at a time. Though the sartorial experiment was actually more (no pun intended) short-lived, it would still go down as the single most embarrassing moment in White Sox history, making the 1976 squad's piss-poor 64-97 record seem mildly respectable by comparison. Even so, Mrs. Veeck steadfastly refused to disown the shorts. "They were not totally a gag thing," she insisted with a straight face. "It got very hot in Comiskey Park."

In 1979, the Phillies introduced a fashion experiment that lasted for only a single game. The team's front office initially wanted the Phils players to sport an all-burgundy combo for every Saturday home game; but after getting shelled 10–5 by the Expos in the uniform's inaugural outing (May 19, 1979) and enduring the taunts of the fans and local media alike over the hideous new look, the players understandably chose to forgo another wearing of the "Saturday Specials."

The generally tradition-oriented Chicago Cubs likewise attempted a more flamboyant look in the late '70s—a strange "reverse pinstripe" road uniform, which featured white stripes over light blue pants and jerseys. This stylistic departure lasted four whole seasons, and continues to divide Cubs fans to this day. For some, the "blue pajamas" remain an utter embarrassment; for others, they still conjure fond memories of Dave "Kong" Kingman's monster 1979 season, in which he jacked 48 homers, drove in 115 runs, and batted a career-high .288.

Kingman probably didn't mind the 'blue pajamas"; after all, during 1977—a season in which the moody slugger played for four different teams—he'd worn a far uglier uniform as a member of the San Diego Padres. The Padres were cursed from the start with a mustard-and-fecal-brown color combination, held over from the team's days in the Pacific Coast League, and their raglan-style jerseys and two-tone caps gave off what can only be described as a total fast-food employee vibe—which was perhaps appropriate, given that the team was purchased in 1974 by McDonald's mogul Ray Kroc.

Kingman was at least lucky to miss out on wearing the team's 1978 jerseys, which had "Padres" written across a white torso in large lowercase yellow letters, and "San Diego" placed awkwardly in smaller brown letters over the right breast; it looked like something a bargain-basement T-shirt manufacturer had come up with for a local Kiwanis Club softball team. Incredibly, there was also an even more unsightly variant with brown sleeves, yellow torso, and matching yellow pants, which made the players look like mustard-slathered hot dogs.

But even at their worst, the Padres' uniforms could not approach the pupil-gouging horror of the Houston Astros', circa 1975–79. "They look like Hawaiian softball uniforms," chortled Dodger knuckleballer Charlie Hough, and he wasn't too far off the mark—though something about them also smacked of chain motel bedspread or 747 jumbo-jet upholstery. The sleeves and the bottom two-thirds of the Astros' jerseys featured horizontal stripes in various gradations of orange, with a navy blue star placed over the left side of the rib cage and "Astros" in plain navy lettering on a white field below the neck. The first incarnation of these jerseys featured a weird white circular "cutout" on the back, where the player's number was placed. For reasons that have never been fully explained, the player's number was also affixed to the right front of the ensemble's white pants—a crotch-accenting fashion choice that was thankfully phased out in 1980, never to return. For extra roller disco flair, the pants also featured orange rainbow piping that mirrored the pattern on the jersey.

The Astros liked their "tequila sunrise" jerseys so much, they wore almost identical versions of them at home *and* on the road. (The road unis had a barely perceptible shade of gray on the upper chest.) While the orange test pattern admittedly made a warped kind of sense within the "futuristic" (and also quite orange) confines of the Astrodome, it looked horribly out of place in the other parks. Perhaps the team, which had been mediocre or worse since arriving in the NL in 1962 as the Houston Colt .45s, was merely trying to achieve a built-in edge against its opponents; standing in against an Astros fireballer like J. R. Richard must have been nerve-racking enough without being additionally distracted by something out of Jasper Johns's mescaline nightmare. Alas, the uniforms didn't seem to help much; in 1975, the year the jerseys were introduced, the Astros finished at 64-97, their worst showing in team history.

During the late '70s, nothing quite evoked the phrase "do not attempt to adjust your set" like a color TV broadcast of an Astros-Pirates game. The Pirates took the Athletics' gaudiness and mix-and-match unpredictability to uncharted levels, commissioning a Japanese ski-clothing company named Descente to design three different basic uniforms—one black with gold lettering, one gold with black lettering, and a third that was white with black-and-gold lettering and black-and-gold double pinstripes spaced five inches apart. And just to complicate things further, there was also a dizzying assortment of undershirts, stirrups, socks, and caps that came in black or gold.

The array of Pirate possibilities was mind-boggling; and when 6-foot-5 Bucs star Dave Parker topped off any of the uniforms with a gold earring and chains, as was his wont, the effect was outrageous, even by the glitzy standards of the disco era. NBC *Game of the Week* announcer Joe Garagiola spoke for many baseball purists when he expressed his distaste for the uniforms during one broadcast, saying he thought the Pirates looked like "big yellow canaries" in their all-gold ensembles, "undertakers" in their black ones, and "convicts" in the pinstripes. But for fans of the late-'70s Pirates, the new uniforms were merely emblematic of the team's brash confidence and charisma.

As memorable as the Pirates' togs were, their caps were actually the most important element of the whole ensemble. In 1976, a handful of teams—the Pirates, Mets, Cardinals, Reds, and Phillies—adopted flat-topped, striped, pseudo-19th-century versions of their regular caps as a salute to the National League's centennial. (NL umpires wore them on occasion as well—black ones with white stripes and a "76" in the center.) Though the four other teams occasionally wore these "pillbox caps" as alternate or road caps (and ditched them once the season was over), the Pirates embraced the retro caps as full-time headgear, sporting them well into the 1980s. During spring training of 1979, Willie "Pops" Stargell, the team's 39-year-old first baseman and captain, began awarding gold cloth stars to his teammates, who affixed them like medals to these throwback caps. The store-bought stars were given out in honor of timely hits, sparkling fielding plays, and clutch pitching performances, as well as more subtle things that didn't show up in the box scores, like advancing the runner in a crucial situation. "I saw the football helmets with buckeyes all over them for intercepted passes, downfield blocking, special-team tackling," Stargell explained. "Baseball just said 'Nice going!'"

Rather than handing them the stars in private, Stargell would call a postgame meeting to praise his colleagues and award them the stars in front of the entire team—which proved a highly effective motivational ploy, even for a bunch of well-paid baseball players. "We fought for those stars," Pirates outfielder Bill Robinson would later recall. "Those were precious. If he forgot to give you one, we'd be at his locker saying, 'Willie, I did this' or 'Willie, I did that.' To get those stars from your leader and captain, that was special." For three straight seasons, the Pirates had finished in second place in the NL East behind the Phillies. But in 1979, the "We Are Family" Pirates went all the way to the World Series, where they beat the Orioles in seven games. It's amazing what a man will do for a gold star.

Though less dramatically obvious than the shifts that occurred in the jerseys and pants of the era, the '70s brought about some important changes in protective gear, too. In the spring of 1971, baseball's Rules Committee finally put its collective foot down about the use of batting helmets. Since 1905, teams had been experimenting with a variety of attachable pads and hard plastic inserts. But the use of batting helmets as we know them didn't really begin until the early 1950s, when Pirates GM Branch Rickey ordered his players to wear them in every game.

For most teams, though, wearing batting helmets had been strictly optional—until the Rules Committee made them mandatory in 1971. Major leaguers who had previously gone helmetless were "grandfathered in" and allowed to use the plastic inserts under their regular caps, if they so preferred. Tigers first baseman Norm Cash and Red Sox catcher Bob Montgomery were among the few such holdouts; Montgomery, who was fated to spend most of his career as Carlton Fisk's backup, would at least go down in history as the last major leaguer to step up to the plate—on September 9, 1979—without an actual batting helmet.

Batting helmets with single protective flaps (worn on either the right or left side of the helmet, depending on which cheek would be facing the pitcher) were commonplace, but wouldn't be made mandatory until 1983, and many '70s players—Hank Aaron, Reggie Jackson, Ron Cey, Reggie Smith, Ted Simmons, and Pete Rose among them—preferred to remain unencumbered by the extra plastic. For switch-hitters like Smith, Simmons, and Rose, going flapless meant that they had to use only one helmet, regardless of whether a righty or lefty was pitching. Dick Allen actually wore his flapless helmet out in the field, a habit he acquired during his unpopular 1960s tenure with the Phillies, when Philadelphia fans threw pennies at his head. Other players, like Brooks Robinson (who'd by his own estimation "been hit three or four times in the head" during his professional career), appreciated the additional protection, though the Orioles' legendary third baseman felt that the protective flap and longish brim of the standard-issue batting helmets combined to interfere with his vision. Robinson solved this problem by cutting an inch and a half off the brim with a hacksaw and taking an additional half inch off the flap, thus clearing his sight line.

Though Robinson's home hardware project created a unique-looking helmet, it looked as bland as the Osmonds next to the uniquely fearsome face protectors worn during the 1978 and 1979 seasons by the Pirates' Dave Parker. On June 30, 1978, in a game against the Mets, Parker tried to score the winning run in the ninth on a short fly to left; when he found Mets catcher John Stearns waiting at home with ball in hand and what Parker later termed a "a satisfied look on his face," he hit him head-on, football-style. Stearns had kept his mask on, however, and the 6-foot-5, 230-pound Parker got the worst of the collision, completely shattering his right cheekbone upon impact.

After enduring extensive surgery to fix the right side of his face, Parker insisted upon returning to the lineup only 11 games later. In order to protect his cheek while he batted and ran the bases, the Pirates' training staff teamed up with their Steelers counterparts to rig up a dual-flap batting helmet with a reinforced, running-back-style face mask from a football helmet. Unlike regular batting helmets, the contraption made its wearer look extremely formidable—but not as much as the hockey goalie mask Parker wore in his first game back on July 16, when he appeared as a pinch hitter against the Padres. Combined with the pin-striped uniform he wore that day, the mask made him look like a cross between crazed killer Jason Voorhees of *Friday the 13th* and the Baseball Furies of *The Warriors*, though it actually predated both films. (Someone in Hollywood clearly missed the boat on a lucrative horror franchise concept.)

Tremendously intimidating as it was, Parker quickly ditched the sporty serial-killer look in favor of the football mask, which allowed for better range of vision; and after three weeks in the running-back mask, Parker felt sufficiently healed to switch to a helmet fitted with an even less obstructive two-bar, late-1960s style football face guard. Several players, including Gary Roenicke (who used one after getting beaned by Lerrin LaGrow in 1979) and Ellis Valentine, would follow Parker's face-guard-attachment example in future seasons, though no one ever looked quite as badass as Parker did while wearing them.

Nearly a year before Parker's fateful collision with Stearns, "the Cobra"—clearly not shy about uncoiling on opposing catchers—bowled over Dodgers backstop Steve Yeager in a similar play at the plate, knocking Yeager out of the lineup for a week. Yeager, whose sun-bleached locks, weathered good looks, and penchant for wearing aviator shades made him look like an L.A. record executive or an extra from *The Rockford Files*, was highly respected among his peers for his ability to call a game and his powerful throwing arm, which no less an authority than Lou Brock dubbed "the best in baseball." Still, Yeager would make his most lasting mark on the game not with his play, but with his protective gear.

On September 6, 1976, Yeager was standing in the on-deck circle during a game in San Diego, waiting for his turn at bat against Padres ace Randy Jones. Bill Russell, the batter ahead of him, got jammed by an inside pitch and broke his bat; Yeager, who was flirting with a girl in the crowd at that moment, didn't see the broken barrel of Russell's bat sailing toward him until it was too late. The jagged end of the barrel stabbed Yeager in the throat, piercing his esophagus—and miraculously missing a major artery by a fraction of an inch. It took over 90 minutes of surgery to remove nine splinters from Yeager's throat and close up his wound; but in less than three weeks the Dodger catcher was, amazingly enough, ready to return to the lineup.

Still, there was some concern that Yeager might not be able to catch again. Foul tips to the throat are one of the occupational hazards of the position, and another blow to Yeager's could reopen his wound, ending his career or even possibly killing him. To prevent this from happening, Dodgers trainer, Bill Buhler devised a plastic protective flap that attached to the bottom of Yeager's catcher's mask; it hung loosely enough to not interfere with Yeager's mobility, yet was solid enough to deflect an errant ball. Often humorously likened to the ceremonial mummy beards in the Tutankhamen exhibit that was touring American museums at the time, Buhler's "King Tut" guard quickly became a de rigueur accessory for major league catchers and home plate umpires, and remained in use for decades afterward, most likely saving a few other careers (and possibly lives) in the process.

CHAPTER 7
1974

Opening Day 1974 was a disorienting one for Yankees fans. For the first time since 1922, their team's first home game of the season was played somewhere other than Yankee Stadium. With New York City's extensive renovation of the crumbling "House That Ruth Built" already well under way—originally budgeted at $27.9 million, the project would eventually cost the city nearly six times that much—the Bronx Bombers were forced to relocate temporarily to the Flushing Meadows home of their erstwhile poor cousins, the New York Mets.

Ten years earlier, the Yankees had been the Kings of the City; the Mets, on the other hand, had been little more than a cellar-dwelling joke—a shabby stand-in for the great New York Giants and Brooklyn Dodgers teams that had skipped town in 1957. Now, the Mets were coming off their second World Series appearance in five seasons, while the Yankees were still recovering from years of benign neglect under the ownership of CBS, which had purchased the team in 1964.

As the team and its stadium had deteriorated, so too had the Yankees' Bronx neighborhood, and there had been some rumblings about the possibility of moving the team to the New Jersey Meadowlands. CBS first proposed renovating Yankee Stadium in 1971, but the Mets organization's refusal to let the Yankees play their "home" games at Shea Stadium squelched the project until a year later, when New York mayor John Lindsay helped broker the city's purchase of the stadium and its parcel of land from Rice University and the Knights of Columbus.

With New York City now owning Yankee Stadium as well as Shea, the Mets had little recourse but to put up their displaced Bronx cousins during the 1974 and 1975 seasons while renovations were completed. For Yankees fans, it had to hurt to see their beloved Bronx Bombers play half their games in a part of town where Tom Seaver and Tug McGraw were far more revered than any of the players on the Yankees' roster. Yogi Berra, one of the all-time Yankee greats, had managed the Mets to within one game of a World Series trophy in 1973; meanwhile, the Yankees, having been thwarted by Charlie Finley in their attempt to hire "retired" A's skipper Dick Williams, were making do with new manager Bill Virdon, who had been fired by the slumping Pirates the previous summer. New York City circa April '74 was definitely the Mets' world; the Yankees were, for now, just lucky to be living in it.

Even so, on April 6, 1974, some 20,744 Yankees fans—up more than 3,000 from the previous season's opener at Yankee Stadium—braved the damp, chilly, and overcast afternoon to see the Yanks' Mel Stottlemyre best Gaylord Perry and the Cleveland Indians in a 6–1 Opening Day contest. One well-known Yankees supporter, however, was rather conspicuous in his absence: George M. Steinbrenner, the Cleveland shipping magnate who had organized and led the group of investors that bought the Yankees from CBS a year earlier (for almost $2 million less than the network originally paid for majority ownership of the team back in 1964), did not attend the home opener. A day earlier, Steinbrenner had been indicted for making illegal contributions to Richard Nixon's re-election campaign; and Bowie Kuhn, always mindful of keeping up at least the outward appearance of propriety, thought it best that the Yankees' owner not show his face at the ballpark until his legal problems were sorted out.

In the nearly two years since five paid operatives of the Nixon Committee to Re-elect the President (a.k.a. CREEP) had been arrested while burglarizing the Democratic National Committee headquarters at the Watergate hotel complex in Washington, D.C., "Watergate" had become a household word, synonymous with the widespread corruption of the Nixon administration. With each passing day in 1973, it seemed as if some new abuse of presidential power was uncovered by the press, or via investigations by the FBI, the Senate, and the House Judiciary Committee. By the fall of that year, evidence had come to light that nearly two dozen American corporations had made illegal contributions to President Nixon's re-election fund, using various ruses and loopholes to funnel donations far exceeding the allowable maximum to his 1972 campaign—money that was then spent on a variety of illegal activities designed to discredit and defeat Nixon's possible Democratic opponents. And Steinbrenner's American Ship Building Company was one of the offending corporations on that list.

According to the 14-count indictment slapped on him by federal officials, Steinbrenner had knowingly circumvented campaign-contribution limits by giving a total of $100,000 in bonuses to several of his employees, then ordering them to contribute the money in their own names to the Nixon campaign. The Feds also alleged that once Steinbrenner had gotten wind of their initial investigation, he'd tried to "influence and intimidate employees into lying to a grand jury" in order to cover his own ass regarding the infractions.

In just a few years, Steinbrenner would become infamous as one of the most hands-on owners in the history of the game, But for now, Kuhn's stay-away edict meant that Steinbrenner would be unable to involve himself in the day-to-day doings of his ballclub during the 1974 season. Not that he didn't have more pressing matters on his plate; Steinbrenner contested the federal charges all through the spring and summer, before finally entering a plea bargain in which he copped to knowingly violating the campaign-finance laws and attempting to obstruct the investigation. Convicted and fined $15,000 for his transgressions (with an extra $20,000 penalty levied against American Ship Building), Steinbrenner thus managed to avoid serving jail time. But there was no sidestepping the wrath of Kuhn; in November, the commissioner would ban Steinbrenner from having any further interaction with the Yankees until 1976.

Steinbrenner wasn't the only one reeling from a brush with the law as the 1974 season began. Houston Astros center fielder Cesar Cedeno, whose exceptional combination of speed, range, and power led many to compare him to a young Willie Mays ("He can play all three outfield positions—at the same time," quipped Expos manager Gene Mauch), had spent Christmas and New Year's Eve of 1973 in a Puerto Rican jail cell, accused of the murder of his 19-year-old mistress.

Cedeno evidently loved the ladies—ladies of the night, especially; and after several sorry occasions wherein prostitutes robbed him of cash and jewelry, the married Cedeno took to bringing a .38-caliber Smith & Wesson along with him on his "dates." On December 11, 1973, he and his girlfriend Altagracia de la Cruz checked into a bungalow at the seedy Keki Motel in Santo Domingo, Puerto Rico, where they got into a drunken argument. A wrestling match over his handgun ensued, ending only when the pistol went off and lodged a fatal bullet in the girl's head. In a panic, Cedeno split the scene in his sports car, only to turn himself in to the Santo Domingo police eight hours later.

According to the outfielder's testimony to the police officers, de la Cruz had admired his gun and insisted upon holding it; he tried to pull it out of her hand, he said, but she pulled the trigger before he could do so. The police didn't buy it, and charged Cedeno with voluntary manslaughter. He spent 20 days in jail before a coroner's report corroborated his story, whereupon the charges were downgraded to involuntary manslaughter, and he was released to stand trial. Though the maximum penalty in Puerto Rico for involuntary manslaughter was three years, Cedeno—quite possibly because he was a famous baseball player—got off with a mere fine of 100 pesos, and was free to return to the U.S. in time for spring training.

Kuhn, somewhat surprisingly, took no additional disciplinary action against Cedeno. "We made our best efforts to determine if a cover-up had taken place, and whether there were any facts beyond those brought out in the trial," Kuhn would later recall in his autobiography, "but our efforts produced nothing further." Cedeno refused to talk to the press about the incident, though the massive drop in his batting average during the 1974 season (to .269 after two straight seasons of .320) would seem to indicate that he was at least somewhat disturbed by the whole affair.

While Kuhn's handling of the Steinbrenner and Cedeno cases received relatively little comment from the media, Kuhn's involvement with Hank Aaron's pursuit of Babe Ruth's home run record set off a serious debate among baseball writers, as well as loud howls of outrage from the Atlanta Braves organization.

Aaron came into the 1974 season with 713 homers, one behind Babe Ruth's all-time mark. But with his team scheduled to open the year with three games in Cincinnati, Braves board chairman Bill Bartholomay decided to keep Hammerin' Hank out of the lineup until the team returned to Atlanta for a 10-game home stand, thereby more or less guaranteeing that Aaron's record-tying and –breaking homers would be hit in front of a hometown crowd. "If the Braves wanted me to hit the home run there," Aaron would later reflect, "I didn't have any objections. I sort of liked the idea of being able to show my grandchildren the spots where 714 and 715 landed."

Sentimental considerations aside, Bartholomay desperately needed the box-office lift that the last days of Aaron's Ruth pursuit would surely provide; in 1973, the Braves had drawn an average of fewer than 10,000 customers per game, the second-worst attendance rate in the National League. But when Kuhn got wind of Bartholomay's plan to sit Aaron for the Cincy series, he stepped in and accused the Braves owner of undermining the "integrity" of the game by withholding his best player from competition. Kuhn insisted that because the aging Aaron had taken every third or fourth game off during the 1973 season, he must play at least two out of the three scheduled games against the Reds. Bartholomay protested—but, fearing disciplinary measures against the team, felt he had little choice but to comply with Kuhn's edict.

Thus, when the Braves took on the Reds in the Cincinnati home opener on April 4, Hank Aaron was in the lineup. Martin Luther King had been assassinated in Memphis six years earlier to the day, and Aaron requested that the Reds organization honor the anniversary of the great black leader's death with a moment of silence before the game—and in a heartwarming reminder that despite Ohio's midwestern location, Cincinnati still considered itself a southern city, the Reds ignored Aaron's request. Whatever anger or disappointment Aaron must have felt, he didn't let it affect his performance; with his first swing of the game, he lined a 3-1 pitch off Jack Billingham over the left-field wall for home run number 714. After trotting around the bases, Aaron was greeted at home plate by Kuhn and Vice President Gerald Ford, who stopped the game for a short ceremony commemorating the record-tying clout.

Aaron failed to homer in any of his other plate appearances during the game, but still had to play one more game in Cincinnati before heading home. This didn't sit well with Braves manager Eddie Mathews, who told the press that the Braves "had been fair enough" in playing Aaron on Opening Day, and that he'd decided to keep the team's star attraction on the bench for the rest of the series.

Kuhn promptly blew his top. Mathews was forced to relent and play Aaron in the third game, though even Reds manager Sparky Anderson thought Kuhn had overstepped his boundaries with his repeated insistence that Aaron take the field. "That had nothing to do with integrity," Anderson would later reflect. "[Aaron] belonged to Atlanta. He was the only thing they had going. My God, give them something."

Happily for the Braves and their fans, Aaron failed to go yard in his next game against the Reds, so the stage was set for him to launch number 715 in Atlanta. A record Fulton County Stadium crowd of 53,775 fans—including Sammy Davis Jr., who had already announced that he would pay a $25,000 bounty to any fan that caught the fateful home run ball—converged upon the ballpark on April 8 to see Hank swing the bat against the L.A. Dodgers, and they wouldn't go home disappointed.

After drawing a walk in the second inning off Dodger pitcher Al Downing, who was loudly booed by the fans for not giving Aaron something to hit, Hank came up again in the fourth and drove a 1-0 Downing pitch into the Braves' bullpen in left center.

The stadium erupted, and Britt Gaston and Cliff Courtney—two white, long-haired college students—ran onto the field to jubilantly pat their hero on the back as he made his way toward third base. (Despite the death threats he'd received over the past year, Aaron didn't seem particularly troubled by the sudden appearance of the two young men, perhaps because they didn't exactly look like vengeful rednecks.) Aaron's fellow Braves—including pitcher Tom House, who ran all the way in from the bullpen after catching the historic baseball—bounded out to greet him at the plate.

House excitedly handed the ball to Aaron, thus missing out on his chance to claim Sammy's $25,000 reward; but the young pitcher told writer George Plimpton that he had no regrets whatsoever. "What made it worthwhile was what I saw when I ran in with the ball," House explained. "In that great crowd around home plate I found him looking over his mother's shoulder, hugging her to him, and suddenly I saw what many people have never been able to see in him—deep emotion. I'd never seen that before. He has such cool. He never gets excited. He's so stable. And I looked, and he had tears hanging on his lids. I could hardly believe it."

Though House chose not to cash in on his historic catch, he did receive a color television from Magnavox—the electronics company that had signed Aaron to a million-dollar endorsement deal during the off-season—for his efforts. Aaron's other big advertising deal for 1974 was with the Williamson Candy Company, which used his likeness to help repopularize its Oh Henry! candy bar. (Contrary to popular belief, the chocolate-covered peanuts, caramel, and nougat confection wasn't named after Aaron, but had actually been around since the 1920s.)

As in Cincinnati, the game was delayed for a celebratory ceremony, only this time Bowie Kuhn was absent. Having made a prior commitment to speak to the Wahoo Club, the Cleveland Indians' booster organization, the commissioner opted out of traveling to Atlanta to see Aaron break Ruth's hallowed record. In his stead, Kuhn sent former Negro League and New York Giants great Monte Irvin to represent the Office of the Commissioner; when Irvin name-checked Kuhn during his vale-dictory speech, the Atlanta crowd jeered even louder than it had after Aaron's base on balls in the second.

Aaron, who throughout his career had been far less militant or out-spoken about racism than, say, Jackie Robinson or Dock Ellis, nonethe-less made it crystal clear that he took Kuhn's absence as evidence of the game's ingrained bigotry, as well as a personal affront—one compounded by the commissioner's failure to send even so much as a congratulatory telegram the year before, when Aaron had become just the second player in history to reach the 700-homer mark. "I was deeply offended that the commissioner of baseball would not see fit to watch me try to break a record that was supposed to be the most sacred in baseball," Aaron later wrote in his autobiography. "It was almost as if he didn't want to dignify the record or didn't want to be part of the surpassing of Babe Ruth."

Kuhn would claim until the day he died that there was no racial mo-tivation behind his absence from Atlanta, nor any other factors save his desire to honor a long-standing speaking engagement. "[Aaron] had tied the record when I was present," he explained. "I felt no obligation to fol-low him day to day until number 715 came along. Who could predict when that would be?" Which seemed like a reasonable explanation, ex-cept that everyone involved—including, surely, the esteemed members of the Wahoo Club—was well aware that, given Aaron's good health and still-powerful wrists, Kuhn wouldn't have to endure too many evenings in the Atlanta humidity before Aaron finally broke Ruth's record. And really, what self-professed lover of the game wouldn't jump at the chance to witness such a momentous occasion? "I believed he would have showed more interest in the record if a white player were involved," was Aaron's bitter take on the matter.

Despite the tumultuousness of the times, there was still plenty of fri-volity on tap in America circa 1974, as evidenced by the sudden rise of "streaking." A well-loved student tradition on American college campuses for at least a decade, the sport of running nude through public places exploded in popularity in the spring of '74. *Time* magazine had done a report on the fad the previous December, which was followed shortly thereafter by the release of "The Streak," a novelty song by Ray Stevens—the singer-songwriter previously responsible for such goofy hits as "Ahab the Arab" and "Gitarzan"—that, er, streaked to the top of the charts. When a streaker sprinted across the stage behind actor David Niven during the April 2 televised broadcast of the Academy Awards, it should have served notice that similar stunts would occur when the major league parks opened for business just a few days later. But really, who would want to go streaking in the early-April cold?

The answer, apparently, was White Sox fans. Despite temperatures topping out at a frigid 37 degrees, naked fans (some of them sporting red plastic souvenir Sox batting helmets) repeatedly interrupted the action at Comiskey Park during the White Sox–Angels Opening Day contest. One nude reveler lost his helmet while being chased by security, then returned to retrieve it by doing a moontastic headstand into the helmet, and somersaulted to his feet with it still perched snugly upon his head. Several female fans in the upper deck, appreciative of the eyeful he'd just given them, cheered and flashed their breasts at him. The day was also marked by numerous drunken fistfights in the stands; new White Sox third baseman Ron Santo, who had seen Wrigley Field's "Bleacher Bums" get out of hand a few times during his decade-long stint with the Cubs, was utterly aghast at the South Siders' behavior. "I never saw a crowd that bad," he said. "It took a lot of concentration away from us."

Out west in much warmer San Diego, a streaker also put in an appearance during the Padres' home opener against the Astros, briefly drawing attention away from a very public temper tantrum thrown by new Padres owner Ray Kroc. Kroc, the fast-food entrepreneur who had built the McDonald's hamburger chain into an international empire, had purchased the team in January for $12 million, narrowly averting the sale of the team to Washington, D.C.–area supermarket magnate Joseph Danzansky, who wanted to move the team to the nation's capital. (The Danzansky deal seemed so certain, the Topps Company actually printed about half its Padres baseball cards that year with "Washington National League" as the team name.)

Coming into their home opener, the Padres had been blown out three straight times by the Dodgers in Los Angeles. Now, with the Padres down 9–2 in the eighth, thanks in part to three San Diego errors (including one each by off-season pickups Glenn Beckert and Willie McCovey), Kroc had seen enough. Commandeering the stadium's public address microphone, he sternly excoriated the team in terms that would have shamed the Hamburglar himself.

"Ladies and gentlemen, I suffer with you," he told the near-record crowd of 39,083 San Diegans, whereupon a naked gentleman jumped out of the stands and ran helter-skelter across the field. "Get that streaker out of here!" bellowed Kroc as security gave chase. "Throw him in jail!" As the distracting nude dude was led away, Kroc resumed ranting about his team's poor play. "I've never seen such stupid baseball playing in my life," he fumed.

Most of the fans were bemused by Kroc's outburst, though some of them responded with scattered cheering and laughter. The Padres players, however, were mortified by their new owner's behavior. "This is a shocking thing," said McCovey afterward. "We may have played sloppy. But we're professionals and we know when the hell we play that way. We don't need to be reminded." Within days of Kroc's meltdown, the owner made a public apology to the fans and players at the behest of Bowie Kuhn, National League president Chub Feeney, and Players Association director Marvin Miller.

Despite the presence of McCovey (who led the team with 22 home runs) and future superstar Dave Winfield (20 HRs and 75 RBIs in his first full season), the Padres wound up at the bottom of the NL West for the sixth straight season. Pitcher Randy Jones lost a Padres-record 22 games, and the team's 60-102 mark tied a franchise record for futility, set the previous season. Still, 1974 saw the team draw over a million fans for the first time in history; Kroc's high-energy persona and willingness to try anything to get people out to the park—including "Chef's Night," wherein anyone wearing a chef's toque was admitted free—captured the imagination of the local public, however horribly their team may have played.

In addition to the suddenly ubiquitous streakers, the spring of '74 witnessed several other bizarre incidents on the diamond. On April 14, during a Tigers–Red Sox game at Fenway Park, a foul pop off the bat of Tigers slugger Willie Horton collided with an unsuspecting pigeon, who plummeted out of the sky and landed just a few feet from home plate. "It scared the hell outta me," testified Red Sox catcher Bob Montgomery. "I jumped a foot in the air—and Willie jumped even higher."

Mother nature also made a cameo appearance the same day during a Padres-Giants matchup in San Diego, when a swarm of bees invaded the stadium and hovered around home plate for several minutes, delaying the game. Though the impending invasion of America by killer bees was a hot topic of conversation during the mid-'70s—a made-for-TV movie called *Killer Bees* (starring Edward Albert, Kate Jackson, and Gloria Swanson, and produced by music biz mogul Robert Stigwood) had been broadcast on ABC just five weeks before Opening Day '74—this particular swarm thankfully turned out to be of the nonmurderous variety, and abated in time for the Padres to claim a 6–5 victory.

Other weird occurrences that spring were distinctly *un*natural. Yankees third baseman Graig Nettles, who had hit 22 home runs the season before, started off the season with a Roger Maris–worthy tear, setting a major league record with 11 homers in April. Maris wouldn't need to worry about his record, however, as Nettles's bat soon cooled off considerably; he'd hit only 11 more the rest of the way, enduring two different homer-free droughts of a month or longer.

Two of Nettles's homers would come in a September 7 doubleheader against Detroit, but neither was as memorable as the broken-bat single he stroked in the second game, whereupon six rubber mini Wham-O Super Balls—the kind you'd find in a drugstore gumball machine—came tumbling out of the fractured barrel. While the Yankee Stadium crowd dissolved in fits of laughter, Tigers catcher Bill Freehan scuttled frantically after the madly bouncing balls, trying to scoop them up as evidence. Nettles claimed to have no idea that the balls were in there, and that he'd received the bat as a gift from a nameless fan in Chicago, who told him it would bring good luck. Nettles's single was disallowed, but his homers were allowed to stand, and he was never disciplined for using the "super bat." However, the incident did raise a few questions about the legitimacy of his hot April.

Though corking a bat with Super Balls—which were made with a synthetic rubber that was vulcanized at 1,200 psi, and were advertised as being able to bounce three stories high—might seem like a rather far-fetched solution to increase one's power numbers, Royals slugger Amos Otis apparently swore by them as well. "I had enough cork and Super Balls in [my bats] to blow away anything," he admitted after retiring in the mid-'80s. "I had a very close friend who made the bats for me. He'd drill a hole down the barrel and stuff some Super Balls and cork in it. Then he put some sawdust back into the hole, sandpapered it down, and added a little pine tar over the top of it. The bat looked brand new."

On the morning of April 17, newly acquired part-time Cubs catcher George Mitterwald showed up at Wrigley Field in the throes of a brutal hangover. Expecting to have the Wednesday game off, since he'd played the day before, "Baron von Mitterwald" had gone out on the town Tuesday night and enjoyed all manner of liquid refreshment—only to be informed the next morning by manager Whitey Lockman that his services would be required after all. Despite his addled state, Mitterwald went on to have the game of his life, hitting three home runs (including a first-inning grand slam) and a double while driving in eight runs and setting a single-game franchise record with 14 total bases in the Cubs' 18–9 slaughter of the Pirates at Wrigley Field. Never one to be confused with Johnny Bench, Mitterwald would hit only four more homers in 1974.

That April 17 game at Wrigley also witnessed the final big-league appearance of Pirates pitcher Steve Blass. Blass, who just two seasons earlier had been the ace of the Bucs' staff, was now in the throes of what would come to be known as "Steve Blass disease"—a sudden and inexplicable inability to throw strikes. As far as anyone could tell, Blass had no physical problems, and there seemed to be only minor differences in his motion from his glory days. Blass went to a psychiatrist, tried "visualization therapy," and experimented with different throwing regimens, including pitching while kneeling on the mound. Nothing worked. In his final game for the Pirates, Blass gave up eight runs to the Cubs in five innings, walking seven and serving up two gopher balls. Blass was then sent to the minors, where he fared even worse; though he would return to the Pirates during the season's final pennant stretch, he never pitched again in the majors.

Blass's fiery rotation mate Dock Ellis could still get the ball over the plate—at least when he wanted to. On May 1, with the Pirates already in last place with a 6-12 record, five games behind first-place St. Louis in the NL East, Ellis decided that his listless teammates needed a wake-up call. Before that day's scheduled game against the Reds, Ellis regaled them with a short clubhouse speech: "We gonna get down. We gonna do the do. I'm going to hit these motherfuckers," he promised. Hell-bent on proving to the Big Red Machine that they were the ones who should be intimidated by the Pirates, and not the other way around, Ellis went to the mound in the first inning and immediately began throwing at the Reds hitters. Pete Rose led off the frame, and received an Ellis pitch in the ribs. Joe Morgan followed, and was gunned in the side; Reds third baseman Dan Driessen, turning to get out of the way of a pitch, took it in his back.

The bases were loaded, but Ellis wasn't finished proving his point. He fired four missiles at Tony Perez, but Perez—who must have had a fair idea of Ellis's game plan by now—nimbly managed to avoid each one, and made it safely to first with an RBI walk. Ellis then aimed two straight balls at the head of the next batter, Johnny Bench; he missed twice, whereupon Pirates manager Danny Murtaugh bolted from the dugout to yank Ellis before he could do any further damage, either to the Reds or the score of the game. Ellis had just set a major league record by opening a game with three straight hit batters—and, of course, was entirely unrepentant about it.

"Dock Ellis was without question the most intimidating pitcher of his era," Pirates outfielder Dave Parker later recalled. Parker, who would become one of the big stars of the "We Are Family"–era Pirates, was just a promising 22-year-old on the Pirate bench when Ellis took to the mound that day against the Reds. "Bob Gibson is up there, too, obviously, but with Dock it wasn't just his stuff. It was his flamboyance, his perceived militancy and his fearlessness. When he came and said he was gonna hit all those Reds, I thought, 'You ain't gonna do *nothing*, man.' Then he did it. I gained a lot of respect for him right there."

But if Ellis's one-man beanball war was meant to light a fire under his teammates, it failed. The Pirates, many of whom felt that the 56-year-old Murtaugh was too out of touch to effectively manage a modern baseball team, remained in the lower half of their division until nearly the end of July. It would take another scrap with the Reds—during the second game of a July 14 doubleheader at Three Rivers—to really shake the team from its stupor and turn its season around. This time, it was the Reds who were doing the beaning: Reds pitcher Jack Billingham nailed Pirates hurler Bruce Kison when he came to the plate in the fourth inning. Both benches cleared, and as the two teams milled about on the field, Reds manager Sparky Anderson accidentally stepped on Pirates first baseman Ed Kirkpatrick. When Kirkpatrick responded with a shove, things went completely awry, with Reds utility man Andy Kosco punching Kirkpatrick, and Reds pitcher Pedro Borbon biting and pulling the hair of Bucs reliever Daryl Patterson while pinning him to the ground.

The Pirates won that game, 2–1, then won their next seven straight, and 12 out of the next 17; in August, they finally kicked into high gear with a 20-8 run that put them in first place toward the end of the month. They battled it out the rest of the way with the Cardinals, who had occupied the top of the division for much of the season. The Cards were led by speedster Lou Brock, who hit .306, scored 105 runs, and spent the season laying all-out siege to Maury Wills's single-season stolen base record. On September 10, Brock stole two bases against the Phillies—the first one tied Wills's 12-year-old mark of 104, and the second one broke it.

Brock ended the season with a staggering 118 thefts, but his team ended it in second place, a frustrating game and a half behind the Pirates. With their final game of the season—against the Expos in Montreal—rained out, the Cards were forced to root for the Cubs in their season-ending contest against the Pirates. If the Cubs won, the Cards would have to beat the Expos the next day to force a tie for the division, then fly to Pittsburgh for a one-game playoff. The Cubs led by a run going into the ninth, but blew the lead with some shoddy fielding; Manny Sanguillen singled with the bases loaded in the 10th, and the Pirates were in the playoffs for the fourth time in the last five seasons. The Redbirds, listening to the Pirates-Cubs game on the radio, were crushed. As reliever Al Hrabosky lamented, "We lose the chance to go to the postseason sitting in the lobby of the Queen Elizabeth Hotel."

In addition to the Reds-Pirates altercations, there were several other instances of baseball-related mayhem in 1974, though not always between rival teams. On May 12, in vain pursuit of a line drive off the bat of the Reds' Merv Rettenmund, Bob Watson of the Houston Astros crashed into the left-field wall at Riverfront Stadium. While Rettenmund legged out an inside-the-park homer, a bleeding and barely conscious Watson lay crumpled on the warning track, temporarily blinded by fragments from his busted sunglasses. Rather than try to get up, Watson opted to stay put—since, as he later explained, "I knew glass might be in my right eye and that any tiny movement might scrape my eyeball and cause damage." Several Reds fans in the front row of the left-field seats demonstrated their sympathy for the stricken Astro by pouring beer on him and pelting him with ice and garbage.

"He could have lost an eye," exclaimed a shocked Cesar Cedeno, who was doused with suds when he ran to Watson's aid. "And those damn fans were laughing and throwing beer and stuff down on us and calling us all kinds of names." Riverfront's security guards waded into the crowd with nightsticks and beat the crap out of the offending parties—three of the troublemakers actually ended up at the same hospital where Watson was being treated. Watson declined to press charges, and was back in the Astros lineup in three days.

Ohioans and beer also formed a festive combination on June 4, when Ten-Cent Beer Night was held at Cleveland's Municipal Stadium. Somewhere between 60,000 and 65,000 10-ounce cups of Stroh's were consumed in the stands during the promotion, and—after the by-now de rigueur interruptions by streakers—drunken Indians fans invaded the field to duke it out with Texas Rangers players, ultimately causing the Indians (several of whom wound up being injured by their own supporters) to forfeit the game. *Newsweek* magazine called it "one of the ugliest incidents in the 105-year history of the game."

The day after the Cleveland fiasco, the typically fractious Oakland A's—who had sauntered into first place in the AL West on May 19, and would remain there the rest of the season—witnessed their worst clubhouse fight of the season, a no-holds-barred brawl between Reggie Jackson and Billy North. The fight surprised many of the A's, as Jackson and North were widely perceived to be close friends; the two outfielders lived near each other in Arizona, and had breakfasted together nearly every day during spring training. But the pair fell out early in the season; Jackson believed it was over a girl, while other A's pointed to an incident in May when Jackson had upbraided North for not running out a ground ball during a game. In any case, the two had stopped speaking to each other, and North repeatedly refused to shake Jackson's hand when he returned to the dugout after hitting a home run.

Whatever the cause, the two finally went at it before a game against the Tigers on June 5. North made a cutting remark, and Jackson—completely naked save for a pair of shower thongs—took the bait. "We fought all the time," Jackson would later say of his A's teammates. "When a fight would break out in the A's clubhouse, no one would even look up from their card games." But as one unnamed A's player would tell sportswriter Dick Young, "It wasn't the regular clubhouse fight. There was no backing off. They went at it hot and heavy—twice."

Vida Blue was the first A's player to try to break it up; but since Blue was pitching that night, and Jackson and North seemed out for blood, catcher Ray Fosse took it upon himself to step in. Unfortunately, Fosse's heroism cost him most of his season; someone pushed him into the lockers, shattering the sixth and seventh vertebrae in his neck. The injury would require neural surgery, and Fosse would spend the next 12 weeks on the disabled list for his peacemaking efforts. Jackson and North were finally separated by Sal Bando and Gene Tenace. Though a much larger man, Jackson got the worst of it, bruising his shoulder badly enough that he was unable to swing with his usual power stroke. He wouldn't homer for another month.

A's owner Charlie Finley and new A's manager Alvin Dark—a mild-mannered born-again Christian—were appalled by the North-Jackson punch-up. Finley, well known for being tight with his wallet, had become even stingier in recent years; rather than spring for expensive World Series rings for his 1973 squad, he gave them ones studded with cheesy-looking fake emeralds, and he had recently implemented the cost-cutting measure of forcing the team's coaches and off-duty pitchers to provide the color commentary on A's radio broadcasts. Even so, Finley booked an emergency flight to Milwaukee—the A's next destination on their road trip—out of his own pocket, just so that he could lecture his players in person. "You're World Champions," he scolded. "Stop acting like a bunch of kids!"

Finley needn't have worried; this was just business as usual for the Swingin' A's. "We were all young," Jackson would explain years later. "We were all cocky as hell because we could beat anyone. We were always mad at Charlie. Couldn't beat up Charlie. Had to beat up each other." A number of the Oakland players publicly expressed their disdain for Dark, whose habit of quoting scripture didn't exactly jibe with the salty repartee of the A's clubhouse, and whose handling of the pitching staff often seemed worryingly random. ("He couldn't manage a fucking meat market," was team captain Sal Bando's succinct appraisal of Dark's capabilities.) Unlike Dick Williams, Dark was more than willing to indulge Finley's every whim, and his handling of Finley's latest pet project—"designated runner" Herb Washington—caused a considerable amount of resentment on the team.

A four-time track All-American at Michigan State University, "Hurricane Herb" hadn't played baseball since high school; but he could run the 50-yard dash in five seconds flat, which made him the perfect subject for Finley's designated-runner experiment. "Finley and Dark feel that Washington will be directly responsible for winning 10 games this year," crowed an A's press release during spring training, and Dark's offensive game plan often seemed to revolve entirely around calculating the proper time to put Washington in the game as a pinch runner. Washington pinch-ran in 92 regular-season games for the A's in 1974—a major league record, as were his 92 appearances without ever lifting a bat or touching a baseball. (In 1975, he would also become the only player in history to have his main position listed as "Pinch Run" on a Topps baseball card.)

The other A's felt that since Washington couldn't hit, field, or throw, he was taking up valuable bench space that might be better used to accommodate an extra bat or arm. They also didn't appreciate being lifted from a game, occasionally as early as the fourth inning, just so that Dark could trot out Finley's latest toy. Washington did steal 29 bases for the A's in '74 (he was also caught 16 times) and score 29 runs; but despite being tutored in the art of baserunning by no less an expert than Maury Wills, his presence on the basepaths wasn't quite as game-changing as Finley had hoped.

In the end, it was the usual suspects who brought the A's their fourth straight AL West flag. Bando, though he hit only .243 for the year, hit 22 home runs and led the team with 103 RBIs. Joe Rudi (.293, 22 HRs, 93 RBIs), Reggie Jackson (.289, 29 HRs, 93 RBIs, 25 stolen bases), and Gene Tenace (26 HRs and 73 RBIs, even while hitting only .211) all contributed significantly to the offense; Bert Campaneris had one of his best seasons, hitting .290 and swiping 34 bags, while Billy North led the league with 54 steals. The green-and-gold pitching staff was tops in the junior circuit,

thanks to a Cy Young–winning year for Catfish Hunter (25-12, 2.49
ERA, 23 complete games) and solid seasons from starters Vida Blue (17-
15, 3.25, 174 Ks) and Kenny Holtzman (19-17, 3.07) and closer Rollie Fingers (9-5, 2.65, 18 saves). The intellectually inclined Holtzman, nicknamed
"the Thinker" by his teammates, also distinguished himself in 1974 by
telling *Esquire* magazine that he had recently finished reading all seven
volumes of Marcel Proust's *Remembrance of Things Past* in the original
French. It's highly unlikely that any other major leaguer, before or since,
has ever been able to say the same.

While the A's had no real difficulty winning the West, they had their
white heels nipped at for much of the summer by an unexpected nui-
sance: the Texas Rangers. In their first full season under manager Billy
Martin, the Rangers not only enjoyed their first winning season in the
team's short history, but also improved on their 1973 record by a stunning
27 games, nearly doubling their home attendance from the previous year
in the process. (The Rangers drew 1,193,902 fans in 1974; by contrast, the
A's—whose fans expected them to win, and who were increasingly put
off by Finley's neglect of the already less-than-hospitable Coliseum, drew
fewer than 850,000.)

Texas certainly benefited from the presence of Fergie Jenkins; shipped
from the Cubs to the Rangers in the off-season in exchange for Bill Madlock, Jenkins rebounded from a mediocre 1973 with a 25-12, 2.82-ERA,
225-strikeout season. Martin also got solid offensive performances out of
outfielder Jeff Burroughs (whose .301, 25-HR, 118-RBI output earned him
the AL MVP Award), scrappy third baseman Len Randle (.302, 26 stolen bases), and shortstop Toby Harrah (21 HRs, 74 RBIs)—not to mention eternal reclamation project Alex Johnson, who hit .291 while stealing
20 bases.

Martin was voted Manager of the Year for 1974 by the Associated
Press, but there were a few developments during the season that boded ill
for Martin's future with the Rangers. One was the sale of the team by
owner Bob Short—who had moved the Rangers to Texas and had brought
Martin there as well—to Brad Corbett, president of Robintech, a company that specialized in PVC pipe. Short had given Martin free rein to

make his own personnel decisions, including whether to promote play-ers from the minors; Corbett offered no guarantee that he would do the same. Worse was an incident in September, when Martin got into a drunken argument with Burt Hawkins, the Rangers' traveling secretary, during a team charter flight. Hawkins had innocently brought up the idea (suggested by his wife) of forming a Rangers wives' club; Martin, who believed that such a thing would only promote gossip and weaken team morale—as well as quite possibly expose his own rampant infidelities—immediately vetoed the idea. The conversation became heated, and Mar-tin slapped the elderly Hawkins; though he later apologized, the Rangers' front office put Martin "on probation" in the wake of the incident.

Though none of the other teams in the AL West ever stood much of a chance against the green-and-gold onslaught, the Twins' Rod Carew did win his third straight batting title, this time with a .364 average, and their 23-year-old starting pitcher Bert Blyleven (17-17, 2.66 ERA, 249 Ks) looked on the verge of becoming a star. In Kansas City, emerging Royals ace Steve Busby went 22-14 with a 3.39 ERA and 198 strikeouts, and—thanks to his June 19 no-no against the Milwaukee Brewers—became the first pitcher in major league history to throw no-hitters in each of his first two seasons. The Angels, who finished at the bottom of the division with a 68-94 record, at least could boast a 22-16, 2.82-ERA, 367-strikeout season from Nolan Ryan. The flame-throwing Texan's record was even more impressive considering that the Angels gave him little offensive support, *and* that he served up a jaw-dropping 202 walks over the course of the season. Along with Bob Feller in 1938, he became only the second pitcher to walk more than 200 batters in a season. Ryan also struck out 19 opposing batters in a game on three separate occasions, and 15 on three others—including his season-ending no-hitter against the Twins on Sep-tember 28.

Perhaps the most puzzling episode in the AL West, especially for White Sox fans, was Dick Allen's "retirement." After missing a signifi-cant chunk of the 1973 season with a broken leg, Allen was ready to carry the Sox on his shoulders again; but he clashed repeatedly throughout the '74 season with veteran third baseman Ron Santo, whom the Sox had picked up in the off-season from their North Side rivals. "Santo thought himself a Chicago institution because he had played all those years with the Cubs," Allen explained in his autobiography. "He thought he should be the team leader automatically."

The increasing tension between the two players adversely impacted the Sox, who never managed to push much above the .500 mark, despite fine seasons by 30-something workhorse hurlers Wilbur Wood (20-19, 3.60 ERA, 320⅓ IP) and Jim Kaat (21-13, 2.92, 277⅓ IP). "Chuck [Tanner] came up to me and told me the dissension was ruining the team," Allen later recalled. "He said, 'There's only room for one guy to run this team—and that's me.' That's when I knew things would never be the same. I decided it was time to go home."

On September 14, with two weeks of the season left to play, Allen stunned his teammates with the tearful announcement that he was retiring immediately from baseball and returning to his home in Wampum, Pennsylvania, where he could concentrate on raising his racehorses. Allen's final numbers for 1974 included a .301 batting average, an AL-leading 32 home runs, and 88 RBIs. Santo—whose .221, 5-HR, 41-RBI season with the Sox was the worst of his career—would retire following the end of the season.

Over in the AL East, Cleveland (77-85), Milwaukee (76-86), and Detroit (72-90) all finished in the bottom half of the division without much of a fight. For the Tigers, the most memorable event of the season came on September 24, when Al Kaline notched his 3,000th career hit with a line-drive double off of a longtime Tigers nemesis, Orioles pitcher Dave McNally. Kaline, the face of the Tigers for two decades, retired at the end of the season with 3,007 hits, 399 home runs, and a .297 career batting average.

The upper half of the division belonged, for much of the season, to the Boston Red Sox. Even without their star catcher, Carlton Fisk, who suffered a season-ending knee injury during a home plate collision with Indians outfielder Leron Lee in late June, the Sox were tough to beat. Though it couldn't boast a Reggie Jackson or Jeff Burroughs–type slugger, Boston's lineup did have 34-year-old first baseman Carl Yastrzemski, who led the team with a .301 average, 15 homers, and 79 RBIs.

But there was a youth movement afoot at Fenway as well. Starting right fielder Dwight Evans (.281, 10 HRs, 70 RBIs) was a mere 22 years of age; rookie shortstop Rick "the Rooster" Burleson (.284, 4 HRs, 44 RBIs) was 23, and first baseman/designated hitter Cecil Cooper (.275, 8 HRs, 43 RBIs) and center fielder Juan Beniquez (.267, 5 HRs, 33 RBIs, 19 SBs) were both 24. The Red Sox also got 12 homers and 61 RBIs from 26-year-old Bernie Carbo, a part-time outfielder and full-time flake. Carbo had shown up for spring training with a stuffed gorilla, with whom he often conversed at length; he also, to no one's surprise, became fast friends with Bill "Spaceman" Lee, the team's top lefty starter and preeminent free spirit. "[Carbo] and I would get high together, but only during rainouts," Lee would later recall. "We were the flower children of baseball."

Lee got his nickname not because he was spacey, but because he was definitely "out there" by baseball standards. A graduate of the University of Southern California, the iconoclastic Lee liked to party as much as or more than the average major leaguer; but he was also extremely well read (especially in areas relating to philosophy and spirituality), an ardent supporter of environmental and feminist causes, and one of the more deliciously quotable players of his era. "I can think of a lot worse things in baseball than marijuana or peyote, if used in moderation," he once said. "Things such as walks, designated hitters, and AstroTurf."

Despite being something of a baseball traditionalist himself, Lee had a deep appreciation and affection for the other oddball characters who inhabited the game, including the seemingly ageless Luis Tiant. "Tiant used marijuana," Lee later recalled. "But he never smoked it. He put it in a mixture with honey, liniment, and other herbs. He would have it rubbed into his arm a few hours before he pitched. That was the secret of his longevity." El Tiante was the ace of the Boston staff in 1974, going 22-13 with a 2.92 ERA and 176 strikeouts in 311⅓ innings, while the Spaceman went 17-15 with a 3.51 ERA, winning 17 games for the second straight year. But even this dynamic, cannabis-powered duo—who racked up 41 complete games between them—couldn't carry the team by themselves; and when the Boston bats suddenly went to sleep in late August, a first-place lead that had been as big as seven games as of August 23 evaporated completely.

Which left the AL East open once again for a late-season surge by the Baltimore Orioles, who claimed the crown on their second-to-last game of the season after going 23-6 in September. As with the previous year's AL East winners, the '74 Orioles got by with a mixture of aging vets from the team's '66–'71 glory days (Brooks Robinson, Boog Powell, Paul Blair, Mark Belanger) and promising youngsters like Don Baylor (who led the team with 29 steals) and Bobby Grich, who led the team with 19 homers and drove in 82 runs. The O's leader in batting average (.289) and RBIs (84) was 35-year-old designated hitter Tommy Davis, whose career was clearly prolonged by the creation of the DH. Davis appeared in 158 games during the 1974 season; the last time he'd played in more than 140 was 1967.

As with all the great Orioles squads of the Earl Weaver era, everything came down to a strong pitching staff. Jim Palmer, who spent much of the season dealing with elbow problems, turned in an uncharacteristically poor 7-12, 3.27-ERA record, but the other three regular O's starters more than picked up the slack. Thirty-seven-year-old Mike Cuellar turned in what would be the last great season of his career, going 22-10 with a 3.11 ERA. Thirty-one-year-old Dave McNally, pitching in what would be the last full season of *his* career, went 16-10 with a 3.58 ERA. The biggest surprise, by far, was the performance of first-year Oriole Ross Grimsley. The 24-year-old lefty, who'd clashed repeatedly with the Cincinnati Reds' management over his personal grooming habits, had been traded to the O's in the off-season in exchange for outfielder Merv Rettenmund. Rettenmund hit .216 in 80 games for the Reds during '74, while Grimsley went 18-13 with a 3.07 ERA for the Orioles while leading the team in strikeouts (158) and innings pitched (295⅔). It was embarrassingly obvious which team had gotten the better end of the deal.

Perhaps if the Reds had retained Grimsley (and refrained from hassling him about the length of his hair), they might have been able to pull off another late-season theft of the NL West crown from the L.A. Dodgers. Ultimately, however, the Dodgers were just too deep to let their nearly season-long lead slip away, even when the Reds—led by Johnny Bench (.280, 33 HRs, 129 RBIs, 108 runs), Tony Perez (28 HRs, 101 RBIs), Joe Morgan (.293, 22 HRs, 107 runs, 58 stolen bases), and Pete Rose (who scored 110 runs despite batting under .300 for the first time since 1964)—briefly cut it to a mere 1½ games in mid-September. The Dodgers led the NL in homers and runs, thanks in part to 5-foot-9 center fielder Jimmy Wynn (a.k.a. "the Toy Cannon"), who hit 32 jacks while plating 108 runs. Third baseman Ron Cey racked up 19 homers and 97 RBIs; left fielder Bill Buckner hit .314 and stole 31 bases, while second baseman Davey Lopes's 59 stolen bases would have led any league that didn't have Lou Brock in it. But the unquestionable star of the '74 Dodger lineup was Steve Garvey.

A powerfully built Michigan State grad with matinee-idol good looks, Garvey—previously a hopeless third baseman and outfielder—had been moved to first before the '74 season began; the switch worked marvelously, with Garvey making only eight errors in 156 games, and winning the first of four straight Gold Gloves. But he shone even more brightly at the plate, batting .312 and notching 200 hits, 21 homers, 111 RBIs, and 95 runs scored, numbers which earned him the NL MVP Award.

As impressive as Garvey's stats were, it was his clean-cut, all-American image—the complete antithesis of the unkempt and unruly players increasingly populating the game—that stood out in a year when the headlines were dominated by the Watergate scandal and kidnapped heiress-turned-bank-robbing revolutionary Patty Hearst. Garvey was as square as '70s L.A. was hip; in an era increasingly populated by antiheroes, Garvey made it crystal clear that he wanted to be a *hero*, a throwback to a more idyllic time, and a role model for the youth of America. "I think [the kids are] ready to get away from the antiheroes of the 1960s and move on to the heroes of the '70s," he told Roger Angell. His teammates rolled their eyes, but the press ate up Garvey's act like a high school wrestling team at the Ponderosa Steakhouse buffet, printing every selfless Garvey proclamation as reassuring evidence that not *all* of today's ballplayers were brooding enigmas like Dick Allen, militant black men like Dock Ellis, or rebellious flower children like Bill Lee.

Equally key to the Dodgers' success in '74—but at the opposite end of the personality spectrum from Garvey—was relief pitcher Mike Marshall, who came to the team in the off-season from Montreal in exchange for veteran outfielder Willie Davis. "Iron Mike" had, ironically, also attended Michigan State, where he'd earned bachelor's and master's degrees in physical education, and was currently working on a doctorate in the physiology of exercise. Garvey and his wife, Cyndy, had both been students in one of Marshall's MSU kinesiology classes.

Through his academic studies and research, Marshall had become obsessed with physical conditioning, convinced that the baseball convention of resting pitchers between game appearances was actually counterproductive. Marshall believed he would pitch better if he pitched every day—all he needed was a manager to run him out to the mound as often as possible. In 1971, after the hurler had dealt with several skippers who thought him a complete nutcase, Expos manager Gene Mauch finally gave him the chance to prove his point. Since then, Marshall had increased his workload each year, setting records in 1973 (and nearly winning the NL Cy Young) with his 92 appearances and 179 innings pitched in relief. In 1974, under Walter Alston's approving eye, Marshall shattered *those* records, appearing in 106 games and throwing 208⅓ innings—racking up 15 wins, 21 saves, and a 2.42 ERA in the process.

For Marshall, baseball was a "hobby," a means to make a living while putting his theories to the test, and not an arena for personal aggrandizement. "The only victory for me is in the quality of the competition, not in the final score," he told *Sports Illustrated*. Marshall thought it absurd that a player (Steve Garvey or anyone else) could be considered heroic for his achievements on the diamond, and he refused to sign autographs or even talk to fans. "As an athlete, I am no one to be idolized," he said. "I will not perpetuate that hoax. They say I don't like kids. I think that by refusing to sign autographs, I am giving the strongest demonstration that I really do like them. I am looking beyond mere expediency to what is truly valuable in life."

Though Marshall wasn't exactly a barrel of laughs, Alston and his players loved having him around. "I know what Mike says about winning, and how performance is all that really matters," said Dodger ace Andy Messersmith. "But there's one thing: his kind of performance leads to winning." It was true—in 1974, the Dodgers were 65-41 in games where Marshall pitched.

Messersmith went 20-6 in '74 with a 2.59 ERA, striking out 221 batters in 292⅓ innings, while fellow righty Don Sutton went 19-9 with a 3.23 ERA and 179 Ks in 276 innings. Though Sutton managed to avoid spending a single day on the DL during his 22-year career, he wasn't nicknamed "Black and Decker" in honor of his consistency and reliability; a master of doctoring baseballs, Sutton was alleged to carry a number of illicit "tools of the trade" on his person at any given time.

The Dodger staff suffered a severe blow in July, when lefty starter Tommy John—who was 13-3 with a 2.59 ERA at the time—blew out his elbow in a game against Montreal. It looked like John's career was over, until Dodger physician Frank Jobe suggested the then-radical step of replacing John's torn left ulnar collateral ligament with a ligament transplanted from his right wrist. In September, John underwent the first-ever ligament-replacement surgery, a procedure that would become better known in decades to come as "Tommy John surgery."

Losing a starter like John would have sunk the playoff hopes of most teams; then again, no other team had a reliever like Marshall, who picked up the slack by pitching three or four (and occasionally even five or six) innings, night after night. At one point, Marshall came on in relief for the Dodgers in a record 14 straight games. John, whose physicians gave him a 1-in-100 chance of ever pitching again, strengthened his surgically repaired wing through a variety of seemingly unorthodox rehab exercises, including squeezing golf club handles and lifting iron shot put balls—all of which came courtesy of Dr. Mike Marshall. John would return to the mound in 1976 and go on to pitch in the majors until 1989, regularly crediting Marshall as much as Jobe for his miraculous comeback.

Mike Marshall's workload in the 1974 NLCS was, by his own standards, rather modest—two innings of scoreless relief to solidify Andy

Messersmith's 5-2 win over the Pirates in Game 2, and a one-two-three ninth inning in relief of Don Sutton in Game 4, which saw the Dodgers clinch the NL pennant with a 12–1 slaughter. In the final contest, Steve Garvey put up four of the first five Dodger runs on a pair of two-run homers. Garvey, who in his youth had occasionally served as a spring training batboy for the Dodgers during the Koufax-Drysdale era, was now about to play for them in the World Series; the ever-reliable Sutton, who also shut out the Pirates 3–0 in Game 1, was returning to the Fall Classic for the first time since 1966, when the Orioles humiliated the Dodgers in four straight. The Dodgers wouldn't get the chance to pay back the Orioles, however—after Catfish Hunter gave up three home runs in Oakland's 6–3 Game 1 ALCS loss to Baltimore, the A's pitching staff limited the O's to a single run over the next three contests, returning Oakland to the World Series for the third year in a row.

The first-ever all-California Fall Classic was—predictably enough, given the two stellar pitching staffs involved—a tight, low-scoring affair, with four of the five games being decided by 3–2 scores. In typical A's fashion, there was far more drama off the field than on: Two days before the Series opened at Dodger Stadium, former A's second baseman Mike Andrews announced that he was filing a $2.5 million lawsuit against Charlie Finley over Finley's poor treatment of Andrews during the 1973 season. Finley probably had a good chuckle over Andrews's belated suit; but he wasn't laughing at all the next day, when Catfish Hunter and his lawyer announced that they were charging Finley with breach of contract, saying that the A's owner had reneged on a prior agreement to make a $50,000 life insurance payment in Hunter's name, and that Hunter would be declaring himself a free agent after the World Series if Finley didn't pony up the payment immediately.

Of course, the Athletics' pre-Series festivities also had to include a clubhouse scuffle, this time between Rollie Fingers and Blue Moon Odom. Throughout the playoff series against Baltimore, Fingers had been distracted by the news that his wife was having an affair with another guy, and that the lovebirds were in the process of moving all of the flamboyantly mustachioed reliever's belongings out of his house. Fingers returned to Oakland and briefly reconciled with his wife; but when they came down to L.A. for the Series, Hunter (who was staying in the hotel room next door) heard them fighting all night, and told his teammates about it the next day. "I can't believe this shit," Hunter remarked. "Only thing she's here for is the damn World Series money." Odom, having heard Hunter's tale, greeted Fingers's arrival in the locker room with a tart "Who's leavin' tickets for your wife's boyfriend tonight? You?"

Odom hurt his ankle in the ensuing scrap, putting his participation in the Series in question; Fingers was still able to pitch, despite cutting his head deeply on the corner of a locker. "You guys haven't been here half an hour and I already believe everything I've heard about you," marveled Jim Muhe, the visiting clubhouse attendant at Dodger Stadium, to several A's players immediately following the fight. "I've been around this clubhouse for 15 years and thought I'd seen everything, but in 10 minutes you showed me I hadn't."

Even with his fresh cranial divot, Fingers was able to get the win in Game 1, pitching 4⅓ innings in relief before being taken out of the game with two out in the ninth, a runner on first, and Oakland's lead cut to a single run thanks to a Jimmy Wynn homer. In payback for all of the wins Fingers had saved for him over the past few seasons, Catfish Hunter took the mound and struck out Dodger catcher Joe Ferguson to ice the victory for Fingers.

Back in 1964, Charlie Finley had balked at giving a young college pitcher named Don Sutton $16,000 to sign with the A's—despite the entreaties of A's scout Whitey Herzog, who told Sutton that Finley might be more willing to shell out extra bucks for a pitcher with a nifty nickname. "Heck, I don't care," said Sutton with a shrug. "Tell him my name is Pussyface Sutton if you want, just get me the money." Unmoved, even by such creative nomenclature, Finley let Sutton go to the Dodgers; now, a decade later, he was forced to sit at Dodger Stadium and watch while Sutton mowed down nine A's batters over eight scoreless innings in Game 2.

But Finley's public humiliation intensified in the ninth: After the A's tightened the score to 3–2 on a two-run single by Joe Rudi, Finley ordered Alvin Dark to send Herb Washington into the game as a pinch runner for Rudi. Mike Marshall, on the mound in relief of Sutton, glowered over his muttonchops at Washington, then spun and fired a bullet to Garvey for a successful pickoff. Marshall then struck out Angel Mangual to even the Series at one same apiece.

With the exception of a typically grandiose Finley stunt during Game 3—wherein the Coliseum PA announcer told the crowd that the Oakland owner was phoning President Gerald Ford and the recently resigned president Nixon with invitations to throw out the first pitch in the next two games—Washington's gaffe would be the last embarrassment the A's would suffer in this World Series. (Both Ford and Nixon declined Finley's offers. In Game 5, however, Finley was joined in his owner's box by closeted film icon Rock Hudson and orange juice spokeswoman/antigay crusader Anita Bryant. What the three of them talked about is anyone's guess.)

The outcomes of the remaining three games, though close, were rarely in doubt. Rollie Fingers helped Hunter nail down a 3–2 win in Game 3, then spelled Ken Holtzman (who helped himself by homering off Messersmith) on the way to an easy 5–2 win in Game 4; and while Odom got the win in the climactic Game 5, Fingers notched the save and took home the Series MVP Award. Only one organization had ever won more than two consecutive World Series championships—the New York Yankees, who had done it from 1936 through 1939, and then again from 1949 through 1953. The A's were now the first non-pin-striped team to win three Fall Classics in a row, the true mark of a dynasty and a legendary team.

But even as the players sprayed champagne and whooped it up in the Oakland clubhouse, that dynasty was beginning to crumble. Hunter, believing his lawyer had found the contract loophole that would finally let him break free from Finley, was fully prepared to follow through on his breach-of-contract claim against the A's owner. Hunter's case went to arbitration in November, and in December, Player Relations Committee arbitrator Peter Seitz declared Hunter a free agent.

The full magnitude of Seitz's landmark decision wouldn't be felt for another two years, but for now it set off the biggest bidding war in baseball history. Twenty-two out of 24 teams tried to woo Hunter; only the A's and their NL counterparts in San Francisco didn't offer the pitcher a contract. Though Ray Kroc and the San Diego Padres offered the most money, Hunter inked a five-year deal on New Year's Eve with the Yankees for a reported $3.75 million—the largest salary in baseball history, with Hunter earning at least triple the pay of any other current player. But whatever the pressures of that massive payday, Hunter just seemed relieved to be leaving Finley behind, telling *Sport* magazine that he "felt like I'd just got out of prison." Out of prison, and into the Bronx Zoo.

CHAPTER 8

1975

If any Americans expected that 1975 would bring some sort of respite from the tumult of 1974, they would be sorely disappointed. Instead, the new year delivered more Watergate-related sentences, widespread economic "stagflation," massive layoffs in Detroit's auto industry, the ignominious end of the Vietnam War, the bankruptcy of New York City, the disappearance and probable murder of former Teamsters union president Jimmy Hoffa, the arrest of Patty Hearst, and two separate attempts on the life of President Gerald Ford. Some of the popular films in theaters reflected the uneasy vibe of the times: the futuristic violence-as-sport fantasies of *Death Race 2000* and *Rollerball*; the man-versus-nature showdown of *Jaws;* and the Academy Award–winning, antiauthority drama *One Flew Over the Cuckoo's Nest*. Along with the immortal Pet Rock, the year's hottest novelty item was the Mood Ring, whose liquid crystal "jewel" supposedly changed colors depending on your mood; given the events of the year, a large percentage of these magical baubles were doubtless stuck on amber ("tense") or black ("anxious").

The most poetically apropos baseball moment of 1975 took place on June 10 at Shea Stadium, when the New York Yankees (still playing in temporary exile at the Mets' house in Flushing Meadows) presented a 21-gun salute in honor of Army Day, which celebrated the 200th anniversary of the formation of the U.S. armed forces. The cannons—though loaded with blanks—produced enough of a collective concussion to knock over the center-field fence, set another section of the fence on fire, blow out car windows in the stadium's parking lot, and fill Shea with acrid smoke. Anyone looking for a convenient metaphor for the Pentagon's botched handling of the Vietnam War, or the chaos and danger of New York City circa 1975, wouldn't have had to look much further.

But for any baseball fan who lived through that strange and uncertain year, the first image that 1975 brings to mind isn't the *New York Daily News'* headline "Ford to City: Drop Dead" or the overcrowded helicopters fleeing the fall of Saigon—it's the memory of Carlton Fisk bouncing up Fenway Park's first-base line, mustering every bit of animated body English to wave his 12th-inning fly ball into fair territory. It remains one of baseball's most enduring images, not to mention one of its all-time most memorable home runs, and it ended the best game of what some consider the greatest World Series ever played. But though Fisk's heroic Game 6 blast continues to overshadow just about everything else from the 1975 baseball season (including the awe-inspiring Cincinnati Reds, who actually *won* that World Series), there was no shortage of drama in the months that led up to it.

In 1975, African-American players made up 27 percent of the total major league population, the highest percentage in history. And now, there was finally a black manager as well: Frank Robinson, who in October '74 had been promoted by the Cleveland Indians from outfielder-DH to player-manager, a position that came complete with a $200,000 salary. The 38-year-old Robinson had long been respected for his on-field abilities and his keen baseball brain—as well as his ardent support of the civil rights movement—and he'd already managed for six years in the Puerto Rican winter leagues. All of which seemed to make F. Robby the ideal candidate to be the first black manager in the bigs, though his blunt manner, along with the fact that he made no bones about *wanting* to manage a major league team, had probably scared off some potential suitors.

During the first half of the 1974 season, Robinson (then playing for the Angels) had clashed repeatedly with Angels skipper Bobby Winkles, often bad-mouthing Winkles to the press. Angels ace Nolan Ryan would later claim that Robinson "tried to manage the Angels while he was playing with them, and he was a disruptive factor on the team," echoing sentiments expressed by Winkles in July '74, when—with the team mired in last place with a 30-44 record—the Angels fired the manager. Winkles's replacement, former A's skipper Dick Williams, tried to head off any potential conflict by appointing Robinson team captain and giving him the authority of a team coach. But in September, when the Angels sent the still-potent Robinson (who hit 20 homers for the team that season) to Cleveland in exchange for two scrubs (minor league catcher Ken Suarez and backup outfielder Rusty Torres) and cash, many viewed the oddly one-sided deal as a convenient dump, designed to rid the Halos of a troublesome player. In any case, the trade sent Robinson to a team that was unhappy with its own manager, Ken Aspromonte, and was quite willing to let Robinson take the reins.

"We needed somebody to wake up the city," explained Indians chief executive officer and executive vice president Ted Bonda, in the wake of Aspromonte's firing and Robinson's hiring. "We sold no tickets in advance here. We waited for people to come to the ballpark. We felt we had to generate excitement." On that score, the Indians definitely succeeded—on April 8, 1975, 56,715 Cleveland fans showed up at Municipal Stadium for Robinson's first home game as manager, over two and a half times as many as had shown up for the previous season's Opening Day. Robinson, who had penciled himself into the Indians lineup as the designated hitter, celebrated the occasion in his first trip to the plate by hitting his record eighth Opening Day home run; his old Orioles teammate Boog Powell (who had been traded to the Indians in the off-season) sealed the 5–3 win over the New York Yankees by going 3-for-3 with a double and a homer, while Gaylord Perry cruised to a complete-game victory.

Robinson's inaugural season as manager would not go so smoothly, however. Perry and Robinson clashed before the season even began over what the new manager viewed as the pitcher's lackadaisical spring training regimen; when Robinson insisted that there would be no special treatment for the veteran hurler, who had gone 21-13 the previous season with a 2.51 ERA and 216 Ks in 322⅓ innings, Perry suggested that all parties might be happier if he were traded. By mid-June, both Perry and his older brother Jim—who had combined for 39 of the team's 77 victories in 1974, as well as nearly a third of the staff's total innings pitched—were gone, leaving no doubt behind them as to who was running the team. Robinson also got into it with catcher John Ellis during a game on July 18 (the two men nearly came to blows when Ellis loudly objected to being pulled for a pinch hitter), and had several run-ins over the course of the season with AL umpires, one of which resulted in a three-day suspension.

Troubled by an injured shoulder, Robinson wasn't able to make much of a contribution to the team as a player, appearing in only 49 games and hitting .237 with only nine homers and 24 RBIs, all career lows. Despite the excitement of Opening Day, and for all of Bonda's talk of "waking up" the Cleveland populace, the Indians drew only 977,039 fans in 1975, down from 1,114,262 in 1974. But thanks to an 18-12 showing in September that brought the Indians' final record to 79-80, Robinson's job would be safe for another year.

Elsewhere in the AL East, the Milwaukee Brewers surprised everyone by competing for the division lead into early June before a complete summer collapse took hold. Despite their woes, the team still managed to draw more than 1.2 million fans to County Stadium, thanks to the presence of power-hitting first baseman George "Boomer" Scott (who lived up to his nickname by socking a career-high 36 homers and drove in 109 runs) and a 41-year-old DH named Henry Aaron, who had come over to the Brewers in an off-season trade with the Braves. Milwaukeeans were overjoyed to see Hank playing out his major league career in the same town where he'd begun it back in 1954; and though Aaron's skills were clearly diminished, every one of his at bats was potentially historic—he surpassed Babe Ruth's career RBI record of 2,209 on May 1, and his 12 homers for the season upped his own career round-trippers total to a record-setting 745.

Detroit, a city racked by continuing white flight, skyrocketing drug abuse, and crime, and where industry cutbacks in February had forced the layoff of over one-third of the local automobile workers, sorely needed an exciting Tigers team to take its collective mind off the area's worsening troubles. What it got instead was the second-worst Tigers squad in history, which lost 102 games while winning only 57. During one particularly dire stretch, from July 29 to August 15, the Ralph Houk–managed team lost 19 in a row; an 8-24 June and a 5-21 September didn't help matters much either.

Other than fan favorite Willie Horton (who hit .275, knocked 25 homers, and drove in 92 runs), the lone bright spot for Detroit was Ron LeFlore's first full season with the club. LeFlore, a tough kid from the crime-infested streets of Motown's east side, had originally come to the attention of Tigers manager Billy Martin in 1973 while playing baseball at the maximum-security penitentiary in Jackson, Michigan, where LeFlore was doing time for armed robbery. (Martin received the tip on LeFlore not from a professional scout, but rather—go figure—from a bartender who knew one of LeFlore's prison mates.) Upon his release in July of that year, LeFlore signed on with the Clinton Pilots, the Tigers' Midwest League farm team, and worked his way up to the parent club in August 1974.

The team's leading gate attraction in 1975, the speedy LeFlore stole 28 bases and patrolled Tiger Stadium's spacious center field with considerable skill, committing only nine errors in 134 games, and throwing out 12 runners. Though his 1975 batting average was an unimpressive .258, LeFlore would hit over .300 in three of his next four seasons while blossoming into one of the league's more formidable base stealers. In 1978, his autobiography, *Breakout: From Prison to the Big Leagues*, would be turned into a corny ABC made-for-TV movie called *One in a Million: The Ron LeFlore Story*, starring LeVar Burton of *Roots* fame.

By 1975, LeFlore's benefactor Billy Martin was long gone from the Tigers—and Martin's days with the Texas Rangers were now clearly numbered. He wrangled constantly with team owner Brad Corbett, team president Bobby Brown, and GM Danny O'Brien over trades, roster moves (Martin wanted to send "phenom" David Clyde down to the minors for more seasoning, while Brown worried that such a move would hurt the young pitcher's feelings), and Martin's handling of the starting lineup and pitching rotation. "In '75, Billy wanted to control the field, and other people wanted to control the field and Billy," recalled Rangers second baseman Lenny Randle, who also played third, shortstop, outfield, and catcher at various points during the year. "He would say [to Corbett], 'I don't tell you how to run your pipe business. You don't have to tell me how to run the baseball team. I'm trying to help you win.'"

Martin's drinking, never exactly under control in the first place, escalated along with the growing tension; the situation was worsened by Rangers catcher Jim Sundberg and third-base coach Frank Lucchesi, who regularly reported Martin's indiscretions and outbursts to the team's top brass. On July 21—with the Rangers already 15½ games behind another tough Oakland A's team—Martin was fired and replaced by Lucchesi.

Martin wouldn't be out of work for long, however; on August 1, the Yankees fired Bill Virdon, and the next day they announced that Martin would be their new manager. The fate of Virdon, the *Sporting News* Manager of the Year for 1974, had been sealed in July, when the skidding Yankees went from being a game out of first in the AL East to 10 games behind the Red Sox in just 30 days. Martin, who had played in five World Series with the Yankees back in the 1950s—and who had abruptly been traded from New York to Kansas City in 1957, allegedly as retribution for participating in a drunken brawl at Manhattan's Copacabana nightclub—had always dreamed of returning to the Bronx to manage, and Yankees owner George Steinbrenner was impressed by Martin's fire.

But both men were also quite wary of each other, and Steinbrenner insisted that a number of unusual clauses be inserted into Martin's contract, including a stipulation that Martin could not criticize the Yankees' front office. Steinbrenner also exploited Martin's well-known longing to wear pinstripes again, telling him, "If you don't take the offer now, you will never get it again"—a statement Martin interpreted as a threat. "I had bad vibes about Steinbrenner, his clauses, the way he threatened me," Martin later wrote in his autobiography. "My every instinct argued against signing this contract."

In the end, Martin's desire to be a Yankee won out, and Steinbrenner introduced his new manager in typically dramatic fashion, sending him out onto the field as a surprise guest during Old-Timers' Day festivities at Shea Stadium. With the Bombers already more or less out of contention by the time he came aboard, Martin was free to spend the last two months of the season getting to know the capabilities of his new team. Despite outstanding years from catcher Thurman Munson (who led the team with a .318 batting average and 102 RBIs), right fielder Bobby Bonds (who had come over from the Giants in a straight-up swap for Yankees outfielder Bobby Murcer, and responded by hitting .270 with 32 homers, 85 RBIs, and 30 stolen bases), and Catfish Hunter (who, in what would turn out to be the last great season of his career, earned his gigantic new salary by going 23-14 with a 2.58 ERA in 328 innings), the Yankees just didn't play like a championship-caliber team. But by next spring, when the team returned to its newly renovated home in the Bronx, Martin would change all that.

Considering how closely Carlton Fisk is associated with the 1975 Red Sox season, it's easy to forget that the All-Star catcher didn't even get to swing a bat for Boston until the last week of June. Having sat out the second half of the '74 season with a knee injury, he recovered from that ailment just in time to break his arm during a spring training game in March of '75. He finally returned to the lineup on June 23, and his timing was perfect; the Red Sox, having fought their way into first place in late May following an uninspired 7-9 April start, were in the process of slipping back into second behind the Yankees. Three days later, the Yankees came to Fenway for a four-game series; Fisk went 4-for-11 with a double, a homer, and three RBIs, as the Red Sox took three games out of four from the Yanks and moved into first for the remainder of the season. The Orioles, led by Jim Palmer (who bounced back from a terrible '74 with a

Cy Young–winning 23-11, 2.09-ERA effort), first baseman Lee May (20 HRs, 99 RBIs), and outfielders Ken Singleton (who batted a team-leading .300) and Don Baylor (who hit .282 with 25 HRs and 32 stolen bases), made a late charge, but never managed to get within less than four games of the smokin' Sox.

While Fisk would finish the season with a .331 batting average, 10 homers, and 52 RBIs in 79 games—very tasty numbers for only a half season of play—the key to Boston's success in '75 was the dynamic rookie duo of Fred Lynn and Jim Rice. Boston fans who had witnessed Lynn's steady hitting and fearless catches in center field were well aware that he was something special, but the rest of the country finally took notice on June 18, when Lynn went 5-for-6 with three home runs, a triple, and 10 RBIs in a 15–1 slaughter of the Tigers at Tiger Stadium, tying an AL record with 16 total bases. Rice, who was so strong that he was rumored to have snapped a bat in half on a checked swing, also attracted attention with some memorably mammoth home runs, including a July 18 bomb that sailed over Fenway Park's distant center-field wall to the right of the flag-pole. Only five other players had ever cleared that part of the wall; Sox owner Tom Yawkey called it the longest clout he'd ever seen at Fenway.

Lynn finished the season with a .331 average (only Rod Carew's .359 was higher in the AL), 47 doubles, 21 homers, 103 runs scored, 105 RBIs, and a Gold Glove award; a shoo-in for Rookie of the Year, he also became the first rookie in history to take home the Most Valuable Player award. Rice, whose season ended prematurely on September 21, when a pitch from Detroit's Vern Ruhle broke his hand, finished the season with a .309 average, 22 HRs, 92 runs, and 102 RBIs; he also played 90 games in left field without making a single error. He placed second in Rookie of the Year balloting, and third in the MVP vote.

Over in Oakland, the three-time World Champion A's seemed to be playing better ball than ever, even while their animosity toward Charlie Finley was reaching new heights. Team captain Sal Bando, who in previous years seemed to give Finley the benefit of the doubt, finally lost his cool following a nasty arbitration meeting, when the A's owner told the press that Bando was "the eleventh best third baseman in the league."

"To me, this is like a car dealer buying time on TV and saying he has the worst cars in town," was Bando's response to Finley's insult. "No wonder people don't come to see us play."

In addition to Finley's tightfisted ways—he'd refused to give any of his star players meaningful raises after they'd won their third straight World Series, and he once again "rewarded" their championship efforts with gem-free Series rings—the A's were fed up with Finley's continuing obsession with team speed. On Opening Day, the A's had not one but *three* pinch runners on their roster: Herb Washington was now joined by Don Hopkins and Matt "the Scat" Alexander, undistinguished players whose speed was their primary attribute. Eventually, even Finley realized that someone would have to go; and since Hopkins and Alexander could at least swing a bat and slap some leather, Washington (who could do neither) was deemed expendable and put on waivers in early May. Thus ended the brief and strange career of "Hurricane Herb," who wasn't exactly given a sentimental send-off by the team captain. "I'd feel sorry for him if he was a player," Bando told the *Sporting News* in the wake of Washington's release. "He got a bonus and a salary and a full World Series share, didn't he?"

But for all the bitterness that permeated the Oakland clubhouse, nothing could stop the A's from simply steamrolling the AL West. With the exception of eight April days spent in second place, the team essentially led the division wire-to-wire, finishing in first place with a 98-64 record. The A's lineup was bolstered by the addition of future Hall of Famer Billy Williams, whom the A's had picked up the previous fall in a trade with the Chicago Cubs—and who clubbed 23 homers and drove in 81 runs in his first season on the West Coast, despite hitting an uncharacteristically low .244—and 20-year-old left fielder Claudell Washington, who hit .308 and stole 40 bases in his first full season with the team. Joe Rudi, who'd moved to first base to accommodate Washington, hit .278 with 21 HRs and 75 RBIs; Gene Tenace, now back behind the plate in order to accommodate Rudi's move to first, hit 29 homers, drove in 87 runs, and walked a team-leading 106 times. And Reggie Jackson, despite hitting only .253, led the team (and tied for the league lead) with 36 homers while knocking in 104 runs.

Jackson briefly ran afoul of the commissioner's office in July, after the *Oakland Tribune* published a quote from an uncorrected galley proof of a forthcoming book called *Reggie: A Season with a Superstar*, cowritten by Jackson and Bill Libby. The inflammatory passage revolved around Jackson's admission that he regularly took "boosters, greenies, bennies, whatever," and would "continue to take them unless I get so much shit over this I am forced to stop." Bowie Kuhn let Jackson know that he was not pleased with the revelation, but ultimately took no action against the A's outfielder.

Despite losing Catfish Hunter to free agency, the A's pitching staff remained as tough as ever, giving up the lowest opponent batting average (.236) in the league. Vida Blue went 22-11 with a 3.01 ERA and 189 strikeouts, while Ken Holtzman turned in another solid season, going 18-14 with a 3.14 ERA. Between them, Blue and Holtzman accounted for over a third of the total innings pitched by the A's; the relief corps, headed by Rollie Fingers (10-6, 2.98 ERA, 24 saves), Jim Todd (8-3, 2.29, 12 saves), and Paul Lindblad (9-1, 2.72, seven saves) picked up more of the slack than usual. Nowhere was this all-hands-on-deck participation more evident than in the last game of the season, in which Blue, Glenn Abbott, Lindblad, and Fingers combined to no-hit the California Angels—the first time in history that four pitchers had ever shared a no-no.

Not wanting to burn Blue out before the AL playoffs, A's skipper Alvin Dark had decided that his ace pitcher would go only five innings in the meaningless season finale; when Blue's five innings were up, Dark lifted him despite the fact that he still had a no-hitter going. Abbott and Lindblad each pitched 1-2-3 innings after him, and Fingers—who willfully flouted baseball tradition not just by mentioning aloud that the team had a no-hitter going, but also by betting Holtzman five bucks that he would be the one to successfully close it out—set the last six Angels down in order to clinch the victory and a place in the Hall of Fame. Blue, who had hit the showers after leaving the game, was oblivious of the fact that history was being made until his triumphant teammates came bounding into the clubhouse. "It's great," Blue told reporters, "but I don't even know who pitched it after I left."

Nolan Ryan made no-hit history of his own on June 1, when he threw the fourth no-hitter of his career in a 1–0 victory over the Orioles, tying Sandy Koufax for the all-time career no-no mark. Five days later, Ryan came close to passing Koufax, throwing five hitless innings against the Brewers before Hank Aaron broke things up with a sixth-inning single. (Ryan allowed only one other hit in the contest, which the Angels won 6–0.) Plagued throughout the season by arm problems, Ryan missed several starts in August and sat out September; he ended the season with a 14-12 record, a 3.45 ERA, and 186 strikeouts, missing out on leading the AL in Ks for the fourth consecutive year. Taking his place on the top of the strikeout heap was fellow Angel fireballer Frank Tanana, a 21-year-old lefty who whiffed 269 batters (including 17 Rangers on June 21) while going 16-9 with a 2.62 ERA. Ed Figueroa (16-13, 2.91 ERA) also had a surprisingly solid season for the Halos, and it looked like the Angels were on the verge of developing a formidable rotation. But Figueroa would be shipped off to the Yankees over the winter, and the Angels' pitching woes over the next three seasons would inspire the popular maxim, "Tanana, Ryan, and two days of cryin'."

California center fielder Mickey Rivers, who would go to the Yankees in the same trade as Figueroa (the Angels would receive Bobby Bonds in return), embodied the team's "nowhere fast" attack under Dick Williams. Rivers led the league with 70 stolen bases and 13 triples, but hit only a single home run in 1975; the Angels led all AL teams with 220 thefts, but their 55 collective homers were by far the fewest in the league, and the Halos' lack of punch contributed to their last-place finish with a 72-89 record.

Kansas City also placed an increased emphasis on team speed, but actually seemed on the verge of turning it into a winning strategy. When manager Jack McKeon was fired in July, the Royals replaced him with Whitey Herzog, who understood how to exploit his new team's AstroTurf-carpeted home to its advantage, and immediately began transitioning fast young players like outfielder Al Cowens and second baseman Frank White into the Royals' lineup. Of course, it didn't hurt that he already had George Brett at third—the 22-year-old posted his first great season in '75, hitting .308 with 35 doubles, 13 triples, 11 homers, and 89 RBIs—power-hitting John Mayberry at first (.291, 34 HRs, 106 RBIs, 119 walks), and a young pitching staff that included Al Fitzmorris (16-12, 3.57 ERA), Steve Busby (18-12, 3.08), and Dennis Leonard (15-7, 3.77). Under Herzog, the Royals finished second in the AL West, seven games behind Oakland, with a 91-71 record, and it was obvious that they would be a team to be reckoned with in 1976.

While the Royals appeared poised to challenge the A's in the AL West, the Philadelphia Phillies seemed just a few players away from wresting the NL East from the grip of the Pittsburgh Pirates. Though they wound up in second place, 6½ games behind the Pirates, their 86-76 record under manager Danny Ozark was their best since 1966. Third baseman Mike Schmidt—who led the league with 38 home runs and drove in 95 runs while leading the Phils with 29 stolen bases—and left fielder Greg "the Bull" Luzinski (who hit .300 while smacking 34 homers and knocking in a league-leading 120 runs) had developed into a feared power-hitting tandem. Over at the keystone, second baseman Dave Cash (.305, 111 runs, 40 doubles, and a league-leading 213 hits) and shortstop Larry Bowa (.305, 24 stolen bases) provided punch in the lineup and speed on the base paths. New center fielder Garry Maddox, picked up from the Giants in exchange for first baseman Willie Montanez, hit .291 and stole 24 bases in 99 games with the Phillies, and his astonishing speed and fielding range proved invaluable on the artificial turf of "the Vet."

Dick Allen, who had been traded by the Braves (to whom he'd refused to report) to the Phillies in May, put up relatively poor numbers (12 HRs and 62 RBIs) but proved to be a positive influence on the team, taking Schmidt and Luzinski and several other players under his wing. Allen, who'd left the Phillies under a dark cloud in 1969, was pleasantly surprised by how at home he felt in the Veterans Stadium clubhouse.

"The brothers on the team—Dave Cash, Ollie Brown, and Garry Maddox—represented a new generation of black ballplayer," he later recalled. "They were talented and proud of it, and they didn't take a back seat to anybody. . . . I remember thinking that maybe with this bunch I could get myself a World Series ring after all."

Not this year, though. The Pirates had the NL East in the bag from early June onward—though they did stumble a bit in August, at one point letting the Phillies get to within half a game of the division lead. Willie Stargell (who finished the year with a .295 average, 22 homers, and 90 RBIs) spent most of that month on the bench with a rib injury, and controversy erupted when Dock Ellis (who else?) delivered a clubhouse "pep talk" that accused manager Danny Murtaugh and general manager Joe Brown of "messing with the minds" of several players and implored his teammates to band together and win *despite* Murtaugh and Brown, statements that so incensed the Pirates manager that he offered to fight Ellis right there in the locker room. Though the team fined Ellis $2,500 and suspended him for two weeks over the incident, his teammates were unstinting in their support for the voluble pitcher. "I think Dock's the key to this ballclub," Al Oliver told Pittsburgh's *Score!* magazine. "He keeps everybody loose, so if there's any tension at all, it's left in the clubhouse. Dock brings it right out of us."

One could easily have argued that the outfield of Oliver, Richie Zisk, and Dave Parker was also a key to the Pirates' success in 1975. Oliver posted one of the lowest batting averages of his career—hitting "only" .280—but still managed 39 doubles, 18 homers, and 84 RBIs, while Zisk hit .290 and contributed 20 HRs and 75 RBIs of his own. But it was 24-year-old Dave Parker, playing in his first full season for the Bucs, who really impressed. Nicknamed "the Cobra" for his coiled batting stance (and the deadly efficiency with which it struck), the 6-foot-5 Parker hit .308 with 35 doubles, 10 triples, 25 homers, and 101 RBIs, and led the league with a .541 slugging percentage. For the rest of the decade, he would be one of the most feared hitters in the NL; once his powerful throwing arm became more accurate, he would also become one of its most respected outfielders.

Far less intimidating at the plate than Parker, second baseman Rennie Stennett was actually the one Pirate who carved himself a place in the record books in 1975, thanks to a seven-hit batting performance during a 22–0 takedown of the Cubs on September 16. Aside from Stennett becoming the first player to go 7-for-7 in a game since Wilbert Robinson in 1892, the contest also boasted the biggest score ever run up in a modern-era major league shutout game. Stennett, who had recently injured his ankle, didn't think he was even supposed to be playing that day, as evidenced by his meager pregame breakfast of two York Peppermint Patties—a repast that Stennett had basically concocted to outwit Stargell, who had a habit of scamming stray sausages and pieces of toast from his teammates' breakfast plates. "So this day I said he's not getting nothing from my plate," Stennett recalled. "All I had was two Peppermint Patties and he came down and looked at me—'What's happenin', man? You eatin' this morning?' I said, 'No, man, not today.'"

Elsewhere in the division, the Mets seemed to be gradually slipping into decline, utterly lacking the fire of their 1973 NL champion squad. Like his American League counterpart Jim Palmer, Tom Seaver at least managed to bounce back from a disappointing 1974 with a Cy Young–winning season, finishing with a league-leading 22 wins and 243 strike-outs, and posting a 2.38 ERA. Between the revitalized Seaver and new Mets gate attraction Dave "Kong" Kingman, who crushed 36 homers and drove in 88 runs while also striking out 153 times, New York's NL franchise managed to draw more than 1.7 million fans to Shea, but the brand of baseball they played was generally as mediocre as their 82-80 season record. Other than Seaver's sheer excellence, the most memorable aspect of the Mets' '75 season (albeit regrettably so) was the infamous Cleon Jones press conference.

During the spring, the popular Mets outfielder had been arrested in St. Petersburg, Florida, near the Mets' spring training complex, for sleeping nude in a parked van. Jones was accompanied by an equally unclothed young woman at the time—a 21-year-old "unemployed waitress" named Sharon Ann Sabol—who also happened to be in possession of marijuana and drug paraphernalia. When the cops asked Jones why he and the young lady were sleeping naked in a vehicle on one of St. Petersburg's main drags, the outfielder simply told them, "We ran out of gas."

The "indecent-exposure" charges against Jones were eventually dropped, since no complaints had actually been made about the couple, and the incident should have quickly faded from memory. But Mets chairman M. Donald Grant, self-righteously insisting that "we have to restore the Mets' image," fined Jones $2,000 for "failing to abide by training rules," and insisted that Jones appear at a press conference at Shea Stadium to publicly confess to his sins. A thoroughly mortified Jones, wife Angela by his side, dutifully read a written apology, telling assembled reporters, "I was at the wrong place at the wrong hour doing the wrong thing." He was then forced to stand there and listen while Grant ran down a detailed list of Jones's indiscretions.

It was a bizarre spectacle indeed, made that much weirder by the fact that New York City circa 1975 was hardly a puritan enclave where people would be shocked by the idea of a black man sleeping with a white woman who wasn't his wife. Marvin Miller of the Major League Baseball Players Association accused the Mets of "a tasteless display of economic power" and of intentionally seeking to humiliate Jones. Jones, who probably just wanted to put the whole sorry incident behind him, chose not to appeal the fine, but his time as a Met was running out; after arguing repeatedly with manager Yogi Berra over his demotion to a late-inning defensive replacement, Jones was released by the Mets in late July. Berra was fired soon after, replaced for the remainder of the season by Mets coach Roy McMillan.

In the NL West, the long-standing rivalry between the Los Angeles Dodgers and San Francisco Giants—imported from New York back in 1958—had been almost entirely eclipsed by the competition between the Dodgers and the Cincinnati Reds, which had intensified considerably following the introduction of divisional play in 1969. During the 1970s, there would be only two seasons (1971 and 1979) when the Dodgers and Reds didn't finish in the top two slots of the division.

With the exception of their division-winning 1971 season, the Giants finished in third place or worse every year from 1970 through 1979; even when they managed to finish 10 to 15 games over .500—as in 1970, 1973, and 1978—it simply wasn't enough to be a good team in a division dominated by two great ones. 1975 wasn't one of the franchise's better years; the Giants finished in third place with an 80-81 record, 27½ games behind the Reds, and drew a league-worst 522,919 fans to their home at frigid Candlestick Park. They did, however, have a rookie hurler named John Montefusco.

Nicknamed "the Count," Montefusco had a Dizzy Dean–like flair for self-promotion, predicting to Giants broadcaster Al Michaels that he would win 30 games for San Francisco in 1975. Montefusco wound up winning only half that number in his first full season, but his 215 strikeouts—the most by an NL rookie since Grover Cleveland Alexander's 227 in 1911—and 2.88 ERA made it clear that this New Jersey–born kid had the goods to back up at least some of the bold statements that came tumbling out of his mouth. He won the NL Rookie of the Year award for '75, as well as the hearts of Giants fans—a Montefusco home start typically brought an additional 10,000 customers through Candlestick's turnstiles—and players, many of whom had their hair permed in emulation of Montefusco's chosen hairstyle.

But like the soft-tossing Randy Jones's 20-win, 2.24-ERA Cy Young runner-up season for the noncontending Padres, or the complete collapse of the Astros (who never fully recovered from the January death of star pitcher Don Wilson, who was found dead in his car of accidental carbon monoxide poisoning)—Montefusco's fine rookie year was ultimately just a mildly diverting sideshow from the title-card bout between the Reds and the Dodgers. After losing three straight games against the Reds to open the season, the Dodgers appeared to pick up where they'd left off in '74, jumping out to a 5½-game lead over Cincy by mid-May. Mired in third place on May 17 with an 18-19 record, the Big Red Machine suddenly kicked into overdrive and laid waste to virtually everything in its path, winning 90 of its remaining 125 games on the way an NL-record 108 wins. The Reds laid claim to the division pennant on September 7—the earliest clinching date in NL history.

As was so often the case throughout the 1970s, the Reds' '75 starting lineup was filled with an embarrassment of riches. Second baseman Joe Morgan, whose method of timing pitches while standing at the plate—by flapping his left elbow like a man doing one-half of the "Funky Chicken"— would have seemed ridiculous if it hadn't consistently produced exemplary results, won his first NL MVP Award by batting .327, scoring 107 runs, driving in 94 more, stealing 67 bases, and leading the league in walks (132) and on-base percentage (.466). But even with those kind of numbers, Morgan's intrinsic importance to the team was often overshadowed by the presence of Bench (who hit .283 with 28 HRs and 110 RBIs, despite playing most of the season with an injured shoulder), Tony Perez (.282, 20 HRs, 109 RBIs), and Pete Rose (who hit .317, scored 112 runs, and notched his 2,500th career hit). George Foster (.300, 23 HRs, 78 RBIs), Ken Griffey (.305, 16 stolen bases), and Dave Concepcion (.274, 33 stolen bases) were no easy outs, either; and if center fielder Cesar Geronimo (.257) was the Reds' lone offensive weak link, he made up for it with his glove, making only three errors all season. It was the kind of lineup that could beat you in a multitude of ways, with a different hero emerging every day.

With his judicious handling of the Reds' pitching staff, manager Sparky Anderson more than earned his nickname of "Captain Hook"; three different Reds starters (Jack Billingham, Gary Nolan, and Don Gullett) won 15 games, but none of them pitched more than 211 innings. At one point between mid-June and the end of July, the Reds went 45 games without a complete game from a starter, and the staff's year-end total of 22 complete games was the lowest in the majors. Instead of stretching his starters to their breaking point, Anderson preferred to let his crack relief corps shoulder the late-inning load: Closer Rawly Eastwick (5-3, 2.60 ERA, 22 saves) and fellow relievers Will McEnaney (5-2, 2.47, 15 saves), Pedro Borbon (9-5, 2.95, five saves), and Clay Carroll (7-5, 2.62, seven saves) threw more than 90 innings apiece.

Even with stellar performances from Steve Garvey (.319, 18 HRs, 95 RBIs) and Andy Messersmith (19-14, 2.29 ERA, 213 Ks), a career year from Ron Cey (.283, 25 HRs, 101 RBIs), and Davey Lopes setting a major league record with his streak of 38 straight successful steal attempts (on his way to leading the majors with 77 thefts), the defending NL champion Dodgers had no chance against the Reds, and finished 20 games back with an 88-74 record. "Iron Mike" Marshall, whose record 106 relief appearances had been so integral to the Dodgers '74 success, was limited to 57 games in '75 by knee and rib cage injuries, while Bill Buckner, Bill Russell, Jimmy Wynn, and Joe Ferguson also suffered injuries that compromised their numbers and their playing time. But the biggest blow against the Dodgers would come after the season had ended: on October 7, Players Association attorney Dick Moss filed a lawsuit on behalf of Messersmith, contending that the Dodgers' ace was now a free agent.

Messersmith, still peeved about his cross-town trade from the Angels in 1972, had insisted after the 1974 season that the Dodgers add a no-trade clause to his contract. Dodgers owner Walter O'Malley offered Messersmith more money and a longer-term deal, but refused to acquiesce on the subject of a no-trade clause—all of which made Messersmith a prime candidate for Marvin Miller's next challenge to the reserve clause. Messersmith played the 1975 season without a contract, as did Dave McNally, the aging former Orioles ace who had been traded against his will to Montreal at the end of the 1974 season; while McNally had retired in all but name in June, after losing six straight decisions, both men were now free, at least in the eyes of the Players Association, to sign new deals with whichever team they chose.

Commissioner Bowie Kuhn (who had recently been reelected by the owners to a new seven-year term) adamantly opposed this notion, opining that widespread free agency would open the door to "potential anarchy" that could conceivably lead to the total destruction of major league baseball. But Player Relations Committee arbitrator Peter Seitz—who had, amazingly enough, been retained by the owners despite his 1974 ruling that allowed Catfish Hunter to leave Oakland—ruled in favor of Messersmith, McNally, and the Players Association. This time, the owners fired Seitz, and moved to challenge his decision in federal court. The case would drag on into the spring of '76, when the court ruled that Messersmith was indeed a free agent, a decision that would have a more profound long-term effect on the game than anything else (even the designated-hitter ruling) that occurred during the 1970s.

But as the 1975 postseason got under way, the impending Messersmith mess seemed like just so much background noise. The Reds and Pirates met in the NL playoffs for the third time in six seasons; and once again, the Reds dashed the Pirates' hopes of making it to the World Series. Cincinnati had won 10 of its last 11 regular-season games, and the accumulated momentum rolled the Big Red Machine over the Bucs in three straight games. It would be the last time the Pirates would play in the postseason until 1979.

The A's, returning to the ALCS for the fifth straight year, were slightly favored over the Red Sox. But even without the injured Jim Rice, Boston wasted no time in driving a stake into the heart of the green-and-gold dynasty, sweeping the A's in three straight. How seriously the A's missed the departed Catfish Hunter became nakedly apparent in Game 3, when Alvin Dark (under pressure from Finley) brought out Ken Holtzman—who had already pitched seven innings in Game 1—to start the game on two days' rest. The Red Sox drove Holtzman from the mound in the fifth inning, and clinched the AL pennant with a 5–3 victory. Asked afterward by a reporter from *New York Newsday* if letting Hunter go was the biggest blunder in history by a major league franchise, Sal Bando just laughed. "If it wasn't the biggest," he said, "I haven't heard of any bigger." Finley fired Dark on October 17; by the following October, most of the key players from the Athletics' dominant five-year run would be gone as well.

Ultimately, the 1975 playoffs were just an unremarkable appetizer for the toothsome main course that was the Reds–Red Sox World Series. During the ALCS, Reggie Jackson had praised Luis Tiant (who had won 18 games during the regular season) as "the Fred Astaire of baseball"; and in Game 1 of the Series, the Cuban hurler put on one of the finest dance recitals of his career, shutting out the Reds 6–0 at Fenway. Most of the Reds players had never faced El Tiante before, and thus were fairly mystified by his wide array of whirling windups—as was National League umpire Nick Colosi, who called a balk on Tiant in the fourth inning for "illegal use" of his leg. *New Yorker* sportswriter Roger Angell, dazzled by the pitcher's performance, broke Tiant's windup dances down into a number of humorously named categories, including "Call the Osteopath," "Falling Off the Fence," and "The Slipper-Kick"—"In the midpitch, he surprisingly decides to get rid of his left shoe."

Bill Lee, the cosmic Sox lefty who had just won 17 games for a third straight season, went up against 15-game winner Jack Billingham in Game 2. The Red Sox held on to a 2–1 lead until the top of the ninth, when Johnny Bench stroked Lee's outside pitch to right for a double, and—with two outs—Boston reliever Dick Drago gave up successive run-scoring hits to Dave Concepcion and Ken Griffey. Asked after the 3–2 Reds victory how he'd characterize the Series thus far, the normally garrulous Lee paused and looked thoughtfully off into the distance while considering the reporter's question. "Tied," he said.

The 10-inning Game 3 was, in retrospect, like a rough early version of the baseball masterpiece that Game 6 would turn out to be—the characters and sense of drama were already in place, but the outcome was slightly different and somewhat less satisfying. The winning run of the Reds' 6–5 victory was put in scoring position by a controversial play (and subsequent controversial ruling), wherein Reds pinch hitter Ed Armbrister tried to bunt Cesar Geronimo to second, then collided with Carlton Fisk while leaving the batter's box. Fisk tried to nail Geronimo at second, but his hurried throw ended up in center field. Fisk and Boston manager Darrell Johnson argued that Armbrister had interfered with the play, but their appeals were overruled by umpires Larry Barnett and Dick Stello; and two batters later, Morgan singled in Geronimo to win the game. Many in the Red Sox dugout felt that the umpires had completely blown the Armbrister call, and that Johnson hadn't argued Fisk's case forcibly enough. "If it had been me out there," groused Lee, "I would have bitten Barnett's ear off. I'd have Van Goghed him!"

Game 4 was another one-run nail-biter, with all of Boston's runs in their Series-tying 5–4 victory coming in the fourth inning, when the Sox sent 10 men to the plate. Tiant, once again the star of the show, labored harder than he had in Game 1, needing 155 pitches to clinch his second complete-game win of the Series. In Game 5, it was Don Gullett's turn to shine, striking out seven Red Sox in 8⅔ innings as the Reds coasted to an easy 6–2 win. The Series returned to Boston, with the Reds up three games to two, and looking to finish the Red Sox off for good in Game 6.

They would have to wait five days for their chance, as heavy rains lashed the Boston area, forcing Kuhn to postpone the game three different times. When the teams finally met up again on dry grass, Tiant— whom Johnson had initially been saving for Game 7—was rested enough to make the start. Fred Lynn staked El Tiante to a 3–0 lead with a three-run homer in the bottom of the first off of Reds starter Gary Nolan, who lasted only two innings and would be one of eight Reds pitchers used in the contest, a World Series record. But Tiant seemed rusty, and the Reds tied it up in the top of the fifth on a two-run triple by Griffey and an RBI single from Bench, then went ahead 5–3 in the top of the seventh on a two-run double by George Foster. When Cesar Geronimo smacked a solo homer in the top of the eighth to make it 6–3, Johnson finally yanked Tiant and brought in Rogelio "Roger" Moret, who had gone 14-3 during the year splitting time between the Boston rotation and the bullpen. Moret set the next three Reds down in order, advancing the game to the bottom of the frame.

With two outs and two men on in the bottom of the eighth, Johnson sent Bernie Carbo up to pinch-hit for Moret—a decision that looked dubious when Carbo swung wildly at an inside fastball from Eastwick, missing it by a mile. He worked the count to 3-and-2, then barely managed to foul off an Eastwick slider. "I'm thinking, 'I just took the worst swing in the history of baseball,'" Carbo later said of his helpless cut. His next swing was the best—and certainly most important—of his career, as it smashed an Eastwick fastball deep into the center-field bleachers to tie the game. The Fenway faithful went completely mad as Carbo careened exultantly around the bases. "Don't you wish you were this strong?" he joked to former teammate Pete Rose as he passed him at third base. "This is what the World Series is about," Rose yelled back. "This is fun."

Dick Drago, who had let Game 2 get away, set the intimidating trio of Morgan, Bench, and Perez down one-two-three in the top of the ninth. The Red Sox loaded the bases with no one out in the bottom of the inning, but blew the opportunity when second baseman Denny Doyle tried to score on Lynn's fly to left, and was nailed at the plate by Foster's laserlike throw. Neither team scored in the 10th, but the Reds got off to a good start in the top of the 11th when Drago nicked Rose's uniform with a pitch. Griffey grounded to second, forcing Rose; Morgan then lashed a line drive to right that looked destined to land in the seats, but was snared by Dwight Evans with a twisting, turning stab at the fence. Griffey was running from the moment Morgan made contact, and Evans easily doubled him off first to end the inning.

After Pat Darcy set the Red Sox down one-two-three for the second straight inning, Johnson brought in Rick Wise to face the Reds in the top of the 12th. Wise, who had led the Red Sox staff with 19 wins in '75, hadn't pitched a single inning in relief all year, but still managed to keep the Reds at bay. Due up first for the Red Sox in the bottom of the 12th: Carlton Fisk.

By now, it was past midnight on the East Coast, but more than 70 million viewers were still glued to their TV sets as Fisk strode to the plate to face Darcy. The Reds had already intentionally walked Fisk twice during the game; but now, with the score tied 6–6 and nobody out, Darcy had little choice but to pitch to the Boston catcher. Fisk golfed Darcy's second pitch on a high arc down the left-field line, then hopped slowly toward first, frantically waving and gyrating and willing the ball into fair territory while keeping his eyes firmly fixed upon its flight.

Lou Gerard, NBC's left-field cameraman, was under orders from network game director Harry Coyle to track the trajectory of any ball Fisk hit in his direction. But Gerard, who was stationed inside the Fenway scoreboard, was too spooked and distracted by the sudden approach of one of the ballpark's infamously gigantic rats to follow Fisk's fly. However, since Gerard's camera was already trained upon home plate, it was able to unintentionally broadcast every second of Fisk's dance—and his celebratory leap when the ball finally clanged off the top of the left-field foul pole—for the millions of viewers still watching at home, and capture the dramatic moment for posterity.

Fisk had just won one of the most exciting games in World Series history, tying the Series at three games apiece. For most teams, losing a roller-coaster game in extra innings would have completely taken the wind out of their sails, but not so the Reds: "Skip, that's the greatest game I've ever played," a grinning Rose told Sparky Anderson as the team walked up the tunnel to the Fenway parking lot in the wee hours of the Boston morning. "Relax," Rose assured him. "We're going to win it tomorrow."

They almost didn't. In Game 7, the Red Sox sent nine men to the plate against Gullett in the bottom of the third, scoring three runs on a single and two bases-loaded walks, and Lee held the Reds scoreless for five innings. The Reds finally drew blood in the top of the sixth when Lee, having previously taunted Tony Perez with his slow-arcing "Lee-phus Pitch" (a psychedelic variation on 1930s hurler Rip Sewell's "Eephus Pitch"), decided to throw him another; Perez timed his swing perfectly, and launched the ball over the Green Monster for a two-run homer. In the seventh, Lee walked Griffey with one out, and was promptly removed from the game by Johnson; Moret, his replacement, blew the lead when Rose singled Griffey home. Griffey scored again in the top of the ninth on Morgan's looping single to center off rookie reliever Jim Burton, as the Reds took a 4–3 lead. The Red Sox hitters, who had been almost completely shut down since the fifth by Reds relievers Billingham and Carroll, fared no better against McEnaney in the game's final frame. Yaz flew out to center to end it all, and the Reds had their first World Series trophy since 1940, coming out on top in the most exciting Series anyone could remember. "We didn't win the Series, but we didn't lose it, either," Lee later reflected. "Baseball won."

CHAPTER 9
ROWS, 'FROS, ANYTHING GOES

In the late 1960s, a time when American writers, musicians, fashion designers, and filmmakers were all pushing the accepted boundaries of stylistic self-expression, most players still looked like clean-cut throwbacks to the Eisenhower era. Major league baseball, of course, exhibited little tolerance for players who chose to let their freak flags fly; and while neat sideburns were generally permissible, mustaches and beards had long been strictly off-limits and hair that extended below the collar was virtually unthinkable. But as the 1960s turned into the 1970s, and all but the oldest or most conservative American males began to adopt shaggier manes and/or facial growth, it was only a matter of time before ballplayers started expressing their individuality in similarly hairy ways.

Ironically, the first major leaguer of the era to sport a groovy do on the diamond was actually wearing a toupee: Joe Pepitone, who is also widely credited with being the first player to bring his own hair dryer into a major league clubhouse, typically alternated between two hairpieces—a short but wavy "gamer" worn under his cap, and a more luxuriously leonine one for off-the-field play.

A free swinger in several senses of the term, Pepitone brought a bushy-sideburned insouciance to Leo Durocher's Cubs when he was traded to Chicago from Houston in 1970. In early 1972, "Pepi" opened Joe Pepitone's Thing, a Division Street singles bar widely rumored to be backed by mob money; he could usually be found holding court at the saloon after Wrigley day games. Unfortunately, Pepitone's peacockish persona rubbed many of his teammates and managers the wrong way, especially once his hard-partying, skirt-chasing ways began to take a serious toll on his hitting. Out of baseball by 1974, Pepitone looked back upon his decadent career in a 1975 memoir, *Joe, You Coulda Made Us Proud*, a book that still reads like a cross between *Goodfellas*, *Ball Four*, and *Penthouse Forum*.

For African-Americans of the day, letting one's hair go "natural"—as opposed to spending time and money processing it with a variety of pomades and straighteners—was a profound expression of black pride, symbolic of their refusal to conform to white society's notions of attractiveness. Appropriately enough, the majors' first real Afro belonged to the Phillies' Dick Allen, who was well aware that his hip appearance and self-confident attitude did not sit well with many of the team's fans. "I represented a threat to white people in Philadelphia," Allen would later reflect. "I wore my hair in an Afro. I said what was on my mind."

Though they were certainly sartorial pioneers, Pepitone and Allen were far too controversial to inspire follicular emulation on the part of their peers. But everyone loves a winner—and when the 1972 Oakland A's sprouted long hair and mustaches on their way to their first World Series championship, players around the majors quickly began to follow suit.

The saga of the A's "Mustache Gang" began in February 1972, when Reggie Jackson showed up at spring training camp in Arizona sporting a bushy mustache. This in itself wasn't unusual; players often grew mustaches or beards during the winter, only to shave them before the regular season began. But Jackson bragged to teammates and reporters that he would continue to wear his mustache during the regular season—and that he might just grow a beard, too, if he felt like it. A's owner Charlie O.

Finley, who'd clashed several times in the past with his temperamental young star, instructed manager Dick Williams to tell Jackson to shave it off. When Reggie refused, Finley countered with a little reverse psychology, telling other players on the team that they should grow mustaches as well. In Finley's mind, Reggie's mustache was just another way of drawing attention to himself; if other A's were also sporting facial hair, he reasoned, it would steal Reggie's thunder as an "individual" and force him to go clean-shaven.

Finley's plan backfired. By May, the A's had become the hairiest team in baseball, yet Jackson's mustache remained willfully intact. But the A's owner, whose reputation as a carnival-type huckster belied his savvy marketing skills, simply turned the team's 'stache surplus into another promotional opportunity. Figuring that a team with funky facial hair just might appeal to the Bay Area's "turned-on" youth demographic, he offered a $300 bonus for any player who would grow a mustache in time for the June 18 Father's Day game against the Indians at the Oakland Coliseum. Billed as "Mustache Day," Finley's promotion offered free admission to any guy with a mustache.

At a time when the average baseball salary was only a little over $34,000—and many A's were making substantially less—Finley's offer of $300 was a healthy inducement, and most of the team took the bait. "For $300," relief pitcher Rollie Fingers admitted at the time, "I'd grow one on my rear end." Only pitcher Vida Blue, still smarting from a nasty contract dispute with Finley, refused to join in the fun.

"Mustache Day" was a resounding success; not only did the promotion draw over 26,000 fans to the game—nearly 15,000 more than A's home games typically averaged—but it also firmly cemented the team's rough-and-tumble "Mustache Gang" image in the minds of fans and writers everywhere. Though many of the A's players shaved their mustaches shortly after the game, most of them resumed their hairy ways as the AL West pennant race began to heat up, reasoning that their mustaches had not only brought them luck, but also symbolically brought them together as a team. When the A's faced off against the clean-cut Cincinnati Reds— one of the few teams who had a written policy expressly forbidding facial hair—in the 1972 World Series, the media had a field day covering the "Hair vs. Square" matchup. "Hair" won the Series, four games to three, conclusively proving to baseball's conservative establishment that you could look like a hippie and still play winning baseball.

One Cincinnati player undoubtedly taking note was pitcher Ross Grimsley, who'd haggled with the Reds organization over the length of his hair since coming up as a rookie in 1971. During one spring training, the Reds marched Grimsley to a Florida barber, then sent him back three more times before his tresses finally conformed to team standards. In 1974, the Reds finally tired of Grimsley's nonconformist attitude and shipped him to Baltimore, where he was finally free to let his brown curls mushroom—he grew a dandy "porn 'stache" as well—while giving the Reds ample reason to regret the trade. Grimsley went on to win 18 games that year for the Orioles, and won another 20 in 1978 as an even hairier member of the Expos. Grimsley, whose nickname was "Scuz," was notorious for refusing to bathe when he was pitching well. In 1977, Yankees manager Billy Martin accused Grimsley of throwing a "greaseball," claiming that the pitcher was hiding lubricant in his hair. Grimsley denied the charges, and none of the umpires were willing to stick their fingers into the pitcher's unwashed mane to find out for sure.

Grimsley's late-'70s Orioles teammate Don Stanhouse also sported a famously unruly white 'fro, which he accessorized for a time with a pretty formidable walrus mustache. An erratic reliever who often walked more hitters than he struck out, Stanhouse was nicknamed "Full Pack" by O's manager Earl Weaver—because the skipper would usually go through a full pack of smokes whenever Stanhouse took the mound.

Dave LaRoche, a reliever who threw for the Angels, Twins, White Sox, and Indians during the '70s, was best known for his low-speed "eephus"-style pitch, which he humorously dubbed "La Lob"; he took a similarly eccentric approach to his facial hair, sometimes sporting a pencil mustache à la Lee Van Cleef in *The Good, the Bad, and the Ugly*, and other times wearing mod muttonchops that made him look like the Z-Man character from *Beyond the Valley of the Dolls*.

Without question, the most memorable mustache of the decade belonged to Rollie Fingers. While his Mustache Gang teammates Catfish Hunter, Joe Rudi, and Sal Bando sported 'staches that looked straight out of a 1970s singles bar, Fingers's Snidely Whiplash handlebars were pure 1890s. The future Hall of Famer cut such a dashing figure that Finley made a special point of including $100 worth of "the best mustache wax available" in Fingers's 1973 contract.

Fingers left Oakland after the 1976 season, signing with the Padres as a free agent. Though they finally managed a winning season in 1978, the Padres of the late '70s weren't an exceptionally talented bunch; but with Fingers leading the way, they were veritable facial hair all-stars. Bob Shirley, Bill Almon, George Hendrick, Derrel Thomas, Rick Sweet, Fernando Gonzalez, and Fingers's old A's teammate Gene Tenace sported an almost encyclopedic array of mustaches, while Dave Winfield, Gene Richards, Oscar Gamble, and Ozzie Smith all paired their mustaches with spectacularly angled sideburns.

While a few clubs like the Reds, Astros, and Expos continued to insist upon clean upper lips, mustaches were sprouting like dandelions everywhere else by the mid-'70s. At times, it almost seemed like a flamboyant mustache was the de rigueur accessory for the top relief pitchers of the day—in addition to Fingers, Mike Marshall of the Los Angeles Dodgers, Sparky Lyle of the New York Yankees, and Al Hrabosky of the St. Louis Cardinals were all top firemen with fearsome fuzz.

For Marshall, who often spoke out against what he perceived to be the game's antiquated approach to physical training and conditioning, the Fu Manchu/muttonchops combo he wore was simply another expression of his individuality. Ditto for Lyle, an incorrigible prankster—his "party piece" involved taking off his pants and sitting on the birthday cakes of his hapless teammates—whose outsize walrus mustache also served to hide his mischievous grin.

But for Hrabosky, the mustache took on an almost talismanic degree of importance. The most exciting member of a Cardinals team that slowly slid into mediocrity as mainstays like Bob Gibson, Joe Torre, and Lou

Brock got older or retired, Hrabosky was known as "the Mad Hungarian," thanks to a highly entertaining mound act that involved stomping around like an angry bull while muttering to himself, and fixing the batter with a homicidal stare before finally throwing the pitch. "My controlled hate routine," Hrabosky said of the ritual, which he performed before every pitch.

During a 1974 contest with Chicago, Cubs third baseman Bill Madlock tried to get under Hrabosky's skin by imitating the pitcher; as Hrabosky was about to go into his windup, Madlock stepped out of the batter's box, retreated halfway to the dugout, and began to stomp around and mutter to himself. Hrabosky watched the comic performance impassively; but when Madlock finally returned to the plate, Cards catcher Ted Simmons delivered his review in the form of a right hook to Madlock's face.

Through a combination of good pitching and sheer intimidation, Hrabosky became one of the most dominant relievers in the National League. But in 1977, his mustache (and Simmons's long raven locks) ran afoul of new Cardinals manager Vern Rapp, who insisted that all his players be clean-shaven and wear short hair. "I didn't come here to be liked," announced the defiantly unhip Rapp. "I'm not trying to treat [the players] like little kids. It's just that they haven't been accustomed to discipline. Today it's do your own thing, be a free soul, live for today because tomorrow may never come. But reality has got to come sometime."

After initially threatening to file a grievance through the Players Association, Hrabosky grudgingly ditched his Fu Manchu, and proved remarkably less effective without it—his ERA ballooned to 4.38, leading St. Louis sportswriters to speculate over whether the pitcher's true powers lay in his arm or in his mustache. At the end of the season, Hrabosky was traded to Kansas City, where he regained both his mustache and his impressive form in 1978, saving 47 games and posting a 2.88 ERA.

The Milwaukee Brewers' 1975 roster boasted an impressively high Fu Manchu quotient, with George Scott, Jim Colborn, Darrell Porter, Pete Broberg, and Kurt Bevacqua among the players flying the Fu. But in 1976, new Brewers manager Alex Grammas declared the Milwaukee clubhouse a mustache-free zone, and promptly led them to two straight mediocre seasons. However, when George Bamberger took over in 1978 and relaxed his predecessor's grooming restrictions, the Brewers suddenly transformed themselves into a dangerous team.

Bamberger's hirsute Brew Crews of the late '70s—who confounded all expectations by actually giving the Yankees and Orioles serious pennant competition in '78 and '79—were extraordinarily popular with fans all over the country, and their down-to-earth appeal was best personified by the shaggy likes of outfielder Gorman Thomas. Whether he was making circus catches in center field, belting tape-measure home runs, or striking out with a force that could be felt on the other side of Lake Michigan, Stormin' Gorman always seemed in danger of becoming completely overwhelmed by his mushrooming blond mane, which often seemed to have a life of its own.

Some players grew facial hair as a form of protest. When Expos pitcher Steve Renko (a mainstay of the Montreal rotation since 1970) found himself relegated to the bullpen at the beginning of the 1976 season, he expressed his dissatisfaction by complaining loudly to the local media—and growing a mustache. Within weeks, he found himself shipped to the Cubs, for whom he started 35 games over the next two seasons. The Yankees' irascible Thurman Munson, who seemed to sport a perpetual three-day scruff as prickly as his personality, grew a beard for a few weeks during the 1977 season as a symbolic middle-finger salute to Yankees owner George Steinbrenner for bringing Reggie Jackson into the Bronx clubhouse. Steinbrenner had no problem with mustaches on his players, but he absolutely despised long hair and beards; on Opening Day in 1976, "the Boss" was so horrified to see photos of long-haired Yankees in the Bronx Bombers' new yearbook, he insisted that team publicist Marty Appel recall the entire print run.

Steinbrenner's edicts notwithstanding, beards became a fairly common sight on the diamond over the course of the decade, whether in the form of groovy goatees worn by the likes of Pirates/Phillies/Expos second sacker Dave Cash and A's/Rangers/White Sox outfielder Claudell Washington, or the full-on mountain-man thickets that sprouted on the faces of Phillies/Braves ace reliever Gene Garber and Expos pitcher Bill Lee—the latter of whom celebrated his trade from Boston to Montreal in 1979 by growing a bushy beard that would have shamed Dan Haggerty from TV's *The Life and Times of Grizzly Adams*. Bill "Soup" Campbell, one of the AL's top closers in '76 and '77 with the Twins and Red Sox, sported a neatly trimmed beard that made him look almost professorial, though he later ditched it in favor of a Village People–style mustache. Bill North, the speed demon who played center field for the A's, Dodgers, and Giants, wore a beard that so perfectly matched the thickness and shape of the hair on his head, it was impossible to tell where one ended and the other began. In certain photos, North looked like a dead ringer for a '70s-vintage G.I. Joe doll.

A number of '70s players—like Cardinals catcher Ted Simmons, Dodgers backstop Steve Yeager, and Brewers shortstop Robin Yount—actually looked good with long hair. Tigers phenom Mark "the Bird" Fidrych's Harpo Marx mop totally suited his happy-go-lucky persona, while no less an authority than Dick Allen gave serious props to Mike Schmidt's natural do. "Schmitty was an honorary black," said Allen of his teammate on the '75-'76 Phillies. "He was also sporting an Afro at the time, even if it was a bright red one."

However, the perms worn by Padres ace Randy Jones, Cleveland Indians hurler Wayne Garland, and journeyman outfielder Bernie Carbo simply made them look like high school math teachers who hoped to get lucky at the local disco during the upcoming weekend. Ironically, Carbo—a self-professed flower child who would later tell the *Sporting News* that "[baseball] management in my day was Nixon, and I was Woodstock"—actually went on to style hair for a living, opening Monsieur Bernardo's Beauty Salon in Detroit after he retired from baseball.

In the late '70s, Cubs pitcher Paul Reuschel and third baseman Steve Ontiveros followed the toupee trail blazed by Joe Pepitone by appearing in print and TV ads for Hairline Creations, a Windy City hair-replacement outfit. Combined with his ever-present droopy mustache, Ontiveros's collar-length black hairpiece made him look like a very poor man's Freddie Prinze from TV's *Chico and the Man*.

Dave Heaverlo took his own tonsorial cues from a TV star at the opposite end of the follicular spectrum. The right-handed reliever, who threw 130 innings for the A's in 1978, after coming to Oakland as part of the eight-player deal that sent Vida Blue across the bay to San Francisco, was nicknamed "Kojak" for his decision to go with a completely shaved dome. Telly Savalas surely would've been proud.

With the exception of Dick Allen, African-American ballplayers of the late '60s had mostly been reluctant to "go natural," or generally emphasize their own blackness in a sport that had been integrated—kicking and screaming at that—just two decades earlier. But by the mid-1970s, the Afro had thoroughly permeated American popular culture: "Rows, 'fros, anything goes!" trumpeted the TV ads for Afro Sheen, a motto that was finally starting to apply to a large number of black baseball players as well.

Predictably, these hirsute expressions of black pride made some of the white folks in baseball's boardrooms squirm with discomfort. Pittsburgh Pirates pitcher Dock Ellis, never exactly a shrinking violet, didn't mix well with authority figures—a trait that once resulted in a face full of Mace, courtesy of a Riverfront Stadium security guard. Ellis regularly gave the baseball establishment fits, most memorably in July 1973, when he appeared in the Wrigley Field bullpen before a Pirates-Cubs contest with his hair in curlers. (Ellis's "Superfly" hairstyle had recently been featured in a photo spread in *Ebony* magazine, and he needed the curlers to create said do.)

When word came down to the Pirates clubhouse that commissioner Kuhn and Pirates owner Joe Brown were both concerned about the potentially adverse effect of Ellis's curlers upon baseball's "image," Pirates skipper Bill Virdon gently took his volatile pitcher aside. "Look, Dock, I don't care what you wear," Virdon told him. "But the front office doesn't like it, the umpires don't like it, and if you're not careful, you're going to get fined."

Ellis agreed to ditch the curlers, but not before venting his frustration over the situation to the *Sporting News*. "There are many black men who wear curlers to help their hair," he fumed. "Baseball is getting behind the times again. Four or five years ago, they wouldn't let players wear moustaches, goatees, long hair, or long sideburns. Look around now." To another reporter, he added, "They didn't put out any orders about Joe Pepitone when he wore a hairpiece down to his shoulders."

After he retired, Ellis would reveal that his infamous curlers had been about more than just self-expression. "That's when I was throwing spitballs," Ellis told Hall, author of *Dock Ellis in the Country of Baseball*. "When I had the curlers, my hair would be straight. Down the back. On the ends would be nothing but balls of sweat." Ellis would reach back between pitches and get a little grease on his fingertips, "just one touch at a time."

By 1975, most major league rosters boasted at least one player—like the Cubs' Jose Cardenal, the Mets' Nino Espinosa, the Dodgers' Reggie Smith, the Phillies' Garry Maddox, the Cardinals' fabulously named Bake McBride, and journeyman hurler Jim Bibby—whose oversized 'fro would have caused them to be mistaken for a member of the Spinners, the Chi-Lites, or any other 'frotastic contemporary act that appeared on TV's *Soul Train*. Maddox, whose muttonchop sideburns were nearly as puffy as the hair on his head, spent parts of the 1969 and 1970 seasons serving in Vietnam as a U.S. Army infantryman. During his tour of duty, Maddox was exposed to various chemicals that left his facial skin prone to rashes; though he was one of the first major leaguers to wear abundant chops, they were less of a fashion statement than an easy way to protect his sensitive face from the glare of the sun and the irritation of daily shaving.

Luis Tiant, Boston's inscrutable Cuban hurler, went his contemporaries one better after the 1975 World Series, when he commissioned a custom-made Afro toupee to cover his balding pate. The bespoke hairpiece—which cost El Tiante a cool $750—was created by none other than Monsanto, the same chemical industry giant that manufactured artificial turf for major league stadiums. Perhaps the crafty pitcher was merely seeking a competitive edge; if any batter had lined a screamer back through the box, Tiant's "turf-toupee" probably could have deflected it to the nearest infielder.

Baseball's most awe-inspiring Afro unquestionably belonged to journeyman slugger Oscar Gamble. To this day, Gamble's 1976 Topps "Traded" baseball card is still prized by many collectors—not because of its rarity or Gamble's abilities, but simply because it showcases the biggest, most thoroughly badass Afro ever to appear on a major league diamond. A native of Ramer, Alabama, Gamble came up with the Cubs in 1969, then spent a couple of undistinguished seasons with the Phillies; it wasn't until his trade to the Cleveland Indians in 1973 that he—and his Afro—truly blossomed. From 1973 to 1975, Gamble averaged 18 home runs a season as a platoon player, all while sporting a voluminous Afro that added a good four inches to his height and appeared to measure as much as two feet across. Gamble typically crowned his luxuriant growth with a cap several sizes larger than he would normally have required—in truth, he probably could have fit two additional caps on the Afro puffs that protruded from either side—and his powerful swings would often cause batting helmets to pop right off their precarious perch on his head. "I had a lot of pitchers want to throw a ball at my head to see if it would stick in my hair," he later recalled.

Gamble was traded to the Yankees prior to the 1976 season, and was immediately informed by manager Billy Martin that he would have to have his hair cut before he could be fitted for pinstripes. When Yankees public relations man Marty Appel turned Gamble's shearing into a media event, Gamble—ever the reliable role player—endured the publicity stunt with typical good humor, though his wife, Juanita, wept as she saw her husband's do reduced to a more conservative circumference.

But Gamble would have his revenge: Traded the next year to the Chicago White Sox for shortstop Bucky Dent, Gamble slugged 31 homers (a significant increase from the 17 he hit for the Yankees in '76) as his hair returned to its earlier jaw-dropping abundance. As writer Dick Young noted in the *Sporting News*, "Oscar Gamble, returning to Yankee Stadium with the White Sox, took pre-game practice bare-headed, no doubt to flaunt a flourishing Afro that he was made to trim down when a member of the Yankees."

Alas, Gamble would have to get his 'fro trimmed again in 1979, when he returned to the Yankees via a midseason trade with the Texas Rangers. But by then, the oversize Afro was beginning to fall out of fashion—a development surely not lost on Gamble, who owned a hip discotheque, Oscar Gamble's Players Club, in Montgomery, Alabama. There would be no place for badass Afros in Ronald Reagan's America, and Gamble's dynamite do was ultimately fated to fade into legend. Referring to the circuslike atmosphere of the Yankees' clubhouse, Gamble once uttered the immortal line "They don't think it be like it is, but it do." For a few years in the 1970s, those words could easily have applied to his unbelievable hair as well.

The very definition of "badass": AL MVP Dick Allen juggles baseballs and smokes while carrying the entire 1972 White Sox squad on his back.

(John Iacono/Sports Illustrated. Courtesy of Getty Images)

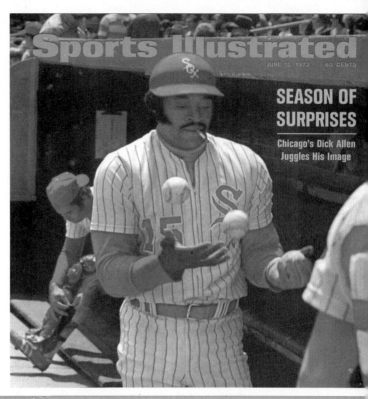

Hank Aaron hammered away at Babe Ruth's home run record with his usual level of class and dignity, but the strain of the constant media attention—and the hate mail and death threats he received—invariably took its toll.

(Courtesy of Steve Dewing)

Johnny Bench was the greatest catcher of the 1970s; Rollie Fingers sported the decade's finest moustache. They would face off against each other in the "Hair vs. Square" World Series of 1972.

(Courtesy of Steve Dewing)

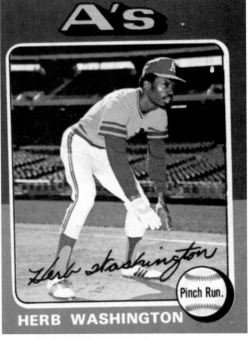

HERB WASHINGTON

Two Bay Area icons of the 1970s—
Dirty Harry star Clint Eastwood and
controversial A's owner Charlie
Finley—enjoy a seventh-inning
stretch at the Oakland Coliseum.

(Courtesy of Steve Dewing)

The guinea pig for Finley's "designated
runner" experiment, former Big Ten
track star "Hurricane Herb" Washington
appeared in ninety-two games in 1974—
all without touching a bat or a baseball.

(Baseball card courtesty of Topps Company, Inc.)

OPPOSITE BOTTOM: Pete Rose brawls with Bud Harrelson
in Game 3 of the 1973 NL playoffs. Mets fans responded to the fight
by pelting Rose with garbage, nearly causing their team to forfeit
the game.

(AP Photo/Marty Lederhandler)

Former Orioles first baseman Boog Powell found new life as the Indians' DH, but had trouble adjusting to their all-red road uniforms. "I look like the world's biggest Bloody Mary," he complained.

(Courtesy of Steve Dewing)

The most 'fro-tastic baseball card of all time. "I had a lot of pitchers want to throw a ball at my head to see if it would stick in my hair," Oscar Gamble recalled.

(Baseball card courtesy of Topps Company, Inc.)

OPPOSITE: Separated at birth: The late Mark "The Bird" Fidrych and Sesame Street's Big Bird, taken at the height of the Detroit phenom's short-lived flight.

(Lane Stewart/Sports Illustrated. Courtest of Getty Images)

The inimitable Dock Ellis clowns with jazz musician
Chuck Mangione before a Yankees game, April 1977.
Given Ellis's proclivities, this probably wasn't the kind
of "toot" he had in mind.

(AP Photo/Ray Stubblebine)

Billy Martin and Reggie Jackson share
a rare laugh before Game 5 of the 1977
World Series. Along with Yankees
owner George Steinbrenner, the two
men produced enough drama to fill
every theater on Broadway.

(AP Photo)

Houston Astros star hurler J. R. Richard.
His 6'8" frame and 100 mph fastballs were as
intimidating as the Astros' "tequila sunrise"
uniforms were ridiculous.

(Courtesy of Steve Dewing)

Dave "The Cobra" Parker, one of the key
players of the "We Are Family" Pirates,
seen here in one of their subtler uniform
ensembles.

(Courtesy of Steve Dewing)

Bill "Spaceman" Lee dons
his Sunday best for an
ACLU press conference,
shortly after being fined
by Bowie Kuhn for
talking about sprinkling
pot on his pancakes.

(AP Photo)

Disco Demolition Night rocks Comiskey Park. "I could smell marijuana the moment I walked onto the field," remembered umpire Durwood Merrill.

(AP Photo/Fred Jewell)

CHAPTER 10
1976

America's Bicentennial year arrived not a moment too soon. The first six years of the 1970s had been plagued by war, recession, social unrest, and political scandal; but with Richard Nixon gone and the Vietnam War finally over, the advent of 1976 seemed like a signal for the exhausted nation to relax, take a deep breath, lighten the mood, and attempt to salve a collective psyche that had been battered relentlessly since John F. Kennedy's assassination in 1963.

The country's renewed appetite for feel-good entertainment was vividly reflected by many of 1976's popular obsessions. Peter Frampton's *Frampton Comes Alive*, the best-selling rock album of the year, was the very essence of "mellow good vibes." *Rocky*, Sylvester Stallone's old-fashioned root-for-the-underdog boxing flick, was the year's biggest box-office smash, while *Happy Days* and *Laverne and Shirley*—two ABC sitcoms that took place in a sanitized post-Elvis/pre-Beatles nostalgia zone—were the year's top-rated TV shows. (*Charlie's Angels*, the ultimate eye-candy show of the 1970s, would debut in the fall.) And why even *watch* TV when you could just plug Atari's new *Pong* into the set and lose yourself in hours of thrilling video table tennis, or listen in to truckers' conversations on a CB radio?

Then, of course, there was the Bicentennial celebration itself. The

United States' 200th birthday party was an all-year event, one marked by patriotic displays both dazzling (the July 4 convergence of 50 warships and 16 tall ships in New York Harbor) and humble (communities slapping red, white, and blue paint jobs on their fire hydrants and park benches). If their country's recent past was still too painful and divisive for most Americans to contemplate, they could at least unite in their appreciation of the courage, resilience, and foresight of the original patriots.

Foresight, however, was not a quality shared by most of major league baseball's owners; nor, for that matter, did many of these gentlemen seem particularly adept at gauging the general mood of the American people. For at a time when people were still buzzing in the wake of what many were calling the greatest World Series ever played—and excitement about the forthcoming season was accordingly high—the owners announced that they were locking their players out of spring training.

Over the winter, Los Angeles Dodgers hurler Andy Messersmith— who'd won 19 games in 1975 while playing without a contract—had officially been declared a free agent by a federal judge, meaning that the right-hander was now free to auction his services to the highest bidder. This didn't sit well with the owners, who foresaw the Messersmith decision as a harbinger of higher salaries and increased negotiating leverage for their players.

Thus, on February 23, the major league owners tried to push through a new labor agreement, which stipulated that all players would be indentured to their teams for nine years—eight seasons, plus one in which they could play out their option and *then* decide to offer their services elsewhere. Until the players signed this agreement, the owners announced, they would be locked out of spring training.

But the Players Association, aware that it—and not the owners—was operating from a position of strength, steadfastly refused to sign the agreement. Barred from entering their training camps, many players began limbering up individually or in small numbers in high school gyms or ballfields across Florida, waiting for the call to go back to work. That call came on March 17, when commissioner Bowie Kuhn—having wisely deduced that it would be sheer idiocy to shut down the national pastime during the Bicentennial year—ordered all team training facilities to be reopened; the owners were given 48 hours to comply.

At this point, A's owner Charlie O. Finley decided to take matters into his own hands: Right before Opening Day, Finley traded Reggie Jackson and Ken Holtzman—two A's stars who'd been in perpetual contract disputes with Finley, and who would most likely test the free-agency waters at season's end—to the Baltimore Orioles. Jackson held out for a month before agreeing to terms with the Orioles, thus handicapping the team while the Yankees got off to their hot start. "We'd have won if Reggie had been there all year," Orioles manager Earl Weaver would bitterly reflect.

On April 10, after entertaining offers from five other teams, including the Yankees and the San Diego Padres, Andy Messersmith finally signed a three-year, $1 million contract with the Atlanta Braves. New Braves owner Ted Turner promptly added fuel to the furor over his big-bucks acquisition when he assigned Messersmith a jersey with the number 17 and the nickname "Channel" on the back. Turner had already placed nicknames on the backs of several other Braves' jerseys—knuckleball specialist Phil Niekro wore "Knucksie," while the uniform of speedster outfielder Ralph Garr read "Roadrunner"—but this time Turner went too far, at least in the eyes of National League president Chub Feeney. After all, Channel 17 just happened to be the spot on the UHF dial where Turner's Atlanta TV station WTCG resided, and Feeney strongly objected to Turner transforming his new megabucks signing into a human billboard. Forced by Feeney to choose another name, Messersmith picked what he claimed was his *real* nickname: "Bluto."

Feeney's edict would prove but a minor speed bump on Turner's journey to media moguldom. Before the end of the year, Turner would rename the channel WTBS—for Turner Broadcasting System—link its signal to a satellite transponder, and offer the country's first "superstation" free of charge to cable operators across the U.S. Many team owners were less than enthused about this development, believing that Turner was encroaching upon broadcast territory that was rightfully theirs. But even with their new million-dollar baby Messersmith (who would go 11-11 with a 3.04 ERA), the Braves wound wind up last in the NL West with a 70-92 record. It would be a few more years before owners in other cities had to worry about fans switching their allegiance to Turner's team.

The return of Bill Veeck was another 1976 development that baseball owners were less than thrilled about. The master showman and former Indians/Browns/White Sox owner had been out of major league baseball since 1961, when poor health forced him to sell Chicago's AL franchise. But when rumors surfaced in late 1975 that the American League was planning to move the bankrupt White Sox to Seattle, Veeck—backed by capital pieced together from 40 different investors—bought the team again, vowing to keep the franchise in Chicago.

Though his fellow owners took a dim view of Veeck's carny persona and progressive attitude about labor relations—he'd testified on behalf of Curt Flood in the latter's 1970 suit against baseball, and he was the only owner to vote against the 1976 spring training lockout—White Sox fans were ecstatic over his return. Almost immediately after Veeck repurchased the team, White Sox season ticket sales jumped over 40 percent from the year before; even if Veeck couldn't duplicate the pennant-winning magic of his '59 "Go-Go Sox," the South Side fans knew his flair for outlandish promotions would at least make things interesting again at their old ballpark.

On Opening Day at Comiskey Park, Veeck got the season off to a patriotic start, treating more than 40,000 White Sox fans (the club's biggest Opening Day turnout in years) to the sight of a live reenactment of Archibald Willard's iconic painting, *The Spirit of '76*. Marching across the field were White Sox business manager Rudie Schaffer on drums, manager Paul Richards carrying the Revolutionary Army flag with thirteen stars, and (of course) the team's new owner—who'd lost a leg as the result of a combat wound sustained in World War II—as the peg-legged fifer. "If you've got the guy with the wooden leg," said Veeck, "you've got the casting beat."

But with the exception of a July 28 no-hitter pitched by John "Blue Moon" Odom and reliever Francisco Barrios—the second tag-team no-no of Odom's career—the 4–0 Opening Day victory over the Kansas City Royals would be pretty much the high point of Veeck's first season back with the Pale Hose. (1976 saw three other major league no-hitters: a July 9 one against the Expos by the Astros' Larry Dierker, one on August 9 by John "Candy Man" Candelaria against the Dodgers, and a September 29 no-no by John "the Count" Montefusco of the Giants over the Braves.)

In May, Wilbur Wood, the Sox' potbellied, knuckleball-throwing iron man—who'd averaged 21 wins and 336 innings pitched during the previous five seasons—had his kneecap shattered by a line drive hit by Ron LeFlore of the Tigers. Though the injury would eventually lead to Wood's early retirement, at least he was spared the indignity of playing in the team's home doubleheader against the Royals on August 8, when Veeck had his players take the field wearing the infamous blue Bermuda shorts and striped kneesocks.

A far more popular Veeck move was his brief reactivation of 53-year-old Minnie Minoso, one of the stars of Veeck's 1950s White Sox teams, including the 1959 AL champion squad. Veeck brought Minoso back in September, allowing him to go into the books as a four-decade major leaguer; Minoso managed only one single in eight at bats, but that was still enough to put the Cuban outfielder in the record books as the second-oldest major leaguer in history to get a hit, behind Jim O'Rourke of the 1904 New York Giants, who had hit safely at the age of 54.

Veeck also inaugurated one tradition in 1976 that would become one of the best-loved rituals in Chicago baseball: the singing of "Take Me Out to the Ballgame" by White Sox broadcaster Harry Caray during the seventh-inning stretch. On several occasions, Veeck had heard Caray humming along (in a decidedly tone-deaf fashion) with Sox organist Nancy Faust's rendition of the baseball standard, and the owner was so amused by it that he asked Caray to lead the crowd in the seventh-inning sing-along. Veeck knew it would be a hit with the South Side fans, who already totally related to Caray's straight-talking, beer-swilling, working-class persona. But Caray refused—and only relented once Veeck revealed that he'd already surreptitiously tape-recorded the broadcaster's hums, and threatened to play them over the Comiskey PA system if Caray didn't cooperate. Thus blackmailed, Caray reluctantly went along with the gag, and was pleasantly surprised when his braying version of the song was met with roars of approval. Within no time, Caray was belting it out at every home game. In 1981, when "the Mayor of Rush Street" moved up-town to take over the Cubs' broadcast booth, he would bring the seventh-inning tradition with him to Wrigley, where both Caray and the sing-along would become synonymous with the Cubs.

Eight hundred miles east of Comiskey, the New York Yankees' home opener also involved a rousing celebration of history, as Yankee legends like Joe DiMaggio and Mickey Mantle returned to mark the unveiling of the newly renovated Yankee Stadium. Elevators had been installed, view-blocking support posts removed, and seats widened from 18 to 22 inches in order to more comfortably accommodate the ever-expanding American backside. Three million dollars was spent on just a new scoreboard; when it failed to work on Opening Day, various wags suggested that perhaps Babe Ruth's spirit was less than pleased with the changes that had been made to his former stomping grounds. Still, it didn't turn out to be a bad omen for the contest or the season; in their first game back in the Bronx, the Yanks beat the Minnesota Twins 11–4, part of a hot start to a year that would see them cruise into the postseason for the first time since 1964.

The Chicago Cubs, as usual, would fall far short of postseason glory in 1976, but at least the Wrigley faithful enjoyed a memorable April. On April 14, New York Mets slugger (and future Cubs star) Dave "Kong" Kingman blasted what is generally believed to be the longest home run ever hit at Wrigley Field, variously estimated at between 530 and 600 feet. The ball sailed over the left-center-field bleachers, cleared Waveland Avenue entirely, and caromed off a house on nearby Kenmore Avenue.

Three days later at Wrigley, with the wind blowing out, Mike Schmidt of the Philadelphia Phillies tied a major league record by launching four homers in a row, leading the Phils—who'd been down 12–1 in the third—to an 18-16 extra-inning victory.

The most newsworthy Cubs item of the entire season was center fielder Rick Monday's rescue of the American flag during an April 25 game at Dodger Stadium. While warming up between innings, Monday was surprised to see two fans—37-year-old William Errol Thomas and his 11-year-old son—jump over the left-field wall and start running across the outfield grass. Left fielder Jose Cardenal let them pass, thinking they were just goofballs trying to get on TV; but when the pair knelt down, unfurled an American flag, and began to douse it with lighter fluid, Monday—a six-year veteran of the Marine Reserves—immediately sprang into action. Running at a full sprint, he reached down and snatched the flag away before Thomas could set it aflame. Thomas chucked the can of lighter fluid at him, but Monday didn't stop running until he reached the Dodgers' dugout, whereupon he handed the flag to Dodger pitcher Doug Rau for safekeeping.

Monday's patriotic intervention touched a nerve with the public, and transformed the solid but unremarkable player—whose 32 homers and 77 RBIs in 1976 were by far the best offensive numbers of his 19-year career—into a hero overnight. He received commendations from President Gerald Ford, commissioner Bowie Kuhn, Chicago mayor Richard J. Daley, and the Illinois House of Representatives, as well as thousands of letters from fans and veterans. "It's refreshing to find out how many people love their flag," Monday said at the time. "I don't know what those clowns were trying to demonstrate and frankly I don't care. All I know is if they don't like it here, there's nobody standing there at the border telling them they can't leave. Take a hike."

Down the road in Anaheim, the California Angels were facing their own countercultural challenges. The May 1 issue of the *Sporting News* reported that an estimated 400 to 500 marijuana plants had been discovered growing in the outfield of Anaheim Stadium. The plants were alleged to have originated from seeds that were inadvertently scattered during a

Who concert at the ballpark on March 21, where roughly a fifth of the 55,000 fans in attendance had been allowed onto the field. The stadium manager of "the Big A" ordered the demon weeds to be eradicated with herbicide, and cautioned the groundskeeper against taking on any volunteers who were willing to work on the grounds for free.

Despite the Bicentennial-year fuss over Monday's flag-saving heroics, the success of *The Bad News Bears*, which hit theaters that spring, proved that Americans hadn't exactly lost their taste for subversive entertainment. One of the funniest baseball movies ever made, *The Bad News Bears* also delivered a rather cutting commentary on competition in the adult world, even if it revolved around a team of gloriously foulmouthed Little Leaguers coached by a beer-swilling Walter Matthau. Though some viewers expressed shock and dismay at the film's nonstop vulgarity and brief bursts of violence, the mayhem on screen was truly child's play compared to what transpired between the Red Sox and Yankees on May 20.

When the two teams met at Yankee Stadium that day for the start of a four-game series, the defending AL champions were already six games behind their bitter rivals from the Bronx. The Yankees were feeling cocky, the Red Sox frustrated, and the ever-present tensions between the two teams were clearly primed to explode. During the first game of the series, Yankee DH Lou Piniella bowled over Sox catcher Carlton Fisk on a play at the plate, setting off the season's biggest bench-clearing brawl. Fisk and Piniella came up swinging at each other, but the fight's worst casualty was Sox pitcher Bill Lee.

While trying to restrain Yankee outfielder Otto Velez, Lee was sucker-punched in the back of the head by Yankee center fielder Mickey Rivers, then picked up and dropped on his shoulder by Yankee third baseman Graig Nettles. "The Spaceman" tried to take a retaliatory swing at Nettles, only to realize that he no longer had any feeling in his pitching arm; Nettles, for good measure, landed another blow to Lee's head.

Impatient for Nettles to finish the job, a crazed Yankee fan jumped onto the field and tried to attack Lee, who somehow managed to keep him at bay with his cleats until security came. "The entire episode became a Fellini movie," the pitcher recalled in his autobiography. "I saw the trainer examining my arm while I'm lying on the floor and I've got some poor son of a bitch nailed to the dugout wall with my spikes perforating his chest. And 45,000 Yankee fans are screaming for the lions to devour the Christians. It was insane."

One of the mainstays of the Boston staff, Lee would be out for two months with a torn ligament in his left shoulder. By the time he returned to the rotation, the Sox were mired in fifth place in the AL East, 17 games behind Billy Martin's unstoppable pinstripe brigade.

Though the Yankees looked like shoo-ins for the AL East flag, the race still might have turned out differently if Charlie Finley had succeeded in his efforts to shop Rollie Fingers and Joe Rudi to Boston for $1 million apiece, and ace left-hander Vida Blue to the Yankees in exchange for a cool $1.5 million. Dubbed the "Tuesday Night Massacre" by the media, Finley's fire sale was announced right before the midnight trading deadline of Tuesday, June 15. The A's owner claimed his hand was forced by "astronomical and unjustified" demands for higher salaries; since he had little hope of re-signing Fingers, Rudi, and Blue for '77, he reasoned, he was just trying to get a decent return on his investment.

But to many fans and most of Finley's fellow owners, the sale of Blue, Rudi, and Fingers seemed to realize their worst fears about free agency—that richer teams would snap up all the best players, and thus completely eradicate any semblance of competitive balance. Rather than let the Tuesday Night Massacre set what he viewed as a dangerous precedent, commissioner Bowie Kuhn handed down one of the most momentous rulings of his entire tenure, which voided all three of the transactions and sent Blue, Rudi, and Fingers (the latter two of whom had already suited up with the Red Sox) back to the A's. "[Kuhn] sounds like the village idiot," thundered the thwarted Finley, but the ruling stood.

By June 28, when the Yankees arrived in Detroit to take on the Tigers, Billy Martin's team held a comfortable nine-game lead over second-place

Cleveland in the AL East; even without the help of Vida Blue, they were well on their way to capturing the division crown. But first, the Yankees would have to face Mark "the Bird" Fidrych.

On the morning of that June 28 game, Fidrych was a gangly rookie right-hander with a surprising 7-1 record and an even more impressive 2.18 ERA. By the time the Tigers finished beating the Yankees 5–1 that night, Fidrych had practically become a rock star. Thanks to ABC's *Monday Night Baseball* broadcast, millions of fans around the country got their first look at Fidrych and his eccentric work habits: When he took the mound between innings, Fidrych dropped to his knees and smoothed out the cleat marks in the dirt; when a Tiger infielder made a good play, Fidrych would run across the diamond to congratulate him. And then there was his conversational rapport with the baseball itself; between pitches, Fidrych would speak directly to the ball, offering gentle words of encouragement before sending it off on another 60-foot-6-inch journey to the plate. If he felt a ball "had a hit in it," he would immediately return it to the umpire and ask for another. "I want to get it back in the ball bag and goof around with the other balls there," Fidrych explained to reporters. "Maybe it'll learn some sense and come out as a pop-up next time."

Flaky? You bet. But, as every initially skeptical team that faced him soon found out, the young man from Worcester, Massachusetts, could flat-out pitch. He didn't have a blistering fastball like Nolan Ryan's, or a vicious slider like Steve Carlton's; over the course of his rookie season, he would fan an underwhelming 97 batters in 250 innings. But the Bird worked with astonishing control and efficiency—for all his mound antics, it wasn't unusual to see Fidrych finish a complete game in two hours or less, having thrown fewer than 100 pitches.

Nicknamed for his marked physical resemblance to the Big Bird character from the PBS children's show *Sesame Street*, the Bird went about his life and his profession in a similarly guileless manner. (His rush-released 1977 autobiography would be titled *No Big Deal.*) He seemed genuinely mystified by his sudden celebrity; after the victory over the Yankees, with 47,855 Tigers fans on their feet and chanting "We want the Bird!" Tigers

DH Rusty Staub practically had to drag Fidrych back out on the field to take a curtain call.

Fidrych handled the avalanche of fan mail and interview requests—everyone from *Rolling Stone* to the children's magazine *Dynamite* came knocking on his door—with a goofy, good-natured grace, always insisting that he was just happy to be playing in the major leagues. When the Beach Boys played a concert in the Detroit area in the summer of '76, drummer Dennis Wilson personally asked Fidrych to emcee the show; the pitcher modestly declined, opting instead to watch the concert from up on the lighting rig, six-pack in hand.

Named the American League's starting pitcher in the '76 All-Star Game (he gave up two runs and was tagged with the L, but still put on a good show), Fidrych would finish 1976 with a 2.34 ERA and a 19-9 record—not bad at all for a kid who began the season in the minors, and didn't get his first major league starting assignment until May 15. His numbers were good enough to win the AL Rookie of the Year Award; he also finished second behind Jim Palmer of the Orioles (22-13, 2.51 ERA) for the AL Cy Young, and 11th in the AL MVP voting behind the Yankees' Thurman Munson.

But the most impressive stats Fidrych put up were in the attendance column. In 1976, even though the Tigers finished fifth in their division with an undistinguished 74-87 record, the team still boasted the fourth-highest attendance figure in the entire league—in only 18 starts at ancient Tiger Stadium, Fidrych accounted for nearly half of the season's 1,476,020 paying customers. The Bird was such a major gate attraction that other teams begged Detroit general manager Jim Campbell to make manager Ralph Houk alter the Tigers' pitching rotation so that Fidrych could draw more fans to their parks as well. When word got out that Fidrych's rookie salary was only $16,500, Detroit fans started a "Send a Buck to the Bird" fund-raising drive on his behalf. Fidrych sent the money back, saying, "I'm making more money now than I need. If they gave me a raise, I'd probably get cocky and pitch lousy."

With Mark Fidrych's mound theatrics and Charlie Finley's ongoing war with Bowie Kuhn (and his own players) dominating the sports pages in the spring and summer of '76, other newsworthy events seemed to go all but unnoticed. On May 27, Tigers center fielder Ron LeFlore tripled to lead off a home game against the Baltimore Orioles, running his hitting streak to 30 consecutive games, the longest such skein in the AL since Joe DiMaggio's 34 in 1949.

On June 22, Randy Jones of the San Diego Padres tied Christy Mathewson's 63-year-old NL record of 68 innings pitched without giving up a walk. Like Fidrych, Jones was a bushy-haired hurler whose pinpoint control more than made up for his lack of heat. Jones's "fastball" wouldn't have cracked the bubble window of an AMC Pacer, yet in 1975 and 1976 he was one of the top pitchers in the majors. Jones finished the first half of the '76 season with a 16-3 record, which earned him a starting job opposite Fidrych in the All-Star Game. Though he would cool off considerably in the second half—thanks to woeful run support from a Padres lineup that managed only 64 round-trippers all season—his final record of 22-14 with a 2.74 ERA was good enough to beat out the Mets' Jerry Koosman (21-10, 2.69), the Dodgers' Don Sutton (21-10, 3.06), and the Phils' Steve Carlton (20-7, 3.13) for the NL Cy Young Award.

By the time Jones and Fidrych faced off against each other at the July 13 All-Star contest in Philadelphia, the four division races looked to be all but over. Led by the hot hitting of team captain and AL MVP Thurman Munson (.302, 17 HRs, 105 RBIs), AL home run champ Graig Nettles (32 HRs, 93 RBIs), and new center fielder Mickey "Mick the Quick" Rivers (.312, 43 stolen bases), the Yankees were already 9½ games ahead of the Red Sox in the AL East. In the AL West, the Kansas City Royals were seven games ahead of the second-place Texas Rangers, while the once-dominant Oakland A's lingered 8½ back in third.

The Phillies, powered by Mike Schmidt (who led the league in homers for the third straight year with 38, and knocked in a team-leading 107 runs) and Greg "the Bull" Luzinski (.304, 21 HRs, 95 RBIs), boasted a starting rotation that included Steve Carlton (who'd gotten his slumping career back on track once the Phillies picked up Tim McCarver, who'd been

Carlton's favorite catcher when they were both with the Cardinals) and Jim Lonborg (18-10, 3.08 ERA), and possibly the best overall bullpen in the majors—Tug McGraw, Gene Garber, Ron Reed, Ron Schueler, and Wayne Twitchell would combine for 40 saves and a collective 2.49 ERA. The Phils had already racked up a 56-25 record—the best in the majors—by the All-Star break, and looked set to run away with the NL East.

The defending World Champion Cincinnati Reds were "only" six games up on the L.A. Dodgers, but with a lineup that included Joe Morgan (on his way to a second straight NL MVP Award, thanks to hitting .320 with 27 HRs, 111 RBIs, 113 runs scored, and 60 stolen bases), Pete Rose (.323, 215 hits, 130 runs), George Foster (.306, 29 HRs, 121 RBIs), and Ken Griffey (.336, 34 stolen bases), few were foolhardy enough to bet against the Big Red Machine.

All four teams were still in first by the time October rolled around, but the Yanks and Reds were the only ones who actually cruised to their division crowns. The Royals went 12-16 in September, giving the A's a fighting chance to run their string of division titles to six; but the speed-crazed A's, who set an AL record with 341 stolen bases—including 31 by "designated runner" Larry Lintz, who had exactly three official plate appearances all season—ultimately weren't strong enough in their other offensive categories to catch Kansas City. The Royals finally clinched the title on September 29 with a 4–0 victory over the A's in Oakland; when they returned to Kansas City, Royals shortstop Freddie Patek and utility man Cookie Rojas celebrated by taking a victory lap in Royals Stadium's outfield fountains.

But the Royals' regular season ended on a far less joyous note. On October 3, when the Royals and Twins met in Kansas City for the final game of the year, Royals third baseman George Brett and Hal McRae, the team's fiery DH, were locked in a dead heat for the AL batting title with Rod Carew of the Twins. Carew went 2-for-4 in the game, raising his average to .331. But by the time Brett and McRae were due up in the ninth inning, both players had already gone 2-for-3, which meant the batting race would literally come down to the last swing.

With one out, the bases empty, and his team down by three runs,

Brett blooped a short fly to left field; Twins outfielder Steve Brye was playing Brett unusually deep, and when the ball bounced off Royals Stadium's AstroTurf and over Brye's head, Brett tore around the bases for an inside-the-park homer. McRae, up next, grounded out to short, which meant that Brett had won the batting title, .333 to .332. McRae, an African-American, angrily accused Twins manager Gene Mauch and Brye of conspiring to "give" Brett a hit because they preferred to see a white player win the title instead of him. Mauch denied any such racial conspiracy, while Brye claimed he'd lost Brett's hit in the afternoon sun. Though it apparently never affected the friendship between McRae and Brett, who would play together for another 11 seasons, Brett later admitted that the ugly incident "took a lot of fun out of winning the batting title."

The National League batting race also came down to the wire, though it was resolved with considerably less rancor. Going into the last day of the season, Reds right fielder Ken Griffey was leading the pack with a .338 mark; his nearest challenger, Cubs third baseman Bill Madlock, was five points back at .333, so Griffey decided to sit out the last game of the season and rest up for the postseason. Madlock, who had won the '75 NL batting championship, defended his title by going 4-for-4 in the Cubs' final game against the Expos, raising his average to .339. After hearing of Madlock's perfect day, Griffey asked back into the Reds lineup; he struck out both times in his two trips to the plate, finishing second to Madlock with a .336 average.

Like the Royals in the AL West, the Philadelphia Phillies managed to turn a foregone conclusion into a nail-biting pennant race. Up 15½ games over the Pittsburgh Pirates on August 24, they seemed to go cold at the exact moment the Pirates got hot; by September 17, the Phils' lead had dwindled to a mere three games. "Even Napoleon had his Watergate," said Phillies manager Danny Ozark, who had a talent for malapropisms that rivaled Casey Stengel's or Yogi Berra's. Asked if team morale might be a problem, he reassured reporters that "this team's morality is not a factor."

With the bitter memory of their team's epic 1964 collapse still painfully fresh in their minds, Philadelphia fans—and sportswriters—began to panic. But the team went 13-3 down the final stretch, clinching the NL East pennant on September 26 in the first game of a doubleheader against the Expos. The Phillies had reached the postseason for the first time since 1950, but rumors of racial discord in the clubhouse seemed to overshadow the achievement. "The Phillies organization . . . was still behind most of the teams in baseball in terms of racial equality," Allen remembered in his autobiography. "There was a sense that the Phillies were working a quota on us, and the clubhouse started getting divided because of it. We were starting to feel like two teams, white and black."

In the media, much was made of the fact that Allen—who had already threatened to leave the team if Cuban vet Tony Taylor was left off the team's playoff roster—and several black players (including second baseman Dave Cash and outfielder Bobby Tolan, as well as "honorary black" Mike Schmidt) had held a private celebration of their own during the second game of that division-winning doubleheader in Montreal. As with McRae's outburst, the situation in Philadelphia indicated that nearly 30 years after Jackie Robinson broke baseball's color line, racial tensions still festered just below the game's surface.

It would have been exceptionally poetic for the team from "the Cradle of Liberty"—whose home stadium even featured a facsimile of the Liberty Bell—to have won the World Series in 1976. But Sparky Anderson's Reds clearly hadn't been watching CBS's nightly "Bicentennial Minute" segments; the only history they wanted to make was their own. The defending World Champs swept the Phillies in three straight playoff games, winning the third 7–6 on Ken Griffey's bases-loaded single in the bottom of the ninth.

The AL playoffs were a far more suspenseful affair, the series' momentum constantly shifting between the evenly matched Yankees and Royals. With the series tied at two games apiece, the Yanks took a 6–3 lead into the top of the eighth in the Bronx finale, only to watch George Brett tie things up on a three-run homer off reliever Grant Jackson. Then, in the bottom of the ninth, Yankee first baseman Chris Chambliss smoked the first pitch from Royals reliever Mark Littell over the right-field fence, and all hell broke loose at Yankee Stadium.

Yankee fans, ecstatic at the prospect of their first World Series since 1964, swarmed the field in celebration and—this being the Bronx in 1976—promptly set about destroying the place before Chambliss could even circle the bases. After being tripped between second and third, the hero of the playoffs tucked his helmet under his arm like a football to keep anyone from stealing it, then headed for the Yankees' dugout in an impressive display of open-field running, flattening several revelers along the way. In order to make the win official, two NYPD cops had to escort Chambliss back to the field so he could touch third base and home plate—or at least the areas where they'd been formerly situated.

Alas, Chambliss's pennant-winning clout would mark the last celebratory opportunity for Yankee fans in October '76. The Big Red Machine chewed up and spat out the Yanks in four straight, becoming the first team in baseball history to sweep a League Championship Series and a World Series in the same season, the sheer dominance and flawlessness of their play inspiring widespread comparisons to the 1927 Yankees. As Joe Morgan succinctly put it, "How can you have a much better team than this one?"

The 1976 Fall Classic was the first one to feature the designated hitter, the National League finally having acquiesced to its usage on the condition that pitchers would still bat in World Series falling on odd-numbered years. Dan Driessen, a backup first baseman and outfielder, served as the Reds' DH; his home run off Dock Ellis in Game 3, which put that contest out of reach, was the first DH-hit homer in World Series history. But the team's true offensive hero (and World Series MVP) was Johnny Bench; rebounding from a subpar year in which he hit only .234 with 16 homers, Bench mauled the Pinstripes' pitching at a .533 clip, and iced the final game with two round-trippers.

Equally key to the Reds' victory was the way that Pete Rose shut down Mickey Rivers, the Yankees' speedy leadoff man. Positioning himself almost even with the pitching rubber, so close that Rivers could practically smell the Aqua Velva aftershave that Rose hawked on TV ("because a man wants to smell like a man"), the Reds third baseman dared Rivers to line one past him. Utterly psyched out by Rose's aggressive stance, Rivers—who walked like an old man, yet led the '76 Yankees with a .312 average and 43 stolen bases—went completely cold in the Series, eking out only three singles in four games for a meager .167 average. (The Yankees collectively hit .222 for the Series; the Reds combined for a .313 average.)

Rivers's bat wasn't the only frigid aspect of the '76 World Series. NBC had offered baseball an additional $750,000 to broadcast the second game of the Series on a Sunday night, so as not to interfere with its football programming earlier in the day. Bowie Kuhn accepted NBC's offer, then showed up to watch Game 2 in nothing warmer than a sports jacket, even though the nighttime temperatures at Riverfront Stadium were hovering in the low 40s. Kuhn's sartorial gesture was widely mocked by the fans, players, and sportswriters who shivered their way through the contest; Yankees third baseman Graig Nettles even had to place a hot water bottle on his Louisville Slugger to keep it from turning into a batsicle. But like so much else with baseball in the second half of the '70s, money was dictating the changes—and everyone would simply have to find a way to adjust.

On November 2, Jimmy Carter defeated Gerald Ford in the 1976 presidential election, thus wiping the final residue of the Nixon years from the White House, if not the American psyche. Carter's election certainly marked a major turning point in American history, and an equally momentous event would occur in baseball history only three days later, when the first free-agent reentry draft was held at the Plaza Hotel in New York City. Thereafter, the financial side of baseball—and its effect upon the game in the front office, in the dugout, and on the field—would be forever changed.

Several teams—including the Cubs, Twins, Reds, Royals, White Sox, and, to no one's surprise, Charlie Finley's A's—refused to participate in the proceedings, citing either penury or the unwillingness to contribute to what they saw as an ominous precedent for labor relations. Even so, most of the 24 players eligible to auction off their services wound up signing deals worth far more than they'd ever believed it was possible to make. "You gotta be kidding," Orioles 20-game winner Wayne Garland reportedly exclaimed when the Indians offered him a 10-year, $2.3 million deal. "Quick, gimme a pen before they change their mind."

Angels owner Gene Autry rounded up all-star second baseman Bobby Grich from the Orioles and Joe Rudi and Don Baylor from the A's for a combined $4.9 million in contracts, while Padres owner Ray Kroc dished out $3.4 million in deals to A's exiles Rollie Fingers and Gene Tenace. Still smarting from what he saw as his team's (and thus his own) humiliation in the World Series, Yankee owner George Steinbrenner outspent everyone, first luring pitcher Don Gullett away from the Reds for a six-year deal worth $2 million, then wooing Reggie Jackson to the Big Apple—over the vocal objections of Yanks manager Billy Martin—for a $3 million, five-year contract. Jackson's deal was a massive one for the time, but the events it set in motion would be positively Shakespearean in scope. In 1977, Steinbrenner would get what he paid for, and then some.

CHAPTER 11

1977

For two cities that loved to dwell with distaste upon each other's differences, New York and Los Angeles experienced remarkably similar 1977s. It was a year in which each city produced or inspired some of the decade's most enduring films—L.A. with Hollywood fantasies *Star Wars* and *Close Encounters of the Third Kind*, and New York with urban sketches *Annie Hall* and *Saturday Night Fever*. Vibrant disco and punk scenes were thriving in both metropolises, and each city contributed some of the year's (and decade's) most enduring music, including such L.A.-spawned albums as Fleetwood Mac's *Rumours*, Steely Dan's *Aja*, and Jackson Browne's *Running on Empty*, and such intrinsically Noo Yawk platters as the Ramones' *Rocket to Russia*, Television's *Marquee Moon*, and Billy Joel's *The Stranger*.

For both cities, 1977 was also a year of significant and unexpected challenges. The worst West Coast drought in memory caused L.A. and 67 other California cities and towns to pass mandatory water-rationing measures, forcing residents to drain their swimming pools, use recycled water to nourish their gardens, and cut back significantly on their showers, laundry, and even the use of ice cubes. In New York, brutally hot July weather (combined with a freak lightning strike at a Con Edison substation on the Hudson River) caused a massive electrical blackout across four of the city's five boroughs, leaving more than 9 million people in the dark for over 25 hours, and triggering some of the worst looting and rioting in the city's history. There were even serial killers at large in both cities—Son of Sam (a.k.a. David Berkowitz) in New York, and the Hillside Strangler (actually two men, cousins Kenneth Bianchi and Angelo Buono) in Los Angeles.

In baseball, too, it was the best and worst of times for the major league franchises of New York and Southern California. Fans of the Yankees and Dodgers, two teams that hadn't won World Series trophies in over a decade, were treated to exciting seasons that led to a memorable meeting in the Fall Classic, while Mets and Angels fans were left to shake their heads and wonder why it all had gone so horribly wrong.

During the 1975 playoffs, A's slugger Reggie Jackson had memorably mused to reporters, "If I played in New York, they'd name a candy bar after me." While he was correct in thinking that his mighty left-handed swing and eminently quotable mouth were tailor-made for the short right porch of Yankee Stadium and the bright glare of the Big Apple media, the former AL MVP made a poor fit with his new pin-striped teammates.

There had been no superstars on the pennant-winning Yankees of 1976, only a bunch of talented, hardworking players who let Billy Martin (and, to a lesser extent, team captain Thurman Munson) run the show. When Yankee owner George Steinbrenner made it clear to Martin that he intended to spend some serious cash at the 1976 free agency reentry draft, Martin had begged Steinbrenner to go after A's outfielder/first baseman Joe Rudi, whose reliable play, low-key demeanor, and rock-solid work ethic perfectly meshed with Martin's vision of what "being a Yankee" was about. Instead, Steinbrenner signed Don Gullett, who had pitched well in the '76 Series against the Yankees despite having been injured for much of the year; and, over Martin's heated objections, he signed Jackson as well.

In Martin's eyes, there wasn't enough mustard in Coney Island to cover a hot dog like Jackson, and he was wary of having to deal with his new outfielder's highly developed ego, as well as the intrusions that Steinbrenner would inevitably make on behalf of his new $2.9 million baby. Jackson preferred to bat cleanup, but Martin made it clear during spring training that he wanted first baseman Chris Chambliss in the four hole—ostensibly because Chambliss struck out a lot less than the free-swinging Jackson, but also because Martin wanted to draw a preemptive line in the sand for everyone to see, demonstrating that *he* was the man in charge when it came to actually running the ball games.

With the off-season addition of not only Gullett and Jackson, but also White Sox shortstop Bucky Dent and Braves outfielder Jimmy Wynn, the Yankees could now boast All-Stars at every position—which meant that Martin had no excuse not to go all the way in '77. Not that the new additions would all pan out as hoped: Gullett would put up a 14-4 record for the Yankees, but still miss about half the season with arm troubles; Wynn proved a total bust and was released outright in July, having hit only .143 with a single home run in 30 games.

But the very presence of "George's boys"—i.e., anyone Steinbrenner had signed without Martin's consent—frustrated the already agitated Yankee manager, and injected a massive dose of tension into a clubhouse that had just a season earlier been one of the happiest in the big leagues. Many of the players, Munson, Graig Nettles, Sparky Lyle, and Mickey Rivers included, were angered that Steinbrenner hadn't adequately rewarded them for winning the pennant in 1976; and now he was spending nearly $3 million to land Jackson, a player that none of them wanted on the team. Martin tried to put on a happy face about Steinbrenner's acquisition of Jackson, but his choice of words often betrayed his real feelings about being saddled with the superstar slugger. "You never say no to getting a Reggie Jackson, because he can help this team," he told one reporter, helpfully adding, "I'd play Hitler and Mussolini if it would help us win."

Jackson was too sensitive to handle the sardonic jabs of acid-tongued teammates like Graig Nettles and Sparky Lyle, and he later admitted feeling hurt that his former A's teammates Catfish Hunter and Ken Holtzman kept their distance from him when he first arrived in the Yankees' clubhouse. Not that Jackson helped his own standing much with the comments he made to *Sport* magazine's Robert Ward during spring training, when the two men shared cocktails and conversation at a Fort Lauderdale bar called the Banana Boat. Ward's account of the exchange appeared in the May 23 issue of *Sport*, and included the immortal Reggie quote, "I'm the straw that stirs the drink. It all comes back to me. Maybe I should say me and Munson . . . but really he doesn't enter into it. He's being so damned insecure about the whole thing." That inflammatory salvo was followed in the piece by Jackson's even more damaging comment that "Munson thinks he can be the straw that stirs the drink, but he can only stir it bad."

Jackson claimed that Ward took the quotes (and several others in the piece) out of context; he also later called the article "the worst screwing I've ever got from the press." But for most of his new teammates, especially Munson, the *Sport* interview merely confirmed all of their negative suspicions. The lukewarm reception Jackson had originally received from the Yankee players in spring training seemed like a hero's welcome compared to the freeze-out he now got from his fellow players. Munson refused even to listen to Jackson's apology; Mickey Rivers and Carlos May moved their lockers away from Jackson's; and one anonymous Yankee left a note in Jackson's locker bearing the friendly message, "Suck my ass."

"The crazy times [with the Yankees] really began after Reggie announced he was 'the straw that stirred the drink,'" Nettles later reflected. "Of course, Billy right away wanted Reggie to know that he, Billy, was the straw. And all the while, there was George, sitting in his office thinking *he* was stirring the drinks." It made for a combustible cocktail, to say the least; and the fact that the Jackson-Martin-Steinbrenner drama was being played out in front of the New York tabloids ensured an exponential potential for subsequent bad vibes. "I didn't think the situation could get any worse," said Jackson. "I found out differently in the dugout at Fenway Park three weeks later."

After losing eight of their first 10 games, the Yankees had righted their fractious ship sufficiently by June 17, when they came into Boston for a three-game weekend series against the Red Sox; they were atop the AL East, 10 games above .500 and a half game ahead of their Beantown rivals. The Red Sox won the first game, 9-4—they would sweep the series, hitting a record 16 homers in three games—and were up 7–4 in the sixth inning of the nationally televised second game when Jim Rice blooped a hit to short right; Jackson, not wanting the ball to skip past him, took his time getting to it, which allowed Rice to make it into second. Martin, incensed because he thought Jackson was loafing on the play, sent outfielder Paul Blair out to take Jackson's position in right. "What the hell is going on?" Jackson demanded of Blair. "You've got to ask Billy that," mumbled Blair, refusing to meet Jackson's gaze.

Jackson jogged back to the third-base dugout, still somewhat unclear about what was happening—at least until he came face-to-face with Martin's angrily twisted visage. "What the fuck do you think you're doing out there?" Martin barked. "Anyone who doesn't hustle doesn't play for me." Jackson tried to explain that he wasn't loafing, then added, "But I'm sure that doesn't matter to you. You never wanted me on this team in the first place. You don't want me now. Why don't you just admit it?"

"I ought to kick your fucking ass," Martin replied.

Now it was Jackson's turn to lose his cool. "Who the fuck do you think you're talking to, old man?" he yelled. Martin, in full view of NBC's cameras, lunged toward Jackson, but was restrained by coaches Yogi Berra and Elston Howard before he could throw a punch; Jimmy Wynn, making his only real contribution to the '77 Yankees, held Jackson back. While Martin continued to scream, Jackson skulked back to the locker room and waited to duke it out with the manager in private; backup catcher Fran Healy, one of Jackson's few friends on the team, finally convinced him to leave the ballpark before the game ended. That night, Phil Pepe of the *New York Daily News* and two other sportswriters found Jackson shirtless and teary-eyed in his room at the Sheraton-Boston Hotel, completely beside himself with frustration and anger, and on the verge of "a breakdown." "It makes me cry the way they treat me on this team," the outfielder told the reporters. "I'm a big, black man with an IQ of 160, making $700,000 a year, and they treat me like dirt."

Steinbrenner, who took his manager's actions toward Jackson personally, wanted to fire Martin, but club president/general manager Gabe Paul and Jackson—both of whom knew that firing Martin would further alienate the other Yankees—talked him out of it. Still, Steinbrenner couldn't resist the impulse to twist the knife in Martin's back; not only did he let Martin know that he was treading on thin ice, but he spent the rest of the season planting rumors in the press that Martin was on the verge of being fired. When those rumors only resulted in an outpouring of fan support for Martin, Steinbrenner fed the press dubious tales of how Munson and other Yankees were coming to the owner and begging him to fire the skipper.

In one of the weirder turns of an already strange season, Steinbrenner and Martin actually filmed a TV commercial together that summer, one of a popular series of spots that featured sports figures arguing over the virtues of Miller Lite beer. "If I don't fire him by the All-Star break, I'll be glad to do it," was Steinbrenner's reply when he was first approached to do the spot. Martin, approached separately, couldn't believe his ears. "Are you fucking nuts?" he asked. But when the pair finally signed on, and time came to roll the tape, the assembled camera crew and ad agency people were amazed that Steinbrenner and Martin were not only on their best behavior, but genuinely seemed to enjoy each other's company. "You'd have thought they were lovers," marveled Marty Blackman, the ad exec who put the commercial together. "There was no clue of acrimony." The ad, of course, ended with Steinbrenner growling, "Billy, you're fired!"

But just as New York punk had recently exploded from the grim surroundings of the Bowery, and the nascent hip-hop movement would shortly emerge from the burned-out South Bronx—its birth partially midwifed by the neighborhood's massive per-capita increase in purloined turntables and sound systems following the July blackout—the Yankees somehow managed to win despite the tension and insanity that surrounded them. They won 50 of their last 70 games, moving into first place for good on August 23, and then hanging on to beat out extremely talented Red Sox and Orioles squads to win the AL East pennant by 2½ games.

Jackson hit .286 with 32 home runs and led the team with 110 RBIs (he made 17 of 20 stolen-base attempts as well), but there were heroes up and down the '77 Yankee lineup. Nettles led the team with 37 long balls and 99 runs scored, and drove in an additional 107; Munson hit .308 with

18 HRs and 100 RBIs; Chambliss hit .287 with 17 HRs and 90 RBIs; Rivers, though his stolen-base total was about half of the previous season's, hit .326. The team also received significant contributions from part-time players: Lou Piniella, who split most of his 103 games among left field, right field, and the DH slot, hit .330 with 12 HRs, while backup catcher/part-time DH Cliff Johnson—a midseason pickup from the Houston Astros—cranked 12 homers in only 142 at bats.

Though Hunter and Gullett were hampered throughout the season by health issues, the Yankees got solid performances out of starters Ed Figueroa (16-11, 3.57 ERA), Mike Torrez (14-12, 3.82), and a skinny Cajun lefty named Ron Guidry, who put up a 16-7 record with 176 strikeouts and a 2.82 ERA in his first full season. The year's AL Cy Young Award went to Sparky Lyle, who made 72 relief appearances, going 13-5 with 26 saves and a 2.17 ERA on his way to becoming the first AL reliever to win a Cy Young. Lyle, an inveterate wiseass, told a credulous reporter that he was going to put his Cy Young plaque in "a big glass case on my front lawn with a big spotlight and display it," modestly adding, "I'm only going to leave it out there for ten years."

If the Yankees often reflected the chaos, absurdity, and dog-eat-dog mentality of life in the Big Apple, then the Dodgers were like a Malibu motivational retreat in double knits. When longtime manager Walter Alston retired in late '76, Tommy Lasorda—a company man who had stayed loyal to the Dodgers organization for decades, despite offers to manage other teams—finally attained his dream job, and wasted no time putting his stamp on the team. Lasorda had already managed many of his players (including Steve Garvey, Ron Cey, Davey Lopes, and Bill Russell) in the minors, and from 1973 onward had served as one of Alston's coaches, so making the transition to Dodger manager wasn't hard; but the contrast between Alston's and Lasorda's managerial styles was enormous.

Alston was the strong, silent type, a man of few words who had managed Brooklyn's "Boys of Summer" to their first (and only) World Championship back in 1955, three years before Walter O'Malley moved the Dodger franchise to Los Angeles. He'd managed the team to three more World Championships in 1959, 1963, and 1965; but by the mid-'70s, the Dodger brass had begun to feel that Alston was becoming a museum piece, a man from another era who didn't understand the modern breed of ballplayers—and some of those ballplayers clearly felt the same way. "The generation gap had grown," explained Doug Rau, a left-hander who averaged nearly 15 wins a season for the Dodgers from 1974 through 1978. "It was time."

Unlike the reserved Alston, Lasorda reveled in being the center of attention, and was gregarious enough to charm (and hold his own with) Hollywood stars like Frank Sinatra and Don Rickles, with whom he hobnobbed regularly. But though Lasorda loved the spotlight, he also knew when to shine it on his players. Lasorda made it a point to know the names of everyone's wife and kids, find out what made each of his players tick, and constantly praise, flatter, encourage—whatever it took to get them to play winning baseball. In front of an open microphone, Lasorda was a veritable font of Dodger propaganda, running at the mouth to reporters about how he "bled Dodger Blue" and gave thanks and praises to "the Great Dodger in the sky." While many players thought Lasorda's "Dodger Blue" shtick was corny, most of them appreciated his competitive fire and personal touch.

"Lasorda came to me [at the beginning of the 1977 season] and said, 'I need you,'" remembered Reggie Smith, a talented outfielder who had had difficulties getting along with previous teams in Boston and St. Louis. "No one in baseball ever said that to me. So how could I let him down?" "The minute Tommy was named manager, we were revitalized," pitcher Burt Hooton told *Sports Illustrated*. "When he told us how much confidence he had in us, it lifted us. Walt never said things like that."

The 1977 Dodgers responded immediately to Lasorda's positive vibrations, exploding out of the gate at a 22-4 clip; Ron "the Penguin" Cey hit 11 homers in April, his 29 RBIs setting a record for that month. Whenever a Dodger player hit a home run, Lasorda made a point of greeting him at the top step of the dugout and hugging him like a proud uncle, a ritual that further fostered the image of the Dodgers as one big happy family enjoying themselves in the California sunshine.

The Reds, who had left the Dodgers in the dust in three of the previous four seasons, weren't buying it for a second. Reds manager Sparky Anderson needled Lasorda in the press, calling him "Walking Eagle" because "he's so full of it he can't fly," and predicting that the Reds would catch up to the Dodgers in midsummer, just like they usually did. "We will win our 95 games," added equally skeptical Reds hurler Jack Billingham. "If the Dodgers win 105 they'll beat us. But they aren't that good."

Only, the '77 Dodgers *were* that good—not good enough to win 105 games, perhaps (they finished 98-64), but good enough to spend all but three early April days in first place, and good enough to finish the season 10 games ahead of the second-place Big Red Machine. The Dodgers became the first team in history to have four players crack 30 or more home runs in a season—Steve Garvey hit 33 (while also batting .297 and leading the team with 115 RBIs), Smith hit 32, and Cey and left fielder Dusty Baker each hit 30. When Baker joined the 30-HR club on the last day of the season, backup outfielder Glenn Burke greeted him at the plate with raised palms, which Baker cheerfully slapped; this wordless exchange has since gone down in sports history as the first recorded "high five."

A former pitcher himself, Lasorda did a masterful job of handling the Dodger staff in 1977, employing the then-unusual practice of utilizing a set five-man pitching rotation, with excellent results. Sutton (14-8, 3.18 ERA), Rau (14-8, 3.43), Hooton (12-7, 2.62), Tommy John (who made an incredible comeback from "Tommy John" surgery, going 20-7 with a 2.78 ERA), and Rick Rhoden (16-10, 3.74) started all but four of the team's games in 1977. The Dodgers, who had always drawn well since moving to L.A., set a major league record by pulling in 2,955,087 fans during the season.

The Big Red Machine's 88-74 record—its worst showing since 1971—certainly wasn't attributable to the starting lineup. Johnny Bench, bouncing back from his previous season's shoulder troubles, batted .275 with 31 HRs and 109 RBIs; Joe Morgan's average dropped to .288, but he still hit 22 homers, scored 113 runs, and stole 49 bases; Ken Griffey hit .318 and scored 117 runs; Pete Rose hit .311; and George Foster, who had been runner-up in the MVP voting the year before, laid full claim to the trophy with a monster season in which he hit .320 with 52 home runs and 149 RBIs.

Though Foster would be the only player to hit the 50-homer mark in the 1970s, it's worth noting that balls were flying out everywhere in 1977—the 3,644 home runs hit by NL and AL players were an all-time major league record, and a massive jump from the 2,235 hit in 1976. The power surge was generally blamed on the Rawlings Sporting Goods Company, which had recently replaced Spalding as the official manufacturer of major league baseballs. Sportswriter Roger Angell joked that the balls, which were made at the Rawlings plant in Haiti, might have been "secretly polished there with applications of Haitian ju-ju oil," while a *Sports Illustrated*–commissioned study confirmed that the new balls were indeed harder and livelier than their predecessors.

For all their power, the 1977 Reds suffered from a lack of reliable pitching—Anderson used 12 different starters over the course of the season. But many observers blamed the trade of Tony Perez to the Montreal Expos at the end of the 1976 season for the Reds' slip in '77. Dan Driessen, now the Reds' full-time first baseman, actually put up some rather Perez-like numbers, hitting .300 with 17 homers and 91 RBIs, but the problem was that Perez's charisma and leadership were missed even more than his bat. "Losing Tony took so much chemistry away," lamented Reds president Bob Howsam. "He had more of an effect on our team—on and off the field—than I ever realized."

The Reds' season might have turned out even worse had they not picked up Mets great Tom Seaver in a June 15 trade for pitcher Pat Zachry, infielder Doug Flynn, and outfielders Steve Henderson and Dan Norman, a trade initiated by the Mets as part of the infamous "Midnight Massacre," which also sent Dave Kingman to the Padres for Bobby Valentine and Paul Siebert.

(Before the season's end, Kingman would be released by the Padres, picked up by the Angels, and traded to the Yankees, becoming the only player to homer for teams from all four divisions in a single year, as well as the only player to homer for the Mets and Yankees in the same season. Kingman would play only eight games with the Bronx Bombers, but he homered in half of them; though the team left him off its postseason roster, the Yankee players did vote him a $200 World Series share.)

The Seaver trade shocked Mets fans and players alike; more than anyone, Seaver had been the face of the Mets' organization since the late '6os, the player whose immense talents had carried the team (and its fans) through years both glorious and miserable. But Seaver's outspoken involvement with the players' union made Mets chairman M. Donald Grant's blood boil, as did Seaver's request for a $250,000-a-year salary. Seaver, who craved job security even more than a raise, was willing to sign a contract extension with the team, but negotiations broke down when Grant planted an item in the *New York Daily News*—via sportswriter Dick Young (who had been taking the Mets' side on stories about Seaver's salary demands)—alleging that Seaver wanted more money solely because his wife, Nancy, was jealous of the raise their old friend Nolan Ryan had recently received from the Angels. Disgusted that the Mets would stoop so low as to drag his wife into the controversy, Seaver called off further talks. That night, Grant traded him to Cincinnati.

The trade worked out very well for the Reds: Seaver pitched in 20 games for Cincinnati in 1977, going 14-3 with a 2.34 ERA, ending the season with 21-6 record, a 2.58 ERA, and 196 strikeouts. For disgruntled Mets fans, the rest of the season would hold only two lasting memories: the Cubs-Mets "blackout" game of July 13, and Seaver's return appearance at Shea on August 21, during which he struck out 11 Mets, doubled off his old teammate Jerry Koosman, and scored two runs in front of a crowd of 46,265, most of whom cheered wildly for their exiled hero and booed the Mets as they lost 5–1. After that bittersweet occasion, the team (managed by third baseman Joe Torre, who had taken the reins from Joe Frazier in May) found it difficult to draw anyone to the park; for the rest of 1977, it wasn't uncommon to see fewer than 5,000 people in the stands at Shea.

In the July 13 game, the citywide power outage occurred just as Lenny Randle came up to bat in the sixth; with only a rudimentary emergency light setup to fall back on, Bud Harrelson, Craig Swan, and some of the other Mets players drove their cars onto the field, then pantomimed a game in the vehicles' headlights for the crowd's amusement. Unlike in other parts of the city, there were no injuries or incidents of looting at Shea, though getting home from the ballpark through the darkened streets was certainly a challenging experience for all involved. When the Cubs players finally returned to their hotel, they had to walk up as many as 16 flights of stairs in complete darkness, to rooms without working air-conditioning. The two teams were supposed to meet again the following afternoon; but since the power still wasn't on, and Shea Stadium's toilets worked on an electric ejector system, the game had to be postponed on account of a lack of working restroom facilities. It seemed a fitting epitaph for the sixth-place, 64-98 Mets team of 1977, which stank as badly as Shea's commodes.

Over in Anaheim, Nolan Ryan—the pitcher whose lucrative Angels contract had allegedly inspired so much jealousy from the Seavers—posted his best season in several years, going 19-16 with 341 strikeouts and a 2.77 ERA, though he also issued 204 bases on balls along the way. Frank Tanana went 15-9 with a 2.54 ERA and 205 strikeouts. Bobby Bonds led the team with 37 homers, 115 RBIs, and 41 stolen bases (tied in the latter category with second baseman Jerry Remy), and new free-agent signing Don Baylor hit 25 homers, drove in 75 runs, and stole 26 bases.

But the team still finished in fifth place in the AL West with a 74-88 record, 11½ games behind fourth-place Minnesota, whose first baseman Rod Carew snagged his sixth career AL batting title—and first MVP Award—hitting .388 with 38 doubles, 16 triples, 14 homers, 100 RBIs, and 128 runs scored. At least Seattle and Oakland, who finished behind the Angels, had excuses for their lousy years; the Mariners were a first-year expansion team that narrowly missed finishing in the division cellar, while Charlie Finley had completely gutted the A's of every last player from the Oakland dynasty years save Vida Blue.

Ryan's powerful pitching performance was good enough for third place in the AL Cy Young voting, while second place went to his old rival Jim Palmer, who enjoyed yet another 20-win season, posting a 2.91 ERA and striking out 193 hitters in the process. Palmer's '77 Orioles squad was a typically solid Earl Weaver–run team, mixing dependable starting pitching—Rudy May, picked up the previous season from the

Yankees, notched 18 wins, while Mike Flanagan and Ross Grimsley won 15 and 14, respectively—with a tough lineup highlighted by the emergence of 21-year-old first baseman/DH Eddie Murray, who was named the AL Rookie of the Year after hitting .283 with 27 homers and 88 RBIs, a performance that he would repeatedly better over his 21-season Hall of Fame career. (Murray's Rookie of the Year counterpart in the NL was the Expos' young outfielder Andre Dawson, who hit .282 with 19 HRs, 65 RBIs, and 21 stolen bases.)

By contrast, the Red Sox, who also came within a hair of winning the AL East, lacked the balance of the Yankees or Orioles. Thanks to the power-hitting contributions of Jim Rice—who led the AL with 39 home runs while hitting .320, driving in 114 runs, and adding 15 triples for good measure—first baseman George "Boomer" Scott (33 HRs, 95 RBIs), third baseman Butch Hobson (30 HRs, 112 RBIs), Carl Yastrzemski (.296, 28 HRs, 102 RBIs), and Carlton Fisk (.315, 26 HRs, 102 RBIs), the Bosox set a franchise record with 213 home runs.

But despite the presence of Luis Tiant, Fergie Jenkins, Rick Wise, and Bill Lee, who had finally recovered from his brawl with the Yankees the year before, Boston's pitching was a total mess. Lee laid the blame squarely at the doorstep of first-year Red Sox manager Don Zimmer. "Zimmer hurt us that year," Lee later testified. "He didn't have a clue on how to run a pitching staff. . . . At one point, he had eight guys moving in and out as starters. He also held out pitchers so they could face certain teams. . . . It was a half-assed way to run things." With the exception of closer Bill Campbell, who went 13-9 with 31 saves, no member of the Red Sox staff won more than 12 games in 1977.

Lee, Jenkins, and Wise made no attempt to hide their disdain for Zimmer. Lee referred to him as "the Gerbil" because of the manager's chubby cheeks, while Jenkins dubbed the Red Sox skipper "Buffalo Head," since the buffalo was not known to be a particularly bright creature. In Zimmer's honor, Lee, Jenkins, Wise, Carbo, and relief pitcher Jim Willoughby formed a drinking (and smoking) club that they christened the Loyal Order of the Buffalo Heads. "Zimmer thought we were a danger to his ballclub," Lee explained. "He was of the old school, and we were part of the counter-culture. He and the front office thought that we were going to corrupt the morals of the rest of the team." Mostly, though, they just corrupted their own livers; Jenkins was supposedly so hung over during a September 18 game in Baltimore that he fell asleep in the bullpen cart, a move that didn't exactly improve relations between him and Zimmer.

To no one's surprise, Jenkins, Willoughby, and Wise would be gone by the time the '78 season rolled around. Wise would be traded to Cleveland in exchange for a brash young fireballer named Dennis Eckersley—who would turn out to be even a hardier partier than Wise. "Eck" provided the lone highlight of the Indians' dire 1977 season on May 30, when he pitched a no-hitter against the California Angels, striking out 12 and walking only one batter in the process. Eckersley spent much of the game heckling Angels starter Frank Tanana, who pitched a good game himself, giving up only one run on five hits. When Angels center fielder Gil Flores came up in the ninth with two outs, Eckersley became frustrated with the way Flores kept stepping out of the batter's box, and told him so. "Get in there," he shouted. "There's one more out, and you're it!" True to Eck's prediction, Flores struck out to end the game and clinch the no-hitter.

For Mark Fidrych, Eck's eccentric counterpart on the Detroit Tigers, 1977 was as frustrating as 1976 had been magical. In March, he tripped over a sprinkler while horsing around in the outfield before a spring training game, and had to undergo surgery to repair the cartilage in his left knee. Fidrych was back on the mound only two months later, but probably returned too soon; he messed up his mechanics by favoring his injured knee, and wound up damaging his shoulder as a result. By mid-July, Fidrych was out for the rest of the season, and the Tigers—despite impressive seasons by Ron LeFlore (.325 with 212 hits, 100 runs scored, 10 triples, 16 HRs, and 39 stolen bases), rookie pitcher Dave Rozema (15-7, 3.09 ERA), and 22-year-old first baseman Jason Thompson (.270, 31 HRs, 105 RBIs), the Tigers wound up in fourth place in the AL East, 26 games behind the Yankees.

Despite losing the Bird, the Tigers still managed to finish higher than the Indians (71-90), the Brewers (67-95), and the newly hatched Toronto

Blue Jays, who drew more than 1.7 million fans despite a 54-107 record and (more unbelievably) an Ontario ordinance that forbade the sale of beer at professional sporting events. When Ontario premier Bill Davis, whose government was responsible for the ruling, showed up at the Blue Jays' snow-covered inaugural home game on April 7, he was greeted by irate chants of "We want beer!" from the assembled spectators. Though the Blue Jays were partly owned by Labatt Breweries, their fans would have to wait another five years before they could enjoy a cold brew at Exhibition Stadium.

There was plenty of beer a-flowin' in Chicago during the summer of '77, however, and for the first time in ages, the fans at Wrigley Field and Comiskey Park weren't drinking to drown their sorrows. No one had expected the Cubs or the White Sox to be remotely competitive; and yet, as play wound down for the All-Star break, each team stood atop its division with a 2½-game lead. Attendance was booming at both parks—Sox owner Bill Veeck even installed a public shower in the Comiskey centerfield bleachers to cool off the sweltering crowds—and Windy City watering holes buzzed incessantly with talk of an all-Chicago World Series.

With the exception of Bobby Murcer, who had come from the Giants in exchange for two-time NL batting champ Bill Madlock, and Bill Buckner, who the team had received from the Dodgers in return for Rick Monday, the Cubs were a bunch of no-names; but from the end of May to the first week of August, the North Siders somehow managed to hold on to first place in the NL East. Murcer led the team with 27 homers and 89 RBIs, and Buckner hit .284, but the team also got steady contributions from some unlikely sources: third baseman Steve Ontiveros, who had been a throw-in in the Madlock/Murcer deal, hit .299; shortstop Ivan DeJesus, who had come over from the Dodgers with Buckner, led the team with 24 steals and 91 runs scored; and outfielders Jerry Morales, Larry Biittner, and part-timer Greg Gross hit .290, .298, and .322, respectively.

But what really kept the Cubs in business for most of the season was the standout pitching performances from beefy starter Rick "the Whale"

Reuschel (20-10, 2.79 ERA in 252 innings) and closer Bruce Sutter, who put together one of the most dominating seasons of any reliever in history, going 7-3 with a 1.34 ERA, 31 saves, and 129 Ks in 107⅓ innings. The secret of Sutter's success was the "split-fingered fastball," a forkball-like pitch he'd developed that could break in any direction he chose, depending on how much pressure he applied with his index or middle digit. "It comes in like a fastball for 55 feet," testified Cubs catcher George Mitterwald. "Then it explodes." Opposing batters found the pitch nearly impossible to hit; unfortunately, since the rest of the Cubs bullpen had difficulty getting anyone out, Sutter wound up pitching in 44 of the team's first 88 games. He couldn't take the Mike Marshall–style pace, and arm troubles kept him on the bench for most of August, during which the Cubs slid inexorably into fourth place, where they would finish the season with an 81-81 record.

Down on the South Side, the White Sox began the season in seemingly even direr straits than their North Side neighbors. Too broke to pick up any big-name free agents, Veeck took a chance on a couple of reclamation projects, pitcher Steve Stone (who had a torn rotator cuff, an injury no pitcher had previously come back from) and third baseman Eric Soderholm, whose knees were in worse shape than the city's derelict Robert Taylor Homes housing project. Veeck also shipped All-Star shortstop Bucky Dent to the Yankees in exchange for outfielder Oscar Gamble and cash, and star pitchers Rich Gossage (whom Veeck had unsuccessfully tried to convert to a starter in '76) and Terry Forster to the Pirates for outfielder Richie Zisk. The fact that both Zisk and Gamble would be free agents at the end of the year didn't deter Veeck; even if the team finished in last place, he figured, fans would come out to see his rent-a-sluggers hit home runs.

Veeck turned out to be more correct than even he could have imagined. The 1977 "South Side Hitmen," as they were dubbed, couldn't field, run, or (for the most part) pitch—but they sure could knock the living crap out of a baseball. Gamble, who under Veeck's merry regime was free to let his voluminous Afro grow as large as he pleased, responded with the best season of his career, hitting a team-leading 31 homers, batting

.297, and driving in 83 runs. Zisk, whose long bombs inspired the Comiskey denizens to hoist signs with slogans like "Pitch at Risk to Rich Zisk," hit 30 and led the team with 101 RBIs. Soderholm hit .280 and added 25 homers while committing only eight errors at third; of course, he would probably have made more had he actually been able to reach most of the balls hit at him. Shortstop Alan Bannister, his noodle-armed partner on the left side of the diamond, made a whopping 40 errors. Twenty-two-year-old center fielder Chet Lemon hit 19 HRs and led the team with 99 runs scored; left fielder Ralph Garr hit .300; second baseman Jorge Orta hit 11 homers and drove in 84 runs; part-time first baseman/DH Lamar Johnson hit .302 with 18 HRs; and Jim Spencer, a journeyman first baseman who had previously kicked around with the Angels and Rangers, added another 18 round-trippers, and enjoyed two different two-homer, eight-RBI games that season at Comiskey. They all helped set a team record of 192 home runs, up considerably from the previous top Chisox mark of 138.

The Hitmen resonated with South Siders in a way that no Sox team had since 1959. "I think our fans especially love this team because, by today's standards, it seems down and out, unsung and lower class," Veeck told *Sports Illustrated*. Fans packed Comiskey all summer, setting a franchise attendance record of 1,657,135. The feeling at the old ballpark was electric and celebratory; along with participating in Harry Caray's seventh-inning "Take Me Out to the Ball Game" sing-along, Comiskey's denizens spontaneously developed the ritual singing of "Na-na-na-na-hey-hey-hey goodbye!"—the chorus of the 1969 song "Kiss Him Goodbye" by one-hit wonders Steam—whenever the Sox put a game out of reach, and rewarded Sox sluggers with standing ovations and curtain calls nearly every time they socked one over the distant Comiskey fences.

While the '77 Sox didn't completely collapse like their uptown cousins, they ultimately proved too one-dimensional to hang with the well-rounded Kansas City Royals, who burned up the diamond at a demonic 45-16 pace throughout August and September. The '77 Royals squad was their strongest of the decade, with right fielder Al Cowens (.312, 32 doubles, 14 triples, 23 HRs, 112 RBIs), DH Hal McRae—who hit .298 and drove in 92 runs while also racking up 54 doubles, 11 triples, and 21 HRs, becoming the first player since Joe Medwick in 1937 to top 50 doubles, 10 triples, and 20 homers in a season—and George Brett (.312, 32 doubles, 13 triples, 22 HRs, 88 RBIs) all making an excellent case for team MVP. five-foot-four shortsop Freddie Patek led the league with 53 stolen bases, while center fielder Amos Otis and second baseman Frank White added 23 bags each. The team also got a 20-12, 3.04-ERA, 244-strikeout performance from staff ace Dennis Leonard, while Paul Splittorff went 16-6 with a 3.69 ERA and Jim Colborn (whose May 14 no-hitter against the Rangers was the first ever thrown at Royals Stadium by a Kansas City pitcher) went 18-14 with a 3.62 ERA. They finished the season with a 102-60 record, the best in the majors. The White Sox finished in third place, 12 games back, with a 90-72 record.

The Sox were tough customers, but the Royals' stellar season was also very nearly preempted by the Texas Rangers, whose surprising 94-68 record was surely the best-ever single-season showing by a team that played under four different managers. The Rangers' first 1977 manager was Frank Lucchesi, whose run-in with infielder Lenny Randle during spring training made the subsequent Martin-Jackson contretemps seem tame by comparison. Randle, a hard-nosed player in the Pete Rose mold, had been frustrated over being benched in favor of rookie Bump Wills; when Lucchesi called Randle a "punk" for complaining about the situation, Randle—a black belt in karate—responded with a flurry of damaging punches to his manager's face and torso. Lucchesi was sent to the hospital; Randle was suspended for 30 days, fined $10,000, and sent to the Mets.

But 62 games into the season, with the team treading water at 31-31, the Rangers' front office decided to fire Lucchesi, claiming he'd lost control of his players. Lucchesi's replacement was Eddie Stanky, the 60-year-old former Brooklyn Dodger, who hadn't managed a team since 1968. After only one game with the Rangers, Stanky handed in his resignation, pleading "homesickness." Coach Connie Ryan took over for six games until the team found another taker for the vacant position, who turned out to be Orioles coach Billy Hunter. Under Hunter, the team—led by shortstop Toby Harrah (27 HRs, 87 RBIs), first baseman Mike Hargrove (.305, 18 HRs), Jim Sundberg (who was quickly developing into one of the majors' best defensive catchers), and a pitching rotation that included Doyle Alexander (17-11, 3.65 ERA), Gaylord Perry (15-12, 3.37, 177 Ks), Bert Blyleven (14-12, 2.72, 182 Ks, and a September 22 no-hitter against the Angels), and Dock Ellis (10-6, 2.90)—went an impressive 60-33 the rest of the season, though that still wasn't enough to catch the Royals.

But for sheer absurdity, the Rangers' managerial revolving door couldn't come close to touching Ted Turner's brief career as Atlanta's skipper. Already in hot water with commissioner Bowie Kuhn, who charged the Braves owner with "tampering" with free-agent outfielder Gary Matthews—i.e., making inappropriate contact with Matthews while he was still a Giants player—Turner sent Kuhn's blood pressure through the roof on May 11, when Turner briefly installed himself as manager of his last-place team.

No baseball owner had managed his own team since 1950, when Connie Mack retired after 50 years of wearing both hats for the Philadelphia A's. Mr. Mack, of course, knew a few things about baseball; Turner, who had only owned the Braves for a little over a year, was still rather unschooled in that particular department. But he knew that he wasn't happy about his Braves losing 16 straight games, so he gave skipper Dave Bristol a paid vacation and attempted to right the ship himself. "You're crazy," Bristol replied. "But go ahead. It's your team."

Suiting up in full Braves uniform (complete with backward stirrups and cleats he'd snagged without asking from Cito Gaston's locker), Turner announced to his incredulous players that he'd be managing the team for the next 10 days. The Braves players had become used to Turner hanging around the clubhouse, organizing team poker tournaments, and running out onto the field to congratulate them after their rare home runs—activities that Kuhn and NL president Chub Feeney distinctly disapproved of—but this was too much. "I couldn't look at him," remembered Braves pitcher Buzz Capra. "I had to look away because it was the funniest sight you'd ever want to see, him in a baseball uniform. Let alone now he's going to manage."

Turner's managerial tenure lasted for exactly one game, a 2–1 loss to the Pirates that extended the team's losing streak to 17. Feeney immediately moved to bar Turner from the Braves' dugout, citing baseball rule 20-E, which forbade an individual from managing a team in which he owns stock. Though the rule was intended to guard against potential conflicts of interest, Feeney and Kuhn were more than happy to apply it to the Turner situation. Third-base coach Vern Benson took over until Bristol got back, and broke the team's losing skid in his first game as interim manager. The Braves celebrated the rare win by breaking out beer and champagne, provided of course by their owner and former manager. "Let's play again right now," whooped Jeff Burroughs, whose 41 homers and 114 RBIs would be the best things about the Braves' dismal season. "We're hot!"

In the NL East, the Phillies, Pirates, and Cardinals spent much of the season battling for a distant second place far below the Cubs, then suddenly found themselves in the thick of a pennant race as the Cubs collapsed. The Cardinals eventually slid downward as well, leaving the Phillies and Pirates to duke it out. Though the Cards' speedy 21-year-old shortstop Garry Templeton wowed fans by hitting .322 with 200 hits, 18 triples, and 94 runs scored, it was a teammate nearly twice his age who made some of the year's biggest headlines: On August 29, Lou Brock stole two bases against the Padres, tying and then breaking Ty Cobb's record of 892 stolen bases.

Though it didn't get as much coverage in the media as Hank Aaron's passing of Babe Ruth's home run mark, Brock's achievement was considerable; not only had Cobb's 892 stood almost a decade longer than Ruth's 714, but the analytical way Brock went about stealing bases was completely antithetical to Cobb's slide-and-slash intimidation tactics. "About as quickly as a pitcher can throw to his catcher and have his catcher throw to second is 2.9 seconds," he explained to *Sports Illustrated*, shortly before breaking the record. "I know I can get to second in 3.4 seconds or less. I am daring them to make that play in 2.9 and be on target. I know I'll always be there in my 3.3 to 3.4. I can't outrun the ball, but a catcher can't throw it until he gets it." Brock, who had come up in an era of station-to-station baseball, when most managers and players preferred to "wait for the long ball," was pleased to note that the game had changed considerably in the 1970s. "There [used] to be a gentlemen's agreement not to run," he explained. "But that attitude is changing. Now running is totally acceptable. Everybody does it."

The Pirates were definitely running, leading the league with 260 steals—shortstop Frank Taveras led the majors with 70 swipes of his own. Bucs right fielder Dave Parker led the league with a .338 batting average, and also chipped in 44 doubles, 21 homers, 88 RBIs, and 107 runs scored. Parker, who ruffled the feathers of more than a few baseball purists by sporting a gold earring and necklaces on the field, was once asked why he wore a Star of David medallion. "Because I'm David, and I'm a star," he replied. But even brilliant seasons from John Candelaria (20-5, 2.34 ERA) and closer Rich "Goose" Gossage (11-9, 1.62 ERA, 26 saves, and a team-leading 151 Ks in 133 innings) combined with Parker's star power weren't enough to make the Phillies walk the plank. The Bucs finished five games in back of the rival Phils, who won 101 games for the second straight season.

The defending NL East champs initially got off to a sluggish start, going 7-9 in April. As manager Danny Ozark memorably put it, "the players expected the season to be a cheesecake." But as the Cubs' fortunes declined, the Phillies made their move, taking over first place for good in August while running off a franchise-record 13-game winning streak. Steve Carlton, who won his second Cy Young with a 23-10, 198-K, 2.64-ERA performance, was the ace of the Phillies' staff, but 23-year-old Larry Christenson came through with 19 wins of his own, while bullpen mainstays Gene Garber, Ron Reed, Warren Brusstar, and Tug McGraw pitched over a quarter of the team's total innings among them, combining for 46 saves and a collective 2.59 ERA.

It was on offense, though, that the Phillies really took their opponents apart. They led the NL with a .279 team batting average and 847 runs scored, and their club-record 186 homers were second in the league only to the Dodgers' 191. Mike Schmidt's .274 batting average was the lowest among the Phils' starting regulars, and he still scored 114 runs while collecting 104 walks, 27 doubles, 11 triples, 38 homers, and 101 RBIs. His teammate Greg "the Bull" Luzinski had an even better season, hitting .309 while doubling 35 times, stroking 39 long shots, and driving in 130.

Luzinski also showed that his heart was as big as his bat, buying out a 126-seat section in the fifth level of Veterans Stadium's left-field stands for the entire season (at a personal cost of over $20,000), and donating the tickets to a different underprivileged children's charity for each Phillies home game. Luzinski also offered to pay $100 to the charity of choice for any player whose home run reached "the Bull Ring," as Section 573 became known.

The Phillies were also a serious threat on the base paths; Larry Bowa, their scrappy shortstop, stole 32 bases in 35 tries, while center fielder Garry Maddox (who hit .292 with 10 triples, 14 homers, and 74 RBIs) stole 22 out of 28, and outfielder Bake McBride stole 27 out of 31 after coming over from the Cardinals in a midseason trade. The slap-hitting McBride, whose 31-inch bat was the shortest in the majors, batted .339 in 85 games with the Phillies, and surprised everyone by socking 11 homers in the same span. Part-time outfielder and full-time cutup Jay Johnstone couldn't run so well, but he did hit .284 with 15 homers, and helped keep the clubhouse loose. With Dick Allen no longer on the team—the aging slugger had signed with the A's in the off-season as a free agent, then retired for good after playing 54 games for Oakland—it was up to Johnstone to organize the team's monthly "cold duck parties," postgame bull sessions wherein the players could relax and air their gripes over several glasses of cold duck, the '70s version of wine coolers. Allen and Tony Taylor had started the tradition; now Johnstone was carrying it on.

"Nobody *had* to show up," Johnstone explained, "but we strongly suggested that they make it—sort of a command performance to clear the air—and it really worked. . . . You would be amazed at how petty little things can grow into major issues. So we would let it rip and throw it all out for discussion. Play a little music, tell a few jokes, maybe even hire a dancer or two, and above all, have some laughs. . . . It helped us become a team."

Unfortunately for the Phillies, it would take more than togetherness and cheap wine to defeat the Dodgers in the NLCS. They did manage to win

7–5 in Game 1, despite a Ron Cey grand slam off Steve Carlton. Luzinski hit a mammoth two-run shot off Tommy John in the first inning, then watched from home plate as Dodger reliever Elias Sosa balked home the Phillies' seventh and final run in the top of the ninth. It was the first Phillies postseason victory since the 1915 World Series; it would also be their last of 1977.

The Dodgers won Game 2 7–1, paced by a Dusty Baker grand slam off of Jim Lonborg, and won 6–5 in Game 3, thanks to a succession of defensive meltdowns on the part of the Phillies in the top of the ninth. Baker struck the fatal blow in a rain-drenched Game 4—NL president Chub Feeney refused to postpone the game, despite the steady downpour throughout—with a two-run homer in the second inning, running his playoff series total of RBIs to an NL-record eight. Tommy John, whose career had looked like it might be over just a year earlier, pitched a complete game, striking out McBride in the ninth to clinch the 4–1 victory and the NL championship. "In this one," claimed a jubilant Lasorda, never one for understatement, "the script was written by God."

If God penned the NLCS, then the ALCS rematch between the Yankees and Royals was scripted by Martin Scorsese. There was no shortage of tough-guy posturing or gritty drama throughout the series, which once again went the full five games. After sailing to a 7–2 victory in Game 1 on home runs by John Mayberry, Al Cowens, and Hal McRae, the Royals finally awakened the slumbering Yankees in the sixth inning of Game 2, when McRae upended Willie Randolph while breaking up a double play. Billy Martin called McRae's body block "a cheap shot," while McRae pleaded innocent. "If I was trying to hurt a guy," the infamously hard-nosed player retorted, "I would cut him around the knees." The Yankees, fired up by the incident, scored three runs in the bottom of the sixth, and won the game 6–2.

The series moved to Kansas City for Game 3, which the Royals won 6–2 on the four-hit pitching of Dennis Leonard. In the first inning of Game 4, Nettles laid a carbon copy of McRae's block on second baseman Frank White, and then the Yankees roughed up Royals starter Larry Gura, driving him out in the third after four runs and six hits. But

New York starter Ed Figueroa couldn't make it through the fourth, and Sparky Lyle—who had pitched 2⅓ innings the day before—came in and held the Royals at bay for 5⅓ innings, allowing only two hits on the way to sealing the 6–4 Yankee victory. "I pitched better because I was a little tired," Lyle said afterward. "When I have too much rest, I become too strong and I muscle the ball, which straightens out my slider."

Game 5's drama began before the first pitch was even thrown. Reggie Jackson had gone 1-for-14 thus far in the series, so Martin decided to bench him against tough Royals lefty Paul Splittorff, penciling Paul Blair into the lineup instead. Jackson felt that Martin made the move to humiliate him, and quietly stewed on the bench while his teammates took the field. In the first inning, George Brett tripled off of Yankees starter Ron Guidry, and fell backward as he slid into third. As Brett tried to regain his balance, Nettles stepped back and kicked Brett in the face. "The funny thing about that is Graig and I were such good friends," Brett later laughed, but the bad blood between the Yankees and Royals was running deeper at that moment than any friendship. Still, Thurman Munson, whose sense of fair play may have been offended by Nettles's sucker kick, jumped on top of Brett and protected him from further blows during the bench-clearing scrum that ensued.

Once the dust cleared, Guidry gave up three runs and left the game in the third inning; but Mike Torrez came in and kept the Yankees in the game with 5⅓ scoreless frames. In the top of the eighth, with two on and one out, Martin sent Jackson into the game as a pinch hitter for DH Cliff Johnson; Jackson, facing reliever Doug Bird, singled in a run, cutting the score to 3–2. The Royals threatened to expand their lead in the bottom of the eighth, but Lyle came in and snuffed out the blaze, striking out Cookie Rojas with two on and two out. The Yankees exploded for three runs in the top of the ninth on a couple of singles, a walk, a sac fly, and a George Brett error, making it 5–3 in their favor. Lyle, pitching for the third straight day, gave up a one-out single to Frank White, then induced Freddie Patek to ground into a series-ending double play.

While the diminutive Patek sat sobbing in frustration in the Royals' dugout, champagne corks popped like rifle fire in the Royals Stadium visitors' clubhouse. In the midst of the mayhem, Martin snuck up behind George Steinbrenner and doused him with bubbly. "That's for trying to fire me." Martin grinned. "What do you mean 'trying'?" the Yankees owner shot back. "If I want to fire you, I'll fire you."

In 1963, the last time the Dodgers and Yankees had faced each other in a World Series, a Sandy Koufax–led L.A. squad had swept the heavily favored Bronx Bombers in four games. This time, the teams seemed evenly matched: The Dodgers had hit only .266 for the season compared to the Yankees' .281, but they'd outhomered them 191–184 and outstolen them 114–93, and the Dodger staff's 3.22 ERA—even allowing for the American League's DH factor—was still substantially more impressive than the Yankees' collective 3.61. But to hear the media tell it, the '77 Fall Classic wasn't about numbers; it was a showdown between the forces of light (fighting on behalf of Lasorda's "Great Dodger in the sky") and the minions of darkness (playing in the service of Steinbrenner and his filthy lucre). Or, as *Sports Illustrated* dubbed it, "The Good Guys Against the Bad Guys."

The Series opened at Yankee Stadium with an appropriately epic Game 1—which was kicked off by Pearl Bailey's equally epic rendition of "The Star-Spangled Banner," which at two minutes and twenty-one seconds was the longest in World Series history. Don Gullett pitched eight strong innings for the Yankees, but the normally reliable Lyle blew the save in the ninth, giving up a hit with two on to tie the game 3–3. Undaunted, Lyle set down Davey Lopes and Bill Russell to end the inning, then mowed through the next nine Dodger hitters he faced. The Yankees finally won it in the bottom of the 12th, when Paul Blair singled off Rick Rhoden to bring Willie Randolph home from second.

Before Game 2, Lasorda appeared on the field accompanied by a priest, and bragged to the assembled reporters about the Dodgers' familial bliss. "I believe in togetherness," he beamed. The Dodgers' 6–1 victory in the second contest was certainly a team effort, with Burt Hooton pitching a complete game, and four different Dodgers homering off Catfish Hunter and the ubiquitous Sparky Lyle. New York fans, unhappy with the game's result, rained smoke bombs and garbage upon the outfield and the Dodger bullpen in the ninth inning, and someone nailed Reggie Smith in the head with a rubber ball tossed from the upper deck.

The game also aggravated the fissures in the Yankees' clubhouse; Hunter hadn't pitched since mid-September, and Jackson fumed to the press that Martin had disrespected his old A's compadre by having him take the mound before he was truly prepared to do so. "How could the son of a bitch have pitched him?" he demanded. Martin, informed of Jackson's comments, told reporters that "Reggie has enough trouble playing right field. Why should I pay attention to him? His teammates don't." Munson, sick of the bickering between Martin, Jackson, and Steinbrenner, spoke openly of his desire to be traded to Cleveland, near his home in Canton, Ohio.

The Series moved to Los Angeles for Game 3, with pop-rock singer Linda Ronstadt—whose new *Simple Dreams* was enjoying a five-week run at the top of the *Billboard* album chart—singing the national anthem before the game began. The Yankees immediately made it clear that they were impervious to Ronstadt's mellow California spell, plating three first-inning runs off Tommy John. The Dodgers tied it up in the third with a three-run Dusty Baker shot off Mike Torrez, but failed to score again. Torrez, in fact, seemed to gain strength as the game went on, striking out a total of nine Dodgers on his way to a 5–3 complete-game victory.

Game 4, a 4–2 Yankees victory, remains best remembered for Lasorda's profanity-laced exchange with Doug Rau when the Dodger manager went to remove the left-hander in the second inning after he'd been touched for three straight hits. In his frustration with Rau, Lasorda must have forgotten that he'd been wired with a microphone for the ABC TV broadcast, or simply didn't care. Either way, the conversation that followed was highly unsuitable for a prime-time broadcast.

"I feel good, Tommy," Rau insisted.

"I don't give a shit if you feel good," Lasorda snapped. "There's four motherfuckin' hits up there!"

"He's a left-handed hitter," Rau said of Graig Nettles, the next batter up. "I can strike this motherfucker out!"

"I don't give a shit, Dougie," Lasorda retorted. "I'll make the fucking decisions here, okay?"

The warm Dodger family feeling came back in time for Game 5. With L.A. down three games to one, Lasorda gave his team a pep talk, telling them that he believed they were the best team in baseball. They came out and played like it, running up a 10–0 lead on Don Gullett and relievers Ken Clay and Dick Tidrow. Don Sutton let a few runs through in the seventh and eighth innings, the last coming on a Reggie Jackson home run. A meaningless solo shot down the right-field line that made the final score a slightly more respectable 10–4, Jackson's homer would gain far greater significance with two days' hindsight.

The Series returned to Yankee Stadium for Game 6, and the Dodgers drew first blood, scoring twice on a Steve Garvey triple off Mike Torrez in the first inning. The Yankees evened it up in the second, when Burt Hooton walked Jackson on four straight pitches, then gave up a homer to Chris Chambliss. Reggie Smith responded in the top of the third with a home run of his own, giving the Dodgers a 3–2 advantage. Then, in the bottom of the fourth, with Munson on first, Jackson swung at the first Hooton pitch he saw—an inside fastball—and drove it into the first row of the right-field bleachers. It was his third home run of the Series, and it gave the Bombers a 4–3 lead. He hit another first-pitch home run in the fifth, this time off Dodger reliever Elias Sosa, widening the score to 7–3; the Yankee Stadium crowd chanted, "REG-GIE, REG-GIE, REG-GIE" as he circled the bases.

When Jackson stepped to the plate in the bottom of the eighth against Charlie Hough, the crowd greeted him with a standing ovation. He'd already tied Babe Ruth's long-standing record of four home runs in a World Series; and on Hough's first pitch—in Jackson's words, "a knuckler that didn't knuckle"—he broke it. Jackson's two earlier home runs had been line drives, but this one was an appropriately majestic blast that landed deep in the stadium's tarpaulin-covered center-field bleachers, 475 feet from home plate. The clout tied Ruth's record for most homers in a World Series game (three), but no one had ever hit three consecutive ones in a game, hit them on three consecutive swings, or (factoring in the

four-pitch walk off Hooton) hit four across two games on four consecutive swings. Jackson's 25 total bases for the Series were a new record, as
were his 10 runs scored.

"Oh, what a beam on his face," enthused legendarily verbose broadcaster Howard Cosell as a grinning Jackson trotted triumphantly home-
ward after his third tater of the night. "How can you blame him? He's
answered the whole world! After all the furor, after all the hassling, it
comes down to this!"

Jackson returned to his right-field post in the ninth inning, then—as
cherry bombs began to explode on the outfield grass—ran back to the
dugout to grab a batting helmet; after the carnage he'd witnessed at the
end of Game 2, he was taking no chances. Neither were the Yankees, who
had quadrupled security for the night's game, including over a hundred
cops in riot gear, in an effort to dissuade the fans from invading the diamond. It didn't work; as soon as Lee Lacy popped out to Torrez for the
final out of the Yanks' Series-clinching victory, thousands of New Yorkers
stormed the field in rabid celebration. Jackson took off his glasses and
zigzagged through the hysterical revelers, who completely overwhelmed
the police and security forces and began tearing up the field. The World
Series MVP hurtled toward the Yankees dugout, leveling a fan with a
shoulder block that would have made Hal McRae proud.

Afterward, Martin and Jackson, united in victory for what would be
the only time, sat in the manager's dingy Yankee Stadium office and
shared a bottle of champagne. The Bombers had won their first World
Series since 1962, and Jackson, who had just put on the greatest spectacle in
World Series history, had forever earned the title "Mr. October" for his
performance. Many of New York's tabloid papers portrayed the Yankees'
triumph as a vindication for both Jackson and the beleaguered Big
Apple—"Who dares to call New York a lost cause?" demanded a *New York
Post* editorial. But like the city itself, Jackson, his manager, and his team-
mates would have to prove themselves all over again in 1978.

CHAPTER 12
CHICKEN SUITS AND CHEAP BEER

Ever since admission was first charged for a baseball game—a July 20, 1858, showdown between New York and Brooklyn all-star teams—the question of how to increase paid attendance has obsessed more than a few owners and general managers. For much of baseball's modern era, conventional wisdom held that star players and winning teams were what drew paying customers, and any promotion more creative than a half-price "Ladies' Day" was an affront to the dignity of the game. During the 1940s and '50s, for example, Indians/Browns/White Sox owner Bill Veeck's oddball promotions and publicity stunts (nylon stocking give-aways, pinch-hitting midgets) were met with the stern disapproval of his fellow owners.

In the 1970s, however, the previously uptight attitude toward "left-field" baseball promotions loosened considerably, as many teams came to the conclusion that there was no shame in upping the entertainment quotient of a day at the ballpark, so long as it made the turnstiles turn. If the resulting flurry of costumed mascots, scantily dressed young women, cash giveaways, and bargain-beer nights produced some of the more memorably embarrassing moments in '70s baseball, it also helped drive the sport's attendance figures to new highs over the course of the decade; in

1979, more than 43.5 million fans would buy tickets to major league base-ball games, a significant increase from the 28.7 million who went to the ballpark in 1970. "Action! Action! Action! With a little blood mixed in—that's what the fans want," Finley told *Time* magazine in 1971. Action, or at least distraction, is what they would most certainly get in the 1970s.

After a brief rough patch in the late 1960s, baseball attendance was already surging to record levels as the new decade dawned. But while attendance was booming at places like Shea Stadium, Busch Stadium, Wrigley Field, and Fenway Park, some teams weren't benefiting from the sport's economic rejuvenation. The Phillies, for example, drew only 708,247 fans in 1970, their final year at Philadelphia's decrepit Connie Mack Sta-dium. Desperate times called for desperate measures—or at least, in the case of the Phillies, the Hot Pants Patrol.

Hot pants, those form-fitting short shorts that made the miniskirt seem positively modest by comparison, were all the rage among liberated young women in 1971; men didn't particularly seem to mind them, either. "You know why I like hot pants?" asked James Brown—then riding high on the charts with his heartfelt ode, "Hot Pants (She Got to Use What She Got to Get What She Wants)." "Because what you see is what you get!"

Reasoning that male baseball fans in Philadelphia most likely agreed with the Godfather of Soul's take on the topic, the Phillies introduced the Hot Pants Patrol—a squad of leggy usherettes who wore tight red tops emblazoned with the Phillies' P logo, matching hot pants, and white go-go boots. Though the short shorts in question weren't quite as scan-dalously brief as the hottest styles of the day, the patrol's "uniforms" raised the ire of feminists and conservatives alike. Still, the Phillies managed to draw more than twice as many fans in 1971 as they had during the previ-ous season. Whether the crowds showed up to enjoy the new Veterans Stadium or to ogle the Hot Pants Patrol remains unclear; but they almost certainly weren't there to watch a miserable Phillies team that would fin-ish dead last in the NL East with a 67-95 record.

Desperate for something to boost attendance after a dismal 1970 season that saw the team rack up 106 losses while drawing barely 6,000 fans a game to Comiskey Park, the White Sox also got in on the act by introducing the Soxettes, a cheerleading squad dressed in Sox caps, jerseys, and scarlet-pin-striped hot pants. Comiskey attendance nearly doubled in 1971, though this probably had more to do with the team's improvement to 79-83—thanks in part to career years from staff ace Wilbur Wood (22-13, 1.91 ERA, 210 Ks) and third baseman Bill Melton (who led the AL with 33 homers)—than with the presence of the Soxettes.

But while the Phillies and White Sox brought hot pants into the ballpark in 1971, Charlie Finley actually put them on the field. Ever the innovator, the Oakland A's owner introduced the first foul-line "ball girls" in 1971, a move that would be imitated by numerous clubs over the next few decades. The A's ball girls, local teenagers Debbie Sivyer and Mary Barry, were attired in green hot pants and A's warm-up jackets; in addition to flagging down foul balls and providing a bit of eye candy, the girls would also attempt to curry favor with the umpires by providing them with lemonade and homemade chocolate-chip cookies between innings. Sivyer, in fact, enjoyed baking the cookies so much that she opened her own cookie shop in Palo Alto in 1977. The shop—Mrs. Fields Chocolate Chippery—would eventually grow into a worldwide empire, netting the former ball girl a substantially larger payday than any A's player ever made under Finley.

Though the Padres fielded a number of notable players during the 1970s, including future Hall of Famers Willie McCovey, Dave Winfield, Ozzie Smith, Gaylord Perry, and Rollie Fingers, none of them ever managed to fire up the hometown crowd like the San Diego Chicken. Though not the first mascot in the major leagues with a removable head—New York's baseball-headed Mr. Met beat him to that honor by nearly a decade—the Chicken was the first to bring his antics onto the playing field, and baseball fans adored him for it.

The strange and wondrous saga of the Chicken began in 1974, when a

San Diego State journalism major named Ted Giannoulas was hired—for the princely pay of $2 an hour—to wear a chicken suit and hand out candy Easter eggs at the San Diego Zoo, as part of a promotion for local radio station KGB. When that promotion ended, Giannoulas—wanting to see some baseball games for free—suggested that he wear the costume to Padres home contests. The Padres, who were willing to consider just about any measure to increase attendance, agreed to let the Chicken go "free-range" and goof around on their field between innings.

It was love at first cluck between the KGB Chicken and Padres fans, who loudly cheered the Chicken's every pratfall and prank—especially when the latter came at the expense of the umpires and visiting players. By the end of the 1974 season, the Chicken's acrobatic clowning at Padres games had turned him into a local celebrity, while the team had drawn nearly half a million more fans than the previous season, despite finishing with an identically awful 60-102 record as in 1973.

The Chicken charmed opposing teams as well. When the Reds were in town, he saluted Pete Rose by imitating "Charlie Hustle's" headfirst slide into home, then immediately followed it up with a slo-mo repeat of the play. Rose got a such a kick out of the Chicken's routine that the Reds extended an invitation for him to come and perform in Cincinnati; similar invitations rolled in from the Cubs, Cardinals, Astros, and Braves. By 1977, the Chicken had become such a San Diego icon that the Padres asked him to throw out the first pitch on Opening Day; he was also given ample time to strut his stuff on national television when San Diego hosted the 1978 All-Star Game.

By the late '70s, the Chicken's immense popularity had inspired several other teams to introduce feathered (or furry) mascots of their own. The Cardinals introduced Fredbird, the Blue Jays had their BJ Birdie, and Pittsburgh came up with the Pirate Parrot. Kevin Koch, the original Parrot, apparently took his morale-boosting duties a little too seriously; during the Pittsburgh drug trials of 1985, it was revealed that Koch had purchased cocaine for Pirates players, and had personally hooked several of them up with a local drug dealer.

Philadelphia's green and fuzzy Phillie Phanatic was introduced in 1978 as an attempt to bring more families to Veterans Stadium, and thereby (in principle, at least) help cut down on the drunken brawls between fans that had become a regular occurrence at Phillies games. Though the Phanatic wasn't particularly successful with the latter mission, the anteaterlike creature proved enormously popular with small children and inebriated fans alike.

The Phanatic was created for the Phillies by the Harrison/Erickson company of New York, which changed its name soon afterward to Acme Mascots. In 1979, Acme created the Expos mascot Youppi! (French for "Hooray!" or "Yippee!"), a hairy orange giant who quickly became as beloved in Montreal as his costumed counterparts were in San Diego and Philadelphia. Contrary to popular belief, Youppi! wasn't the Expos' first mascot—that distinction belonged to Souki, a bizarre, alienlike creature whose spiky, spherical head made him look like Mr. Met crossed with the Sputnik satellite. A far too nightmarish figure to appeal to younger Expos fans, Souki lasted only a year before he was replaced by the much cuddlier Youppi!

Though she wasn't exactly an official team mascot, an exotic dancer named Morganna Roberts seemed to take the field at major league games in the '70s nearly as often as the Chicken himself. Best known as "Morganna the Kissing Bandit," the shapely Roberts would dash out onto the diamond—typically dressed in short shorts and a tight T-shirt that accentuated her already eye-catching 60-inch bust—and plant a big kiss on an unsuspecting ballplayer, before inevitably being wrestled away by security.

Morganna's most famous on-field appearance occurred during the first inning of the 1979 All-Star Game in Seattle, when she invaded the diamond to lay a wet one on a chaw-chomping George Brett. Mariners officials allegedly paid Morganna's way to the event, perhaps wanting to make sure that the game would be a memorable one; though they denied having anything to do with her presence, it's worth noting that she was gently and politely escorted from the field by Mariners security—the same folks who, toward the end of the game, would lay a ferocious gang tackle on a 20-year-old male who had run out onto the Kingdome's field to shake Pete Rose's hand.

The '79 All-Star Game, the only such contest ever played at the Seattle Kingdome, hit something of a trifecta in the famous nonplayer participant department: Not only was Morganna in the house, along with the San Diego Chicken—who did his usual umpire-baiting shtick between innings, much to the crowd's delight—but Rollen Stewart was there as well. Stewart, a.k.a. "Rockin' Rollen" or "the Rainbow Man," was a familiar face in the late-'70s world of televised sports; immediately identifiable with his scraggly beard, oversize glasses, and brightly colored rainbow Afro wig, Stewart had a knack for popping up in front of network cameras during random crowd shots. Though he would later admit that he actually despised sports, Stewart—a former marijuana farmer— attended high-profile sporting events simply because he wanted to be a star, and he figured that acting up in front of a live TV crew would be his quickest ticket to fame.

Stewart's on-camera antics were initially limited to making dual thumbs-up or A-OK hand gestures while bugging his eyes and grinning maniacally, before a 1980 conversion to evangelical Christianity inspired him to add "John 3:16" T-shirts and placards to his repertoire. Rockin' Rollen eventually wound up in jail, serving consecutive life sentences for making terrorist threats in the early '90s against airplanes flying into Los Angeles International Airport; but back in 1979, he just seemed like another harmless post-hippie goofball.

Along with the proliferation of costumed team mascots during the 1970s, the decade also saw a huge increase in one-off promotions designed to pad the attendance figures for individual games. Giveaway promotions like "Team Poster Day," "Helmet Day," "Ball Day," and "Bat Day" became perennial favorites, even though it might not always have been the most prudent idea to put an official baseball or a regulation-size Louisville Slugger in the hands of a rowdy fan. There were more unorthodox promotional stunts as well, like Charlie Finley's greased-pig races after A's games; the A's also held a "Hot Pants Day," when the "foxy little girls in Oakland" (to quote soul singer Rodger Collins's immortal phrase) got in for free, and "Bald Head Day," when chrome-domes received half-price treatment. And then, of course, there were the fabulously ill-conceived promotions like Cleveland's "Ten-Cent Beer Night."

Even taken within the context of a far less abstemious era than our own, it's hard to believe that no one in the Cleveland Indians' front office recognized the folly of offering Indians fans an endless supply of cold brew at a dime a cup; and yet, that was exactly the idea behind "Ten-Cent Beer Night," the promotion that brought 25,134 thirsty patrons to Cleveland's decrepit Municipal Stadium (a.k.a. "the Mistake by the Lake") for a June 4, 1974, night game against the Texas Rangers. More puzzling still is the fact that the club didn't think to beef up security for the game, even though the Indians and Rangers had actually brawled on the field during a contest in Arlington the week before, where Texas fans had added insult to injury by dousing the visitors with beer, and several Indians players had to be restrained from going into the stands to slug it out with the hecklers. This time, it was the Rangers who would be in enemy territory, and Indians fans—who turned out for the game in nearly twice their usual number—were determined to return the gracious hospitality, as well as drink as much beer as possible. Between 60,000 and 65,000 10-ounce cups of Stroh's were consumed that night, an average of nearly a quart of beer per customer.

Predictably enough, trouble flared throughout the game, with at least 20 drunken Indians fans taking turns invading the field and attempting to evade security. One woozy young woman tried unsuccessfully to plant a smooch on home plate umpire Nestor Chylak, while a long-haired teenage boy completely shed his clothes and led security guards on a moonlit chase across the outfield. Still, the mood of the crowd remained surprisingly docile and convivial, at least for the first six innings, possibly due to the copious amounts of pot being openly smoked in the stands. "The marijuana smoke was so thick out there in right field," said Rangers slugger Jeff Burroughs afterward, "I think I was higher than the fans."

But with the Indians trailing 5–3 in the seventh, the mood began to sour. Cleveland fans launched an all-out attack on the Texas bullpen, firing a barrage of batteries, tennis balls, rocks, trash, and firecrackers at the Rangers' relief squad. Texas manager Billy Martin ordered his pitchers into the dugout, which only enraged the crowd further; cherry bombs exploded all over the field, and some fans even dangled strings of lit firecrackers over the edge of the Rangers' dugout. Somehow, the game went on.

Finally, in the bottom of the ninth, all hell broke loose. After the Indians tied the game on John Lowenstein's sacrifice fly with the bases loaded, two Cleveland fans ran onto the field and tried to snatch Burroughs's cap and glove. When the Texas right fielder tried to push them away, several other spectators ran onto the field and attacked him. Both dugouts cleared as Rangers and Indians players—some of them armed with bats—ran to back up Burroughs, who was now in Muhammad Ali "rope-a-dope" mode, trying to keep himself from getting punched in the face by several assailants. Mortal enemies just six days earlier, the two teams were now suddenly united in battle against at least 50 drunken Clevelanders, with hundreds more pouring onto the field around them.

Miraculously, the players suffered only a few minor injuries—Burroughs jammed his thumb, Rangers pitcher Steve Foucault received a black eye, and Indians pitcher Tom Hilgendorf survived with only a few lumps and bruises, despite being clocked on the noggin by an airborne metal chair. Once security finally cleared the field, Chylak (bleeding profusely from a cut on his wrist) declared the game a 9–0 forfeit in favor of Texas, partly because all of the bases had been stolen.

While single-game promotions proliferated throughout baseball during the 1970s, Major League Baseball still had a long way to go in terms of figuring out how to market the sport to the masses. Bowie Kuhn's insistence upon scheduling playoff and World Series games in the evening certainly increased the postseason TV viewership, but the few attempts that MLB made to reach out and expand the sport's fan base were awkwardly conceived and tentatively executed, at best. Though it seems unfathomable from the perspective of the marketing-crazed 21st century, it was almost as if the commish and his cronies felt it unseemly to have to "sell" the national pastime to the youth of America, even while the NFL (and, to a lesser extent, the NBA) were clearly gaining on baseball in terms of overall popularity.

Between the 1974 and 1975 seasons, baseball statisticians calculated that 997,513 runs had been scored thus far in major league history, and that that the 1 millionth would be scored at some point during the 1975 season. Tootsie Roll Industries approached Major League Baseball about sponsoring a nationwide sweepstakes in which entrants could predict which player would score the historic run, along with when and where he would score it; the person with the winning guess would receive $10,000. After much hemming and hawing—Tootsie Rolls didn't have the same long-standing connection with the game as, say, peanuts and/or Cracker Jack—MLB finally okayed the contest, and set up "countdown clocks" in every ballpark so that fans and players could watch as the all-time run total crept inexorably toward 1 million.

Bob Watson of the Houston Astros eventually scored the millionth run when he homered against the San Francisco Giants on May 4, 1975, crossing the plate at Candlestick Park just 12 seconds ahead of the Reds' Dave Concepcion, who was circling the bases at Riverfront Stadium at that very moment. For his historic accomplishment, Watson received a $1,000 digital watch from the Seiko Time Company (which had been roped in to co-sponsor the contest), while the Tootsie Roll folks awarded him 1 million Tootsie Rolls and—in what was surely the most unwelcome gift of $10,000 that anyone has ever received—1 million pennies. Watson donated the pennies to charity; and, since his own children were allergic to chocolate, he donated the candy to the Boy Scouts and Girl Scouts of America.

MLB's other big marketing initiative of 1975—the Bazooka Bubble Blowing Championship—was at least a little more in synch with the intended target demographic. Sponsored by Topps, the leading manufacturer of baseball cards, who also produced Bazooka bubble gum, the competition took place between representatives of all 24 major league teams, and was filmed for that year's World Series pregame broadcasts, with NBC broadcaster Joe Garagiola as the host. Though the contestants included such stars as the Reds' Johnny Bench, the Royals' George Brett, the Twins' Bert Blyleven, the Cubs' Bill Madlock, and the Expos' Gary Carter, the World Series of bubble blowing came down to a face-off between two lesser-known players: Phillies backup catcher Johnny Oates and Brewers utility infielder Kurt Bevacqua. Bevacqua won the championship with a massive bubble that was measured by umpire Dick Stello at 18 inches; though Bevacqua was back in the minors the following year, his bubbletastic feat was immortalized by a special 1976 Topps baseball card, which featured an "action shot" that showed him all but completely obscured by his winning bubble.

In 1975, Atlanta's first year without home run king Hank Aaron, the Braves drew just 534,672 paying customers—and the team's four straight last-place finishes from 1976 to 1979 hardly offered much in the way of turnstile-clicking incentive. But thanks to new owner Ted Turner and team publicity director Bob Hope (no, not *that* Bob Hope), the Braves indisputably led the league in oddball promotions. The Braves already had a mascot by the time Turner arrived on the scene in 1976: the über–politically incorrect Chief Noc-A-Homa, who "lived" in a teepee beyond the outfield walls and did a "Native dance" whenever the Braves hit a home run. But the Chief was old news, having come from Milwaukee to Atlanta with the team back in 1966, and he clearly lacked the Chicken-esque charisma needed to draw fans to Fulton County Stadium. Instead, Turner turned to Hope, who helped him transform the stadium into what Turner proudly called "the most fun ballpark in America" with an unending barrage of offbeat contests and attractions. "So long as the team was losing games, we in the promotions department had nothing to lose," Hope would later explain.

He wasn't kidding. Braves fans in late '70s bore witness to (and often participated in) such ridiculous promotions as bathtub races, tightrope-walking demonstrations, "cow pie"–throwing competitions, blanket- and mattress-stacking contests, and even "Wishbone Salad Dressing Night," wherein contestants dug through a giant bowl of salad in search of keys to a new car. Turner himself often joined in the fun, donning riding silks for ostrich and camel races against local sportswriters, and besting Phillies reliever Tug McGraw in a contest to see who could push a baseball around the bases the quickest using only his nose. Despite playing pathetic baseball, the Braves increased their attendance by an average of nearly 3,500 fans per game in 1976, thanks entirely to Turner and Hope's promotional savvy.

In a move that presaged Turner's late-'80s ownership of World Championship Wrestling (and, perhaps, his marriage to Jane Fonda), the Braves held a "Headlock and Wedlock Night" in the summer of 1976. Before the game, 34 couples were married at home plate in a single ceremony; afterward, a team of pro wrestlers took the field for a no-holds-barred exhibition match. Hope would later admit that the weddings and wrestling matches were actually supposed to take place on different nights; but when he realized they had inadvertently been scheduled for the same game, Hope cheerfully combined the two and acted as if it had been planned that way from the beginning.

Hope was considerably more ambivalent, in retrospect, about the wet T-shirt contest sponsored by the team in May 1977. "We didn't know what we were inventing," he later admitted. "Our 'college night committee' suggested the ridiculous idea. They wanted it topless; I suggested the T-shirt. They countered with the idea of adding water. I assured Ted we would get lots of publicity and lots of tickets. I was certain someone would step in and stop us before the event ever took place. No one did."

In fact, nightclubs on New Orleans's infamous Bourbon Street had been holding wet T-shirt contests since at least 1975, so Hope can't be blamed for their invention. Still, there's no question that the "Wet T-Shirt Night" at Fulton County Stadium was by far the best-attended contest of its sort; some 27,000 fans hung around through a two-and-a-half-hour rain delay, just to whoop and holler while 43 contestants strutted their thoroughly soaked stuff after the game's conclusion. News coverage of the event did much to introduce the mainstream to this novel form of competition; by the end of the decade, the Braves were still mired in last place, but wet T-shirt contests had become a popular fixture in night-clubs, discos, and singles bars across the country.

Of course, any era that produced such a sublime and ridiculous array of promotions was tailor-made for a man who'd once sent a midget into a game as a pinch hitter. So it was no surprise to see Bill Veeck pick up where he'd left off upon his reentry into the major leagues in 1976. "He viewed the baseball park as the theater in which he operated," recalled sportswriter Ed Linn, who coauthored Veeck's hilarious autobiography, *Veeck—As in Wreck*. "And he was bursting with the ideas that had been accumulating for 15 years."

In addition to reactivating Comiskey Park's famous exploding score-board, Veeck boosted White Sox attendance with a string of "ethnic nights" reflective of Chicago's melting-pot diversity—"Italian Night," "Irish Night," "Polish Night," "German Night," "Croatian Night," etc.—all of which fea-tured entertainment related to the nationality being celebrated. "Greek Night" featured belly dancers, while "Mexican Fiesta Night" featured age-less Sox legend Minnie Minoso dressed as a matador and dueling to the "death" with some guy in a bull costume. Veeck also paid tribute to the Windy City's alcoholic working-class tradition with a long-running beer-stacking tournament, wherein thee-man teams from Chitown's various ethnic enclaves competed to see who could stack cases of beer the highest and fastest. Thanks to Veeck, the 1976 White Sox drew an average of 2,000 additional fans per game—despite a 64-97 record that was considerably more dismal than the previous season's 75-86 performance.

But if Veeck's Barnumesque flair made him popular with Sox fans, Sox players often took a dim view of the circuslike atmosphere at the old ballpark. "Baseball at Comiskey Park is a sideshow to belly dancers and beer case–stacking contests," complained pitcher Ken Kravec in the sum-mer of 1979. "It's so bad that most of us look forward to playing on the road. Our record is better there. It's because we don't like playing at home."

Kravec's comments came in the wake of Veeck's most infamous promotion—July 12, 1979's "Disco Demolition Night," an event that rivaled Cleveland's "Ten-Cent Beer Night" for questionable conception and overall mayhem. The event was actually cooked up by Veeck's son Mike—who served as White Sox promotions aide—and popular local radio DJ Steve Dahl. Ostensibly intended as a lighthearted protest against the disco music that had been clogging the nation's airwaves in the wake of *Saturday Night Fever*, "Disco Demolition Night" inadvertently tapped into deep feelings of resentment that many young Chicago rock fans held toward disco and its attendant cultural trappings.

In decades to follow, "Disco Demolition Night" would be singled out by many social and pop-cultural commentators as an example of the racist and homophobic impulses that drove the late-'70s backlash against disco music. While it's debatable that most white rock fans of the era were even vaguely aware of the connection between disco and gay nightlife, there's no question that they generally viewed disco as "black music"—i.e., something that no self-respecting Led Zeppelin or Pink Floyd fan would be caught dead listening to. But mostly, it was disco's innate trendiness that rankled rock fans; in their eyes, white people who bought disco music and danced to it at clubs à la *Saturday Night Fever* were merely vapid followers of fashion, superficial losers who didn't appreciate "real" music. In other words, it all basically came down to a philosophical difference of white polyester versus torn denim, silver coke spoons versus wizard-shaped bongs, and *Dance Fever* on TV versus *Dark Side of the Moon* on headphones.

This division between disco and rock supporters was especially apparent in Chicago, and it was further widened in late 1978, when the popular hard rock station WDAI suddenly announced its plans to shift to an all-disco format, thus enraging the Windy City's blue-collar rock fans. WDAI's competitor WLUP ("Where Chicago Rocks!") made hay of the situation by hiring former WDAI personality Dahl; and when Dahl summarily anointed himself Chicago's most militant antidisco crusader, disenfranchised listeners immediately abandoned "Disco DAI" and turned their FM dials to "the Loop." Dahl's most rabid followers dubbed themselves "the Insane Coho Lips"—a moniker that simultaneously referenced a local Latin street gang (the Insane Unknowns) and a fish (the Coho salmon) commonly found in the Great Lakes. Anytime Dahl made a public appearance, the "Cohos" would show up in droves, chanting "Disco sucks!" like a battle cry.

For "Disco Demolition Night," the hook was simple: Anyone carrying a disco record would be admitted to a Tigers–White Sox doubleheader at Comiskey for a mere 98 cents. The records would be collected by the park's staff, and then destroyed by Dahl in a giant between-games explosion. But despite the virulently antidisco sentiments of WLUP listeners—not to mention the radio station's sharply rising popularity—apparently no one expected "Disco Demolition Night" to draw more than a few thousand extra patrons to Comiskey. Instead, an estimated 90,000 people showed up to the 52,000-capacity ballpark, bringing traffic on the nearby Dan Ryan Expressway to a complete standstill. Of the tens of thousands who were turned away at the ballpark ticket kiosks, several hundred found their way into Comiskey by scaling the walls or bum-rushing the gates, while a large percentage of the rest simply hung outside and partied.

"I knew we didn't have your typical baseball crowd," remembered umpire Durwood Merrill, "because instead of families and kids, I saw a bunch of hard rockers with long hair and spacey-looking eyes. I could smell marijuana from the moment I walked onto the field." Tigers manager Sparky Anderson also caught a whiff of some earthy fragrances at the ballpark. "Beer and baseball go together, they have for years," he would remark at the end of the night. "But I think those kids were doing things other than beer."

Clearly more interested in the impending bonfire than in the baseball action in front of them, the rowdy Cohos in the crowd devoted themselves to swilling Schlitz, smoking weed, and chanting "Disco sucks!" instead of cheering for the home team. On several occasions during the contest, play had to be stopped as vinyl LPs and 45s sailed onto the field; Tigers reliever Aurelio Lopez was pelted with garbage while warming up in the eighth inning, while center fielder Ron LeFlore narrowly missed getting beaned by a golf ball. When the first game finally concluded with a 4–1 Tigers victory, both teams repaired to their respective dugouts for what was supposed to be a 30-minute break, and watched as enough albums and singles to stock a small record store were piled into a giant heap in center field to await Dahl's arrival.

The Cohos howled with glee as Dahl took the field in a jeep, decked out in combat helmet and fatigues, accompanied by Lorelei, WLUP's blond and curvaceous female "mascot." After leading the crowd in yet another "Disco sucks!" chant, Dahl detonated the mound of records, blasting shards of flying vinyl all over the park—and sending thousands of wasted kids tumbling out of the stands and onto the field in ecstatic celebration. Unlike that fateful night five years earlier in Cleveland, where fans physically attacked the players, the "Disco Demolition" hordes were content simply to run zigzag patterns around the field, climb the foul poles, throw handfuls of sod and dirt at one another, wave their "Disco Sucks!" banners (some of which were set ablaze), trash a batting cage that had somehow been loosed from its moorings, and generally frolic amid the flaming mound of vinyl in center field.

When it became painfully obvious that the hesher hordes had no intention of vacating the field in a timely manner—and Bill Veeck and Sox broadcaster Harry Caray proved unable to sweet-talk them back to their seats—Chicago's finest finally moved in, on horseback and in riot gear, to quell the disturbance. Thirty-nine kids were arrested, and six others were taken to the hospital; however, the evening's biggest casualty was the charred and pockmarked field, which Tigers manager Sparky Anderson refused to let his team play on. Crew chief Dave Phillips got AL president Lee MacPhail on the phone for a quick conference, and the two initially decided to postpone the second game of the doubleheader, citing unplayable field conditions; twenty-four hours later, the ruling was changed to a 9–0 forfeit win in favor of Detroit.

Bill Veeck was never quite the same after the night of July 12, 1979. Utterly chagrined by—and widely chastised for—the chaos he'd unintentionally unleashed, Veeck kept a lower profile and seemed to put considerably less energy into White Sox promotions. By January 1981, he was out of baseball for good, having sold the team to an ownership group with much deeper pockets. The end of Veeck's second tenure with the White Sox was indubitably hastened by the increased financial pressures of the free-agency era, but it's safe to say that "Disco Demolition Night" marked the point when Chicago's renewed love affair with the Sox' irascible owner officially began to sour. Not that he ever completely renounced it, of course; asked before his death if "Disco Demolition Night" was his greatest promotion or his greatest disaster, the old showman didn't bat an eye. "Looking at it as objectively as possible," he said, "it was both."

CHAPTER 13

1978

Released right before Christmas 1977, *Saturday Night Fever* cast a white-suited shadow over 1978. Both the film and its Bee Gees–heavy sound track album raked in millions of dollars, bringing disco to Middle America; thousands of new discotheques opened across the country, and everyone from Barry Manilow (who enjoyed a huge summer hit with the discotastic "Copacabana") to the Sears and JC Penney men's departments (which offered up all manner of snazzy three-piece suit ensembles in some of the least breathable fabrics ever created) boogied aboard the disco bandwagon to cash in. Though many cultural commentators decried the disco movement's hedonistic music and attitude, its popularity was at least partly due to the fact that it offered Americans a welcome distraction from some fairly bleak times.

1978 was marked by rising inflation and health costs, as well as the declining power of the U.S. dollar, which was depreciating so rapidly against foreign currencies that the Carter administration was forced to implement an emergency "dollar-rescue plan," which included increasing U.S. gold sales and drastically reducing the amount of money that U.S. banks were allowed to lend, despite the likelihood that such measures would lead to a recession in 1979.

Adding to the pervasive gloom across the country were several labor actions, including a 110-day coal miners' strike and an 88-day newspaper strike in New York City. President Carter declared a federal emergency in New York's Love Canal neighborhood, which turned out to have been constructed on a toxic waste dump; it was so contaminated that more than 50 percent of the children born there between 1974 and 1978 had some form of birth defect. In the Chicago suburbs, professional birthday clown John Wayne Gacy was arrested and charged with the rape and murder of 33 young men and boys; at the Peoples Temple compound in Jonestown, Guyana (a mass suicide following the assassination of U.S. congressman Leo Ryan on a nearby airstrip), left more than 900 American citizens dead. Even the steady pounding of the disco beat couldn't completely disguise the fact that happy days were definitely a long way from here again.

Baseball, on the other hand, was thriving. Perhaps because, like disco music, the sport represented a fairly cheap distraction from the unrelenting parade of bad news, baseball attendance figures—which had already set an all-time record in 1977 with 38.7 million tickets sold—rose above 40 million for the first time in history. The Dodgers, who in '77 had narrowly missed becoming the first team ever to hit the 3 million mark in a single season, surpassed it by almost 350,000 fans, while a record five other teams (the Phillies, Reds, Yankees, Red Sox, and Royals) topped the 2 million figure.

But thanks to the advent of free agency, team owners weren't the only ones cashing in. The second annual reentry free-agent draft was held in November '77, and while the prevailing consensus was that this second crop of free agents was less impressive than the first, the bidding wars they inspired were even more heated—and, for the players, even more lucrative—than in 1976. Orioles starter Ross Grimsley scored a five-year, $1.5 million contract with the Montreal Expos. Journeyman starter Mike Torrez, fresh off his two victories for the Yankees in the 1977 World Series, snagged a seven-year, $2.5 million deal from the Red Sox. George

Steinbrenner, despite the fact that he already had a Cy Young–winning closer in Sparky Lyle, signed Pirates reliever Rich "Goose" Gossage to a six-year, $2.75 million deal, a move that would permanently alienate Lyle, and foster additional tension in a Yankees clubhouse that needed more bad vibes like Central Park needed more muggers.

Some owners, like Calvin Griffith of the Twins, still refused to shell out the big bucks for free agents, either on principle or due to a lack of ready cash in the till. Griffith's team had gone 84-77 in 1977 without the help of any expensive free-agent signings; but while the notoriously stingy Griffith kept his wallet sealed, outfielders Larry Hisle and Lyman Bostock, two of his '77 stars, signed with other teams. Hisle, who had hit .302 with 28 home runs and 119 RBIs, inked a six-year, $3 million contract with the Brewers; Bostock, coming off a career year in which he hit .336 (second in the AL only to teammate Rod Carew's .388) with 36 doubles, 12 triples, 14 homers, 90 RBIs, and 16 stolen bases, signed a five-year, $2.2 million deal with Gene Autry's Angels. Before the '78 season ended, the effects of Griffith's shortsightedness (and tightfistedness) would become apparent to everyone in the Twin Cities but Griffith. Carew would win yet another AL batting title for the Twins in 1978—his .333 beat out Al Oliver of the Rangers by nine percentage points—but it would be his last; angered by Griffith's intransigence, Carew demanded to be traded, though he wouldn't get his wish until early 1979.

Strapped for cash, White Sox owner Bill Veeck simply couldn't afford to sign Richie Zisk and Oscar Gamble, the big guns of his '77 "South Side Hitmen" squad, to new deals, much less enter into the bidding wars for some of the bigger names on the auction block. Zisk signed with the Rangers, who dangled a 10-year, $3 million contract, while Ray Kroc lured Gamble to the Padres with a six-year, $2.8 million deal. "The Angels spent more money than we did last year, and we competed with them all right on the field," Veeck insisted, though he admitted to having doubts about how competitive the White Sox would be in seasons to come. "For a year or two maybe, we can think of some way to equalize the situation," he told *Sports Illustrated*. "But there will come a time, just as in table-stakes poker, when the preponderance of capital will ultimately win."

For now, at least, the cagey White Sox owner would try to patch the many holes in his lineup and pitching staff with budget-priced free agents—like Braves infielder Junior Moore, Twins reliever Ron Schueler, and oft-injured Yankees outfielder Ron Blomberg, who hadn't made more than 100 plate appearances in a season since 1975—and trading promising young catcher Brian Downing to the Angels as part of a multiplayer deal that brought aging slugger Bobby Bonds to Chicago. Unlike Zisk and Gamble, Bonds would prove a bust in Chicago; after he hit only two homers in 26 games, Veeck would ship him to Texas in exchange for outfielder Claudell Washington. It would prove one of the normally savvy Veeck's worst trades; Bonds went on to hit 29 homers, drive in 82 runs, and steal 37 bases for the Rangers in 1978, while Washington's listless offense (he hit .265 with a .290 on-base percentage, slapping six homers and driving in only 31 runs) and indifferent defense inspired Sox fans in the Comiskey bleachers to hoist signs reading "Washington Slept Here."

A's owner Charlie Finley not only refused to participate in the free-agent draft, but seemed almost pathologically determined to strip his team of every last vestige of its once-mighty dynasty—and a fair amount of its remaining dignity as well. In March, after several unsuccessful attempts over the years to deal Vida Blue (all of them scotched for one reason or another by Bowie Kuhn), Finley finally managed to trade the former Cy Young winner to San Francisco, in exchange for seven players and $390,000. (That cash figure was conspicuously just short of the $400,000 limit that Kuhn had recently—and arbitrarily—decreed as the maximum amount that could be exchanged between teams for a player.) Now only one player remained from the glory days of the "Mustache Gang"—outfielder Billy North—and even he wasn't long for Oakland.

In December of 1977, the *San Francisco Chronicle* reported that an all-black ownership cartel had formed with the intention of buying the A's, a group that included comedians Bill Cosby and Redd Foxx, musician Curtis Mayfield, heavyweight fighter George Foreman, and boxing promoter Don King. While it would have been interesting to see if an all-star coalition of African-American entertainers and sportsmen would have fared better than Finley in luring Oakland's predominantly black population to the Coliseum, nothing ever came of negotiations between them and Finley. The A's owner did, however, come quite close to selling the franchise off to Colorado oil mogul Marvin Davis, who wanted to move the struggling team (which had drawn fewer than half a million fans in 1977) to Denver. But the transaction ran aground in late March over a variety of complex issues, including the Oakland–Alameda County Coliseum Commission's insistence that Davis buy out the team's remaining lease at the Coliseum, and thus the A's were fated to remain in Oakland for at least another season.

As if Finley's highly publicized sale attempt hadn't sufficiently alienated Oakland baseball fans, the A's owner perversely decided to sell the radio broadcast rights for the team's first 16 home games to KALX, a student-operated station at the University of California, Berkeley. Because of the station's limited 10-watt range, only listeners within three to four miles of the college campus could pick up the games, which were called by student broadcasters Larry Baer and Bob Kozberg. In May, the team finally negotiated a deal for the rest of the season with the more powerful AM station KNEW, whose broadcast team ironically included Curt Flood, whose fight against the reserve clause had helped set in motion the free-agency revolution that hastened the Mustache Gang's exit from Oakland.

Along with Finley and the aforementioned North, the last remaining participant from the A's dynasty years was Stanley Burrell, the team's 16-year-old "executive vice president." In 1972, Finley had discovered Burrell dancing for spare change in the Coliseum's parking lot; impressed by his spunk, Finley offered the young man a job as an A's batboy, later promoting him to a glorified gofer with a fancy title. Since the A's owner preferred to run the team out of his Chicago office, he paid Burrell $7 a game to give him the play-by-play via telephone, along with updates on the clubhouse gossip. While A's players were initially amused by the presence of this preternaturally mature youngster—who was never shy about saying that he thought a pitcher was tiring, or that the manager was making a questionable move—they soon discovered that anything said in his presence would inevitably make its way back to Finley, and learned to keep their mouths shut around the kid they dubbed "the Pipeline."

To his face, many of the A's players called Burrell "Hammer," a nickname inspired by his uncanny physical resemblance to a young Hank Aaron. In the '80s, Burrell would try to make it as a ballplayer; but when that career path led nowhere, he'd record a rap demo with financial backing from Finley and several former A's players. Under the nom de rap MC Hammer, Burrell would go on to sell millions of CDs while wearing unfeasibly baggy pants.

Despite fielding a bunch of no-name and has-been players—the team's season leader in nearly every offensive category was left fielder Mitchell Page, who hit .285 with 17 homers and 70 RBIs in '78—the A's surprised everyone by going a major-league-best 16-5 in April, briefly vindicating Finley's refusal to play the free-agent game, and making Bobby Winkles seem like a managerial genius. A's fans, however, were unconvinced; after 17,283 showed up to see the team's April 10 home opener against Seattle, the team didn't draw more than 6,000 again until April 30.

But on May 22, with the A's 24-15 and still in first place, Winkles resigned as Oakland's manager, having been driven to the brink of insanity by Finley's incessant phone calls—especially the early-morning ones in which Finley would bark, "Get up! Only whores make their living in bed!" Finley replaced Winkles with Jack McKeon, whom Winkles had replaced just the previous season. McKeon, who had been 26-27 with the A's in 1977 before getting canned, would do an even worse job in '78, leading the team to a 45-78 record over the rest of the season. He would be fired shortly after the final game of the year.

In addition to Oakland's unexpectedly hot start, the spring of 1978 brought plenty of other astonishing developments. The Detroit Tigers, who absolutely no one expected to be a factor in the AL East race, got off to a roaring start of their own, going 13-5 in April, and Mark Fidrych once again inspired numerous "The Bird is Back" headlines by allowing only two earned runs in each of his first two starts, both of which were solid complete-game victories. But on April 17, in his third start of the season, Fidrych had to leave in the fourth inning due to shoulder tightness; five days later, he tried to warm up for a start against the Rangers, but felt too much pain in his right wing to pitch. The tendonitis that had plagued the Bird in 1977 was back, and would keep him from pitching again in '78.

Despite the crushing loss of Fidrych, the Tigers put together their best season since 1972, finishing 86-76 thanks to fine efforts from veterans Rusty Staub (.273, 24 HRs, 121 RBIs) and Ron LeFlore (.297, 126 runs, 68 stolen bases), as well as a hungry group of young players that included first baseman Jason Thompson (.287, 26 HRs, 96 RBIs) and the highly touted rookie keystone combination of shortstop Alan Trammell (who would improve considerably over his .268 batting average) and second baseman "Sweet" Lou Whitaker (who hit .285 and won AL Rookie of the Year honors). Trammell and Whitaker would go on to play 1,918 games together in the Tigers infield, setting an AL record for a double-play combination; and after enduring four straight losing seasons, the Tigers would remain on the right side of the .500 mark for a decade to come.

Across Lake Michigan in the land of Schlitz, the formerly hapless Milwaukee Brewers—led by rookie skipper George Bamberger—were suddenly going for all the gusto they could grab. Even with career years from Giants castoff Mike Caldwell (22-9, 2.36 ERA, and a league-leading 23 complete games) and second-year starter Lary Sorensen (18-12, 3.21, 17 complete games), it was the Brewers' bats that drew a franchise-record 1.6 million fans to County Stadium. "Bambi's Bombers" led the league in batting average (.276), on-base percentage (.342), and home runs (173), thanks to a lineup that included left fielder Larry Hisle (.290, 34 HRs, 115 RBIs), free-swinging center fielder "Stormin'" Gorman Thomas (whose 32 homers and 86 RBIs made up for his 133 strikeouts), and the double-play combination of Robin Yount (.293, 71 RBIs, 16 stolen bases) and rookie second baseman Paul Molitor (.273, 30 stolen bases), who seemed like they might become an even more potent duo than their Detroit counterparts. A thorn in the side of the Red Sox, the Orioles, and especially the Yankees (from whom they would take 10 out of 15 games) all summer long, the Brewers finished in third place with a 93-69 record, an impressive 26-game improvement over 1977—and the team's first winning mark since landing in Milwaukee.

The Cincinnati Reds celebrated their home opener by beating the Houston Astros 11–9—despite also becoming the first major league team in history to strike out into a triple play. With Joe Morgan on third and George Foster on first in the bottom of the seventh, Dan Driessen whiffed on a Joe Sambito pitch while Foster attempted to steal second; Astros catcher Joe Ferguson nailed Foster with a throw to shortstop Roger Metzger, then tagged Morgan out at the plate when he tried to beat the return throw home. 1978 would be a rough season for Morgan in general, as his batting average dropped to .236 from .288 the previous year, and his stolen bases from 49 to 19. Though he would hit his 200th career homer in late August, becoming the first player in history to reach 200 home runs and 500 stolen bases, the two-time MVP's poor overall performance at the plate would significantly hinder the Reds' attempt to retake the NL West from the L.A. Dodgers.

The Yankees' home opener in the Bronx was a particularly sweet affair, and not just because Ron Guidry outpitched Wilbur Wood of the White Sox for a 4–2 win. Ever since Reggie Jackson had uttered his infamous line to a reporter about how they'd name a candy bar after him if he played in New York, it was only a matter of time until someone actually took him up on the concept. In the spring of 1978, Standard Brands of Chicago introduced Reggie!, a fairly disgusting candy bar composed of "chocolaty covered caramel and peanuts," all molded into a round patty approximately the diameter of a baseball, and housed in a garish orange package with a photo of Jackson taking one of his monster swings. The company's unconvincing TV commercial for the bar showed a suave-looking Jackson gingerly sinking his teeth into his namesake treat and proclaiming, "Gee, Reggie! You sure taste good!"

On Opening Day at Yankee Stadium, Standard Brands launched its new product by giving away free Reggie! bars to each person who entered the venerable ballpark. Jackson rose to the occasion by cranking a three-run home run off Wood in the first inning, and the ecstatic crowd celebrated by tossing their Reggie! bars onto the field as he circled the bases.

"It was a hailstorm of Reggie Bars," Sparky Lyle wrote in *The Bronx Zoo*, his acerbic diary of the 1978 season. "They covered the outfield and the home plate area like a lawn overgrown with dandelions." Jackson, sensitive as ever, initially thought the deluge meant that the fans were rejecting his new candy bar.

Faced with a Reggie!-littered diamond, the umpires were forced to call time out while the Yankee Stadium grounds crew picked up the little orange packages. "People starving all over the world, and 30 billion calories are lying on the field," cracked White Sox skipper Bob Lemon. Yankees pitcher Ken Holtzman, whose intellectual curiosity was piqued when a Reggie! bar landed near him in the bullpen, unwrapped the bar and took a bite. "He said it tasted like cowflop," remembered Lyle. Catfish Hunter got in a dig of his own, wryly commenting that "when you unwrap a Reggie! bar, it tells you how good it is."

For the St. Louis Cardinals and their fans, 1978 would be yet another year of frustration and disappointment. After finishing third in the NL East in 1977 with an 83-79 record, they slid back into fifth place with a 69-93 mark—the lone high point of the season being Bob Forsch's April 16 no-hitter against the Phillies, which made him the first Cardinals pitcher since Jesse Haines in 1924 to pitch a no-hitter in St. Louis. (Two months later to the day, the Cardinals would become the victims of a Tom Seaver no-hitter, the first of Seaver's 12-year career.)

Manager Vern Rapp, a strict disciplinarian whose conservative grooming edicts had alienated several Cards players during the '77 season, including star catcher Ted Simmons and closer Al "the Mad Hungarian" Hrabosky, was fired only 17 games into 1978, and replaced by 1960s Redbirds hero Ken Boyer. For team owner Gussie Busch, the final straw came when Rapp referred to Simmons, one of the franchise's best and most popular players, as "a loser" during a postgame interview with team broadcaster Jack Buck.

April 24 saw the Angels' Nolan Ryan set yet another strikeout mark, fanning 15 Mariners to become the first pitcher to strike out that many or more batters on 20 separate occasions. (Even Sandy Koufax, the next hurler down the list from Ryan, had done it only eight times.) Alas, Ryan left the game with the score tied, and the Angels wound up losing 6–5 in the 12th inning. For 1978, Ryan would compile a record of 10-13 with a 3.72 ERA, a mediocre performance by his standards, even if his 260 strikeouts were good enough to lead the league, the sixth time he'd done so in the past seven seasons.

Elsewhere in the AL West, Texas Rangers owner Brad Corbett's wild off-season wheeling and dealing actually seemed to give his team—which now boasted a veteran-heavy pitching staff that included Jon Matlack (who would go 15-13 for the year with a minuscule 2.27 ERA), Fergie Jenkins (18-8, 3.04), Doyle Alexander (9-10, 3.86), Dock Ellis (9-7, 4.20), and Doc Medich (9-8, 3.74)—a fighting chance of catching Kansas City. Unfortunately, they would have to race the Royals without the help of Rogelio "Roger" Moret, whose April meltdown was among the weirder ones in baseball history, even by 1970s standards.

From 1973 through 1975, Moret had been an important (if inconsistent) member of the Red Sox staff, racking up a 36-15 record as a starter and long reliever. Known in his native Puerto Rico as "El Látigo" ("the Whip") for the way his curve audibly snapped as it crossed the plate, Moret had, according to teammate Bill Lee, "the potential to be the next Sandy Koufax. When he threw the ball over the plate, he was unhittable."

Unfortunately, the lanky lefty had numerous personal issues as nasty as his curveball, including intense family pressures, financial problems (having grown up dirt poor, Moret had little clue as to how to handle the relative riches that he earned as a major league player), drug use—though he wouldn't cop to using anything stronger than marijuana, many who knew him back home claimed he also had a fondness for cocaine and a local hallucinogen distilled from the *campanitas* flower—and, worst of all, chronic schizophrenia.

The latter problem didn't explicitly rear its head until 1976, when the Red Sox traded Moret to the Braves; convinced that there were "bad vibrations" in Atlanta, the pitcher downed a witches' brew of rum and kerosene in an attempt to protect himself from the negative energies he felt were swirling around him. It didn't work; during a Braves road trip that summer, Moret became so hysterical in his hotel room that several of his teammates had to restrain him. He spent the next several weeks in New York's Bellevue Hospital; the Braves covered for the disturbed hurler by telling reporters that he was taking time off to deal with "family problems," then traded him to the Rangers in the off-season.

Moret's first year with Texas was relatively uneventful; after missing the first three months of the season due to arm injuries, he started eight games, relieved in another 10, and posted a 3.73 ERA over 72⅓ innings. But on April 12, 1978, Moret—who was scheduled to start that day against Mark Fidrych and the Tigers—suddenly told his teammates during batting practice that he couldn't pitch and was going home. Upon returning to the clubhouse, he stripped down to his underwear and stood by his locker in a catatonic state for the better part of 90 minutes, his left arm extended outward in front of him, while his right hand dangled at his side, holding a shower clog. When attempts to snap the pitcher out of his trance failed, the Rangers' training staff sedated him and packed him off to the Arlington Neuropsychiatric Center, where he spent two weeks under observation.

Moret returned to the team at the end of May, but pitched in only six more games before the voices in his head became too distracting. The Rangers put their troubled hurler on the disabled list for the rest of the season, and released him before the 1979 season began. Moret would never pitch another game in the majors. "I have not been through hell," he later reflected in an interview with *Sports Illustrated*. "Hell has been through me."

Though not in hell, Moret's old pitching mate Bill Lee found himself in an odd state of purgatory as the Red Sox entered 1978. In their effort to rid their team of troublemakers, Boston's front office had purged three-fifths of the Loyal Order of the Buffalo Heads—Fergie Jenkins, Rick Wise, and Jim Willoughby—from the roster, leaving Lee and Bernie Carbo wondering how soon they'd be shipped off to parts unknown. What the Boston brass hadn't figured on was that off-season acquisition Dennis Eckersley (who had come to the team in the deal that sent Wise to Cleveland) partied even harder than any of the exiled Buffalo Heads, and had an eccentric flair of his own that effectively made him the right-handed yin to Lee's lefty yang.

"Eckersley had the world's greatest vernacular," an admiring Lee would later write. "If he threw a 'yakker for your coolu,' it meant you were going to get nailed in the ass with a fastball. 'Cheese for your kitchen' was a fastball up and in. We never went out partying. Instead, we went out to 'get oiled.'" Eckersley and Lee—respectively dubbed "Cheese Master" and "Salad Master" by Eck himself—would get oiled together throughout the '78 season, much to the chagrin of Red Sox manager Don Zimmer. During one road trip to New York City, the wild pair even paid a visit to Xenon, a newly opened midtown Manhattan disco, where they marveled at the variety of weirdly costumed revelers getting down on the dance floor, including two naked, silver-painted individuals wearing *Saturday Night Live*-style Conehead prostheses. "And people think I'm bizarre," mused Lee.

Despite Eck's rowdy ways, he turned out to be a crucial addition to the Sox rotation, as did free-agent signee Mike Torrez. Eck went 20-8 in 1978, leading all Boston starters in ERA (2.99), innings pitched (268⅓), strikeouts (162), and complete games (16), while the dependable Torrez went 16-13 with a 3.96 ERA in 250 innings, delivering 15 complete games of his own. Bob Stanley, an iron-armed 23-year-old right-hander pitching in only his second major league season, gave the staff added depth with his ability to start, close, and do everything in between; it was not uncommon to see Stanley come in during the third or fourth inning when a starter was in trouble, and pitch all the way to the end of the game. He would finish the season with a 15-2 record and a team-leading 2.60 ERA and 10 saves, despite striking out only 38 batters in 142⅔ innings of work.

Even with disappointing seasons from first baseman George "Boomer" Scott (who dropped from 33 taters to 12) and third baseman Butch Hobson (whose homer output declined from 30 to 17, and 43 errors gave him a wretched .899 fielding percentage—the worst any full-time fielder had accrued since the deadball era), the Red Sox lineup was nearly as fearsome as it had been in '77. Fred Lynn (.298, 22 HRs, 82 RBIs) bounced back from a mediocre year, while Carlton Fisk put up typically solid numbers (.284, 20 HRs, 88 RBIs, 94 runs) and Dwight Evans hit 24 homers, breaking the 20-HR mark for the first time in his career. But the indisputable driving force of the Boston offense was Jim Rice, who hit .315 while playing in every single game, and led the league in 15 different categories, including home runs (46), triples (15), RBIs (139), hits (213), and slugging percentage (.600). Rice's 406 total bases not only led the majors, but he became the first player since Joe DiMaggio in 1937 to rack up more than 400. The monster year earned the Red Sox star his first and only AL MVP Award.

After a sluggish 11-9 April, the Rice-powered Sox began to soar, going 41-14 over May and June, moving into first place in mid-May; by July 5, they'd widened their lead over second-place New York and Milwaukee to 10 games. Opposing pitchers initially tried to defuse the Sox' attack by backing Rice off the plate, though that tactic was all but abandoned after an early-May game against the Royals, in which the powerfully built Rice strode out to the mound to calmly inform Kansas City's Jim Colborn that he would tear his head off the next time Colborn threw one up and in on him. "I thought it was all over," Colborn told reporters after the game. "I thought he was going to turn me into Rice-a-Roni."

Though the Red Sox spent the late spring and early summer steamrolling their competition, portents of impending doom began rearing their ugly heads. Various injuries sidelined Evans, Hobson, Carbo, and shortstop Rick Burleson, while Scott's numbers began to nosedive once the portly first baseman went on a crash diet to try to lose some of his excess belly. Despite lacking sufficient bench or farm-system depth to shore up their lineup, the Sox sold Carbo (the team's "10th man," who had hit 15 homers in only 228 at bats in 1977) to the Indians in June for $15,000. Lee, who suspected that the front office had chosen to get rid of the flaky but popular outfielder rather than negotiate a new contract with him, briefly walked off the team in protest, predicting that the Sox had just blown their chance at winning the AL pennant.

With the Red Sox seemingly cruising with ease toward the AL East crown, no one took Lee's dire prophecy seriously, especially since the Spaceman's continuing feud with Zimmer seemed utterly innocuous compared to the bad blood that was boiling down in the Bronx. Sparky Lyle, who in Graig Nettles's memorable phrase had "gone from Cy Young to sayonara" with the arrival of Goose Gossage, found himself relegated to long-relief duty, and let it be known that he wanted to be traded to a team that would use him as a closer. Several other players, including Nettles, Lou Piniella, Roy White, Ed Figueroa, and even team captain Thurman Munson, also expressed their desire to play elsewhere.

On a commercial flight from Kansas City to Chicago in mid-May, Munson goaded manager Billy Martin into a mini-meltdown by repeatedly blasting snippets of Neil Diamond songs from his portable cassette player. Martin, already quite drunk and apparently not much of a Neil Diamond fan, showered Munson with an array of angry expletives and threats, all of which Munson took great pleasure in pretending to ignore. When the team arrived in Chicago, Martin told Munson that he was going to come to his hotel room to settle things man to man; Munson waited patiently for Martin to arrive, but the Yankee manager was either too drunk to find the right room, or chickened out of the confrontation at the last minute.

Team morale was further worsened by injuries to Willie Randolph, Bucky Dent, Mickey Rivers, Don Gullett, and Catfish Hunter, as well as by the three-ring circus that seemed to revolve continually around Martin, Reggie Jackson, and owner George Steinbrenner. And it didn't help matters much that Gossage, the team's new millionaire closer, didn't seem at all like his old dominating self; he blew his first two save opportunities of the season, and lost his first three decisions.

Yankee fans expressed their annoyance at the Goose's lousy April by pelting the Yankees' bullpen car—a pin-striped Datsun 1200—with garbage whenever it ferried Gossage into the game, and his new teammates weren't much kinder. During one game, Munson greeted Gossage on the mound with a "How are you gonna lose *this* one?" In another, Gossage had just finished climbing into the car when Mickey Rivers prostrated himself upon the hood of the vehicle and refused to budge. When one of the umpires, curious about the lull in the action, ran out to the bullpen to see what was going on, Rivers comically implored him to keep Gossage from entering the game. "Pleeeaassse, Mr. Umpire," he begged. "We don't wants Goose to come in. We wants to win this ball game. We don't wants to lose."

Gossage finally notched his first save in early May, and the Yankees began to play again like their World Champion selves, going 19-8 for the month. (Five of those May victories were credited to Ron "Gator" Guidry, a.k.a. "the Ragin' Cajun," who won 13 straight before finally losing to Milwaukee on July 7.) Unfortunately, the team never seemed to gain on the Red Sox. Up by three games over the Yankees at the end of May, Boston increased its lead steadily as spring turned into summer, and a frustrated Steinbrenner began making regular visits to the Yankee clubhouse, ranting about how the team was embarrassing him and the city of New York, and that he'd "clean house" if he had to, replacing the Yankees' starters with minor league prospects.

The Yankee players, of course, had less to fear than Martin, whose head was clearly on the chopping block. Steinbrenner warred constantly with Martin over the manager's preference for sitting Jackson on the bench against tough left-handers, as well as his refusal to let Jackson play right field with any regularity. (Being relegated to a part-time DH didn't make the hero of the 1977 World Series a particularly happy camper, either.) Martin's physical and mental health seemed to be in rapid decline—due, in part, to his prodigious intake of alcohol, the stress brought on by Steinbrenner's constant meddling, and the additional strain of trying to keep his live-in relationship with a 16-year-old South Bronx girl under wraps—and rumors abounded that Steinbrenner and Bill Veeck (whose White Sox were still in the thick of the AL West race as of mid-June, despite playing sub-.500 baseball) were seriously considering swapping Martin even up for White Sox manager Bob Lemon.

Jay Johnstone, the famously flaky Phillies utility man, was traded to the Yankees in mid-June in exchange for reliever Rawly Eastwick, whose vegetarianism and preference for reading *Rolling Stone* over the *Sporting*

News had caused the Yankee coaching staff to regard him with intense suspicion. Johnstone, who despite his goofy demeanor was a fairly perceptive individual, picked up on the dark and chaotic atmosphere in the Bronx as soon as he walked in the door. "Frankly, I felt I was one of the sanest people in the Yankee clubhouse," he later recalled in his autobiography, *Temporary Insanity*, noting that his fondest memory from his brief Bronx sojourn was watching "Mickey Rivers, in one automobile, being chased around the parking lot of Yankee Stadium by his irate wife, who was in another." By Johnstone's count, the squabbling couple severely damaged at least 11 other cars during their impromptu demolition derby.

By most accounts, Reggie Jackson had been making more of an effort to fit in with his Yankee teammates than he had during his first season with the club. But Jackson was growing increasingly frustrated with Martin treating him like a spare part; and on July 17, he finally went over Martin's head and met with Steinbrenner and team president Al Rosen to complain about the situation. To Jackson's shock and surprise, Steinbrenner—who had typically aligned himself with Jackson in conflicts involving his star slugger and manager—sided with Martin, then insulted Jackson's fielding ability and told him, "You better get your head on straight, boy." The conversation deteriorated from there, and Jackson left Steinbrenner's office feeling even angrier than when he'd walked in.

That night, when Jackson came to bat in the top of the 10th against the Royals, with the score tied 5–5, nobody out, and Thurman Munson on first, he was startled to see third-base coach Dick Howser signaling for a bunt. Martin, who had flashed the signal to Howser, intended to have Jackson decoy the Kansas City infielders into playing in, thus giving Jackson more of an opening to smack a hot grounder through the infield. But Jackson, who had been stewing since his earlier meeting with Steinbrenner, took the bunt signal as yet another emasculating affront from his manager; one strike later, Howser flashed the hit-away sign, yet Jackson continued to bunt twice more until he popped the ball foul for an automatic out. The Yankees failed to score in the inning, and wound up losing the game 9–7 in the 11th. They were now in fourth place in the AL East, 14 games behind the Red Sox.

Martin, absolutely incensed by Jackson's insubordination, chose not to confront Jackson physically as he'd done at Fenway in June '77, and merely trashed his office instead. Martin demanded that Steinbrenner suspend Jackson for the remainder of the season for his actions; Jackson, emotionally spent and sick of dealing with both the manager and the owner, secretly hoped for a similar outcome. Steinbrenner, who understood that the Yankees needed Jackson's bat if they were going to make it back to the World Series, handed down a five-game suspension, and Jackson spent the following week cooling his heels at a girlfriend's home in Oakland, emerging only to take in the popular new horror film *Damien–Omen II* at a local cinema.

When Jackson returned to the team in Chicago on July 23, he promptly pissed off his teammates and his manager again by skipping batting practice to speak to reporters about his suspension; instead of offering up a humble mea culpa for the bunt incident, Jackson told the press, "The way I interpret it, I haven't done anything wrong." Martin, informed afterward of Jackson's comments, began to seethe.

That night at O'Hare Airport, while the team waited to board a flight to Kansas City, Martin—who had stopped eating in recent days, and was now basically living on a steady liquid diet of scotch and water—repaired to the nearest airport bar with Murray Chass of the *New York Times* and let fly with a torrent of drunken invective about Jackson and Steinbrenner, bending Chass's ear about how the two men were making his life miserable and his job impossible. "They deserve each other," he said in summation. "One's a born liar, and the other's convicted." Chass asked Martin if he was sure he wanted such inflammatory words reproduced in the newspaper. "Print it," Martin demanded.

Steinbrenner, still rather sensitive about being busted for violating campaign funding laws on behalf of Richard Nixon's re-election campaign, took Martin's rant as the final straw. He sent Al Rosen to Kansas City to fire Martin, but the Yankee manager—knowing full well that his outburst had violated the stipulation in his contract that he couldn't criticize Steinbrenner to the media—attempted to save face by resigning before he could be fired.

Steinbrenner, a puppet master to the last, agreed to pay out the remainder of Martin's contract, but only on the condition that Martin make a public apology and announce that he was resigning due to the precarious state of his health, as opposed to any conflicts he might have had with Jackson or the Yankee owner. In the tearful televised press conference that followed on July 25, a blubbering Martin spoke at length about how much the Yankee tradition meant to him, and how he didn't want to be a distraction to the team. "I'd like to thank the Yankee management, the press and news media," he sobbed, without any trace of irony, "my coaches, my players . . . and most of all . . . the fans."

Bob Lemon, fired by the White Sox in June, was promptly installed as the new Yankee skipper. Lem's replacement in Chicago was Larry Doby, who in 1947 had been tapped by Bill Veeck (then owner of the Cleveland Indians) to become the second African-American to play in the major leagues. Now, thanks to Veeck, Doby became the second African-American to manage a major league team. His managerial stint would be far less distinguished than his Hall of Fame playing career, however; the White Sox went 37-50 under Doby, finishing in fifth place in the AL West. Doby would never manage in the big leagues again.

The volcanic outpouring of fan rage that followed Martin's ouster (despite the public "resignation," his exit clearly had Steinbrenner's fingerprints all over it) took the Yankee owner by surprise. The Yankee Stadium switchboard was deluged by thousands of callers, several of whom threatened to kill Steinbrenner for what he'd done. Even worse, the Mets—who, in the midst of another dismal season and well on the way to their worst attendance numbers since 1962, were desperate to find a way to bring fans back to Shea Stadium—let it be known that they were interested in hiring Martin as their new manager, replacing current manager Joe Torre. The prospect of Martin decamping to the Mets, and thus shifting the attention of New York baseball fans and sportswriters from the Bronx to Flushing Meadows, was too frightening for the egotistical Steinbrenner to consider; only two days after Martin's emotional farewell, the Yankee owner secretly met with Martin at the Carlyle Hotel to negotiate his former manager's return to the team.

On July 29, the Yankees held their annual Old-Timers' Day in the Bronx. Following the introduction of past Yankees greats, including the "Big Three"—Whitey Ford, Mickey Mantle, and Joe DiMaggio—Yankee Stadium PA announcer Bob Sheppard took the microphone and told the 46,711 paying customers that he had "two very special announcements" to make. The first was that the Yankees had given Bob Lemon a contract extension through the end of the 1979 season; the crowd, many of whom brandished angry signs demanding Martin's return, howled with displeasure. Sheppard's second announcement was that, in 1980, Lemon would be kicked upstairs to become the team's GM. The crowd booed some more, forcing Sheppard to plead repeatedly for their attention.

"The Yankees would like to announce at this time," Sheppard intoned, once the noise level finally abated somewhat, "that the manager for the 1980 season and hopefully for many years after that will be number 1 . . . Billy Martin." The packed stadium erupted as a grinning Martin came running out onto the field; the deafening standing ovation lasted for more than six minutes, while the players looked on in stunned silence. In just four days, his former skipper had gone from Steinbrenner whipping boy to the future of the Yankee organization.

"The thought [of Martin being rehired] had never even crossed anyone's mind," Lyle later recalled. "No one, and I mean no one, could believe it." Gossage's jaw practically hit the dugout floor; making the adjustment to the "Bronx Zoo" had been difficult enough, but now he felt like he'd just stepped into *The Twilight Zone*. "Only Rod Serling could dream up something like this," he marveled.

Out in Los Angeles, the Dodgers' season wasn't following the standard Hollywood script, either. After beginning May in first place in the NL West, the Dodgers began to stumble just as the Reds and the Giants were picking up steam; and after losing two out of three to the lowly Cubs during a mid-May homestand, Lasorda's boys found themselves in third place. Dave Kingman, the Cubs' big free-agent signing during the off-season, single-handedly beat the Dodgers in the third game of that

weekend series, hitting three homers and plating eight runs over the course of a 15-inning, 10–7 Cubs victory. After the game, when reporter Paul Olden asked Lasorda what he thought of Kingman's performance, the Dodger manager responded with a harangue that, thanks to it being captured on tape, would go down in history as one of the all-time great managerial tirades.

"What's my opinion of Kingman's performance!?" yelled Lasorda, taken aback by the question. "What the fuck do you *think* is my opinion of it? I think it was fucking horseshit! Put that in [the paper], I don't fucking care. *Opinion of his performance?* Jesus Christ, he beat us with three fucking home runs! What the fuck do you mean, 'What is my opinion of his performance?' How could you ask me a question like that, 'What is my opinion of his performance?' Jesus Christ, he hit three home runs! Jesus Christ! I'm fucking pissed off to lose the fucking game. And you ask me my opinion of his performance! Jesus Christ. That's a tough question to ask me, isn't it? 'What is my opinion of his performance?'"

If Billy Martin had spewed vitriol like that to a New York journalist, it would have been all over the papers the following day. But the L.A. sports media took a much more deferential line with Lasorda, so the outburst went unreported. Nor did L.A. reporters seem especially interested in digging into the motivation behind the Dodgers' May trade of backup outfielder Glenn Burke to the A's in exchange for Billy North, even though the trade made little sense—both men were outfielders who had plenty of speed but little power, and had virtually identical batting averages (Burke was hitting .211 to North's .212) at the time of the trade. Though they were similar players, North was 30 years old and seemed to be on the decline, while Burke was a promising 25-year-old who had yet to see a full season of big-league action. But in his 1995 autobiography, *Out at Home*, Burke would allege that the Dodger brass had a very specific reason for shipping him off—they didn't want a gay player on their team.

Burke wouldn't publicly declare his homosexuality until after he'd retired from baseball; but in the 1970s, he was a well-known and popular figure in the gay communities of Los Angeles and the Bay Area, and he frequented gay bars in most of the cities where the Dodgers played.

Burke claimed that the Dodger brass was well aware of this, and was concerned about the effect it might have upon the team's clean-cut image; according to Burke, Dodger GM Al Campanis tried to convince the outfielder to marry a woman, even offering to pay for the honeymoon. Burke refused to go through with it, and just a few days later found himself wearing A's green instead of Dodger blue. Campanis, for his part, would later confirm his suggestion that Burke get married, but claimed he'd made it only because the Dodgers felt marriage tended to make young players "more serious about baseball."

Ironically, Burke's lover, sportswriter Michael J. Smith, had urged Burke to "come out of the closet" during the 1977 World Series; it had been eight years since the Stonewall riots in New York City ushered in a new era of gay pride, and Smith reasoned that the high-profile coming out of a major league ballplayer (one who was playing in the World Series, no less) would further advance the cause of gay liberation. But Burke, who didn't exactly have the kind of superstar status that would have allowed him to be seen as more than just "that gay ballplayer," feared that retribution from the lords of baseball for such a revelation would be savage and swift. Given that the gay publication the *Advocate* had approached major league teams just two years earlier about doing interviews with "players living gay lifestyles"—only to be upbraided by the publicity director of the Minnesota Twins for "attempting to extend your perversion to an area of total manhood"—Burke was probably correct. In any case, Burke would be gone from major league baseball for good by the turn of the decade.

If 1977 had been a magical season for the Dodgers, 1978 was a hard slog that saw them struggling to keep pace for much of the year with Cincinnati and San Francisco. The addition of Vida Blue gave the Giants a much-needed shot in the arm department—the lefty hurler would go 18-10 for the season with a 2.79 ERA, also becoming the first pitcher to start the All-Star Game for both leagues—but the team also got a great year from 24-year-old southpaw Bob Knepper (17-11, 2.63 ERA, with a league-leading six shutouts), and solid stuff from John "the Count" Montefusco (11-9, 3.81, and a team-leading 177 Ks). The Giants' pitchers gave up only 84 home runs all season, the second fewest in the NL, and their combined 3.30 ERA was good for third lowest in the league.

Offensively, the Giants were less impressive, hitting only .248 as a team. On June 30, 40-year-old first sacker Willie McCovey became only the 12th player in history to reach the 500-homer mark, but his season totals (.228 batting average, 12 HRs, 64 RBIs) indicated that the future Hall of Famer was running out of gas. Thankfully for Giants fans, a new star was emerging at Candlestick: 22-year-old right fielder Jack Clark, who in only his second full season led the team in home runs (25), doubles (46), RBIs (98), and runs scored (90) while batting .306—third on the team behind third baseman Bill Madlock's .309 and first baseman/outfielder Mike Ivie's .308. Clark also stole 15 bases (second only to Madlock's 16), threw out 16 base runners from the outfield, and set a San Francisco record for longest hitting streak by batting safely in 26 straight games, two better than the previous team mark of 24, which McCovey had set in 1963.

Impressive as Clark's run may have been, no hitting streak attracted more attention in 1978 than Pete Rose's. The Reds' third baseman had reached a major career milestone on May 5, singling off of the Expos' Steve Rogers to join the elite 3,000-hit club. As Rose was one of the most consistent hitters of his era, it had been a foregone conclusion that "Charlie Hustle" would eventually reach 3,000 hits. What no one expected was that, at the age of 37, Rose would also mount a serious challenge to Joe DiMaggio's record of hitting safely in 56 consecutive games.

Rose's skein started, as such things often do, in mundane fashion; on June 14, he broke out of a 5-for-44 slump with a pair of singles off of the Cubs' Dave Roberts in a 3–1 Reds victory. It wasn't until July 15, when Rose singled off the Mets' Craig Swan to run his streak to 28 straight games—thereby breaking the Reds' team record of 27, held by Vada Pinson and Edd Roush, and tying the major league record for switch-hitters, set by Red Schoendienst in 1954—that folks outside of Cincinnati really began to pay attention. For the next two weeks, the buzz surrounding his streak grew exponentially louder with each game he hit safely in. The Great DiMag had been only 26 years of age in 1941, the year of his legendary streak; could a player 11 years older actually withstand the pressure, the media attention, and the daily wear and tear long enough to surpass Joltin' Joe?

Rose was clearly having fun with the whole thing, relishing the added attention like Morris the Cat chowing down on a can of 9-Lives. "I like pressure situations," he cheerfully told anyone who put a microphone in his face, which—in the wake of the July 25 contest against the Mets that saw him break Tommy Holmes's modern NL record of 37 straight games—included such illustrious interrogators as *Good Morning America*'s David Hartman, *Today*'s Dick Schaap, and *Donahue* host Phil Donahue. ABC's *Monday Night Baseball*, paying tribute to both Rose's lengthening streak and his almost supernaturally consistent abilities, ran a montage of Rose career highlights set to the tune of Bob Seger's "Still the Same," one of the summer of '78's biggest hits. Rose did admit, however, that his quest for DiMaggio's record was motivated by more than just the love of the game and his desire to be seen as one of its all-time greats. "Baseball is a team sport," he told *Sports Illustrated*, "but you get paid for what you do as an individual. My contract expires at the end of the season, and I want to prove I can still play." And, it went without saying, he wanted to see if he could score a much more lucrative contract in the reentry draft.

On July 31, Rose singled off the Braves' knuckleballer Phil Niekro (who at age 39 was on his way to one of his best seasons—19-18, 2.88 ERA, 248 strikeouts—with yet another lousy Atlanta team) to tie Wee Willie Keeler's all-time NL record of 44 straight games. The fact that Keeler had set the mark in 1897, back before foul balls were counted as strikes, made Rose's accomplishment that much more impressive. But the next night, August 1, Rose's streak finally ran out during a 16–4 loss to the Braves. Six times during the streak, Rose had kept things alive with a hit in his final at bat; but this time he whiffed in the top of the ninth against Braves closer Gene Garber, ending both the game and his hitting streak. A frustrated Rose carped to the press that the reliever should have challenged him with a fastball instead of nibbling the corners with his changeup. "Garber pitched like it was the ninth inning of the seventh game of the World Series," he groused. Given that Rose himself approached nearly every game situation as if the World Series were on the line, his complaint seemed more than a little hypocritical.

Powered by Rose's streak and the slugging heroics of George Foster (who led the NL with 40 HRs and 120 RBIs while hitting .281), the Big Red Machine won 92 games, up four from the previous year, but ultimately couldn't keep Lasorda's boys from repeating as champions of the NL West. Nor could the suddenly competitive San Diego squad, whose 84-78 record gave them the first above-.500 finish in Padres history. Dave Winfield led the team in batting (.308), home runs (24, nearly a third of the team's overall homer total), RBIs (97), hits (181), and doubles (30) while also stealing 21 bases, and shortstop Ozzie Smith's 40 steals and acrobatic glove work were good enough to land him second in the NL Rookie of the Year voting, behind Atlanta slugger Bob Horner. Wily old spitballer Gaylord Perry, who arrived via the Rangers shortly before the season began, went 21-7 with a 2.73 ERA for the Padres, winning the NL Cy Young Award in a landslide. Perry became the first pitcher in history to win the coveted pitching prize in both leagues; at 40 years of age, he became the oldest Cy Young winner as well. Perry's 21 victories also gave him 15 or more wins in 13 straight seasons. The last pitcher to do that? None other than Cy Young himself.

Placing second in 1978's NL Cy Young balloting was the Dodgers' Burt "Happy" Hooton, who led L.A. with a career-best 19 wins while also posting a 2.71 ERA. But while the Dodger rotation got reliably strong years from veterans Tommy John (17-10, 3.30 ERA), Doug Rau (15-9, 3.26), and Don Sutton (15-11, 3.55), it was the contributions of a younger arm that really gave the team an unexpected boost during a crucial juncture in the season. On June 20, Bob Welch, a 21-year-old rookie right-hander barely a year out of Eastern Michigan University, made his major league debut for the Dodgers, throwing two scoreless relief innings in a 5–3 loss to the Astros; the following night, Welch notched his first victory by throwing two more scoreless frames against Houston in an extra-inning win. With their rookie righty sounding the wakeup call, the Dodgers slowly, imperceptibly, began to come to life and gain ground against Cincinnati and San Francisco. During his first two months with the team, Welch would appear in 14 games, saving three and winning five—two of those victories coming in crucial August starts against Ed Halicki and Vida Blue of the Giants. And on August 16, Welch pulled the Dodgers into first place for good with a 5–2 complete-game win over the Phillies.

Ironically, just as the Dodgers appeared finally to be getting it together, an incident occurred that threatened to derail their season completely. On August 20, Don Sutton and Steve Garvey completely blew the team's carefully constructed "one big happy family" image with a vicious fight in the Shea Stadium visitors' clubhouse. The much-publicized scuffle was detonated by a recent *Washington Post* interview with Sutton, in which the veteran pitcher had taken a swipe at Garvey's Madison Avenue image while asserting that Reggie Smith's significant contributions to the team were overshadowed by Garvey's because "Reggie doesn't go out and publicize himself. He doesn't smile at the right people or say the right things." (Smith would lead the Dodgers in 1978 with 29 homers despite missing 34 games due to injuries, and his .295 batting average and 93 RBIs were second on the team only to Garvey's .316 and 113 ribbies.)

Garvey's painstakingly coiffed Mr. Clean persona had rankled many of his teammates over the years—especially Sutton, the longest-serving Dodger on the roster. When Garvey confronted Sutton about the *Post* article shortly before the beginning of the team's August 20 game against the Mets, what initially appeared to be a civil (if somewhat tense) exchange suddenly escalated into a no-holds-barred wrestling match. Sutton "leaped at Garvey and shoved him into the lockers," according to UPI sports editor Milton Richman, who watched the whole thing unfold. "They went down on the floor, clawing and scratching at each other, trying to get in blows." It took the combined strength of Davey Lopes, Bill Russell, Reggie Smith, and Rick Monday to pull the grappling pair apart. "Aw, let 'em go," cracked catcher Joe Ferguson. "Maybe they'll kill each other."

Both players suffered only minor facial cuts in the fracas; Garvey, who had been poked in the eye, looked somewhat groggy as he was led away to the trainer's room, though he recovered sufficiently by game time to go 2-for-4 in the Dodgers' 5–4 victory. But the Sutton-Garvey bout left a sizable bruise upon the Dodgers' previously blemish-free veneer, and the team's PR-conscious front office was mortified by the amount of publicity that the incident received. When the players returned to L.A. later in the week, Sutton was forced to make a public apology to the team and its fans, though his teary mea culpa was noticeably devoid of any apology to Garvey. Still, the team seemed energized in the wake of the fracas, playing 19-7 ball in the four weeks that followed, inflating its division lead to nine games in the process. The Dodgers slipped a bit in the second half of September, going 5-9 over the last two weeks, but managed to hold on and win the NL West crown by 2½ games over the Reds.

In one of the odder twists of the season, Jim Bouton made a brief cameo appearance in the NL West pennant race. Yes, *that* Jim Bouton; after spending several years as a sportscaster and actor—he costarred with Elliott Gould in Robert Altman's 1973 film adaptation of Raymond Chandler's *The Long Goodbye*—the retired knuckleballer and *Ball Four* author had gotten the itch to pitch again. In 1977, Bill Veeck gave him a tryout with the White Sox Class A farm team in Portland, which led to Atlanta owner Ted Turner's giving him a shot in the Braves' minor league system; and after winning 12 games with Savannah in 1978, the 39-year-old pitcher was called back up to "the show." Bouton made his big-league return on September 10 against Sutton and the Dodgers, and pitched three no-hit innings before the Dodgers got the hang of his knuckler and smoked him for six runs. The Dodgers were less than gracious in victory: "It was like facing Bozo the Clown," said Dodger outfielder Rick Monday of Bouton's return. "We're in a pennant race," cracked Reds skipper Sparky Anderson. "Bouton should have to pitch against the Giants and Reds, too."

In fact, Bouton beat San Francisco 4–1 four days later, giving up only three hits in six innings. ("It was the most humiliating experience of my life," moaned Giants third baseman Darrell Evans.) And on September 24, Anderson very nearly had to eat his words; after the Reds eked out a 2–1 win over Bouton, who pitched eight strong innings, the Cincy skipper told the press, "We didn't even hit the ball hard off him and we got two runs we shouldn't have gotten."

Ultimately, Bouton had little actual impact on the NL West race; and, having racked up a 1-3 record in five starts with a 4.97 ERA in his return to the majors, the pitcher decided it was time to retire for good. He'd make his next contribution to baseball with Big League Chew, a brand of bubble gum that was shredded like chewing tobacco, and came similarly packaged in an aluminum foil pouch. Bouton and minor leaguer Rob Nelson first hatched the idea while hanging out in the Portland Mavericks bullpen; introduced in 1980, Big League Chew offered a considerably less addictive and toxic substitute for tobacco, and would go on to sell more than 450 million pouches over the next 25 years. "I'm a little concerned about promoting a product with sugar in it," Bouton admitted at the time, "but I figure I'm morally covered. Our original idea called for brown sugarless wheat germ gum. It just didn't test well."

Like the Reds, the squad the Phillies fielded in 1978 was far less impressive than the 1977 version. The Phils won 11 fewer games in '78 than they had the year before—finishing at 90-72 instead of 101-61—while the team's batting average dropped from .279 to .258, and its total home runs shrank from 186 to 133. Greg Luzinski led the team with 35 homers and 101 RBIs, but his batting average sank to .265 from the previous season's .309, while Mike Schmidt's 21 homers and 78 RBIs were his fewest since his rookie year. No one on the Phils even managed to bat .300; light-hitting shortstop Larry Bowa led the team with a .294 average, while Garry Maddox (who led the team with 33 steals) was second with .288.

The Phillies' pitching staff likewise turned in a solid yet unremarkable collective performance; Steve Carlton led the starters with 16 wins, 161 strikeouts, 247⅓ innings pitched, 12 complete games, and a 2.84 ERA, little more than a mediocre year by his standards, while Larry Christenson (13-14, 3.24), Randy Lerch (11-8, 3.96), and Dick Ruthven (13-5, 2.99) basically did their best to keep the team in the game until relievers Warren Brusstar (6-3, 2.33), Tug McGraw (8-7, 3.21, nine saves), and closer Ron Reed (3-4, 2.24, 17 saves) could come in and seal the deal. The team even drew about 115,000 fewer fans to Veterans Stadium than the year before—not a huge decline, though it certainly trended against the overall boost in major league attendance.

But if the Phillies were less exciting to watch in 1978 than the year before, they still played well enough to snag the NL East crown for the third straight season, despite a gallant late-season charge by the Pirates, led by Dave Parker, who snagged the NL MVP Award by batting a league-leading .334 with 30 home runs, 117 RBIs, and 102 runs scored. Perhaps if Parker hadn't missed 11 games with a broken cheekbone—or if Willie Stargell, who hit .295 with 28 homers and 97 RBIs despite various aches and pains, had been able to play more than 122 games—the Pirates might have been able to rack up enough Ws to push past the Phillies. But when the two teams faced off at the end of the season for a four-game series in Pittsburgh, the Bucs were back 3½ games, which meant they needed a sweep to take the division. Parker and Co. made Philly fans nervous by taking the first two contests, then going up 4–1 in the first inning of the third on a Stargell grand slam. Momentum seemed to be on the side of Pittsburgh, until the Phillies took the lead on a three-run Luzinski homer, and the Philadelphia bullpen hung on to win the game 10–8. For the third year in a row, the Phillies were advancing to the NLCS.

Over in Kansas City, the AL bridesmaids of the previous two seasons mirrored the power outage of their NL counterparts in Philadelphia. The Royals went 92-70 in 1978, winning 10 fewer games than in 1977, while the team batting average dipped to .268 from .277, and the team's home run output dropped from 146 to 98. Center fielder Amos Otis led the team with 22 HRs, 96 RBIs, and a .298 batting average (he also stole 32 bases), while George Brett—like the Phillies' Mike Schmidt—had his worst offensive season since *his* rookie year, hitting an uncharacteristically low

.294 with only nine HRs and 62 RBIs. (Brett's 45 doubles did, however, lead the league.)

But if the Royals were not quite as intimidating at the plate as in previous seasons—partly because they'd sold off Big John Mayberry to the Toronto Blue Jays at the beginning of the season—they still rattled their opponents with speed. The Royals stole 216 bases in 1978, up from 170 the year before; the team leader in thefts was freakishly fast rookie outfielder Willie Wilson, who managed to swipe 46 bags despite hitting only .217 in 198 at bats and appearing in most of his 127 games as a late-inning defensive replacement. "In this park, we don't drop a big bomb on people," explained McRae, referring to the synthetically carpeted fun-house that was Royals Stadium. "We just run them all over the place."

The team also boasted a very tough four-man rotation that featured Dennis Leonard (21-17 with 20 complete games, 3.33 ERA, 183 Ks in 294⅔ innings), Paul Splittorff (19-13, 3.40), Rich Gale (14-8, 3.09), and Larry Gura (16-4, 2.72), while the off-season acquisition of Al "the Mad Hungarian" Hrabosky gave the Kansas City bullpen a much-needed full-time closer. Hrabosky, who had battled with Cardinals manager Vern Rapp over the right to grow facial hair, was allowed to regrow his intimidating Fu Manchu mustache in Kansas City, and responded by going 8-7 with a 2.88 ERA and 20 saves.

Like the Phillies, the Royals moved into first place in their division in June—though, dogged first by Oakland (before the A's completely collapsed), then by the California Angels and Texas Rangers, the Kansas City squad wasn't able to pull away from the pack until mid-September. Both the Rangers and Angels finished the year five games in back of the Royals; the Angels' 87-75 record was an 11-game improvement over their previous season, and the team's first above-.500 finish since 1970, but the murder of right fielder Lyman Bostock left a dark cloud over the team's season.

After signing a multimillion-dollar free agent contract with the Angels in the off-season, Bostock got off to a terrible start in 1978, batting only .209 through the first two months of the season. Afraid that he was letting the team and its fans down with his extended slump, Bostock approached Angels owner Gene Autry and offered to return his April salary. Autry declined Bostock's offer, but told his outfielder that he would help him find a worthy charity to donate that money to. The gesture endeared Bostock to Angels fans, and further solidified his reputation as one of the game's good guys; it would also make his premature death that much harder to fathom.

On September 23, following a 5–4 loss to the White Sox at Comiskey (in which he'd knocked a single and a double), Bostock paid a visit to his uncle, Thomas Turner, who lived in nearby Gary, Indiana. The two men got together whenever Bostock came to Chitown; on this night, Bostock wanted to take Turner and his two goddaughters, Joan Hawkins and Barbara Smith, to dinner. The four piled into Turner's Buick, with Bostock sitting in the backseat next to Barbara, and headed out to a local restaurant. While the Buick was idling at a traffic light, Barbara spotted her estranged husband, Leonard Smith, pulling up alongside Turner's vehicle. Barbara became visibly upset and urged Turner to floor it; he sped through three stoplights with Smith in pursuit.

Unfortunately, the next light Turner came to was at Fifth and Jackson, one of Gary's busier intersections, and Turner didn't want to risk running the red light in the midst of Saturday-night traffic. While both cars were stopped at the light, Smith emerged from his car with a shotgun and fired it into the backseat of Turner's Buick; the shot, intended for Barbara, hit Bostock in the left temple. Turner drove as fast as he could to a local hospital; but after several attempts to save him, Bostock was pronounced dead. He was 27 years old.

While Bostock's murder was surely the most tragic and traumatic event of the 1978 season, the slow collapse of the '78 Red Sox would still be remembered (and bitterly lamented) in Boston decades after Angels fans had forgotten all about their fallen right fielder. Up by seven games over the second-place Yankees on August 30, the Sox should have been able to waltz to the AL East pennant; but the Yankees, under Bob Lemon's relaxed supervision, after going 19-8 in August, had no intention of slow-ing down. "You guys won last year, which means you must have been doing something right," Lemon had told the Yankee players in his first meeting with them. "So what do you say you go out and play just like you did last year, and I'll try to stay out of the way."

Though the Yankee bats slumped to a .267 team average and 125 hom-ers in 1978 (down from .281 and 184 in '77), there was no question that their starting lineup—which was virtually identical to the previous year's—knew how to win games. Lou Piniella (.314) was the only Bronx Bomber to hit over .300 for the season, though Thurman Munson came close with .297, while Reggie Jackson (.274, 27 HRs, 97 RBIs), Graig Nettles (.276, 27 HRs, 93 RBIs), and Chris Chambliss (.274, 12 HRs, 90 RBIs) plated the bulk of New York's runs. Mickey Rivers had one of his worst years at the plate, hitting only .265, but still managed to swipe 25 bases; Mick the Quick's position as top base thief on the team was usurped by 23-year-old second baseman Willie Randolph, who stole 36 bases while hitting .279 and generally playing with the poise of a veteran 10 years his senior. The Yankee bench, which included outfielders Roy White, Gary Thomasson, and Paul Blair, catcher Mike Heath, and in-fielders Jim Spencer, Fred Stanley, and Brian Doyle, was solid enough to keep the team from capsizing when Randolph, Rivers, Piniella, and shortstop Bucky Dent went down with injuries.

But it was pitching that really kept the Yankees in the race during the second half of the season. Ron Guidry's incredible performance (25-3 with 16 complete games, nine shutouts, a 1.74 ERA, and 248 strikeouts—including 18 in a June 17 game against the Angels, setting an AL record for lefties) more than earned him the AL Cy Young Award, but Ed Figueroa (20-9, 2.99) and, despite his rough first month, Goose Gossage (10-11, 2.01, 27 saves, and 122 Ks in 134⅓ innings) were nearly as key to the Yankees' suc-cess in 1978. Between them, Gator, Figgy, and Goose pitched nearly half of the Bronx staff's total innings and accounted for more than half of the team's victories. Catfish Hunter, who'd pitched only six games during the first half of the season due to injuries, returned to the rotation in mid-July and went 10-3 the rest of the way with a 2.88 ERA.

The Yankees were four games behind the Red Sox on September 7, when they arrived in Boston for a four-game series; they wound up slaughtering the Sox by scores of 15–3, 13–2, 7–0, and 7–4. Bill Lee, who pitched in relief in two of the contests, was impressed—and frightened—by the Yankees' merciless drubbing of his team. "Getting on the field with them was akin to stepping into a wading pool with *Jaws*," he said. "Every time we made a move, they would bite off another limb. It was terrifying to watch." "The Boston Massacre," as the sweep came to be known, left the two teams tied for first place with only 14 games remaining. "By the time the Yankees left Fenway," said Lee, "we were walking around in a daze. It was as if the entire team had just returned from Cambodia."

The sweep also marked Lee's final outing in a Red Sox uniform. His long-running feud with manager Don Zimmer had grown so poisonous that Zimmer refused—despite Lee's long history of effectiveness against the Yankees—to start him in any of the four games, even starting a totally green rookie named Bobby Sprowl over Lee on September 10. Sprowl was knocked out of the box in the first inning; Lee eventually got into the game in the seventh, by which time the Yankee victory was a foregone conclusion. Lee claimed Zimmer had been overheard telling someone, "There's no way that California fag"—i.e., Lee—"is ever going to pitch for me." Zimmer denied making the comment, but also showed no further inclination to give Lee the ball, even as the team slipped behind the Yankees in the standings.

Still, the Red Sox had plenty of fight left in them—they went 11-2 over the last two weeks of September, a pace that pulled them back to within a game of the Yankees with only one game left to play. On October 1, the final day of the season, Luis Tiant kept their hopes alive by shutting out the Toronto Blue Jays 5–0 at Fenway, while Rick Waits and the Cleveland Indians beat Catfish and the Yankees 9–2 in the Bronx. The two teams ended the season tied for first place at 99-63, and a one-game playoff was hastily scheduled for the next day to decide which team would advance to the ALCS against the Royals.

For the dramatic final showdown between the two rivals, Zimmer gave Mike Torrez the ball, while Lemon opted to go with Guidry. Visiting left-handers typically had difficulty pitching at Fenway, especially against right-handed power hitters like Jim Rice and Carlton Fisk, but Guidry was no typical lefty; the wiry hurler had already beaten the Red Sox three times during the season, including a two-hit shutout at Fenway on September 9. But when Carl Yastrzemski took Guidry deep with a solo shot in the second, it seemed like the Ragin' Cajun might be vulnerable after all. Torrez was practically untouchable through six innings, and when Rice singled in Rick Burleson in the bottom of the sixth, giving the Red Sox a 2–0 lead, Fenway shook to its rafters with the sounds of celebration.

But Torrez was tiring. With one out in the seventh, Chris Chambliss and Roy White rapped back-to-back singles, bringing Jim Spencer to the plate as a pinch hitter for second baseman Brian Doyle, who had been subbing for the injured Randolph. Torrez got Spencer to fly out to left, and the crowd breathed a sigh of relief as Bucky Dent stepped to the plate. Dent, the team's regular shortstop, was nobody's idea of a slugger, having averaged just over four home runs per season in five full years in the bigs.

After taking Torrez's first pitch for a strike, Dent fouled the second pitch off his front foot, and dropped to the ground writhing in pain. While the Yankee trainer attempted to numb the pain by spraying ethyl chloride on Dent's foot, Mickey Rivers—waiting his turn at bat from the on-deck circle—realized that Dent was using one of Rivers's bats, which had been cracked during batting practice. "Hey, homey, you're using the wrong bat," Rivers told Dent, handing him a different one.

The bat exchange and the treatment of Dent's instep took only three, maybe four minutes to complete, but it was enough to throw Torrez off his rhythm. His next pitch to Dent was intended as an inside fastball, which should have knocked the shortstop off the plate and set him up for an outside slider; unfortunately for Torrez, the pitch tailed into the strike zone, and Dent (who would henceforth be forever known in Boston as "Bucky Fuckin' Dent") smacked it out to left on a high arc. Yastrzemski, playing left field for the Sox, slowly backed his way toward the Green Monster, punching his mitt as he waited for the ball to come to earth. It never did, landing instead in the netting above the wall. The Yankees had taken a 3–2 lead; the ballpark was so quiet, you could have heard the belching of an overfed Fenway rat.

The Yankees got another run in the inning when Thurman Munson scored Rivers with a double off of reliever Bob Stanley, who was pitching on only one day's rest; Reggie Jackson then touched Stanley for a solo shot to center in the top of the eighth. Down 5–2, the Red Sox came clawing back against Gossage in the bottom of the eighth, narrowing the Yankee lead to one with RBI singles from Yaz and Fred Lynn. Despite the rough frame, Lemon opted to stick with Gossage in the bottom of the ninth. The Goose got the first batter, Dwight Evans, to fly to left, then walked Rick Burleson. The next batter, Jerry Remy, slashed a vicious liner that fell in front of right fielder Lou Piniella; Sweet Lou was blinded by the late-afternoon sun (he later admitted he "didn't see the damn thing until it landed about ten feet in front of me") but somehow managed to get his glove up and make the stop. Had the ball gotten past him, Burleson would have scored easily, and the winning run would have been on second or third with only one out. Instead, Burleson had to hold at second.

Next up was Jim Rice, who was coming off one of the most remarkable offensive seasons in history, and could easily have ended the game with one powerful blow; instead, Gossage got him to hit a long fly to Piniella, which advanced Burleson to third. Now Carl Yastrzemski, the Red Sox hero of 1967, came to the plate, hoping to crush a two-out Gossage fastball and thereby become the hero of 1978. Gossage, who by his own admission had "never come close to playing in a game of that magnitude," was petrified; he managed to calm down slightly by telling himself that if he couldn't get Yaz out, the worst thing that could happen was that he'd be headed back home to Colorado to hunt elk. Yaz weakly popped his second pitch to Nettles at third, and the Goose's elk-hunting plans were temporarily put on hold. Bob Lemon was now the first manager in history to win a title after beginning the season with a different ballclub, and the Yankees were returning to the postseason for the third year running.

The Royals, awaiting the outcome of the one-game playoff, were less than enthusiastic to learn that they would, once again, be facing the Yankees in the ALCS. "I think everybody in Kansas City was pulling for the Red Sox," George Brett later recalled, "because we hadn't had any success against the Yankees in the playoffs." They wouldn't have any in 1978, either.

Despite blowing out the Yankees 10–4 in Game 2, thanks in part to a surprise two-run homer by Freddie Patek, and a heroic three-homer performance by Brett in Game 3 (which the Yankees won 6–5 on a mammoth two-run shot by Thurman Munson), the Royals went down in four games. In an ace-versus-ace matchup in the final contest, Ron Guidry outdueled Dennis Leonard for a 2–1 win, with Gossage getting the save. Once again, the Yankees advanced to the World Series, and the Royals went home to lick their wounds.

The Phillies, much to their frustration, encountered a similar fate, losing the NLCS to the Dodgers in four games. The final contest, an extra-inning nail-biter at Dodger Stadium, turned on a rare fielding gaffe by Phillies center fielder Garry Maddox, who somehow failed to catch a Dusty Baker fly ball with two out and Ron Cey on first in the bottom of the 10th. Bill Russell, the next batter, laced a single to center that sent the Penguin waddling home, and set up a rematch between the Dodgers and Yankees.

In keeping with the example set by Dent against Boston, most of the stars of the 1978 World Series weren't superstar sluggers, but gritty infielders who would mostly have gone unrecognized on the street. Davey Lopes, the Dodgers' second baseman whose droopy mustache made him look like a stray member of Santana, was already known for his speed—in 1978, he'd stolen a phenomenal 45 out of 49 bases—and his Gold Glove. But in 1978, he'd found his power stroke, hitting 17 homers out of the leadoff position while batting .278, and he'd hit .389 with two homers in the playoffs against the Phillies. Now, in the opening game of the '78 World Series, he jacked two more off the Yankees' Ken Clay, driving in five runs in an 11–5 Dodger rout in Los Angeles.

In Game 2, Lopes scored on Ron Cey's three-run homer off of Catfish Hunter, a blow that would eventually give the Dodgers a 4–3 victory. The game ended in dramatic fashion, with rookie Bob Welch coming in to face Thurman Munson in the top of the ninth with two on and one out; the flame-throwing Welch got Munson to fly out to right, then fearlessly dueled Reggie Jackson for seven solid minutes, as "Mr. October" worked the count to 3-and-2. "It was like the 15th round of a heavyweight championship fight," an awestruck Dodger outfielder Billy North later told *Time* magazine. "Bob just aired it out and said, 'Hey, Reggie, here it comes. If you can handle it, you deserve it.' It had to end in a home run or a strikeout." Welch fired another fastball; Jackson swung mightily and missed. Somewhere, the Big Dodger in the sky was smiling.

He would not be smiling much longer, however. The Series moved back to the Bronx for Game 3, wherein Graig Nettles conjured up memories of Brooks Robinson's 1970 Series heroics, making four astonishing acrobatic stops at third, as Guidry battled to a 5–1 victory that was far closer than the final score made it seem. In Game 4, Tommy John seemed to be cruising to a Dodger victory until the sixth inning, when Reggie Jackson broke up a sure double play by deflecting a relay throw from Dodger shortstop Bill Russell with his hip, sending the ball bouncing into right field while Munson scored from first to pull the Yankees to within a run. Tommy Lasorda ran out to argue, but the umpires decided that Jackson had done nothing illegal; two innings later, Munson doubled home Paul Blair to tie the game, and then Welch gave up a game-winning single to Piniella in the bottom of the 10th. The Series was now tied at two games apiece.

By Game 5, it was clear just how much the momentum had shifted. Burt Hooton, who had pitched a gem in Game 2, was driven from the mound in the third inning, as the Yankees literally singled the Dodgers to death in a 12–2 victory—out of the Yanks' 18 hits, only two were for extra bases. Munson drove in five runs on three hits, while Dent and

Doyle (the latter once again subbing for Randolph, who was out for the Series with a balky hamstring) collected three hits apiece. Jim Beattie, a New York rookie who had gone 6-9 with a 3.73 ERA during the regular season, pitched the first complete game of his career for the win.

The Series returned to L.A. for Game 6. Lopes, who hit .308 for the Series, led off the first inning with a home run off Catfish Hunter, but it would be the last time the Dodgers would lead in the Series; the Yankees came right back in the top of the second, scoring three runs on a double by Doyle and a single by Dent off of Don Sutton. Doyle and Dent once again smacked three hits apiece, and Reggie Jackson avenged his Game 2 strikeout by crushing a Bob Welch fastball for a long two-run homer in the seventh. The Yankees coasted to a 7–2 win (Hunter's final career World Series victory), clinching their second straight World Championship, and Dent—who hit .417 and drove in seven runs over the six games—was awarded the Series MVP. Jackson, who hit .391 with two homers and a team-high eight RBIs, was uncharacteristically gracious about being passed over for MVP honors, and heaped high praise upon Dent and Doyle, the latter of whom hit .438 for the Series. "We couldn't have won it without them," he told reporters.

The Yankee players' treatment of Bob Lemon was far less classy. Taking Lem's earlier words about "I'll try to stay out of your way" at face value, the players initially voted against granting their manager a World Series share, finally forking over the full share of $31,236 only after months of subsequent bad press regarding their stinginess. Billy Martin, their once and future manager, was voted half a share.

Over in Cincinnati, Sparky Anderson was surprised to find himself the recipient of even shabbier treatment. Despite finishing with a 92-69 record—a 4½-game improvement over 1977, even while piloting an arguably worse team—Anderson was unceremoniously given the boot by the Reds' front office. Having averaged 96 wins a season over nine years with the club, including five divisional titles, four NL pennants, and two World Series rings, Anderson (who still had a year left on his contract) was shocked by the firing, as were many Cincinnati fans and players.

Though deeply disappointed, Anderson managed to retain his sense of humor about the whole affair. In 1979, he would "return" to the Queen City as a guest star on an episode of CBS's hit sitcom *WKRP in Cincinnati*, playing himself as the host of the titular station's new sports call-in show. In the episode, Anderson leers at buxom blond receptionist Loni Anderson and trades witticisms with the rest of the staff, until a series of wacky incidents forces the station manager to give him the ax. "Every time I come to this town I get fired," grumbles Anderson as the laugh track goes nuts.

CHAPTER 14
1979

"These are the good times," sang the influential disco-funk group Chic in their 1979 smash "Good Times," a quite-possibly-coke-fueled ode to upward mobility and urban hedonism. But for many of those in the dugouts and up in the stands, these were the *weird* times. A player or fan who'd lapsed into a coma in 1970 or 1975, only to awaken in the spring of 1979, would have had considerable difficulty wrapping his head around some of the changes that had since occurred in the grand old game.

The Pittsburgh Pirates, for example, could now boast 64 different cap, jersey, and pants combinations, each one more appalling to baseball purists than the last. (Columnist George Will lamented the black-and-yellow Pirate togs as "new forms of gaucherie.") Prerecorded Top 40 hits were now augmenting (if not yet entirely supplanting) the live organ music that had been part of the ballpark experience since the 1940s. And, horror of all horrors, women were now invading the sanctity of major league locker rooms.

The collision between the women's rights movement and Major League Baseball had been brewing for years. As more and more women entered the world of sports journalism in the 1970s—the most high-profile example being Phyllis George, the former Miss America who cohosted the

CBS pregame football show, *The NFL Today*—it was only a matter of time before sports publications began assigning female reporters to cover baseball games. The very thought mortified commissioner Bowie Kuhn, who in the spring of 1975 issued a stern memo to all MLB teams, urging them to make a "unified stand" against allowing female sportswriters into their clubhouses. If *Sports Illustrated* et al. persisted in sending women to the ballpark, Kuhn felt that "in fairness to our players and to the family-sport image of baseball," the women should be made to wait with their notebooks outside the clubhouse door, where they would be allowed to speak to the players as they exited. The players, of course, were under no obligation to speak back.

In late 1977, *Sports Illustrated* reporter Melissa Ludtke, with the backing of parent corporation Time Inc., filed civil suit against Kuhn to obtain the same clubhouse privileges and access as male reporters. Ludtke, assigned by the magazine to cover the '77 World Series, had received a message from the Commissioner's Office prior to the Series that she would not be allowed to enter either team's clubhouse for postgame interviews, despite the fact that the Dodgers had already given her permission to do so. *Sports Illustrated* suggested to Kuhn that if personal privacy was such an important issue for the players, they could easily hide their man-bits with the judicious use of towels or bathrobes. "Anyone who knew the mechanics of a clubhouse would doubt the workability of that suggestion," Kuhn would later huff in his autobiography. "The players were great athletes, not magicians or fan dancers."

Kuhn's prudish sentiments cut little ice with New York District Court Judge Constance Baker Motley, who reasoned that, since television cameras were already being allowed into major league clubhouses, the admission of female reporters hardly constituted a compromise of player privacy. Judge Motley's decision was handed down on September 26, 1978, which meant that a number of female reporters would be on hand to test the ruling in the Yankees clubhouse during the postseason.

Some of the Bronx Bombers reacted less than gallantly to this distaff incursion. "Half these women don't know the first thing about baseball," groused Yanks reliever Sparky Lyle, who estimated that there were at least 30 female journalists in the Yankees' clubhouse during the final week of the regular season. Lyle staged his own protest of their presence by parading around the locker room naked except for the sanitary sock that he'd pulled over his privates. Yanks utility man Jay Johnstone opted for an even less subtle approach, hanging a homemade sign above his locker reading, "U.S. JUDGE CONSTANCE MOTLEY SUCKS RATSHIT!" Johnstone's teammates also overheard him yelling at one female reporter, "Why don't you go back to the kitchen?"

Though the Commissioner's Office considered appealing the verdict, Kuhn and Co. realized that they would get little out of an appeal besides negative publicity. In March of 1979, the commish recanted his 1975 memo, issuing an official notice to all of the clubs that urged them to give reporters of both sexes equal access to their locker rooms.

Female sportswriters weren't the only group at odds with the Commissioner's Office. Major league umpires had staged a one-day walkout on August 25, 1978, in a bid for better wages—NBA officials with 10 years' experience were making roughly $45,000 per season at the time, while umpires with 10 years in the majors were making around $32,500. Though the American and National league presidents were the ones refusing to raise their salaries, the umpires were offended by Kuhn's unwillingness to get involved with the negotiations, even when the umps sat out spring training in 1979, and the AL and NL had to bring in a motley collection of semipro, high school, college, and minor league umpires to call the exhibition games.

Though having games officiated by unqualified umps certainly went against "the best interests of baseball" that Kuhn usually loved to defend, the commish continued to sit on his hands. The umpire strike spilled over into the 1979 season, inspiring the formation of a Chicago-based group of baseball fans that dubbed itself UMPS, for Union of Mortified Protesting Spectators, which encouraged the boycotting of major league games until the real umpires returned. Faced with fan and player unrest—and out-and-out embarrassments like the Pirates-Braves contest of May 9, which saw the scab umps completely lose control of a game that included four bench-clearing brawls, and resulted in the ejection of five players and both managers—league presidents Lee MacPhail and Chub Feeney finally settled the strike by offering "no-cut" contracts that included two-week vacations and salaries up to $55,000. The umpires returned to work on May 19.

Of course, the umpires' collective windfall paled in comparison to what the major league players were making. Thanks to the strength of the Marvin Miller–run Players Association and the onset of free agency, the average annual player salary was now up to $113,558; even adjusted for inflation, this was a significant jump from the $29,303 that the average player had made back in 1970. The days of major leaguers having to take off-season jobs at the local car dealership or insurance agency—or, like Richie Hebner in his early playing years, the local cemetery—just to make ends meet would soon be over forever.

The days of baseball stars playing out their entire careers with the same team were clearly on the wane as well, as more players began to test the waters of free agency. Spring training of 1979 treated fans to the jarring sight of Pete Rose in a Philadelphia Phillies uniform; during the off-season, "Charlie Hustle," who had been synonymous with the Cincinnati Reds since winning NL Rookie of the Year honors for them in 1963, signed a four-year, $3.2 million contract with Philadelphia, making him the highest-paid player in the game. Tommy John and Luis Tiant, who had been major cogs in the L.A. Dodger and Boston Red Sox rotations, respectively, for most of the decade, both signed lucrative deals with the New York Yankees. Rod Carew, who had played his entire career for the Minnesota Twins, was still a year away from declaring free agency; but with no love lost between him and penny-pinching Twins owner Calvin Griffith, the Minnesota front office knew they'd have little hope of re-signing the seven-time AL batting champ. Rather than be left with nothing but Carew's empty locker, the Twins sent their star player to the California Angels in exchange for outfielder Ken Landreaux, pitcher Paul Hartzell, and two minor leaguers.

Even given the time-honored tradition of trading away problem players, it still felt strange to see Sparky Lyle's walrus mustache protruding from under the brim of a Texas Rangers cap, or Bill Lee wearing an Expos jersey. Lyle, chafing at being relegated to second fiddle in the Yankee bullpen behind Goose Gossage, had agitated to be traded for most of the 1978 season; in November, the Yankees finally obliged, sending the former Cy Young winner to the Rangers as part of a 10-player deal in which the Yanks received a top lefty prospect named Dave Righetti. Lee, whose colorful personality and endless criticism of Red Sox manager Don Zimmer had finally sealed his fate in Boston, may as well have been traded to the Montreal Expos for a bucket of baseballs and a chaw of tobacco—all the Red Sox got in return for their "Spaceman" was reserve infielder Stan Papi, who had hit a measly .230 for the Expos in '78.

Though deeply offended by the fact that the Sox had basically given him away, Lee was happy to be playing again in a league that allowed pitchers to hit for themselves, and to be reunited with Expos skipper Dick Williams, who had managed the Red Sox during Lee's rookie year in 1969. Greeted with open arms by both the city and the team, the thickly bearded Lee wasted no time flying his freak flag in the Expos' clubhouse. Before a Red Sox–Expos exhibition game, a Boston reporter asked Lee if he thought his former club had "had a problem with marijuana." Lee, who made no secret of his belief that alcohol, caffeine, nicotine, and animal proteins were far more harmful to the human body than pot, shot back, "Hell no. How could they? I've been using that stuff since 1968, and I've never had a problem with it." He then launched into an extended soliloquy about the many productive and positive aspects of marijuana, including the alleviation of nausea in chemotherapy patients. Of course, that part of the conversation didn't make the papers—but lurid headlines screaming "Lee Admits Smoking Marijuana" did.

Predictably outraged, Kuhn sent one of his staffers, former FBI drug-enforcement agent Art Fust, to meet with Lee and Expos president John McHale. Lee explained to Fust that he'd been misquoted: He'd never actually said that he *smoked* pot, only that he'd "used" it. Asked to elaborate, Lee told Fust that he liked to sprinkle pot into his organic buckwheat pancakes while they were cooking; the frying process absorbed the THC in the pot, and, Lee claimed, the THC made him impervious to the air pollution he encountered on his daily five-mile run to the ballpark.

"I'm not addicted to anything," he said. "If I was, tell me how I could run five miles a day and run faster than any Red Sox player my age."

Unbelievably, Fust bought the explanation, and Lee got off with a relatively light slap on the wrist. A letter from Kuhn soon arrived telling the Spaceman to refrain from saying such things to the press in the future, and instructing him to pay a fine of $250 to the Commissioner's Office, which would donate the money to charity. Rather than make a check out to Kuhn—"I knew if I sent it to his office, it would probably end up in a 'Let's Bring Back Richard Nixon' fund," he joked—Lee wrote out a check for $251 and sent it to St. Mary's Mission in northern Alaska. Asked why he'd added an extra dollar, he told reporters, "I just wanted Bowie to know that I'm worth more than he thinks."

While major league ballplayers were enjoying their highest salaries in history, average Americans weren't doing so well. U.S. inflation hit 13.3 percent in 1979, the highest rate since the stormy years immediately following World War II. Thanks to strained relations with the OPEC nations over U.S. support for Israel, along with political upheaval in Iran—where the Islamic Revolution had overthrown the unpopular Shah Mohammad Reza Pahlavi (a staunch American ally, who had been installed as the head of the Iranian government as part of a 1953 CIA coup)—the price of crude oil had more than doubled, plunging America into its second energy crisis of the decade.

In California, Texas, and several other states, odd-even gas sale days were instituted for motorists: If your vehicle's license plate ended in an odd number, you could purchase gas on an odd-numbered day but not on an even one. Meanwhile, in the East and Midwest, truckers rioted over fuel rationing. President Jimmy Carter urged Americans to cut down on their energy usage, and tried to set an example by installing solar panels on the roof of the White House.

But while baseball owners initially worried that the energy crisis might prevent fans from coming out to the ballpark—because of either increased travel costs or the generally diminishing amount of disposable income in the average baseball aficionado's wallet—the sport set another attendance record in 1979, with major league turnstiles clicking to the tune of 43,550,395 paying customers. A record eight teams—the Dodgers, Yankees, Phillies, Reds, Expos, Royals, Red Sox, and Angeles—drew 2 million or more, while the Brewers fell just short of the mark. In the few cases where local fans actively stayed away, the empty seats in the stands were more the result of the poor quality of play rather than the high cost of living.

The Atlanta Braves and New York Mets certainly offered little incentive for fans to come out to the ballpark. The former drew only 796,465 fans while racking up a 66-94 record; their only real gate attraction was 40-year-old knuckleballer Phil Niekro, whose 21-20 record gave him the league lead in wins *and* losses—the only time in the entire century that any pitcher had topped both columns in the same season. "Knucksie" also compiled an impressive array of additional stats, including leading the NL in innings pitched (342), games started (44, the most by any NL pitcher since 1917), complete games (23), and home runs allowed (41), while also ranking third in the league in strikeouts (208). All the Mets had going for them was 24-year-old hometown heartthrob Lee Mazzilli (.303, 15 HRs, 79 RBIs, 34 stolen bases), and the team's 63-99 performance brought only 788,905 paying customers out to Shea—the lowest attendance figure in team history.

Though they'd been in existence for only three years, the Seattle Mariners also set a team record for lousy attendance. Their tally of 844,447 tickets sold was nearly a half million drop from their inaugural 1977 season, despite the fact that the M's fielded far and away their most formidable lineup in the team's short history. (Of course, the team's inability to win more than 67 games might have kept the turnstiles from clicking.) Veteran DH Willie Horton (.279, 29 HRs, 106 RBIs), first baseman Bruce Bochte (.316, 16 HRs, 100 RBIs), center fielder Ruppert Jones (.267, 21 HRs, 78 RBIs, 33 steals), and third baseman Dan Meyer (.278, 20 HRs, 74 RBIs) all roughed up their share of pitchers, though the lineup also included hot-fielding, weak-hitting shortstop Mario Mendoza, whose .198 average in 373 at bats led to the coining of the phrase "the Mendoza

Line"—i.e., if you pushed your average over .200, you were hitting above the Mendoza Line.

Every one of the Oakland A's regulars hit above the Mendoza Line in '79, and a 20-year-old rookie named Rickey Henderson showed some promise, hitting .274 and swiping 33 bases after being called up from the minors in late June. But that was about the best thing you could say for the Athletics' no-name squad, which finished last in the AL West with a depressing 54-108 record. Only 306,763 fans showed up to the "Oakland Mausoleum" all season, the worst attendance figure in the majors since 1953, when Bill Veeck's Browns played out their final year in St. Louis.

Down on the South Side of Chicago, the novelty of Veeck's presence was wearing off. Though his oddball promotions—including the ill-conceived and equally ill-fated "Disco Demolition Night"—continued to draw the curious to Comiskey, Sox fans would happily have traded in the cavalcade of gimmicks for a reprise of 1977's "South Side Hitmen" excitement. Alas, this year's Sox were a mediocre bunch, fated to finish fifth in the AL West with a 73-87 record. Perhaps Veeck's most apropos promotion of 1979 was the one that resulted from his team's home opener: The Sox played such uninspired ball during their 10–2 Opening Day loss at Comiskey that Veeck offered everyone in attendance free admission to the following game.

Veeck's North Side neighbors didn't fare much better, finishing fifth in the NL East with an 80-82 record. But unlike the Sox, the Cubs had a couple of genuine stars on their roster. Bruce Sutter (6-6, 2.22 ERA, 37 saves, 110 Ks in 101⅓ innings) saved or won more than half of the Cubs' victories, a performance so dominant that he would be awarded the NL Cy Young. After the season's end, Sutter would take the Cubs to arbitration and be awarded a $700,000 salary, at the time a mind-boggling amount to pay for a young pitcher, even one of his considerable talents.

Though the Cubs wouldn't spend a single day in first place all season, 1,648,587 fans—the team's highest attendance mark since 1971—still flocked to the day games at Wrigley in hopes of seeing Dave Kingman crush one (literally) out of the park. Kingman's injury-plagued first season with the Cubs had been something of a disappointment, but in 1979 he put up the best numbers of his career, hitting .288 while leading the league with 48 home runs and a .613 slugging percentage, and driving in 115 runs to boot.

Kingman put on a show all year for the Wrigley faithful, most memorably during a wild 23–22 extra-inning loss to the Phillies on May 17, wherein the two teams tied a major league record by combining for 11 home runs, three of which were Kingman's. Though Cubs fans embraced Kingman, he wasn't the kind of player who wanted to return the embrace. Quiet and introverted at the best of times, brusque and standoffish at others, Kingman feuded constantly with the Chicago press; local columnist Mike Royko regularly parodied him in print as "Dave Ding-Dong." The surly slugger's one awkward attempt to cash in locally on his Cubs success was with Kingman's Landing, a nautical-themed sandwich stand and ice-cream parlor. Situated in a crummy residential neighborhood near Addison and Western, miles away from Wrigley and the lakefront, it whiffed worse than Kingman on a Phil Niekro knuckler.

For the third year running, the L.A. Dodgers led the majors in attendance, but they also experienced the biggest drop-off from 1978; their 1979 figure of 2,860,954 missed the previous year's record mark by nearly half a million. Again, the problem was not so much steep gas prices, but the team's inability to win as they had in the past two seasons. Steve Garvey once again hit like a neatly coiffed machine, putting up a .315 batting average with 28 homers and 110 RBIs, while Ron Cey (.281, 28 HRs, 81 RBIs), Dusty Baker (.274, 23 HRs, 88 RBIs), and Davey Lopes (showing surprising power with 28 HRs and 73 RBIs of his own, as well as swiping 44 bases in 48 attempts) provided the sock, but with the exception of Rick Sutcliffe—whose 17-10, 3.46 record would be good enough to snag him NL Rookie of the Year honors—the Dodger pitching simply fell apart. The team finished in third place in the NL West with a 79-83 record, its first sub-.500 year since 1968. Dodger owner Walter O'Malley passed away on August 9 at the age of 75, adding one more funereal touch to a lost season.

Bob Welch, the previous year's rookie phenom, sank deeply into alcoholism, often showing up to the ballpark completely sloshed; while his record of 5-6 with a 3.98 ERA and 12 saves was a disappointment, it was actually rather impressive when one considered that he was drinking up to two fifths of scotch per day. At the end of the season, the Dodgers would confront Welch about his drinking problem and get him to enroll in a rehab program—a fairly novel concept for baseball players of the era.

But while Dodger fans experienced an unexpected summer of discontent, their counterparts down the 5 Freeway in Anaheim were in baseball heaven, cheering the California Angels to their first title in team history. Jim Fregosi's team pulled a franchise-record 2.5 million fans through the gates of the "Big A," and treated them to a season-long dogfight with the defending AL champion Kansas City Royals. Though the '79 Angels were somewhat shaky from a pitching standpoint—Nolan Ryan (16-14, 3.60 ERA, 223 Ks) and Dave Frost (16-10, 3.57) were the only starters to win more than 10 games, and Frank Tanana (7-5, 3.89) missed half the season with shoulder problems—they led the league in scoring, thanks to a rock-solid lineup that included second baseman Bobby Grich (.294, 30 HRs, 101 RBIs), rookie DH/first baseman Willie Mays Aikens (who socked 21 HRs and 81 RBIs in only 379 at bats), catcher Brian Downing (.326, 12 HRs, 75 RBIs), and third baseman Carney Lansford (.287, 18 HRs, 79 RBIs, 20 stolen bases).

Rod Carew missed two months of his first season with the Halos due to a thumb injury but still managed to hit .318 in 110 games. "Disco" Dan Ford, a former Twins teammate of Carew's—and nicknamed for his penchant for hanging out in the more dance-oriented Minneapolis nightclubs—had come to the team in a separate trade during the off-season, and hit .290 with 21 HRs and 101 RBIs. But the real engine behind the team's success was Don Baylor, who hit .296 with 36 HRs, 139 RBIs, and 120 runs scored, while stealing 22 bases on his way to winning the AL MVP Award. Though technically the first designated hitter to win the award, the misconception that Baylor played all 162 games at that position in 1979 would linger for decades afterward. In fact, he appeared in only 65 games as a DH, splitting the other 97 games between left field, right field, and (for one game) first base.

After fighting it out all season with the Angels, the Royals came into Anaheim on September 24 for one final showdown. Kansas City had gotten phenomenal performances all year from Willie Wilson (.315, 113 runs scored, 13 triples, 83 stolen bases, and no fewer than five inside-the-park home runs), George Brett (who hit .329 with 107 RBIs and 119 runs scored, and whose 42 doubles, 20 triples, and 23 homers made him only the sixth player in history to exceed the 20 double/triple/homer marks in the same season), and catcher Darrell Porter (.291, 10 triples, 20 HRs, 112 RBIs, 101 runs scored). But injuries kept outfielder Al Cowens and second baseman Frank White out of the lineup for more than 50 games between them, and their combined absence took its toll upon the Royals, who now found themselves four games behind the Angels with six left to play. Fittingly, it was Ryan and Tanana—the two pitchers that, for years, had been the Angels' only bright lights—who delivered the coup de grace, beating the Royals 4–3 and 4–1 with back-to-back complete-game victories. Nearly two decades after joining the American League, the Angels were finally going to play in the postseason. And for the first time since 1975, the Royals were staying home in October.

With the Dodgers out of the way in the NL West, and Atlanta, San Francisco, and San Diego posing little in the way of a threat, the race came down to the resurgent Cincinnati Reds and the surprisingly hot Houston Astros. For the latter team, managed by Bill Virdon, it was all about pitching and speed. J. R. Richard, the team's 6-foot-8 right-hander, parlayed his 100-mph fastball and nasty-as-all-hell slider into an 18-13 record while leading the league with a 2.71 ERA and 313 strikeouts, the latter mark an NL record for right-handers. Joe Niekro, Phil's baby brother—who threw a harder version of Phil's knuckler—went 21-11 for the Astros with a 3.00 ERA; Joe tied Phil for the league lead in victories, the first time in history that two brothers had done so. The Astros' bullpen was anchored by closer Joe Sambito, who went 8-7 with a 1.77 ERA and 22 saves while finishing 51 games.

Though power was definitely not their strong suit—the team, led by

Jose Cruz's whopping nine round-trippers, actually hit more triples (52) than homers (49)—and no one in the regular lineup hit higher than .290, the fleet-footed team was a perfect fit for the Astrodome, where ostensible homers regularly turned into easy outs, but hot grounders through the infield could become doubles, triples, or even inside-the-park home runs. The players also turned on the jets once they reached base; led by third baseman Enos Cabell (37 steals), Cruz (36), first baseman Cesar Cedeno (30), and center fielder Terry Puhl (30), the team led the NL with 190 stolen bases.

Other than the obvious absence of Pete Rose, the Reds, under new manager John McNamara, didn't differ much from other Big Red Machine squads of the decade. George Foster (.302, 30 HRs, 98 RBIs), Johnny Bench (.276, 22 HRs, 80 RBIs), and Dan Driessen (.250, 18 HRs, 75 RBIs) delivered the power as usual. Ray Knight, an infielder who had been kicking around in the Reds' farm system for nearly a decade, didn't exactly fill Rose's shoes at third, but he did surprise everyone by leading the team in batting average (.318), hits (175), and doubles (37) while also driving in 79 runs.

The Reds' '79 pitching staff was solid if unspectacular, with Tom Seaver leading all starters with a 16-6 record and a 3.14 ERA. Twenty-three-year-old righty Mike LaCoss, pitching in his first full season, pitched well enough in the first half (9-3, 2.24) to make the NL All-Star team, though he came back to earth in the second half, finishing at 14-8 with a 3.50 ERA. But the Reds' bullpen, always a strong point under Sparky Anderson, was no longer quite the watertight ship it had once been—and it didn't help that Pedro Borbon, who had eaten more than 850 relief innings in the previous seven seasons, was mysteriously shipped off to San Francisco in late June for weak-hitting outfielder Hector Cruz. Borbon was so incensed by the trade that he allegedly put a voodoo curse on the Reds, decreeing that the team would never win another World Series.

Borbon's curse apparently didn't apply to division titles; as the NL West race came down to its final week, the Astros were the ones who appeared to be snakebit. After Joe Niekro defeated the Reds on September 22 to pull within half a game of the division lead, the dudes with the

orange rainbow jerseys proceeded to lose five out of their next six contests. Phil Niekro knocked the Astros out of the race for good on September 26 with a complete-game 9–4 victory, while brother Joe took the loss. Cross words were doubtless exchanged at the subsequent Niekro family Christmas get-together.

The high-priced addition of Pete Rose to the Philadelphia lineup was supposed to help the Phillies win their first NL championship since 1950, but things didn't quite work out as planned. In fact, the Phils were lucky even to make it into fourth place in the NL East with an 84-78 record. Danny Ozark, the manager who had led the team to three straight division titles, was fired at the end of August and replaced by Dallas Green.

The team's disappointing season wasn't Rose's fault; he was the only Phillies player to appear in every game, leading the team in batting average (.331), at bats (628), hits (208—a record 10th time that he'd collected 200 or more in a season), doubles (40), and on-base percentage (.418) while also scoring 90 runs and stealing 20 bases. But with the exception of Rose, Mike Schmidt (.253, 45 HRs, 114 RBIs, 109 runs), and Bake McBride (.280, 12 triples, 12 HRs, 82 runs, 25 stolen bases), everyone else on the team experienced average or subpar seasons. Of the pitching staff, only Steve Carlton (18-11, 3.62 ERA, 213 Ks) and off-season trade acquisition Nino Espinosa (14-12, 3.65) could boast respectable records.

Perhaps the most amazing thing about Rose's 1979 performance was that he managed to put up all those impressive numbers despite experiencing a myriad of personal distractions. *Playboy* magazine's September issue, which appeared on the stands in July, featured Rose as the subject of the magazine's "Playboy Interview," in which Charlie Hustle revealed some interesting (and potentially damaging) things about himself over the course of the conversation.

Asked if he would ever use amphetamines (or "greenies") in order to get up for a game, Rose said, "Yeah, I'd do it. I've done it." But the fallout from Rose's "greenie" admission (which he later denied, claiming he was misquoted) was small compared to the outcry over his other major

gaffe: Asked why he'd become such an in-demand ad pitchman for a variety of products, he cracked, "Look, if you owned Swanson's Pizza, would you want a black guy to do the commercial on TV for you? Would you like the black guy to pick up the pizza and bite into it? Or would you want Pete Rose?"

The Campbell's Soup Company, which owned Swanson, immediately sent out press releases reminding the media and public that it had indeed done ads in the past featuring black football players Rosey Grier and Ed "Too Tall" Jones. The company also quickly cut ties with Rose (who never recanted his comment) and pulled his TV ads for Hungry-Man Pizza—"You know what gets my goat? Striking out and skimpy pizzas!"—off the air.

When Rose told the *Playboy* interviewers that he liked "women with pretty legs and pretty mouths," he wasn't exactly speaking from the perspective of a chaste aesthete. A notorious horn-dog, Rose was known to have at least one girlfriend in every National League city, and had enjoyed several in Cincinnati—a fact that caused the Reds' conservative front office no small amount of anxiety, worrying that their married star's philandering could lead to a public scandal that would tarnish the team's image. Luckily for them, Terryl Rubio, a 25-year-old divorcee from Tampa, waited until Rose signed with the Phillies to file her paternity suit against him. Rubio claimed that she'd been Rose's mistress for three years, and that Rose was the father of her year-old daughter, Morgan. Rose, who didn't contest the charges, settled with Rubio out of court. The next time the Phillies played in San Francisco, fans at Candlestick unfurled a large sign reading, "Pete Rose Leads League in Paternity Suits."

Karolyn, Rose's wife, had put up with Charlie Hustle's hustling ways for 16 years, but finally decided she'd had enough. The final straw wasn't Rubio's paternity suit, nor the fact that she'd recently seen a Philadelphia Eagles cheerleader driving Pete's Porsche around their neighborhood. But when Rose didn't even bother visiting Karolyn in the hospital when she was admitted for a blood clot in her leg, she decided to file for divorce. As with the paternity suit, Rose didn't contest the divorce; he just shrugged it off and kept on hitting. According to Rose, getting rid of a

wife was as simple as swinging at a 2-0 fastball: "Hey, just give her a million dollars and tell her to hit the road," he laughed.

The St. Louis Cardinals enjoyed their best season since 1975, finishing 86-76 thanks to their solid pitching staff (led by Pete Vuckovich and Silvio Martinez, who won 15 games each) and equally solid hitting. In his final major league season, the great Lou Brock hit .304 and stole 21 bases. On August 13, he singled off Dennis Lamp of the Cubs to notch hit number 3,000; he finished the year (and his career) with 3,023. He stole his 938th and final base during a September 21 game against the Mets, topping 19th-century stolen-base king Billy Hamilton by one. Brock's spikes were already in the Hall of Fame; there was no question that the man himself would soon follow.

After hitting only .255 in 1978, Cards first baseman Keith Hernandez had a breakout season in '79, leading the league with a .344 batting average while collecting 210 hits (including a league-best 48 doubles), scoring 116 runs, and driving in 105. The performance would win him the NL MVP Award—though he'd wind up having to share it with the Pirates' Willie Stargell.

Stargell's Bucs duked it out until the final day of the season with the Expos for the NL East pennant. Managed by Dick Williams, who'd already guided the Red Sox and the A's to the World Series, the Montreal team had slowly been accumulating some of the best young talent in baseball—six of the Expos' eight regular position players were 25 or younger. Third baseman Larry Parrish led the team with a .307 average and 30 homers while also knocking in 82 runs. Catcher Gary Carter hit .283 with 22 homers and 75 RBIs, and was already being mentioned in the same breath as Johnny Bench—a comparison given added weight by the fact that "the Kid" gunned down 66 would-be base stealers over the course of the season. Center fielder Andre Dawson (.275, 12 triples, 25 HRs, 92 RBIs, 35 stolen bases), right fielder Ellis Valentine (.276, 21 HRs, 82 RBIs), and left fielder Warren Cromartie (who hit .275 with a team-leading 46 doubles) gave the Expos one of the best outfields in the majors.

"Cro" led the three with 16 assists, but that's only because runners were so afraid to run on Valentine's bionic arm—during a July 10 game against the Giants, Valentine picked up a Darrell Evans line shot to right and nailed him at first before he could reach the bag.

The Expos also boasted one of the top pitching staffs in the NL, with an overall ERA of 3.14 that was the lowest in either league, with Bill Lee (16-10, 3.04) pacing the starting rotation. Montreal fell in love with Les Expos all over again, and more than 2 million fans showed up at Stade Olympique to cheer them on. For the first time in baseball history, there was serious talk of the World Series being played in two different countries.

The Pirates, however, were determined to keep the postseason an all-American affair. As of July 8, nearly halfway through the season, the Pirates had been stuck in fourth place in the division, a solid seven games behind Montreal. But with the help of former batting champ Bill Madlock, who'd come over from the Giants in a six-player trade on June 28, the Bucs went 57-26 the rest of the way. Madlock, who'd been in a batting slump since the Giants had installed him at second base, was able to return to familiar third-base territory with the Pirates, and responded by hitting .328 over the last three months of the season.

Madlock, though, was just one of many key members of the "We Are Family" Pirates. The team's connection to the Sister Sledge disco hit of the same name was almost accidental: Greg Brown—an intern in the team's promotions department, who was in charge of spinning the latest hits between innings over the Three Rivers PA system—heard the song playing in the Pirate clubhouse, and decided to spin it after their next home victory. The Pittsburgh crowd responded rapturously to the song, and Brown began to pull it out after every win, inextricably linking the song with the '79 Bucs. The chorus refrain of "I've got all my sisters with me" notwithstanding, the song really was a remarkably apt choice for a remarkably diverse (racially and otherwise) Pirates team.

With the exception of Willie "Pops" Stargell (.281, 32 HRs, 82 RBIs), center fielder Omar Moreno (.282, 12 triples, 110 runs scored, 77 stolen bases), and right fielder Dave Parker (who hit .310 and led the team with 45 doubles, 25 HRs, and 94 RBIs), none of the Pirate hitters had a particularly remarkable year. The team's power was in its overall consistency: Left fielder Bill Robinson kicked in 24 homers and 75 RBIs; outfielder John "the Hammer" Milner pounded 16 homers in only 326 at bats; second baseman Phil "Scrap Iron" Garner hit .293 with 32 doubles. Though hardly a murderers' row, the Pirates still managed to lead the league in runs scored. And as the team got hot during the second half of the season, new heroes—be they veterans like Lee Lacy and Manny Sanguillen, or youngsters like Dale Berra and Steve Nicosia—seemed to emerge with every game.

Retina-searing uniforms aside, the Pirates' pitching staff wasn't particularly flashy either. Kent Tekulve, the team's closer, looked like Ichabod Crane in mirrored cop shades, but there was nothing comical about his vicious submarine delivery. "Teke" went 10-8 for the season with a 2.75 ERA, racking up 31 saves over 134⅓ innings in 94 appearances. His fellow relief workers included veteran hurlers Enrique Romo (10-5, 2.99, five saves in 129⅓ innings), Grant Jackson (8-5, 2.96, 14 saves), and Jim Bibby (12-4, 2.81), the latter of whom split time between the bullpen and the starting rotation. Of the Pirates starting pitchers, John Candelaria (14-9, 3.22), Bruce Kison (13-7, 3.19), and Bert Blyleven (12-5, 3.60, 172 Ks) were the most consistently tough on opposing hitters.

Managed by the ever-cheerful Chuck Tanner—who deftly handled the team's potentially volatile mixture of rookies and veterans, superstars and scrubs, and black, white, and Latino players—and spiritually guided by "Pops" Stargell, who would hand out "Stargell stars" after each game to every player who had made a key contribution, the Pirates motley crew truly *was* a family. "We're not trying to be sassy or fancy," Stargell would tell reporters at season's end. "But we depended on each of the 25 men. There was a closeness. We worked hard, and we scratched and clawed together. We're a very loose ball club and we work like hell." On the final day of the season, with the Pirates clinging to a one-game lead over the Expos, Pops smacked a solo homer and a sacrifice fly off of Lynn McGlothen as the Pirates beat the Cubs 5–3 at Three Rivers. With Sister Sledge on the sound track, the Family prepared to groove into October.

Back at the beginning of the 1979 season, one of the more hotly debated topics was whether or not the Yankees could win a third straight World Series championship, thus allowing the Bronx Zoo to take its place alongside the Mustache Gang as one of the great baseball dynasties of the last 25 years. With all of the '77-'78 starting lineup returning, and a starting rotation bolstered by the free-agent signings of Tommy John and Luis Tiant, many observers favored the Yanks to go all the way again.

Certainly, there was nothing that George Steinbrenner wanted more, and the pressure he put on his team was even more intense than usual—when the Yankees lost their first six exhibition games, an outraged Steinbrenner imposed a team curfew and stationed guards on every floor of the players' hotel. Team captain Thurman Munson bristled at Steinbrenner's punitive edict, and one night masterminded an escape from the hotel, in which he, Graig Nettles, and three Yankee prospects shinnied down a sheet tied to his second floor balcony, and merrily went off to paint the town red. Unfortunately, Steinbrenner was dining in a nearby restaurant at the time and was able to observe the entire stunt as it went down; the players were all fined the next day.

Though they looked unbeatable on paper, the Yankees were still playing uninspired ball as the regular season began. Part of the problem was that manager Bob Lemon had lost his son to an off-season car accident; in his mourning, the always laid-back Lem became morose and withdrawn. "I just wonder if it's worth it anymore," he told Reggie Jackson. "It's different now. My heart's not in it." And on April 19, when Goose Gossage sustained a torn thumb ligament in a shower-room brawl with backup catcher Cliff Johnson—who'd taken offense at some of the Goose's good-natured ribbing—the chances of the Bronx Bombers making it to the postseason suddenly looked dim. Gossage, whose herculean relief efforts contributed significantly to the Bombers' championship run in 1978, was out three months with his thumb in a cast. With Sparky Lyle now in Texas, the Yankee bullpen was suddenly more vulnerable than it had been in years.

The team barely played above .500 ball through the first two months of the season, leaving them lagging behind Baltimore, Boston, and Milwaukee, and Steinbrenner began to panic—all the more so in early June, when Jackson popped a muscle in his calf and had to be sidelined for a month. Steinbrenner decided that there was only one possible move to make: bring back Billy Martin.

It was, however, a tricky proposition. Steinbrenner had previously promised Yankees president Al Rosen that Lemon (Rosen's old teammate and great friend) would be given a full season in the driver's seat before being kicked upstairs and replaced by Martin. There was also the not-so-small matter of an assault charge filed against Martin in the wake of an incident that had happened in Reno, Nevada, in November 1978, when Martin had coldcocked a *Nevada State Journal* reporter named Ray Hagar. Martin had been in highly publicized brawls before, but never with a member of the press, and Steinbrenner told him he'd need to be cleared of all charges against him before he could return to the Yankees.

But after much legal wrangling and a rather insincere public apology, Martin was able to persuade Hagar to drop the charges. On May 26, the day Martin was cleared, Steinbrenner began seriously plotting to bring his once and future manager back earlier than his original 1980 restart date. Rosen, aware that his friend's head was on the chopping block, insisted that Steinbrenner extend Lemon's GM contract through the 1982 season so that Lem would at least have a financial cushion to fall back on. Steinbrenner acquiesced, then fired Lem following a June 17 loss to the Rangers in Texas. Billy Martin was the Yankees' new manager, effective immediately.

Jackson first heard the news about Martin from the team's beat reporters, and he was absolutely livid. Not only did he have no love for Martin, but he was hurt that Steinbrenner hadn't personally given him the heads-up before announcing Martin's return. "You better trade me, because if you don't, I plan to be hurt all year long," he railed at Steinbrenner in a 3 a.m. phone call. "'Cause I've played for that man for the last time."

"When I want your advice about how to run my baseball team, I'll ask for it," Steinbrenner barked back before hanging up the phone.

Jackson briefly considered walking off the team and heading back to California in protest, but some of his friends wisely talked him out of it. From that point on, relations between Jackson and Steinbrenner would cool considerably, and they would be further chilled by Jackson's subsequent comments to the press about how shabbily Lemon had been treated by the Yankee owner. Steinbrenner, in turn, began egging on Martin to make negative comments about Jackson's performance to reporters. With the George-Billy-Reggie drama back in action, it seemed like old times again.

Except, that is, on the field. Even with the valiant efforts of Jackson (who hit .297 with 29 homers and 89 RBIs despite missing 31 games), Tommy John (who more than justified his free-agent deal by going 21-9 with 17 complete games and a 2.96 ERA in 276⅓ innings), and Ron Guidry (who went 18-8 with a 2.78 ERA and 201 strikeouts despite injuries, and even volunteered to fill in as closer during Gossage's absence), the team played listlessly, and seemed perpetually stuck in fourth place.

Steinbrenner, tired of having to lend Mickey Rivers money to cover his gambling debts, traded the inscrutable center fielder to Texas for Oscar Gamble, who proceeded to hit .389 for the Yanks with 11 homers in only 113 at bats; Steinbrenner also brought back old Yankee hero Bobby Murcer, who hit .273 with eight home runs in part-time play. But even with the addition of those two familiar faces and their solid bats, the team lacked the killer instinct of the previous two seasons, even with the fiery Martin back in the dugout.

Tellingly, the most enthusiasm the Yankees mustered all season was during an off-the-field incident that occurred on August 1, following a game against the White Sox at Comiskey Park. While the team's bus idled outside the ballpark, waiting to take the players back to their hotel, an attractive young woman made her way on board, dropped her pants, and insisted that the assembled Yankees sign her bare butt. *Chicago Sun-Times* columnist Mike Royko got word of the affair the next day from the angry mother of a young baseball fan, who complained that the Yankee players ignored her son's repeated requests for autographs, yet eagerly lined up to sign the woman's backside; some players, apparently, even included middle names in their signatures. Royko wrote about the incident in his regular column, and it might have turned into a major scandal, had it not been almost immediately eclipsed by full-blown tragedy.

While the other Yankees cooled their heels and enjoyed an off day in Chicago before heading back to New York for a series against Baltimore, Thurman Munson had flown home to Canton, Ohio, in his new Cessna Citation twin-engine jet. Munson had taken up flying two years earlier, in order to spend more time with his wife and kids, who still lived in Canton. It soon became an obsession for the gruff catcher. "On the road," Gossage would remember, "instead of having a few beers at the hotel bar, [Thurman] stayed in his room studying aviation manuals."

In 1979, after he'd logged enough hours in the cockpit to start flying solo, Munson—who absolutely hated New York and refused to put down roots in the area—began flying back to Ohio after night games; he'd get home, sleep in his own bed, spend some time with his family in the morning, then fly back to New York in time for the next night game. The grueling travel regimen exhausted him, and he began to lobby for a trade to Cleveland, where he would at least be able to play ball within driving distance of the family home.

Sadly, the trade would never happen. While practicing takeoffs and landings at the Canton-Akron Airport on August 2, Munson miscalculated his approach and crashed the plane about a thousand feet short of the runway. His two passengers managed to escape, but the plane caught fire before they could unhook Munson's seat belt and extricate him from the wreckage. The seven-time All-Star catcher, the first Yankee player to be named team captain since Lou Gehrig, was dead at the age of 32. His teammates, manager, and coaches, all of whom considered him the heart and soul of their team, were utterly devastated.

Almost catatonic with grief, the Yankees dropped their next three games to first-place Baltimore, then flew to Ohio for Munson's August 6 memorial service, where Lou Piniella and Bobby Murcer were among the eulogists. But the final game of the Baltimore series was also scheduled for that night, and the Yankees—no matter how emotionally and physically exhausted they were—had to return to Yankee Stadium for the contest. Down 4–0 going into the bottom of the seventh against Orioles hurler Dennis Martinez, the team pulled within a run on a three-run Murcer homer, then won it in the ninth when Murcer singled home

Bucky Dent and Willie Randolph. Murcer was weeping as his team-mates ran out to embrace him; he later gave the bat that had driven in all five runs to Munson's widow. "There is no way to explain what happened," Murcer said later. "We used every ounce of strength to go out and play that game. We won it for Thurman."

The Yankees wound up the season with an 89-71 record, only good enough for fourth place in the AL East—which was, admittedly, the toughest division in baseball in 1979. With the exception of the Toronto Blue Jays, whose 53-109 record was the worst of their brief three-season existence, every team in the division finished over the .500 mark. The Cleveland Indians, led by Bobby Bonds—who, playing for his sixth team in six years, hit .275 with 25 HRs and 85 RBIs and stole 34 bases, becoming the only player besides Willie Mays to surpass both 300 homers and 300 swipes—went 81-80, a distinct improvement over the previous year's 69-90 mark. The Detroit Tigers, under the tutelage of new skipper Sparky Anderson, who replaced Les Moss halfway through the season, went 85-76, thanks in part to stellar seasons from Ron LeFlore (.300, 78 stolen bases) and youngsters Steve Kemp (.318, 26 HRs, 105 RBIs) and Jack Morris (17-7, 3.28 ERA).

The Red Sox, who'd blown it down the stretch in '78, got yet another dominating season out of Jim Rice (.325, 39 doubles, 39 HRs, 130 RBIs, 117 runs scored), which was matched this time by Fred Lynn (.333, 42 doubles, 39 HRs, 122 RBIs, 116 runs scored), and they led the AL with 194 home runs, thanks to the additional contributions of Butch Hobson (.261, 28 HRs, 93 RBIs), Dwight Evans (.274, 21 HRs, 53 RBIs), and 39-year-old Carl Yastrzemski (who hit .270 with 21 HRs and 87 RBIs, and also smacked his 400th career home run and notched his 3,000th career hit during the season); but injuries to Carlton Fisk and Jerry Remy left gaping holes in the Sox' lineup, and the team's 91-69 record was ultimately good enough for only third place in the division.

Second place in the AL East went to the Milwaukee Brewers, who put on another season-long fireworks display while compiling a 95-66 record, proving that the previous year's success was the real deal. Gorman Thomas, looking more like a dirtbag biker than ever before—*Chicago Tribune* columnist Bob Verdi wrote of Stormin' Gorman, "If he came into your home with your daughter, you'd disown them both"—continued to perform like the American League's answer to Dave Kingman, leading the league in long balls (45) as well as strikeouts (175) while knocking in 123 runs and scoring 97 times. Thomas was also a daredevil in the field, wowing fans and players alike with spectacularly acrobatic catches and a flagrant disregard for his own personal safety.

Unlike Kingman, who was essentially a one-man wrecking crew for the Cubs, Thomas had some help in the Brewers' lineup: first baseman Cecil Cooper hit .308 with 24 HRs and 106 RBIs, right fielder Sixto Lezcano hit .321 with 28 HRs and 101 RBI, and left fielder Ben Oglivie added 29 HRs with 81 RBIs while hitting .282. Shortstop Robin Yount had something of an off year, hitting only .267, but his double-play partner Paul Molitor more than made up for it, hitting a team-leading .322 with 16 triples and stealing 33 bases. When Jerry Koosman of the Twins beat the team 5–0 in the final game of the year, it marked the only time all season that anyone had shut the Brewers out. A franchise-record 1.9 million fans still came out to County Stadium that summer to drink beer, bask in the sun, and watch Bambi's Bombers swing for the fences.

But swing as they might, there was no catching the Baltimore Orioles in 1979. Earl Weaver, Bamberger's friend and former mentor, was the only major league manager of the 1970s who'd made it through the entire decade with the same team, and he marked the achievement on April 6 with his 1,000th victory as the O's manager (a 5–3 win over the White Sox). The Orioles took first place in the AL East on May 1, and they would remain there for all but two days of the rest of the season.

The irascible Weaver was famous for his constant haggling with star pitcher Jim Palmer. "See these gray hairs?" Weaver would joke. "Every one of them has number 22 [Palmer's uni number] on it." But in 1979, with Palmer plagued by injuries (he would appear in only 23 games, going 10-6 with a 3.30 ERA), Weaver was free to relax and enjoy the view as lefty Mike Flanagan picked up Palmer's Cy Young slack, going 23-9 with 16 complete games, a 3.08 ERA, and a team-high 190 strikeouts in 265⅔ innings. Though the rest of Weaver's rotation didn't make anyone forget his "Big Four" of the early '70s, Dennis Martinez (15-16, 18 complete games, and a 3.66 ERA in 292⅓ innings), Steve Stone (11-7, 3.77), and Scott McGregor (13-6, 3.35) all pitched consistently well enough to keep the O's in the game, and his bullpen—including Tippy Martinez (10-3, 2.88), Tim Stoddard (3-1, 1.71), and closer Don "Full Pack" Stanhouse (7-3, 2.85, 21 saves)—made it extremely difficult for opponents to score in the late innings.

No one in the Orioles lineup hit over .300 in 1979, though right fielder Ken Singleton (.295, 35 HRs, 111 RBIs) and first baseman Eddie Murray (.295, 25 HRs, 99 RBIs) came close. Like the Pirates, the Orioles had more reliable role players than stars: center fielder Al Bumbry hit .285 and stole 37 bases; DH Lee May added 19 HRs and 69 RBIs; left fielder Gary Roenicke hit 25 HRs in only 376 at bats; and utility man John Lowenstein cranked 11 homers and drove in 34 runs in only 197 at bats while also stealing 16 bases. And where the lineup was weakest from an offensive standpoint—like catcher Rick Dempsey, who hit only .239 for the season, or second baseman Rich Dauer, who hit .257—the players made up for it with excellent defense. Third baseman Doug DeCinces, who'd been groomed for years to be Brooks Robinson's replacement, hit only .230, but his Brooksian fielding made him an essential part of the team.

The Orioles had little difficulty waltzing to the AL East title, winning it by eight games over Milwaukee with a 102–57 record, which meant the final month of the season was pretty much a nonstop victory celebration at Memorial Stadium. The atmosphere at the ballpark was far more festive (and fragrant) than in recent years, thanks to an influx of teenage and college-age fans—a new development attributed to the fact that O's games were now being broadcast on local rock station WFBR. The stadium's upper deck was often shrouded in a cloud of pot smoke, and the fans would thrill to the antics of a hirsute, beer-bellied, cowboy-hatted cabdriver named "Wild" Bill Hagy, who would stand in front of section 34 and lead his rowdy fellow Birds watchers in a chant of O-R-I-O-L-E-S while contorting his body into the shape of each letter.

"The Roar from 34," as it was dubbed, became as integral a part of the O's winning season as "We Are Family" was for the Pirates.

The American League playoffs pitted the Angels, who led the league in runs scored, against the Orioles, who led the league in not letting runs score. In Game 1, an old-school matchup between Nolan Ryan and Jim Palmer, the teams battled each other to a standstill for the first nine innings. Then, in the bottom of the 10th, with the score tied 3–3, John Lowenstein, pinch-hitting for shortstop Mark Belanger, belted a three-run homer off of Angels reliever John Montague to win it.

In Game 2, the O's staked Mike Flanagan to a 9–1 lead, thanks in part to a homer and four RBIs from Eddie Murray, and sent Angels starter Dave Frost packing after only 1⅓ innings. But the Angels continued to pick away at Flanagan, and did the same to reliever Don Stanhouse. In the top of the ninth, down 9–8, the Angels loaded the bases against Stanhouse with two outs. Stanhouse then got Brian Downing to ground to DeCinces, ending the threat and the game.

The series then moved to Anaheim, where the Angels celebrated the first-ever postseason game at the Big A by winning 4–3 in the bottom of the ninth on an error by Al Bumbry (who'd gotten a late start on a Bobby Grich fly ball because he couldn't hear the crack of the bat over the deafening roar of the Anaheim crowd) and a pinch-hit double off Stanhouse by Larry Harlow. In Game 4, the O's took a 3–0 lead off Chris Knapp, but found themselves in trouble in the bottom of the fifth, when the Angels loaded the bases off Scott McGregor with nobody out. McGregor then got Rick Miller to fly out to left, too shallow to score the runner from third. The next batter, Jim Anderson, smashed what looked like a sure bases-clearing double down the third-base line; but DeCinces dove hard to his right, speared the ball while brushing the bag with his leg, then threw to first to nail Anderson. The wind taken out of their wings by DeCinces's masterful play, the Angels never threatened again, and the Orioles piled on five more runs in the seventh for good measure, and went home with their first AL flag since 1971.

For the fourth time this decade, the Pittsburgh Pirates and Cincinnati Reds faced off against each other in the NL playoffs. The Reds had won all three of the previous matchups; and when the Pirates arrived at Riverfront Stadium for the opening game of the series, they found a newspaper clipping tacked to the wall of the visitors' clubhouse, in which an unnamed major league scout had given the Reds the edge at six out of eight starting positions. "Some people seem to think we don't belong here," Willie Stargell wryly noted, before crushing a three-run homer off of Reds reliever Matt Alexander in the 11th inning to win the game 5–3.

Game 2 went into extra innings as well, the Pirates finally winning it 3–2 in the 10th on a Dave Parker RBI single off Reds reliever Doug Bair. After using five pitchers in the first game and six in the second, the Pirates were able to give their bullpen a rest in Game 3, as 10-year veteran Bert Blyleven won his first-ever postseason game, striking out nine Reds and cruising to a 7–1 complete-game victory. Stargell, who hit his second homer of the series in the third inning off of Fred Norman, was named the NLCS MVP, but it was clear that this Pirates team was firing on all 25 cylinders. "They're a better team than they were during the season," remarked a stunned George Foster, who'd fanned twice against Blyleven.

And so the rematch of the 1971 World Series came to pass. Of the players on the 1979 Orioles, only Palmer and Belanger had seen action when these two teams last met in the postseason, while Stargell, Bruce Kison, and reserve catcher Manny Sanguillen were the only holdovers from the '71 Pirates. But the most glaring difference, as Earl Weaver saw it, was the matter of the designated hitter, which hadn't existed in 1971. The National League had agreed to allow the use of the DH in the World Series in even-numbered years, but this was an odd one—which meant that Lee May, the O's main DH, would have to ride the pine, and Weaver wasn't very happy about it. "When we put our club together in spring training," he complained, "it was with the DH in mind."

Still, one would never have known something was amiss by the way the Orioles drove Bruce Kison from the mound after only a third of an inning in Game 1 at Memorial Stadium. Doug DeCinces smacked a two-run homer off Kison, and the other runs scored as a result of a Phil Garner throwing error and a Kison wild pitch. It was a sloppy game all around; Stargell and shortstop Tim Foli also committed errors for the Pirates, and the normally sure-handed DeCinces muffed two for the Orioles. In the top of the ninth, as the Orioles tried to hang on to a 5–4 lead with one out, Dave Parker attempted to steal second; Rick Dempsey's throw had him nailed, but Mark Belanger dropped the ball and couldn't make the tag. Mike Flanagan then got Bill Robinson to ground out, and Stargell to pop out to Belanger, who held on to it this time for an Oriole victory.

Game 2 started out as a fine pitchers' duel between Palmer and Blyleven, but both veterans were gone from the game by the time pinch hitter Manny Sanguillen singled off of Standhouse in the top of the ninth, scoring catcher Ed Ott to give the Pirates a 3–2 lead. Tekulve came in and struck out Rick Dempsey and shortstop Kiko Garcia, then got Al Bumbry to ground to short to ice the game and the save. The Series then moved to Pittsburgh, where Garcia went 4-for-4 with a double, a triple, and four RBIs as the Orioles—down 3–0 after two innings—coasted to an easy 8–4 Game 3 win, with Scott McGregor getting the complete-game victory. In Game 4, the Pirate bats came alive, knocking 17 hits against four Oriole pitchers, including Stargell's second homer of the Series; but Baltimore still pulled out a 9–6 victory, thanks to a major Tekulve meltdown in the top of the eighth that led to six runs for the O's.

Down three games to one, with only one home game left to play, the Pirates had their black-and-yellow backs to the wall. "All we need is three one-day winning streaks," Stargell enthused to anyone who would listen; but just to make sure he got the point across, Stargell called for a team meeting, and brought in comedian and social activist Dick Gregory to give his fellow Bucs a pep talk. "We talked until two in the morning," said Rennie Stennett. "Gregory was telling us all about positive thinking and believing in ourselves. He was trying to put us in the right frame of mind for the rest of the Series. We came out of that meeting, and we felt we were going to win."

Win they did in Game 5, touching Mike Flanagan and three other

Orioles pitchers for seven runs and 13 hits in a 7–1 victory. Bert Blyleven, who'd pitched only six innings in Game 2, was fresh enough to relieve Jim Rooker, who'd been pinch-hit for in the fifth; he pitched four scoreless innings to get the win. The Series then returned to Baltimore, but the Orioles seemed to have left their bats back in Pittsburgh. Jim Palmer and John Candelaria dueled to a 0–0 tie for six innings before the Candy Man was lifted for a pinch hitter in the top of the seventh. The Pirates got two runs in the seventh on a Parker RBI single and a Stargell sac fly, then got two more in the eighth off Palmer via a Bill Robinson sac fly and an Omar Moreno RBI single; that would be all they needed, as Tekulve nailed down the 4–0 win with a three-inning save. The Orioles managed seven hits but couldn't even buy a walk, much less a run, off Candelaria or Tekulve.

The momentum had shifted toward the Pirates, but when Rich Dauer hit a solo homer off of Jim Bibby in the third inning of Game 7, it seemed like Baltimore still had a chance to take the Series. Then, in the top of the sixth, with one on, one out, and the score still 1–0, Stargell lofted a Scott McGregor off-speed pitch in the air to right; Singleton raced back toward the wall to catch it, but ran out of room as the ball sailed into the right-field seats. The Pirates scored two more in the ninth; but with the Oriole bats still cold—Eddie Murray, Al Bumbry, Doug DeCinces, and Gary Roenicke went a combined 14-for-88 in the Series, an average of .160—the game, and the Series, were essentially over as soon as Stargell's homer traveled over the wall. Pops, who hit .400 in the Series, along with four doubles and three homers for a Series-record seven extra-base hits, was named the Series MVP, but it took a full Family effort to beat the Orioles: Tekulve, who saved Game 7, tied a Series record with three saves; scrappy Phil Garner went 12-for-24; Dave Parker hit .345; and Omar Moreno, who had slumped badly in the first few games of the Series, wound up hitting .333.

Stargell insisted on giving full credit to his teammates, but his teammates gave it all right back to him. "He taught us how to take what comes and then come back," Parker told reporters as the champagne sprayed and "We Are Family" boomed away in the background. "He taught us how to strike out and walk away calmly, lay the bat down gently, then get up next time and get a home run. From him we learned not to get too high on the good days or too low on the bad days, because there's plenty of both in this game."

In mid-November, Stargell would complete his MVP triple crown for the year, adding the NL MVP Award to his plaques for the NLCS and World Series. The idiosyncrasies of baseball awards voting—writers at the time were allowed to "split" votes between players—resulted in the first (and highly controversial) co–MVP Award, with Keith Hernandez and Stargell sharing the prize. Two weeks later, Twins third baseman John Castino (who hit .285) and Blue Jays shortstop Alfredo Griffin (who hit .287) wound up tied for the AL Rookie of the Year Award, and the two deadlocked votes would result in significant changes in the way that votes were cast and tabulated. But even if Stargell hadn't received the nod (or the half nod) from the baseball writers, the guys with the gold stars on their pillbox caps would surely, and unanimously, have named him their MVP.

Two weeks after the World Series ended, Reggie Jackson was enjoying a solitary drive near his home along California's Monterey Peninsula, listening to some music on the radio and generally just "trying to get my mind clear and right after all the unhappiness" of the 1979 season. The music briefly subsided, giving way to the hourly news report. New York Yankees manager Billy Martin, the announcer read from the news ticker, had gotten into a fight at a hotel bar in Minnesota with a traveling marshmallow salesman named Joseph Cooper. True to form, Martin had sucker punched the man when he wasn't looking. Cooper needed 20 stiches to close a split lip, and Martin was most likely out of a job. Again.

"I pulled the car over to the side of the road and pondered all that for a minute," Jackson later wrote. "And then I just started to laugh. If anybody had pulled up to me, it would have been a curious sight. Me. Car stopped, but engine still running. Laughing and laughing."

EPILOGUE
THE PARTY'S OVER

On the field, at least, there was little about the 1980 baseball season to differentiate it significantly from the 10 seasons that had come before it. If anything, the 1980 season was pretty much a direct extension of the 1970s, with most of the dominant players and teams from that decade figuring heavily in 1980's outcome.

The Philadelphia Phillies and Kansas City Royals made it back into the playoffs after taking an involuntary one-year hiatus from postseason play—and it was somehow perfect, even poetic, that the two teams faced off against each other in the 1980 World Series. Both teams had come painfully close to making the Fall Classic so many times during the 1970s, only to be denied by the glitzier, higher-profile, higher-paid Yankees, Reds, and Dodgers squads. The fact that the 1980 Series was the first one to be played entirely on artificial turf only added an extra layer of '70s déjà vu—as did the sight of flamboyant Phils reliever Tug Mc-Graw (whose battle cry of "You gotta believe!" had sparked the 1973 Mets to the NL championship) celebrating his Series-clinching strikeout of the Royals' Willie Wilson by dancing on the Veterans Stadium mound. But there was nothing remotely 1970s about the battalion of helmeted Philadelphia riot squad cops that circled the field to deter any potential invasion of would-be rioters; in retrospect, it seemed more like a glimpse of the cold, hard Reagan years to come.

It's been said many times that the American 1940s didn't really end until Elvis showed up during the first Eisenhower administration, and that the 1950s hung on until the Beatles landed at New York's newly renamed JFK Airport in February 1964. And whether "the '60s" as we know them actually ended with the Rolling Stones' tragic Altamont concert in December 1969, the May 1970 Kent State shootings, the re-election of Richard Nixon in 1972, Nixon's resignation in 1974, or the fall of Saigon in 1975 remains very much open to debate.

The door on the 1970s, however, slammed shut fast and hard. Jimmy Carter, who'd surfed into the White House in 1976 on a wave of Bicentennial optimism, would be out of office by 1981, his presidency doomed by the country's dire economic difficulties, the Soviet Union's December 1979 invasion of Afghanistan, and the ongoing diplomatic nightmare of the U.S. embassy hostage crisis in Iran. For Americans still filled with angst over their country's ignominious exit from Vietnam, the U.S. government's inability to find immediate solutions to any of these issues gave rise to additional feelings of anger and impotence, which Ronald Reagan was able to exploit successfully during his 1980 run against Carter for the Oval Office.

Shortly after being sworn in on January 20, 1981, Reagan set in motion massive cuts in government spending, which seriously truncated (or eradicated entirely) many of the Carter administration's social programs for the poor, the elderly, and the mentally ill. Meanwhile, Nancy Reagan, the new president's fashion-plate First Lady, spent over $800,000 redecorating the White House living quarters, including over $200,000 for new china. The message was clear: compassion and sacrifice were out; greed and opulence were in. "After years of Jimmy Carter empathizing with our malaise and telling us to lower our expectations and carry our own suitcases," wrote author Jay McInerney, "the Reagans were unself-conscious advocates of the good life."

Greed would become a dominant factor in baseball as well. Each year since 1976 had brought higher contracts for free agents, and in 1980, Nolan Ryan busted through the $1 million ceiling with his four-year, $4.5 million Astros contract, making him the highest-paid player in baseball. While players flexed their newfound earning power and scrambled after larger and more lucrative deals, baseball owners desperately tried to put the free-agency genie back in its bottle and hold on to their cash.

On December 31, 1979, the Basic Agreement between the players and owners expired. The owners, though not having much of a leg left to stand on, insisted that the new agreement should give them compensation for any player lost to free agency; the players, believing that compensation would be counterproductive to their cause, disagreed vehemently. The dispute would result in a strike-riven 1981 season that cast the sport in a darker, lucre-colored light that it would never be entirely able to shake. Lingering owner bitterness over having to keep up with skyrocketing player salaries would eventually lead to the collusion scandal of 1985–87 and the players' strike of 1994, which forced commissioner Bud Selig's cancellation of the 1994 World Series.

By the time of the 1981 strike, Charlie O. Finley and Bill Veeck, two of the most flamboyant owners of the 1970s, had already fallen victim to the economics of the free-agency era. Finley got out in November 1980, when he sold the Oakland A's to Levi Strauss chairman Walter Haas Jr.; Veeck followed suit two months later, selling the White Sox to an ownership group headed by Jerry Reinsdorf and Eddie Einhorn. However grating Finley's blowhard personality and Veeck's populist hucksterism could be at times, baseball would be a much quieter and far less interesting game without those two men around.

Though many major leaguers of the 1970s used everything from amphetamines and marijuana to cocaine and LSD, it wasn't until 1981 that the sport experienced its first major drug scandal—the "Phillie Seven" trial, wherein the team physician from one of the Phillies' minor league franchises was accused of illegally prescribing amphetamines to Phillies players Pete Rose, Steve Carlton, Tim McCarver, Larry Christenson, Randy Lerch, Larry Bowa, and Greg Luzinski.

But the Phillie Seven trial was small potatoes compared to the "Pittsburgh Drug Trials" of 1985, which—while specifically implicating 11 players, including Joaquin Andujar, Keith Hernandez, Dave Parker, and Claudell Washington—revealed the rampant use of cocaine throughout baseball. Next to Tim Raines's testimony that he only slid headfirst on the basepaths so as not to break the vials of coke in his back pocket, Bill Lee's admitted fondness for marijuana-dusted organic pancakes sounded downright wholesome.

Just as the popularity of cocaine in baseball reflected the increased pervasiveness of the drug in American society, major league players seemed to march in lockstep with the cleaning up and buttoning down of the newly yuppified America. The exuberant experimentation and self-expression of the 1970s were now passé—and while the "porn 'stache" would still flourish above players' lips throughout the coming decade, the Afro hairdo would be as dead as disco by the early '80s. Team uniforms gradually became, on the whole, less colorful, and so did the players themselves. While the occasional flake like "Super Joe" Charboneau— the Indians outfielder who won AL Rookie of the Year in 1980, and became legendary in Cleveland for such off-the-field stunts as doing his own dental work and fixing his broken nose with a pair of pliers and a couple of shots of bourbon—still appeared on the scene, there no longer seemed to be much room in the sport for the wild-haired, wild-eyed characters who so colorfully populated baseball in the '70s.

The game itself, so fast and exciting to watch on artificial turf, began to slow down as the 1980s progressed and more teams began trading in their plastic grass for the real stuff, while more managers began to rely upon offensive strategies that boiled down to "wait for the three-run homer" instead of base stealing and hit-and-running; and the increased emphasis on home runs would play a part in the proliferation of steroid use throughout the sport. The increased specialization of relievers would also contribute to the lengthening of games, as managers began reserving their top relievers for ninth-inning save situations only; no longer would top firemen like Goose Gossage, Rollie Fingers, and Mike Marshall pitch three or more innings in relief.

Going by numbers alone, the 1970s hardly constituted a golden baseball era: Nobody hit .400 in a season, or won 30 or more games. Only one player—George Foster in 1977—managed to hit more than 50 home runs in a season during the entire decade. (The steroids-tainted 1998 season, by contrast, had four 50-plus guys.) But in those categories that continue to defy statisticians—weirdness, hairiness, overall funkiness, and sheer amusement—the 1970s still tower over every other baseball decade before or since. Long may the spirit and memory of the Mustache Gang, the Big Red Machine, the Bronx Zoo, Bambi's Bombers, and the South Side Hitmen, and all those other charismatic rebels, flakes, and hard-nosed hustlers in the form-fitting polyester uniforms, endure.

ACKNOWLEDGMENTS

By the time you read these words, it will have been over 10 years since the day I decided to write this book. I am incredibly grateful to my agents Lyn DelliQuadri, Jane Lahr, and Ann Tanenbaum at LTD Editions, and to Rob Kirkpatrick, my editor at St. Martin's, for their belief in the project; it's not blowing smoke to say that they bear considerable responsibility for making my '70s daydream a reality. Rob's helpful suggestions—offered as much from the perspective of a true baseball fan as from an editor's need to get this manuscript down to a manageable size—lent me some much-needed focus at times when I was completely overwhelmed by the daunting task of tackling this insanely colorful decade. I also owe considerable gratitude to Margaret Smith at St. Martin's, for shepherding my book through the copyedit and production stages.

I'd also like to thank a number of friends, colleagues, and acquaintances for inspiring me to keep on keepin' on with this book. I'm sure I'm forgetting some folks (for which I'll apologize now), but Michael Ansaldo, Michael Azerrad, Soren Baker, Greg Barbera, Fred Baron, Tom Beaujour, Josh Bernstein, Will Fulford-Jones, Randy Bookasta, Jerry Cook, Bill Crandall, Jennifer Dorn, Rebecca Epstein, Paul Gaita, Erik Himmelsbach-Weinstein, Sean Kelly, Lynda Keeler, MJ Knappen, Dean Kuipers, Adam

Langer, Dr. LaWanda, Bob MacKay, Betsy McLaughlin, Josh Mills, Michael Moses, Dave Mundo, Morgan Neville, Betsy Nichols, Bruno Oliver, Chris Perry, Carole Pixler, Gary Poole, James Saft, Bob Samiljan, Stu Shea, Max Stevens, Erik Sugg, Brad Tolinski, Jaan Uhelski, David Ulin, Loana DP Valencia, Don Waller, and Don Zminda all offered substantial encouragement, ideas, insight, advice, and moral support for the project at crucial junctures in the writing process. Thank you all for recharging my enthusiasm at times when this labor of love started to feel more like a labor than a love.

Special shout-outs go to Rebecca Fain, who was wonderfully helpful in guiding me through the maze of photo research, and Steve Dewing, whose jaw-dropping photo archives provided me with several of the rare images you see in this book. (Check out his amazing Web site, Steve's Baseball Photography Pages, at www.thatsmyboy03.com.) And many thanks to Rob Neyer and Paul Lukas from ESPN.com—the former for his photo research advice, and the latter for helping me come to grips with the full horror of the Chicago White Sox "softball shorts" incident. Uni Watch, Paul's enormously entertaining blog, was also a valuable and inspiring resource for my chapter on uniforms. You can visit his site (and, if you're as hard-core as I am about the aesthetics of diamond wear, become a member) at www.uniwatchblog.com.

The explosion of baseball information on the Internet over the last decade has made research and fact-checking a lot easier than it was back when I first began this project. Web sites I found particularly valuable and inspirational included Baseball-Reference.com, Baseball-Almanac.com, Ballparks by Munsey & Suppes (www.ballparks.com), ballparksof-baseball.com, Clem's Baseball Blog (www.andrewclem.com/baseball), Josh Wilker's cardboardgods.net, Al Yellon's bleedcubbieblue.com, the SI Vault (www.sportsillustrated.cnn.com/vault), the *Time* magazine archives (www.time.com/time/archive), and the sadly now-vanished *Sporting News* archives at Paper of Record, all of which enabled me to delve deeply into the decade while relaxing at home with a beer in my hand and some righteous '70s jams on the stereo.

And finally, I'd like to take a moment to pay tribute to two of my all-time baseball heroes, Dock Ellis and Mark Fidrych, both of whom passed away during the final stages of this book. I had the pleasure of watching and rooting for both pitchers as a kid, but it's only in recent years that I've realized how much Dock's iconoclastic attitude and the Bird's playful approach to life rubbed off on me at an early age, inspiring me to live as truthfully and as joyfully as possible, and forever wave my own freak flag high. Those two gents were "keepin' it real" long before that dubious phrase entered the popular lexicon; and while they'll never be elected to the Baseball Hall of Fame, they've long been permanently enshrined in mine.

BIBLIOGRAPHY

Adelman, Tom. *The Long Ball*. Little, Brown, 2003.

Allen, Dick, and Tim Whitaker. *Crash: The Life and Times of Dick Allen*. Ticknor & Fields, 1989.

Angell, Roger. *Five Seasons: A Baseball Companion*. Simon & Schuster, 1977.

———. *Once More Around the Park: A Baseball Reader*. Ivan R. Dee, 2001.

———. *The Summer Game*. Viking Press, 1972.

Ballew, Bill. *The Pastime in the Seventies: Oral Histories of 16 Major Leaguers*. McFarland & Company, 2002.

Bouton, Jim. *Ball Four (Twentieth Anniversary Edition)*. Macmillan, 1990.

———. *I'm Glad You Didn't Take It Personally*. Dell, 1971.

Burke, Glenn, with Erik Sherman. *Out at Home: The Glenn Burke Story*. Excel Publications, 1995.

Cantor, George. *The Tigers of '68*. Taylor Publishing, 1997.

Conner, Floyd. *Baseball's Most Wanted*. Potomac Books, 2000.

Delson, Steve. *True Blue*. William Morrow, 2001.

Down, Fred. *Major League Baseball 1973*. Pocket Books, 1973.

———. *Major League Baseball 1975*. Pocket Books, 1975.

———. *Major League Baseball 1976*. Ballantine Books, 1976.

———. *Major League Baseball 1977*. Ballantine Books, 1977.

Durocher, Leo, with Ed Linn. *Nice Guys Finish Last*. Simon & Schuster, 1975.

Edelman, Rob. *Great Baseball Films*. Citadel Press, 1994.

Editors of Total Baseball. *Baseball: The Biographical Encyclopedia*. Total / Sports Illustrated, 2000.

Einstein, Charles, ed. *The Fireside Book of Baseball*. Vol. 4. Simon & Schuster, 1987.

Falls, Joe. *Detroit Tigers*. Collier Books, 1975.

Felder, Rob, ed. *Great Baseball Writing: Sports Illustrated 1954–2004*. Sports Illustrated Books, 2005.

Fidrych, Mark, and Tom Clark. *No Big Deal*. J. B. Lippincott, 1977.

Garruth, Gorton. *The Encyclopedia of American Facts and Dates*. 10th ed. HarperCollins, 1997.

Golenbock, Peter. *Wild, High and Tight: The Life and Death of Billy Martin*. St. Martin's Press, 1994.

———. *Wrigleyville: A Magical History Tour of the Chicago Cubs*. St. Martin's Press, 1996.

Gossage, Richard "Goose," with Russ Pate. *The Goose Is Loose: An Autobiography*. Ballantine Books, 2000.

Gutman, Dan. *Baseball Babylon*. Penguin Books, 1992.

Hall, Donald, with Dock Ellis. *Dock Ellis in the Country of Baseball*. Fireside, 1989.

Honig, Donald. *The American League: An Illustrated History*. Crown Publishers, 1983.

———. *The National League: An Illustrated History*. Crown Publishers, 1987.

Jackson, Reggie, with Mike Lupica. *Reggie: The Autobiography of Reggie Jackson*. Villard Books, 1984.

Johnstone, Jay, with Rick Talley. *Temporary Insanity*. Contemporary Books, 1985.

Jordan, David M. *Occasional Glory: The History of the Philadelphia Phillies*. McFarland & Company, 2002.

———. *Pete Rose: A Biography*. Greenwood Publishing Group, 2004.

Kuenster, John, ed. *At Home and Away: 33 Years of Baseball Essays*. McFarland & Company, 2003.

———. *From Cobb to "Catfish": 128 Illustrated Stories from Baseball Digest*. Rand McNally, 1975.

Kuhn, Bowie. *Hardball: The Education of a Baseball Commissioner*. Times Books, 1987.

LaBlanc, Michael L. *Hotdogs, Heroes, and Hooligans: The Story of Baseball's Major League Teams*. Visible Ink, 1994.

Lee, Bill "Spaceman," with Dick Lally. *The Wrong Stuff*. Penguin Books, 1988.

LeFlore, Ron, with Jim Hawkins. *Breakout: From Prison to the Big Leagues*. Harper & Row, 1978.

Lyle, Sparky, with Peter Golenbock. *The Bronx Zoo*. Triumph Books, 2005.

Mahler, Jonathan. *Ladies and Gentlemen, the Bronx Is Burning*. Farrar, Straus & Giroux, 2005.

Maraniss, David. *Clemente: The Passion and Grace of Baseball's Last Hero*. Simon & Schuster, 2006.

Markusen, Bruce. *A Baseball Dynasty: Charlie Finley's Swingin' A's*. St. Johann Press, 2002.

———. *The Team That Changed Baseball: Roberto Clemente and the 1971 Pittsburgh Pirates*. Westholme Publishing, 2006.

Martin, Billy, and Peter Golenbock. *Number 1*. Delacorte Press, 1980.

McCollister, John. *Tales from the 1979 Pittsburgh Pirates*. Sports Publishing, 2005.

———. *The Tigers and Their Den: The Official Story of the Detroit Tigers*. Addax Publishing Group, 1999.

McLain, Denny, with Dave Diles. *Nobody's Perfect*. Dial Press, 1975.

Nash, Bruce, and Allan Zullo. *The Baseball Hall of Shame*. Wallaby Books, 1985.

Nemec, David, et al. *20th Century Baseball Chronicle: A Year-by-Year History of Major League Baseball*. Publications International, 1993.

Nettles, Graig, and Peter Golenbock. *Balls*. G. P. Putnam's Sons, 1984.

Okkonen, Marc. *Baseball Uniforms of the 20th Century*. Sterling Publishing, 1993.

Pepe, Phil. *Talkin' Baseball: An Oral History of Baseball in the 1970s*. Ballantine Books, 1998.

Pepitone, Joe, with Berry Steinbeck. *Joe, You Coulda Made Us Proud*. Playboy Press, 1975.

Preston, Joseph G. *Major League Baseball in the 1970s*. McFarland & Company, 2004.

Reichler, Joseph. *Baseball's Great Moments*. Bonanza Books, 1987.

Reidenbaugh, Lowell. *Take Me Out to the Ball Park*. Sporting News Publishing, 1983.

Reston, James, Jr. *Collision at Home Plate: The Lives of Pete Rose and Bart Giamatti*. University of Nebraska Press, 1997.

Rieland, Randy. *The New Professionals: Baseball in the 1970s*. Redefinition, 1989.

Ritter, Lawrence S. *Lost Ballparks: A Celebration of Baseball's Legendary Fields*. Penguin Studio, 1992.

Rivers, Mickey, and Michael DeMarco. *Ain't No Sense Worryin'*. Sports Publishing, 2003.

Rosen, Ira. *Blue Skies Green Fields: A Celebration of 50 Major League Baseball Stadiums*. Clarkson Potter Publishers, 2001.

Ryan, Nolan, with Bill Libby. *The Other Game*. Word Books, 1977.

Shea, Stuart, with George Castle. *Wrigley Field: The Unauthorized Biography*. Brassey's, 2004.

Smith, Red. *Red Smith on Baseball*. Ivan R. Dee, 2000.

Smith, Ron. *The Ballpark Book: A Journey Through the Fields of Baseball Magic*. Sporting News, 2000.

Spatz, Lyle, ed. *The SABR Baseball List and Record Book*. Scribner's, 2007.

Stanton, Tom. *Hank Aaron and the Home Run That Changed America*. William Morrow, 2004.

Thorn, John. *The Relief Pitcher: Baseball's New Hero*. E. P. Dutton, 1979.

Thorn, John, ed. *The Complete Armchair Book of Baseball*. Galahad Books, 1997.

Thorn, John, et al. *Total Baseball.* 6th ed. Total Sports, 1999.

Veeck, Bill, with Ed Linn. *Veeck—As in Wreck.* University of Chicago Press, 2001.

Zimmer, Don, with Bill Madden. *Zim: A Baseball Life.* Contemporary Books, 2001.

INDEX